Mandate
of
Heaven

A New Generation of Entrepreneurs,

Dissidents, Bohemians, and Technocrats

Lays Claim to China's Future

Orville Schell

Simon & Schuster

New York · London · Toronto · Sydney · Tokyo · Singapore

SIMON & SCHUSTER
Rockefeller Center
1230 Avenue of the Americas
New York, New York 10020

Designed by Levavi & Levavi
Manufactured in the United States of America

1   3   5   7   9   10   8   6   4   2

Library of Congress Cataloging-in-Publication Data

Schell, Orville.
Mandate of heaven: A new generation of entrepreneurs,
dissidents, bohemians, and technocrats lays claim to China's
future/Orville Schell.
p.   cm.
Includes index.
1. China—Politics and government—1976-   2. China—History—
Tiananmen Square Incident, 1989.   3. China—Economic
conditions—1976-   4. China—Social conditions—1976-   5. Human
rights—China.   I. Title.
DS779.26.S34   1994
951.05′8—dc20   94-16065
                                                    CIP

ISBN: 0-671-70132-0

Edited portions of this book have been previously published
in the *Atlantic, Granta*, the *Los Angeles Times Magazine*,
the *Nation, Vanity Fair*, the *New Yorker, Travel Holiday*,
and *Vogue*.

Acknowledgments

Completing this book would have been almost impossible without the help I received from several people. The thoughtfulness and painstaking thoroughness with which my dear friend and former editor Tom Engelhardt read the manuscript and made suggestions and comments for changes were crucial in helping me see the way during times of uncertainty and confusion. The insightful editorial work and tireless research assistance of Todd Lappin, who also collaborated with me on the chapter about China's stock markets, was invaluable in keeping me moving forward.

For taking time to review the manuscript and for offering everything from broad critical insights to minor corrections, thanks are due James H. Williams, Zhang Xiaogang, John Despres, Richard Gordon, Carolyn Wakeman, and Robin Munro. Special thanks are also due my agent, Amanda Urban, for her usual timely ministrations and encouragement. And to my editors Alice Mayhew and Elizabeth Stein at Simon & Schuster, dual thanks are in order—for suffering my tardiness and then for their prompt and helpful editing.

I wish also to thank the Center for Chinese Studies at the University of California, Berkeley, whose library served as a crucial resource in the researching of this book.

Orville Schell

San Francisco, April 1994

FOR BAIFANG WITH MUCH LOVE

The simplest and most adequate way of describing the history of China would be to distinguish between two types of periods: (1) the periods when people wish in vain to enjoy a stable slave condition; and (2) the periods when people manage to enjoy a stable slave condition. The alternation of these two states is what our old scholars called "the cycle of chaos and order."

Lu Xun, "Random Thoughts Under the Lamp,"
April 29, 1925

Contents

Part V
The Boom

PROLOGUE

Tiananmen Square as History

Tiananmen Square is one of those places whose immensity and potency as a symbol cannot be adequately grasped until you have actually visited it for yourself. Photographs have a curious way of making Tiananmen Square, the world's largest public quadrangle, seem as flat and unimpressive as a parking lot at an American shopping mall. But when one actually stands in the middle of it and looks first north to Tiananmen, the Gate of Heavenly Peace, which leads into the ancient Forbidden City, and then back around the frieze of monumental socialist architecture that lines the peripheries of its hundred acres, one cannot help but be overwhelmed. As the nation's foremost seat of authority, "the Square," as most Chinese call it, is China's ultimate political reference point. It is the center of the country's center, and as soon as one arrives in Beijing, one feels oneself in its thrall, as if it emitted its own unique field of lateral gravity.

Almost twenty years later, I can still remember with perfect vividness the morning I saw Tiananmen Square for the first time. I had arrived in China late one April night in 1975 while Mao Zedong still lived and the country was still infused with the political militancy of the Cultural Revolution. After trying to reach Beijing for many years, now that I had at last been allowed in, I could not help feeling somewhat furtive, as if I had mistakenly been given entrance into a forbidden realm.

I awoke the next morning at dawn with Tiananmen Square already tugging at me. Knowing it was just moments away from the Beijing Hotel, where I was staying, made going back to sleep impossible. In 1975 the authorities still frowned upon "foreign guests" setting off on unchaperoned expeditions around the city, but the thought of watching the sun rise over this long-heralded place was so irresistible that I dressed, took the elevator downstairs, and then hoping that no watchful comrade would notice my exit, crossed the hotel's cavernous empty lobby. Stepping out onto the Avenue of Eternal Peace was like walking into a dream.

As I headed west under the canopy of budding sycamore trees that fringe the vermilion wall of the ancient Forbidden City, the eastern sky was just beginning to be suffused with a hint of matinal gray. The half-light created the feeling of a great chimerical openness rather than a clearly defined place in front of me. When at last I approached the very end of the sidewalk with the oceanic vastness of the Square stretching away in front of me, my heart was pounding. Stepping out onto the checkerboard of cement paving stones, I felt the same kind of breathless excitement that I remembered as a child the winter I had first dared venture out from shore alone to ice-skate out across the enormity of the frozen reservoir that lay behind our New England house. I was so intoxicated by the thought of finally being in Tiananmen Square that it was not until I was nearing its center that I allowed myself to stop and actually look around and see Tiananmen Gate itself, rising up like a mountain above a flat plain at the Square's northern end.

There are no words that adequately convey the grandeur of China's great *men*, or gateways, which were the only means of entry through the thick, towering walls that once surrounded the Forbidden City and Beijing, as well as many other Chinese towns and cities. Capped by two tiers of sloping yellow-tiled roofs, Tiananmen is a massive ten-story-high stone rampart painted imperial maroon, a color that traditional Chinese associated with the North Star. As Confucius said, "He who exercises government by means of virtue may be compared to the north pole star, to which all other stars are attracted."

Running through Tiananmen Gate's base were five tunnel-like portals that before the fall of the last dynasty in 1911 were kept closed except when the son of heaven himself emerged out of the central and largest one accompanied by a retinue of thousands of attendants. And just above, flanked by two latter-day inscriptions—"Long Live the Unity of the Peoples of the World" and "Long Live the People's Republic of China"—like a prize jewel set at the center of a royal diadem, was Mao's famous portrait.

I'm not sure how long I stared at Tiananmen Gate that morning, but when I finally turned away, the sky was beginning to glow red in the east, and the colossal Museum of the Chinese Revolution and the Museum of History on the east and the Great Hall of the People on the west were being transformed before my eyes from shadowy blurs into sharply limned images like a photograph developing before my eyes. I stood alone in the middle of this vast man-made expanse and watched the sun slowly climb into the sky. The early-morning cold was bone-chilling, but having arrived at long last here at the figurative center of what was, for Americans at least, one of the most elusive and impenetrable countries in the world, I did not care.

As the day broke over the museums and the sun began shining fiery orange down on the Square, it would not have surprised me if one of those electronic carillons that the Party often rigged at train stations and in the cupolas of government buildings had suddenly begun to peal forth with the old Party anthem, "The East Is Red":

> The red in the East raises the sun,
> China gives forth a Mao Zedong.
> He works for the happiness of the people,
> He shall be China's saving star.
> The East is red!

In the years since that first visit, I have visited China so many times that the excitement of arrival in Beijing has long since receded. Still, each time I return, I sense the Square's ferocious pull, and feel disoriented until I have made a pilgrimage to this hub of the Chinese nation. The way it radiates political and spiritual authority out across the land and the crucial role it plays as a unifying symbol for China would only slowly become evident to me as I traveled around the country during the next two decades. For instance, while working on the Dazhai model agricultural brigade in northwestern Shanxi Province later that spring, I heard the local children sing the Party-sanctioned jingle "I Love Beijing's Tiananmen" over and over again:

> I love Beijing's Tiananmen,
> The sun rises over Tiananmen Gate.
> Our great leader Chairman Mao Zedong
> Will guide us into the future.

Because I had actually visited this sacred place, during rest breaks the children would ply me with endless questions: What was it like to stand in the middle of the Square, to visit the Great Hall of the People, and to see Tiananmen Gate? Even though my own experience had been extremely limited, they were so eager to hear more that often I had to repeat myself, and even embellish a little, to satisfy their craving.

Several years later while in Hunan Province I came across a wall map of China in a Changsha high school that showed Beijing with a crimson line drawing of Tiananmen Gate so big that it covered much of Hebei Province. Emanating from it were scores of black lines protruding like cracks in a pane of glass around a bullet hole. At first, I thought I was looking at a Beijing airline route map, but when I studied the drawing more closely, I realized that the lines were simply cartoonlike depictions of the Square's figurative aura pulsing out across the country.

And while on the way to a trekking and climbing expedition on the Tibetan Plateau in Qinghai Province, I encountered a fifteen-foot replica of Tiananmen Gate fashioned entirely out of yak butter. It had been made by monks at the Ta'er Monastery outside of Xining as part of a winter festival competition for artwork sculpted in this unique traditional medium. As I marveled at its bizarreness, not to mention its rancid odor, local Chinese and Tibetans gazed at it like Christians beholding a purported piece of the cross.

Tiananmen Square may have been constructed by Mao as a secular shrine to the Party and the Revolution, but it also had a divine dimension. It is what journalist Zhang Xiaogang calls "China's state cathedral," a sacred shrine that many view as a physical incarnation of what it means to be Chinese. Visits are anticipated with almost the same expectation as that of the faithful making pilgrimages to Mecca or the Vatican. In fact, when Mao used to appear on top of Tiananmen Gate during ceremonial occasions, in many ways the atmosphere in the Square resembled the scene around the Great Mosque during the hajj, or in the huge piazza in front of St. Peter's Basilica when on holy days the Pontiff recites homilies to hundreds of thousands congregated below. Few provincial Chinese visit Beijing without arranging to have a ritual photograph snapped in front of Mao's renowned portrait.

Because of the Square's unique centrality, it has also served as a curiously accurate barometer of China's prevailing political mood. For years the propaganda billboards and the choice of Mao quotations painted on them along the Avenue of Eternal Peace leading into it have provided subtle clues about the Party's current political state of mind. If the quotes stressed Mao's utterances on class struggle, one could surmise that the Party leaders were on a leftist tack. If the quotes stressed unity and production, one could assume that they were in a more practical and moderate frame of mind. And the Square's May Day portraiture shed light on the shifting balances of power among factions and competing ideological "lines" within the Central Committee. When towering likenesses of Marx, Lenin, Engels, and Stalin were still erected facing Mao's immutable visage, one knew that hard-line views were still in favor. But when this quartet of hirsute Europeans gave way to the neutral Sun Yat-sen—who had led the revolution against China's last imperial dynasty and established the Republic of China—it was a signal that the more pragmatic wing of the Party was in ascendancy.

Perhaps the Square's most telling political barometer was the Chinese people themselves. Like arctic animals whose coats change color with the seasons to help them blend in with their surroundings, the haberdashery displayed by Chinese tourists provided a telling indication of the prevailing ideological climate. This became particularly true after 1978 as Party prohibitions against such bourgeois fashions as dresses, short skirts, bell-bottomed trousers, and Western suits were first relaxed, and the People's Republic began to come alive with new fashion crazes every few months. With so many visitors from the provinces, the Square became the perfect control setting for judging how deeply new designs in clothing, hairstyles, and makeup had penetrated society at large. Such details as whether men wore Mao tunics and pug-nosed caps or Western-style suits and neckties; whether women wore shapeless jackets and baggy trousers or brightly colored dresses and high heels; or whether young girls got perms and young males wore their hair long or short reflected the Party's ever-fluctuating attitudes toward such things as individualism and the outside world. Eavesdropping on conversations and observing the casual behavior of these visitors was also revealing. Were they respectfully silent, or did they banter among themselves as they trooped through the Great Hall of the People on guided tours? Were they somber like pilgrims as they snapped obligatory photos standing in front of Mao's portrait, or smiling like tourists? Did they mention politics as they waited in line to "pay their respects to Chairman Mao" in his mausoleum at the south end, or joke and jabber away about money? And how much of their hard-earned cash did they part with when they emerged to buy official Mao memorial chopsticks, sun visors, wristwatches, and tote bags at the souvenir stands that had sprung up near the exit from Mao's final resting place as a result of Deng Xiaoping's marketization of the economy?

As the centuries-old symbolic and literal seat of political power, the space in front of Tiananmen Gate has long been the place where ruler and subjects—indeed "all things under heaven"—merged in China. One classical text described Tiananmen as a kind of littoral where "earth and sky meet, where the four seasons merge, where wind and rain are gathered in, and where *yin* and *yang* are in harmony."

But while the Square was the locus where these forces ideally came into harmonious union, it could also be a place of great political tension. In fact, sometimes the Square seemed as if it were on a fault line dividing slipping tectonic plates of politics, as Deng Xiaoping learned in 1989. At the same time, neither Deng nor any other ruler could long endure if denied the aura of legitimacy that symbolic possession of the Square conferred on a government. Even after the student protesters had been physically ousted by troops, Deng's government needed to have its title to the Square cleared and relegitimated in order to show that the Party rather than its opponents was the Square's rightful heir. What made repossession so difficult was that Party leaders found they confronted not a unified symbolic image, but two contradictory versions of the Square, each with its own deep historical roots.

Over the past five centuries, Tiananmen Gate has linked the Forbidden City's 250 acres of grounds and 9,000 rooms, attended by some 70,000 imperial eunuchs, to the outside world. As such, the great Gate and the area in front of it became the most potent symbol of imperial power in the land. For the *laobaixing*, or ordinary people, this was as close as they could get to the "great within" and the emperor on the other side of the wall.

However, with the fall of the Qing Dynasty in 1911, Tiananmen Gate began to take on a second, shadow identity that intruded repeatedly on its traditional identity as the locus of establishment authority. The space in front of the gate became the country's preeminent forum for political dissent, a lodestone for those Chinese wishing to petition their government for relief from hardship and injustice. In a very real sense the 1989 struggle between the students and the Party, and the later battle between the people of Beijing and the People's Liberation Army (PLA), revolved not only around the question of who would physically control Tiananmen Square, but around which of these conflicting identities would henceforth prevail in the minds of the Chinese people.

Most of the present Square was originally covered by buildings housing imperial offices and palaces constructed by the Yongle Emperor during the Ming Dynasty after he decided to move the imperial capital from Nanjing to Beijing in 1421. Along with the Forbidden City itself, this complex of buildings was part of a grand design that placed the "dragon throne" at the very center of Beijing. What made this area in front of the Forbidden City so important was that it was bisected by a central axis running directly from the emperor's throne room, out Tiananmen Gate, across the public space that would ultimately become "the Square," through the Front Gate of the City Wall, to the Temple of Heaven in the southern reaches of the capital, and then out across China. It was believed that imperial power was transmitted from the emperor to his empire along this axis.

It was from atop Tiananmen Gate that military expeditions were launched and the names of those who passed the highest imperial examinations were announced. It was also from these exalted heights—no surrounding building was allowed to be taller—that important imperial edicts were read aloud before being lowered down in the mouth of a gilded wooden phoenix or "cloud tray" to officials prostrated below so that they could be remanded to the Ministry of Rites for copying and circulation throughout China. It was also in front of the Gate that the Imperial High Court sat twice each year to review all death sentences. And finally, it was through Tiananmen Gate that with awesome pomp and ceremony the emperor himself passed whenever he left the Forbidden City to travel the empire or make his annual pilgrimage to the Temple of Heaven, where he performed rituals to protect the dynasty from losing the favor of heaven.

An emperor's ability to rule was said to reflect the cosmic sanction bestowed on his reign by *tianming,* or the "mandate of heaven," which Chinese believed was signified by peace and harmony within his realm. Traditional political philosophers held that moral legitimacy was a vital component of *tianming* and that if the moral bonds between ruler and ruled were irrevocably violated, the all-embracing forces of "heaven" from which an emperor drew his "mandate" to rule as "the son of heaven" would be withheld and his dynasty would collapse. Before such a fall, it was believed that "heaven" would signal its displeasure with such portents as natural disasters and popular rebellions. "We are informed that when heaven gave life to the human race it instituted rulers to look after its members and to keep them in order," explains the *Hanshu,* a first-century history of the former Han Dynasty. "When a ruler of mankind is not possessed of appropriate qualities, or when his administrative measures are not fair, heaven points out these failings by means of calamity so as to give warning of disorders."

Almost two millennia later the idea of *tianming* still retained such popular currency among ordinary Chinese that when the modern notion of "revolution" came to China from the West, an old term, *geming* (*ge* meaning to "to remove" or "break," and *ming* meaning "the mandate" or "will of heaven") was borrowed from the classic *Book of Changes*. So it was quite natural that when demonstrations broke out in front of Tiananmen Gate, even after the last emperor was swept from the Forbidden City, many continued to view them as a signal that the "mandate of heaven" was slipping from the grasp of whatever regime was in power.

Even in the prerevolutionary era when Tiananmen Gate was the preeminent symbol of imperial sovereignty, it already harbored suggestions of the shadow identity that would develop only later. Just in front of the five balustraded marble bridges (standing for the five cardinal Confucian virtues) that span the Stream of Golden Waters in front of the Gate stand two marble *huabiao* (pillars) topped with stylized wings and mythical animals, one facing the palace and the other the city, reminders to the emperor of the indissoluble connection between ruler and ruled. Although the cultural origin of these pillars is murky, some scholars believe that they originally served as representations of the right of ordinary people to watch over the emperor's conduct and to report injustices to the Imperial Board of Criticism and Protest. It is said that in ancient times such *huabiao* were made of wood so that subjects could inform the court of their true sentiments by carving criticism onto them. Even after the *huabiao* were redone in marble, their presence served as reminders that at the same time that the Square served as the seat of state power it was also a place where citizens were entitled to remonstrate.

Despite the vigil maintained by these vestigial sentinels, the area in front of Tiananmen Gate did not erupt with large-scale public protests until after China's last dynasty fell in 1911 and its once unimpeachable aura of political authority was greatly diminished. On May 4, 1919, shortly after the end of World War I, patriotic young Chinese took to the streets with banners and placards proclaiming "Protect Our Sovereignty!" and "International Justice!" to protest their government's agreement to accept the ceding of Germany's territorial concessions in China to Japan at Versailles. The warlord government ruling North China at the time responded by beating and arresting scores of demonstrators, even killing one. But instead of ending their protest, students widened it by dispersing throughout the city and delivering political speeches on street corners about the corruptness of the government and its humiliating appeasement of Japan.

Although the May Fourth Incident itself lasted only one afternoon, it spawned a whole movement that grew until other elements of society began joining protesting students. In fact, what finally persuaded the government to renounce the terms of the Versailles Treaty was the participation of tens of thousands of sympathetic Shanghai workers. These events marked not only the first time that China witnessed street demonstrations but that Chinese intellectuals, shopkeepers, and workers joined hands in a common cause. They presaged a decade of nationwide political and cultural ferment. The May Fourth Movement inspired a whole generation of political activists to try and modernize China through a technological and cultural "renaissance" and rescue it from further humiliation at the hands of the Great Powers. Ever since then, the two characters for *wusi* (the fourth day of the fifth month) have come to occupy a place in China's political consciousness synonymous with the idea of patriotic student activism and of China's educated elite serving as a conscience for the nation. The May Fourth generation's spirit of protest and its preeminent slogan, "Science and Democracy," continued until the present to be celebrated by freethinking Chinese.

Although Communist Party organizers did not support the May Fourth Movement's emphasis on freedom of inquiry and expression, they did embrace its spirit of patriotic activism to "save the country" from dismemberment by foreign imperialists. The May Fourth Incident baptized Tiananmen Gate for Communists and non-Communists alike as China's most hallowed place of protest. In the following decades, protesters gravitated to the space in front of the Gate to take issue with their rulers so often that by the middle of the century it was ineradicably identified with morally upright challenges to the political status quo.

On June 10, 1925, two weeks after British police killed thirteen people at an anti-imperialist demonstration in Shanghai that came to be known as the May Thirtieth Movement, more than 100,000 Chinese rallied again in front of Tiananmen Gate to call for the abolition of the system of unequal treaties that gave foreigners extraterritorial immunity from Chinese law.

On March 18, 1926, thousands of students and workers marched to Tiananmen Gate to protest warlord Zhang Zuolin's capitulation to new Japanese demands. Zhang became the first Chinese leader in modern times to consecrate the Square with blood when he ordered his troops to open fire, killing fifty people and wounding several hundred more. The tragedy prompted China's greatest modern essayist, Lu Xun, to pen the well-known epitaph, "This is not the conclusion of an incident, but a new beginning. Lies written in ink can never disguise truths written in blood. Blood debts must be repaid in kind; the longer the delay, the greater the interest."

Although the central city of Nanjing was then serving as China's official capital, another mass protest broke out in the Square on December 9, 1935, when thousands of students rallied against Nationalist Party leader and President Chiang Kai-shek's refusal to form a united front with Mao Zedong's Communist guerrilla forces against Japan's military incursions in North China. This time, however, instead of firing live ammunition at the crowd, sophisticated Nationalist military commanders sprayed protesters with fire hoses—a tactic that proved equally effective in repelling demonstrators during Beijing's freezing winter weather.

Not until after Japan's occupation of China ended in 1945 did Tiananmen once again see such mass political demonstrations. On October 1, 1949, when Mao stood atop the ancient gate before an enthusiastic crowd to proclaim that the Chinese people had finally "stood up," he was, in effect, dedicating this space to the establishment of yet another Chinese dynasty. Standing beneath a row of new national flags featuring five gold stars (signifying the unity of the Chinese people under the Party) on a crimson field (symbolizing the Communist revolution), Mao proclaimed the founding of a New China. Insisting that this People's Republic would be the ultimate embodiment of justice and virtue in which political opposition would be superfluous, he was eager to lay to rest Tiananmen's identity as a place of protest. Mao wished to claim the Square for his revolution so that it might lend his new People's Republic historical ballast and continuity. One of the government's first acts was to adopt the silhouette of Tiananmen Gate itself as a national emblem, making it not only the centerpiece of China's new national crest, but putting it on stamps and banknotes as well. While the expropriation of this ancient symbol for revolutionary purposes was perhaps understandable, it was also an act of patent contradiction—as if the Bolsheviks had made the Winter Palace the symbol of the USSR.

This early effort to borrow Tiananmen's iconographic power was only the beginning of a far more extensive effort to link this symbolic place with China's socialist revolution in the minds of the "broad masses." After significantly enlarging the area in front of the Gate, Mao initiated an urban redevelopment scheme that rivaled Napoleon and Louis Napoleon's design for the Arc de Triomphe, the Champs Élysées, the Place de la Concorde, the Bois de Boulogne, and the Louvre. To complete his grandiose plan for transplanting a socialist heart into the chest cavity of China's most imperial capital, Mao put tens of thousands of "volunteers" to work around the clock to build not only a vast new Square and an imposing skyline of edifices around its perimeters, but an immense new boulevard running from east to west past the old Gate, to be called the Avenue of Eternal Peace. On the Square's east side he built the Stalinesque museums of the revolution and history. On the west side he constructed the even more imposing Great Hall of the People as a place for state functions. And at the very center of this grandiose public *Platz,* Mao commanded that a towering granite obelisk, the Monument to the Martyrs of the People, be erected and inscribed in his own hand with the epigram "Eternal Glory to the People's Heroes." On the plinth of this cenotaph, a frieze of ten bas reliefs was carved depicting China's revolutionary history, including such *qiyi* (insurrections) as the Wuchang Rebellion against the Qing Dynasty in 1911, the May Fourth Incident of 1919, the May Thirtieth Incident of 1925, and the Nanchang Rebellion of 1927 against the Nationalists, all venerated by Communists as prototypes of "people's revolution." And, of course, Mao had his own visage hung on Tiananmen Gate, beaming out like a lighthouse beacon across what was, when completed, a parade ground several times larger than even Red Square in Moscow.

Mao's new *guangchang* (broad field) was a propagandist's dream come true. Everything about it was gargantuan. It called out for the kinds of impressive statistics that socialists love to bandy about when touting grain harvests and outputs of steel tonnage. The Square is over 100 acres in size; the Monument to the Martyrs of the People is over 100 feet tall; the slab of stone bearing Mao's gilded inscription weighs more than 60 tons and the reliefs around its plinth depict 170 life-sized figures; the reviewing stands on either side of Tiananmen Gate hold over 20,000 people; and the Great Hall of the People is more than 1,000 feet long and has a banquet hall capable of seating more than 5,000 guests.

Once Mao's remodeling had been completed, Party leaders set about quashing the Square's legacy of political protest, the hortatory depictions of "insurrections" on the base of the Monument not withstanding. Shortly after Mao came to power, Beijing University—the epicenter of so many earlier student movements—was moved from its downtown location behind the Forbidden City to the outlying Haidian District. In the years that followed, the new government relocated most major institutions of higher learning to the suburbs. Henceforth, if students ever got the urge to march on the Square again, they would first have to negotiate many miles of no-man's land where they could easily be stopped.

Propagandists then went about turning the Square into a staging ground for ostentatious spectacles of obedience to the Party and loyalty to Mao. May Day rallies, National Day parades, and celebrations of other Communist devotional holidays and anniversaries were held there just as state-sponsored displays of pomp and power had been enacted in the days of yore. Now, however, instead of processions of sedan chairs bearing dynastic officials adorned in brocade robes, peacock feathers, and imperial emblems, Mao launched parades modeled after those held by China's "socialist big brother" in Red Square. These epic displays typically included phalanxes of ruddy-cheeked workers; defiles of youths flourishing crimson banners; acres of pom-pom girls who with a flick of the wrist could spell out "Long Live Chairman Mao" or "Down with American Imperialists and Their Running Dogs"; units of goose-stepping soldiers; columns of tanks, missiles, and rockets; towering motorized statues of Chairman Mao; floats of factory workers wielding hammers and sickles; peasants holding sheaves of golden wheat; and endless political placards in series arranged like oversized Burma Shave ads. And at the end came the inevitable release of doves and balloons followed by fireworks displays unparalleled anywhere else in the world.

By the time Mao died in 1976, Tiananmen Square had become so closely identified with his revolution that it was virtually unthinkable for him to be entombed anywhere else. So in order to create a permanent reliquary for the "Great Helmsman," the Party put 700,000 more "volunteers" to work around the clock to erect yet another socialist colossus in the Square. In less than a year the Mao Zedong Memorial Hall had been completed at its southern end. Here the ex-Chairman's taxidermicized remains were draped with a Party flag, laid out on a slab of stone from sacred Mount Tai under a crystal sarcophagus, and then brought up each morning on a special elevator from a subterranean refrigerated room for public viewing. In the following years millions of people trooped past his bier to catch a glimpse of the now less-than-worldly remains of this revolutionary demigod.

Each time I visited Mao's ponderous mausoleum and glimpsed his waxy face—many whispered that the embalming job had been so botched that his real corpse had long since been replaced by a Madame Tussaud's Wax Museum–like replica—it seemed to me that nothing short of an immense tidal wave could ever succeed in flushing the Square clean of his spirit. But as aggressive as Mao had been in linking his party and his revolution to the Square, its alter ego as a place of dissent managed to survive. Even before he died, this stubborn shadow identity began to assert itself once again.

Ironically, it was Mao himself who first revived the notion of using the Square as a place for mass expressions of anti-Party sentiment.

Aware that other leaders had turned against his vision of ceaseless class struggle and were maneuvering to oust him, in 1966 Mao virtually hijacked the Square from the Party and turned it into a marshaling yard for his own private Red Guard army. Standing atop Tiananmen Gate again, he exhorted millions of young followers to "put politics in command" and to "bombard the headquarters" of the Party apparatus in order to root out those "capitalist roaders" he claimed were still lurking within.

It was not until the end of the Great Proletarian Cultural Revolution that a new wave of true May Fourth–style protest erupted. The exhaustion Chinese felt from all the struggle and violence of the Cultural Revolution finally goaded them back to the Square and to engage in the kind of political protest symbolized by the May Fourth spirit. After Premier Zhou Enlai, who had a reputation as one of China's more moderate and fair leaders, died, on April 5, 1976, tens of thousands of mourners defied a government ban and, on the day of the annual Qing Ming festival, when Chinese pay respects to their ancestors, poured into the Square to place funeral wreaths and poems at the foot of the Monument to the Martyrs of the People. They were not only protesting the extreme ideological policies espoused by Zhou's adversaries within the Party—especially the "Gang of Four," led by Mao's wife, Jiang Qing—but for the first time since 1949 they were raising a public cry for democracy. "China is no longer the China of before," read one poem. "Its people are no longer wrapped in ignorance. Gone for good is the feudal society of the First Emperor."

Other than the chaos of the Cultural Revolution, the Tiananmen Square Incident, as the 1976 demonstration came to be known, was the first impromptu outburst of true mass dissent to erupt in the People's Republic. Although riot police quickly suppressed it and labeled it "counterrevolutionary turmoil," the event turned the Monument into what one student called a "lightning rod" for those who no longer wished to march in lockstep with the Party. The incident was also an eye-opening reminder that by taking to the Square and the streets, the "people" could still shake the Party and government to its political fundaments. As student activist Feng Congde explained in 1991, "After decades of Communist Party education, every time people want to stage a democracy movement they think about the May Fourth Movement which happened at Tiananmen. Tiananmen is taken as a symbol, a symbol of democracy."

The next outburst of spontaneous dissent came in the fall of 1978. This time the protest centered around an unimposing brick wall situated at the intersection of the Avenue of Eternal Peace and Xidan Street just west of the Square. When on November 15, 1978, the government—now led by Deng Xiaoping, who had just made his third political comeback—"reversed the verdict" on those charged with counterrevolutionary crimes during the Tiananmen Square Incident, hundreds of disaffected people began gathering at this wall to paste up *dazibao* (handwritten wall posters) to criticize past Party policies, hold discussion groups, and give extemporaneous speeches. At first, Deng supported this unique zone of free expression. "Let the people say what they wish, the heavens will not fall," he declared, evidently pleased that most of the attacks targeted his "leftist" opponents within the Party hierarchy. "A range of opinions is good for a revolutionary party leading the government. When people are free to speak, it means that the Party and the government have strength and confidence."

With each passing day, however, critiques of the government became bolder, and by December, habitués of Democracy Wall, as the Xidan wall had come to be known, were indicting the whole Maoist era and calling for a more democratic political system. As attacks by activists such as Wei Jingsheng escalated against Mao, and then finally against Deng himself, Deng began to reconsider his support.

Wei Jingsheng, a young electrician working at the Beijing Zoo and editor of a samizdat-style publication called *Explorations*, became one of the most trenchant critics. On December 5, 1978, he posted a critique of Deng's Four Modernizations program that insisted that modernizing agriculture, industry, science and technology, and national defense without also embracing a "fifth modernization," namely democracy, was futile. "What is true democracy?" his wall poster asked. "It means the right of people to choose their own representatives who will work according to their will and in their interest. Only this can be called democracy. Furthermore, the people must have power to replace their representatives any time so that these representatives cannot go on deceiving others in the name of the people."

While Deng was willing to countenance a certain amount of Party-directed reform from the top down, he was not about to tolerate giving "the masses" power to elect their own leaders. Nor was he about to tolerate the likes of Wei attacking him and the Party with impunity. Deng may have been a reformer, but he was no democrat. What evidently really turned him against Wei was an essay entitled "Democracy or New Autocracy?" that Wei published in March of 1979 as a response to a call by Deng for all Chinese to heed his "Four Cardinal Principles," a bouquet of socialist prescriptions that required adherence to the "socialist path," "the leadership of the Party," "Marxism-

Leninism and Mao Zedong thought,'' and ''the dictatorship of the proletariat.''

''We hold that people should not give any political leader unconditional trust. Does Deng Xiaoping want democracy? No he does not,'' asserted Wei. Then, as if he were engaged in an actual face-to-face debate with Deng, Wei rhetorically asked, ''We cannot help asking: What do you think democracy means? If the people do not have a right to express their ideas freely, how can one speak of democracy? If refusing to allow other people to criticize those in power is your idea of democracy, then what is the difference between this and what Mao euphemistically called the 'dictatorship of the proletariat'? ''

Wei was soon arrested and sentenced to fifteen years in prison on charges of having sold state secrets to a foreigner. In jail he became a troublesome reminder of the Party's arbitrary power to suppress political opposition, until he was finally released in the fall of 1993 in an effort by the Chinese government to enhance its chances of bringing the 2000 Olympic Games to Beijing.

It was not until the end of 1986 that the next wave of student protest—this time against the slow pace of democratization—swept China. On January 1, 1987, this nationwide movement culminated when several thousand Beijing students breached several cordons of police and again succeeded in reaching the Square. Like their precursors, they were animated by an almost primal belief that no political protest in China could be considered legitimate until its demands were articulated before Tiananmen Gate. As in the past, however, their protest only presaged another hard-line political crackdown. Hu Yaobang, the relatively liberal general secretary of the Communist Party, was forced from office, and three prominent dissident intellectuals—astrophysicist Fang Lizhi, investigative journalist Liu Binyan, and essayist Wang Ruowang—were expelled from the Party for having allegedly spread subversive political ideas among China's youth.

Each time a group of protesters managed to reach Tiananmen Square and *zai fotou dongtu* (dig up the earth right under the Buddha's nose), the Party's myth of having created a monolithic socialist society in which political opposition was outmoded lost a little more credibility, and the Square's standing as a forum for patriotic protest grew. Seeking to staunch this upsurge of oppositional sentiment among China's newest generation of intellectuals, Deng made it clear that while he would tolerate, and even encourage, economic reforms, he would continue to oppose fundamental political changes, especially those that promoted the May Fourth ideals of Western-style democracy and freedom. Whereas seventy years ago students had rallied around the slogan "Science and Democracy" as the key to China's modernization, Deng now wanted to emphasize "science" alone. However, with so many Western ideas beginning to flow through Deng's own "open door," Chinese students grew increasingly discontent with the idea of leaving their country's political system frozen in the past.

While Deng seemed to believe that he could radically transform China's economic system without fundamentally altering the political structure that he had inherited from Mao, his critics insisted that unless complementary political change was forthcoming, economic reforms would sooner or later founder. Without a system that made the government accountable to the people or guaranteed orderly succession, they argued, China would never attain the level of political stability needed to sustain long-term economic growth. Each view had its own historical roots and compelling logic, and each had its analogue in one of Tiananmen Square's confluent but conflicting identities. During the late 1970s and the 1980s, these contrary tendencies collided frequently without ever being resolved, locking the country in a series of repetitive epicycles in which economic reform seemed ineluctably to generate political upheaval, which, in turn, necessitated the Party to crack down ideologically. By the beginning of 1989 this schizophrenic state of affairs had coupled with widespread frustration over the failure of economic reform to deliver all that Deng had promised, and brought China to a dangerous boiling point.

Part I

The Square

1

The Year
of the Snake

By the time the Chinese New Year ushered in the Year of the Snake in February 1989, the city of Beijing was seething with a discontent so poisonous that many people began to whisper that the government's heavenly mandate to rule was running out. The optimism that had been generated in 1978 when Deng Xiaoping formally proclaimed his ambitious program of pragmatic reform and "opening up" to the outside world had been all but dissipated by deepening economic problems and a growing disillusionment with the slowness of political change. Ironically, this feeling of disaffection had grown despite the fact that, for most Chinese, living standards were far higher and life far more comfortable than at any time since the Cultural Revolution. But the fact that China's gross national product had grown by an astonishing 11.2 percent over the preceding year while the value of industrial production jumped by an even more dramatic 21 percent, making China the world's third-fastest-growing economy of the decade, only fueled more extravagant expectations.

For all too many, hopes of joining China's nascent bourgeoisie were now collapsing into a black hole of disappointment and pessimism. Having tried for a decade to wrench sectors of the economy free from state ownership and the stifling grip of the central planning apparatus, reform-minded officials led by Party General Secretary Zhao Ziyang now found themselves trapped between the leadership's ongoing commitment to a highly centralized one-party system that took its cues from Mao Zedong and a program of free-market reforms that looked to Adam Smith. After countless bureaucratic skirmishes with hard-liners (who included neo-Maoist ideologues as well as leaders who continued to believe in state ownership and central economic planning), many reformers were nearly spent from trying to build what Deng had dubbed "socialism with Chinese characteristics." It did not help that China's headlong dash toward economic development had created rampant profiteering, corruption, and nepotism among Party and government officials. At every level, from the children of ranking leaders to low-level bureaucrats, officials were on the take. With key resources in scarce supply, prices for basic industrial building blocks such as steel, coal, cotton, and electricity began to rise rapidly, sparking an inflationary spiral that affected virtually every part of society. China's retail price index increased by an alarming 18.5 percent in 1988, and then shot up to 26.7 percent during the first four months of 1989. State-sector workers found the buying power of their fixed salaries reduced almost daily by an inflation rate that was higher than it had been at any time since the 1940s. Subsidies to moribund state-run enterprises, many of which had become little more than state-funded welfare societies for workers and their families, had increased by a factor of seven since 1978 and were sucking up a third of the state's total budget. In many cities cash-strapped local governments were so desperate that they began requiring factory workers to buy government bonds, while in the countryside many peasants were forced to accept IOUs in exchange for the grain that they were required to turn over to the state at artificially low prices.

Meanwhile, students and intellectuals on stipends so meager that they were barely able to get by chafed at the government's refusal to liberalize controls over politics and culture more rapidly. One of the stillborn dreams of many educated Chinese was for a legal system that could protect their right to freedom of inquiry, expression, assembly, and worship. "If the media is free then it can discuss and test various policy options before they are carried out . . . and correct them before they cause damage," declared an article in the *World Economic Herald*. Despite endless rhetoric about "socialist legality" and the revival of legal codes and courts, the judicial system remained the hostage of the Party, which continued to be able to order the arrest and imprisonment of anyone it wished. After a decade of reform, the Public Security Bureau (PSB), the "People's Courts," and the prison system were no less available for government and Party use than when Mao still lived. To make matters worse, urban crime was rising rapidly. Under the circumstances, the best that many intellectuals could imagine was to find some way to escape abroad.

When I arrived back in Beijing that February, I had never seen people so frustrated, cynical, and ill mannered, or heard them heap such contempt on government leaders. Once proud of being "the first to endure hardships and the last to enjoy life," Party cadres were now viewed as the embodiments of venality and self-aggrandizement. The Party itself seemed to have lost every reason for existence—except the protection of its privilege and survival.

In the absence of any other officially sanctioned avenues for ordinary people to express their grievances, a welter of sardonic *shunkouliu* (limerick-like folk rhymes that distorted old political slogans and ridiculed the Party's most sanctified ideological notions) were making the rounds. Bitterness over the high rate of inflation was expressed in this piece of doggerel:

Mao Zedong was bad, so bad,
But if you had a dollar you knew what you had.
Deng Xiaoping is fine, so fine,
But a dollar's only worth a lousy dime.

Criticizing Deng's penchant for throwing his weight behind rapid reform at one moment and then supporting hard-line crackdowns the next, another declared:

Chairman Mao was like the sun—roasting us morning, noon, and night.
Deng Xiaoping is like the moon—ever changing his mind about what
   is right.

Few things, however, attracted more scorn than the way officials spent public funds to buy fancy foreign cars and then used them for their own personal purposes.

A Japanese limo that costs big bucks,
From the blood and sweat of the people is sucked,
And inside a fat son-of-a-bitch is tucked.

Although China's political climate had become increasingly relaxed under the relatively liberal stewardship of Zhao Ziyang (who had been designated by Deng to replace Hu Yaobang as Party general secretary in February 1987 after student demonstrations swept the country), and although there was lively debate in a whole host of new publications about China's political future, political reform had not kept pace with economic reform. When coupled with the atmosphere of cynicism that prevailed, the Party's relatively hands-off posture only emboldened intellectuals to complain that, politically speaking, the reform movement was "all thunder and no rain." Searching for some sort of *tupo* (breakthrough), many of them looked hopefully toward that spring when, like intersecting planetary orbits loaded with astrological significance, three highly symbolic political anniversaries were concentrated within a period of a few months. March 29 was the tenth anniversary of Wei Jingsheng's arrest and the symbolic end of the Democracy Wall Movement; May 4 the seventieth anniversary of the May Fourth Movement; and July 14 the two hundredth anniversary of the French Revolution. To top it off, October 1 would be the fortieth anniversary of the founding of Mao's People's Republic.

Perhaps the most symbolically loaded anniversary was May 4. As the revisionist Marxist theoretician Su Shaozhi wrote in *China Youth* that January: "The May Fourth Movement sounded a clarion call to struggle against feudal despotism in modern China. . . . The immense contrast between the ideals of the May Fourth Movement and the reality of China today merits special reflection and vigilance by contemporary Chinese youth." Su went on to proclaim that "no Chinese of conscience can fail to recognize the fact that [the advancement of] science and democracy in China are extremely incomplete. . . . If feudal despotism is not toppled, there is no hope for democracy and science."

No one exemplified the May Fourth spirit better than astrophysicist Fang Lizhi, who had been the vice-president of China's prestigious University of Science and Technology. Before the last round of student demonstrations in 1986, Fang had toured university campuses speaking out with an unprecedented candor. In September at a conference on political reform in Anhui Province, where the University of Science and Technology was located, Fang had astonished listeners by saying, "The idea that we can modify a few chosen aspects of society while leaving everything else intact is a pipe dream. . . . We have to acknowledge the reality of our situation; namely, that backwardness is ubiquitous in China and no aspect is exempt from the need for reform."

Two months later at Shanghai's Tongji University, Fang told another audience that "speaking quite dispassionately, I have to judge this era [of socialism] a failure . . . in virtually every aspect of economic and political life." He went on to insist that "the key to understanding democracy lies first of all in recognizing the rights of each individual. Democracy is built from the bottom up. Every individual possesses certain rights, or to use what is a very sensitive term indeed in China, everyone possesses 'human rights.' Although we seldom dare utter the words 'human rights,' actually human rights are very basic."

Never before had a prominent figure dared to issue such a sweeping condemnation of the Chinese Revolution, much less publicly proclaim that all Chinese possessed universal human rights that transcended class rights. Young listeners found Fang's message electrifying, and it was not long before he began being referred to as "China's Andrei Sakharov." When nationwide student democracy demonstrations followed in the late fall of 1986, Deng Xiaoping responded uncompromisingly. "Firm measures must be taken against any student who creates trouble at Tiananmen Square," he said. "No concession should be made in this matter. . . . They must be dealt with unhesitatingly."

Much of the blame for these demonstrations was heaped on Fang. "I have read Fang Lizhi's speeches, and he doesn't sound like a Communist Party member at all," Deng fumed. "People who start rumors and spread slander can't be allowed to go around the country with impunity stirring the masses up to make trouble." Alluding to the Democracy Wall Movement and the arrest of Wei Jingsheng, Deng boasted that "a few years ago we punished . . . some exponents of liberalization who broke the law. Did that bring discredit on us? No! China's image was not damaged. On the contrary, the prestige of our country is steadily growing." Fang was promptly fired from his job and expelled from the Party.

On January 6, 1989, Fang was back in the news after making a simple but eloquently symbolic gesture that stunned China's intelligentsia and Party leaders alike. In his own hand, Fang penned a public letter to Deng. "This year is the fortieth anniversary of the founding of the People's Republic of China, and the seventieth anniversary of the May Fourth Movement," he wrote. "In view of this, I would like to offer my sincere suggestion that on the occasion of these two anniversaries a nationwide amnesty be declared, and that it especially include the release of political prisoners such as Wei Jingsheng." Saying that he felt such a "humanitarian act" would "improve the atmosphere of our society,'' Fang urged Deng to look upon such a release as a way of demonstrating his concern for China's future.

Although the government had incarcerated tens of millions of people for political reasons since "liberation" in 1949, no prominent figure had ever before publicly raised the extremely sensitive matter of "political prisoners." In fact, the idea of dissenters exiled or locked up for "ideologically incorrect" thoughts was so commonly accepted that many Chinese hardly seemed to question it. Now, like the Zen master who jolts his students into *satori* with a *koan*, Fang's letter jarred intellectuals into facing up to the reality of the Chinese gulag.

Deng, who had personally ordered Wei Jingsheng's arrest and Fang's firing, was reported to have seethed with anger at this latest effrontery. Although he never officially responded to Fang's letter, Chinese intellectuals did. On February 16, marking the occasion of the fortieth anniversary of the U.N. Declaration of Human Rights, the well-known avant-garde poet Bei Dao secured the signatures of thirty-three prominent Chinese on a petition supporting Fang and sent it to both the Standing Committee of the National People's Congress and the Party Central Committee. A month later forty-two senior members of the Chinese Academy of Sciences signed a petition drafted by the eminent historian of science and translator of Albert Einstein, Xu Liangying, calling for the release of those "youth imprisoned or sent to reform-through-labor camps for ideological problems." The petition also insisted that "world history as well as China's own experience shows us that political democratization, including [the establishment of] a legal system, are necessary to guarantee economic modernization."

At this time China's university campuses were also coming alive with iconoclastic political energy. Reveling in experimental fiction, obscure poetry, Freudian psychoanalytical theory, rock music, outlandish Western fashions, and libertine sexual mores, university students were contagious with heterodoxy. Significantly, these were the elite of China's young generation, those very youths being trained to lead the country in the future. In this sense there were few places more important in China than the university quarter in Beijing's northwestern Haidian District where most of the capital's institutions of higher education are located. At many of the most prestigious universities, such as Beijing University (Beida) and Beijing Normal University (Beishida), students had been holding informal *shalong* (salons) to discuss everything from new currents in philosophy and physics to the theory and practice of democratic pluralism, human rights, and nonviolent protest as advocated by Martin Luther King, Jr., and Mahatma Gandhi. Guest lecturers included Fang Lizhi who told students, "China cannot have economic development without democracy," and dissident journalist Dai Qing who told students that it was time for them to stand up, speak out, and "pledge allegiance to no authority but your conscience." A growing intellectual fascination with personal identity and individual autonomy made this generation far bolder and more interested in challenging orthodoxy and authority than their parents.

While most reform-minded officials looked upon these errant ideological tendencies as unavoidable side effects of efforts to integrate China into the modern world, neo-Maoist hard-liners were disturbed. Even though the Party had repeatedly launched campaigns against "spiritual pollution" and "bourgeois liberalism," un-Maoist, foreign ideas became increasingly corrosive, creating deeper tensions than ever between political factions. It was into this politically volatile situation that U.S. President George Bush stumbled on an official state visit late in February. Although he carefully avoided publicly criticizing China's human rights record, he did invite Fang Lizhi and a number of other intellectuals identified with China's nascent opposition movement to a farewell banquet at Beijing's Sheraton Great Wall Hotel, one of China's first large-scale joint-venture projects with American investors. Because the invitation provided both a welcome measure of respectability to his dissident ideas and some real protection from future detention or arrest, Fang gladly accepted. After all, since he had just provoked Deng anew with his January letter, there was no telling what the government might do next.

On the night of the banquet Fang and his wife, physicist Li Shuxian, decided to drive to the hotel with Princeton University Professor Perry Link and his wife, Jean Wong, at the last minute. But as the two couples came within sight of the hotel, their car was suddenly pulled over and surrounded by a phalanx of armed police. At first, Link and Fang thought that they had been stopped for a routine security check. When they tried to get out and walk to the hotel, even after Fang displayed his official presidential invitation, the way was blocked. Only after both men had made several requests to speak to someone in authority did a man finally identify himself as "the main person in charge of security for President Bush's visit." He informed Fang that neither he nor his wife were on "the guest list provided by American security," and that he was thus unable to allow them to proceed to the banquet.

"I thought that this was quite an amazing statement," Fang later recalled with a chortle, "for the truth was that they had not yet even asked us for our names!"

Fearful of what might happen to Fang if they were separated, Link was determined to stick with his friend. "If Fang had been alone, I don't know what the police would have done with him," he later said. "But the unanticipated presence of my white face probably made it 'inconvenient' for them to do whatever they had originally planned."

In the confusion that reigned on the street, the four managed to hail a cab. But after going for only a few blocks, the cab, too, was pulled over and the driver was charged with having a defective headlight. Abandoning their second impounded vehicle, they tried next to board a series of public buses. Each time a bus approached the stop where they were standing, however, agitated police waved it away. Seeing no other alternative, the four set off on foot for the American embassy, followed by a retinue of walkie-talkie-toting plainclothes tails.

Meanwhile, back at the banquet, Chinese President Yang Shangkun was standing in front of an enormous Texas flag sanctimoniously extolling Sino-American "friendship." By then, however, foreign reporters—there were hundreds of them from the world's leading television networks, news magazines, wire services, and newspapers on the presidential trip—were paying little attention because they had noticed that Fang's assigned seat remained mysteriously empty.

Fang's "strange little band," as he dubbed the four of them, finally reached the residence of U.S. ambassador Winston Lord only to find it empty because everyone was at the banquet. As they stood outside the guardhouse in the dark wondering what to do next, a Canadian diplomat passed by and, happening to recognize Fang from photographs, invited him to his nearby apartment.

I arrived in the lobby of the Great Wall Hotel just as the banquet was ending to find journalists frantically calling around the city on the house phones trying to find out what had happened to the celebrated guest. Being a friend of Fang's, I immediately phoned his apartment and reached his youngest son. Fang Zhe told me that his father had just called in and he gave me the rough outlines of what had happened. At that moment, he said, his parents and the Links were being driven to the Shangri-La Hotel, where the White House press office had been set up. Hopping a cab, I raced across town.

Not until about 1:30 A.M. did Fang arrive at the Shangri-La. The glittering lobby was a bedlam of reporters. As he entered, he crossed a symbolic line in the coming-of-age of Chinese political dissidence. Outside lay the world of the Party, with its secrecy, censorship, intimidation, and control. Inside lay a free-for-all of camera-wielding photographers, TV crews, anchormen, and reporters all clamoring to scoop the unexpurgated story of Fang's disappearance. It was the first time since the founding of the People's Republic that a Chinese political dissident in Beijing was being thrown together with so many foreign journalists for an uncensored press conference. It was, in short, the Chinese government's worst nightmare.

Fang edged his way through the crowd into the hotel's grand ballroom, where reporters eventually quieted down long enough for him to make a brief statement. Bathed in klieg lights between Chinese and American flags, he explained what had happened. Then, holding up his invitation embossed with the presidential seal, he spoke sorrowfully of the humiliation he felt his country was inflicting on itself by stifling the democratic rights of its citizens. "What we are calling for is extremely basic; namely, freedom of speech, press, assembly, and travel," Fang said. "However, it is all too easy to see from this incident what the human rights situation is like here in China."

Then hands began shooting up. One reporter asked him if he thought President Bush should intervene in his behalf. "Democracy is a world concept common to every human being," said Fang somewhat obliquely. "Democracy is not just a Western right, but a human right." Another reporter asked if he had been frightened during that night's game of cat and mouse. "How can I tell you I was not afraid?" Fang replied. "But since such human rights violations happen so often here, I am somewhat used to them by now." Before the night was out, Fang had not only given a press conference, but had been interviewed by three major U.S. networks and done what no one had previously succeeded in doing in forty years—put a human face on China's dissident movement for the outside world to see.

Although China's official press ignored the incident, word about the government's clumsy efforts to prevent Fang from attending the banquet, and of his uncensored responses to the questions of foreign reporters, quickly spread via the Chinese-language services of the Voice of America (VOA) and the British Broadcasting Corporation (BBC). Previously, such public acts of opposition politics had seemed almost unimaginable to most Chinese. But now Fang had shown others who also harbored grievances against their government but had not yet dared speak out that public opposition was not only possible in China but could also earn the respect of the world. As Lu Xun had written in

1936, "It doesn't matter whether at first there is any hope. Hope is like a path. In fact, even though there is no path, once many people have trod there, a path appears." Only a few months later, thousands of other Chinese were also treading Fang's figurative path, this time back to Tiananmen Square.

2

A Funeral in
Counterpoint

On the afternoon of April 15, 1989, an announcer interrupted
regular programming on Radio Beijing to report that the former general secretary of the Chinese Communist Party, Hu Yaobang, had
died of a heart attack at the age of seventy-three. A curious combination of Party loyalist and quixotic maverick, Hu had been Deng
Xiaoping's protégé and designated successor until 1987. While Hu
had never openly defied the dictates of the Party's Central Committee leadership, during his seven-year tenure as general secretary he
gained a reputation both as an adversary of Cultural Revolution–type
political campaigns and a defender of reform-minded officials and
liberal intellectuals when they ran afoul of Maoist hard-liners. Hu
was also known for his quirky spontaneity and the emotional, almost
childlike way he responded to certain issues, especially to the plight
of those who had been treated unjustly. And of all ranking Party
leaders, there were few less besmirched by rumors of selfishness,
scandal, and corruption. Thus many were angered when after the
1986 student demonstrations Hu was scapegoated for the unrest and
unceremoniously forced to resign.

As the news of Hu's death spread that spring day in 1989, Beijing
university campuses spontaneously began to blossom with banners and
wall posters eulogizing the disgraced reformer. "Yaobang Is Gone.
We Mourn," read a message printed on a long piece of computer paper

hung from a dormitory window at Beida. "The Star of Hope Has Fallen," lamented a wall poster.

Such feelings of loss were not the exclusive province of the younger generation. The venerated eighty-nine-year-old May Fourth–era writer Bing Xin penned a eulogy praising Hu's honesty and righteousness: *"Gaisi meisi, bugaisi que sile"*—"The one who should not have died is dead, while those who should have died remain alive"—a blunt reference to the disappointment many felt that it was Hu rather than Deng who had passed away. Almost immediately these words were adopted as an epitaph for Hu and began appearing on the flurry of wall posters that went up inveighing against the rampant corruption and official incompetence that Hu was viewed as having opposed. A poem pasted up at Beishida hinted that popular disgust with the Party's treatment of Hu was symptomatic of a far deeper malaise:

> The privileged class, "officials of the people,"
>   you live a life to make immortals envious;
> Opening up and reform—what good opportunities—
>   if you don't make money now, then you never will.
> Children of officials violate the law and run wild,
>   and the law barely touches them.
> Although their sons and daughters are idiots,
>   they can choose between Beijing and Qinghua Universities.
> These privileged souls accompany foreign guests, eating
>   and drinking for free . . .
> Chartered trains and planes deliver gifts,
>   delicacies from every land, fresh year-round.
> The whole family happily resides in Zhongnanhai,
>   their palatial second homes and villas scattered
>   from the mountains to the sea.
> Luxurious gleaming buildings, clubs, and hotels—
> The people can only look on and sigh. . . .

Just as a previous generation of students had used the death of Premier Zhou Enlai as a pretext in 1976 to protest the policies of the Gang of Four, now politically attuned students began to organize another ritual of mourning for Hu. For those who had been looking to the upcoming May Fourth anniversary to protest the Party's corruption and its refusal to initiate real political reform, Hu's passing presented a perfect opportunity to speed up their plans. In his autobiography, Shen Tong, a biology student at Beida who was to play a prominent role in the upcoming protest, remembers glibly telling a fellow student, "Hu Yaobang's death has the potential to start a student movement."

Such statements reflected a new sophistication about political tactics that had begun to temper the naive idealism characteristic of the student protests of 1986. After all, students cleverly reasoned, who could fault them for commemorating a leader whom Party obituaries were hailing as "a loyal fighter for communism [and] a great proletarian revolutionary"?

"Hu Yaobang was not that important, and the regard heaped on him was excessive," Fang Lizhi openly acknowledged when interviewed by University of Toronto History Professor Timothy Brook several months later. "But in China, a leader's death provides an excuse for people to assemble. . . . [And] it's only when people can assemble that something can be achieved."

The paradox of students launching a protest movement by supporting a former Communist Party chief was not lost on Liu Xiaobo, an iconoclastic thirty-two-year-old essayist and critic from Beishida who had flown back from Columbia University in New York just after Hu's death to join the demonstrations. "Why is it that the Chinese feel so much more deeply for tragic heroes like Zhou Enlai, Peng Dehuai, and Hu Yaobang than for ones like Wei Jingsheng?" Liu asked in an essay published a short while later. "All these tragic heroes have one thing in common: They were loyal but not trusted, they told the truth and were condemned for it. . . . Not even in his wildest dreams could Wei Jingsheng or his fellows ever hope for such treatment . . . [even though their] agonies . . . in prison have been far greater than anything Hu Yaobang experienced following his fall from power."

In pointing to the tendency of Chinese intellectuals to focus their feelings on individual political leaders rather than on the political system that sustained them, Liu was highlighting one of the key historical weaknesses of political-opposition movements in China. What he did not mention was that in a repressive society where the price of opposing the status quo invariably meant state-sponsored persecution, prison, or death, circumlocution was the only way to express discontent without risking catastrophe. Since state funerals were, as Fang noted, one of the few occasions when people could actually expect to gather en masse without fear of arrest, it was hardly surprising that the deaths of relatively benign leaders were seized upon as occasions for expressing all kinds of grievances.

It was telling that on April 15 the first people to place a funeral wreath at the base of the Monument to the Martyrs of the People were a group of workers from the Ministry of Textiles. Although the next day about three hundred Beida students appeared in the Square, it was not until April 17 that the first organized march in remembrance of Hu took place as thousands of students from many different campuses poured into the Square. By then the base of the Monument was heaped with commemorative wreaths and banners and Hu's reputation as a fallen hero had swollen to unreal proportions. But as the wall posters and banners made clear, students were not simply mourning Hu's passing and the way in which the Party had impugned Hu's legacy as a liberalizer, but they were also criticizing the dictatorial way in which Deng and his supporters ruled in his stead.

Denied access to China's mass media, the students were forced to create innovative modes of guerrilla propaganda. Donning black armbands, bearing funeral wreaths draped with white sashes inscribed in classical Chinese, and carrying mock ancestral tablets made out of Styrofoam, they were careful to play on the traditional symbols. They also appropriated more contemporary symbols that until then had been the exclusive preserve of the Communist Party. Marching through the streets under the national flag, singing the "Internationale" and China's national anthem, and in some cases toting portraits of Chairman Mao, demonstrators sought to cultivate the same image of nationalism and patriotic zeal that the Communists themselves had sought by opposing Japanese aggression when they were an opposition party during the 1930s and 1940s. And since the Party had adopted Tiananmen Square as its most cherished emblem, it was hardly surprising that this new generation of protesters was again drawn to it. By commandeering this symbol of Party legitimacy, the students were, in Maoist parlance, "waving the red flag to attack the red flag."

The next day, Tuesday, April 18, was beautiful and sunny, and the crowds of students and curious bystanders gathered in the Square were larger than ever. Despite the initially funereal aspect of their commemoration, by then the atmosphere had become almost festive. People milled around reading the inscriptions on the sashes of memorial wreaths and studying the handwritten wall posters pasted up all around the Monument's base. "Openly Reevaluate Comrade Yaobang's Successes and Mistakes!" and "Reveal the Truth About Comrade Yaobang's Resignation!" demanded inscriptions on two banners. Daring demonstrators delivered extemporaneous speeches and shouted slogans. "Old ideas and institutions can no longer satisfy the needs of the people!" declared one. "Seventy years have passed since the May Fourth Movement and still we have no freedom and democracy!" complained another to an accolade of cheers.

Meanwhile, self-appointed student leaders began to coalesce and formalize demands. They called on the Party to reassess "the verdict" on Hu's political career; renounce the use of mass political campaigns; publicly disclose their incomes and assets; take measures to halt official corruption; increase funding for education; abolish prohibitions against street protests; and permit greater press freedom so that journalists could cover their protest activities. Standing in front of the Great Hall of the People that day, student representatives even requested that an official come out and accept a petition containing these seven demands. It was not until after dark, however, that three lowly deputies from the National People's Congress emerged to receive the petition, promising only to pass it along to "superior government departments."

Since students knew that it was unlikely that high-level Party leaders would ever reply to their demands, later that night thousands of them marched from the Square along the Avenue of Eternal Peace and rallied outside Xinhuamen, or New China Gate, which leads into the Zhongnanhai leadership compound adjacent to the Forbidden City. Here they began chanting for Premier Li Peng to come out and accept their petition.

As the night progressed, some of the rowdier demonstrators—which by this time included many nonstudent *geti hu* (private entrepreneurs) and unemployed youths—began crowding and pushing up against the police guarding the gate. The situation might have become far more grave were it not for the fact that the attitude of most demonstrators was actually more playful than hostile and that police acted with commendable restraint.

The apparent ease with which the students had been able to flood into the Square that day and then to rally outside of Xinhuamen left them flushed with a sense of unexpected power. Not since the founding of the People's Republic had any group demonstrated against the government so openly at such important symbolic locations.

"We were almost drunk with success," one young participant later told me. "We had all spent our lives heeding authority, and our parents were always warning us that insubordination would spell disaster. Then when we found ourselves protesting against the government in the middle of Tiananmen Square and out in front of Zhongnanhai as if we owned the place . . . *and* were able to get away with it, everything seemed suddenly so different that it was hard to imagine ever becoming so obedient again."

Since by the morning of April 19 senior Party leaders had still not responded to the students' seven demands, tens of thousands of demonstrators once again flooded back into the Square. "Down with

Dictatorship'' and ''Support Peaceful Petitioning,'' their banners proclaimed. Instrumental in shaping the students' decision to return was a
slender, bespectacled young undergraduate in history from Beida
named Wang Dan, who edited a student magazine called *New May
Fourth* and was one of the organizers of a weekly campus ''salon''
called the Democracy Forum. It had been here as a guest speaker at one
of the forum's outdoor sessions held in front of a statue of Cervantes
that Fang Lizhi had reminded students that Beida had been founded on
the principles of intellectual freedom expressed by an earlier generation of students who had made ''Democracy and Science'' their rallying cry. The decision on April 19, 1989, to continue this latest protest
not only gave the nascent student democracy movement a second wind
but also thrust the twenty-one-year-old Wang into a major leadership
position.

That morning a group from the Central Academy of Fine Arts triumphantly hoisted a huge black and white oil painting of Hu Yaobang
inscribed with the words ''Wither have you gone? May your soul
return'' up onto the granite pedestal of the Monument directly facing
the portrait of Chairman Mao on Tiananmen Gate. Looking out from
their respective frames, the two deceased Party leaders were perfect
emblems for the opposing forces now faced off in the Square. ''It was
as if Beijing suddenly had two rival sources of authority, the two
patrons of different visions of communism staring each other down
across the Square,'' wrote Andrew Higgins and Michael Fathers from
the British paper the *Independent*. Suddenly, the struggle over who
would possess the mantle of the Square—Chairman Mao, the Party,
and the legacy of state dominance; or Hu Yaobang, the students, and
the legacy of May Fourth—was joined in the most graphic way.

Late that night, some 20,000 demonstrators again flocked to Xinhuamen demanding that Li Peng come out for a dialogue. They
chanted, ''Let Cixi retire!''—an unflattering equation between Deng
and the autocratic Empress Dowager Cixi who ruled during the last
years of the Qing Dynasty. Just as their pushing and shoving against
beefed-up phalanxes of police threatened to get out of hand, another
twenty-one-year-old student happened to bicycle past on his way back
to campus from the Square. When Wu'er Kaixi, who was studying
education at Beishida and had already played a significant role in
organizing his own campus's response to Hu's death, stopped to find
out what was going on, it became obvious to him that the situation
might soon erupt in violence. Wu'er began calling for the mob to sit
down on the pavement. Almost miraculously, he succeeded in trans-

forming the dangerous shoving match between demonstrators and police into a free-form teach-in with himself serving as moderator.

"I told them that we needed organization, not just a bunch of people getting together and making noise," he later remembered. "They were really hungering for someone to stand up and lead." With a flair that became his trademark, Wu'er told the crowd, "I know you're afraid, but I'm not afraid. If you want to say something, write it on a piece of paper and give it to me, and I'll read it. I'll read anything!"

As Wu'er read aloud sentiments that students did not dare to utter themselves, he kept up a running repartee of humorous comments that quickly captivated the crowd. "It was beautiful," he said later with his characteristic lack of self-effacement. "All the students needed was a bit of organization!" What Wu'er had provided was a demonstration of chutzpa in the face of authority, traits that would in the days to come perfectly complement Wang Dan's quiet, cerebral abilities as a thinker and tactician.

Despite Wu'er's charismatic efforts to defuse the situation, events took a turn for the worse later that night. Around 3 A.M., when only a few hundred demonstrators remained in front of Xinhuamen, Public Security Bureau (PSB) loudspeakers suddenly burst forth: "A small number of people" have been "attacking and insulting Party and government leaders," "spreading rumors," shouting "reactionary slogans calling for the overthrow of the Chinese Communist Party," and "poisoning minds," a voice ominously declared. Such politically charged terminology had seldom been heard in China since the tumultuous days of the Cultural Revolution, and its revival now indicated that high Party leaders were not only losing patience, but might be on the verge of reverting to Maoist forms of repression. Indeed, a short while later, policemen waded into the midst of the remaining demonstrators with clubs flying. "They beat students with belts and kicked them with jackboots," claimed one student eyewitness. "Some students' glasses were broken and blood covered their heads and faces. . . . Some of the girls' clothes were torn. Others were beaten so badly they begged for mercy, but the police would not let up." It was the first outbreak of violence that spring, and as Party leaders might have foreseen, it served only to further incense demonstrators and encourage them to continue.

The next day freshly painted wall posters blossomed all over university campuses, hailing those beaten and arrested in front of Xinhuamen as "martyrs" and condemning the police attack as a senseless outrage against nonviolent demonstrators who were only exercising their constitutionally guaranteed right of free assembly. "The state has finally resorted to violence and lied in order to maintain its rule over the people," read one such poster. "We young students are very worried and angry, but [now] we know all the more that we must change this incompetent and shameful way of ruling."

A group of workers who had also been at Xinhuamen put out a "Letter to the People of Beijing" in which, with a panache typical of these days, they mockingly demanded that the Party respond to a series of questions about privilege and corruption. How much, they wanted to know, did Deng's son, Deng Pufang, bet when he went to Hong Kong to play the horses? And who paid Zhao Ziyang's greens fees when he teed off at the golf links each week?

A commentary in the April 21 edition of the Party's flagship paper, the *People's Daily,* did nothing to calm the situation. It warned that "those who take advantage of mourning for Comrade Yaobang to loot, smash, rob, or set fire to offices of the Communist Party or the government will be condemned by history. In dealing with the 'very small number' of people doing these unlawful activities, the government has until now exercised restraint. If some people consider this weakness, they will face bitter consequences."

April 22 had been set aside as the day when the government would hold an official funeral ceremony for Hu in the Great Hall of the People. However, fearful that student protesters would once again fill the Square, leaders banned all further demonstrations and ordered that the Square be closed off, beginning early that morning. Acting with a cleverness, swiftness, and discipline that surprised many, around midnight on the night of April 21 before the government had a chance to seal off access with police, a huge crowd representing almost every institution of higher learning in Beijing poured back into the Square.

"It was a magical scene," wrote Higgins and Fathers of the procession through the city. "In the darkness, they seemed to come from nowhere, their chants and songs echoing through otherwise deserted streets. Lights flickered on in apartment buildings as people peered out to watch the parade. Late-night buses stopped to let them pass, the passengers leaning out the windows to gaze, smile, and sometimes cheer."

All along the route students sang, chanted, and waved banners inscribed with slogans: "Grieve for the Soul of China!" "Mr. Democracy and Mr. Science, We Have Been Expecting You for Seventy Years!" and "Whoever Conducts Real Reform Will Get Our Support!" When troops finally appeared early that morning, there were already over 100,000 students in the Square, and there was nothing commanders could do other than cordon off the entrance to the Great Hall where the funeral ceremony was scheduled to begin at 10 A.M.

Actually, the students were far from eager for confrontation. The dustup in front of Xinhuamen had given them a preview of what lay in store if things turned violent. Fortunately, Hu's funeral provided a perfect opportunity for them to challenge the Party again in a nonviolent way.

Although it had been cloudy and raining, April 22 broke a beautiful sunny spring morning. Fuzz from the freshly budded willow and poplar trees that line the streets drifted through the air as students gathered around the Monument, where a huge placard inscribed with the character for "Sorrow" had been placed next to Hu's funerary portrait. In a gesture obviously aimed at foreign television, just below hung a banner in English inscribed with the single word "Liberty." Students solemnly raised the flag of China, bowed to Hu's portrait, and then began singing the national anthem, whose words were paradoxically appropriate:

> Arise, ye who refuse to be slaves,
> With our very flesh and blood
> Let us build a new Great Wall!
> The peoples of China are in a most critical time.
> Everybody must roar with defiance,
> Arise! Arise! Arise!

Then they broke into the "Internationale":

> Arise up ye prisoners of starvation,
> Arise ye wretched of the earth,
> For justice thunders condemnation.
> A better world's in birth,
> The earth shall rise on new foundations,
> We have been naught, we shall be all . . .

> No one will give us deliverance;
> No god, no czar, no hero;
> We'll arrive at our freedom
> Only by our own hand.

As the hour of the official funeral ceremony approached, thousands of Party leaders began trooping up the enormous front stairs of the

Great Hall, furtively glancing over their shoulders at the massive crowd below that stretched almost to the wreath-strewn and banner-draped Monument. Wanting to avoid the indignity of entering in full view of so many protesters, Deng slipped in through a back entrance as students out front smashed bottles on the pavement. In Mandarin, "Xiaoping," or "Small Peace," which is Deng's given name, is a homophone for "small bottle." During the late 1970s when his reputation as a reformer made Deng a popular figure, students tied glass bottles onto picket signs and paraded them in public to signify their support. Now that they had become disenchanted with his halfway reforms, they inverted the ritual.

Just before 10 o'clock, outdoor speakers were turned on so that the students could hear the ceremony inside, which was also being broadcast nationwide via Central Chinese Television (CCTV). The scene within the Great Hall stood in stark contrast to the youthful hubbub outside. Arrayed before Hu's body draped in a Chinese flag under a crystal sarcophagus was a sea of doddering septuagenarian and octogenarian Party leaders in dark Mao suits. "A lot of them were deaf and wearing hearing aids and some had to be carried by their nurses or secretaries or shuffled their feet step by step, hardly able to walk," remembered Chen Yizi, director of the Research Institute for Economic Structural Reform and an advisor to Party Chief Zhao Ziyang. Chen went on to describe how at meetings before the funeral these elderly leaders "sat in wheelchairs, dragged oxygen bottles around, and during meetings pissed and shit in their pants," would suddenly emit "big snores as some of them fell asleep, drooling at the mouth." And sometimes when they made speeches, "they would suddenly turn to their secretaries and ask, 'What was I just talking about?' " Nowhere in the world was there a government leadership so visibly tired and aged as the one arrayed around Hu's corpse that morning.

As Zhao Ziyang gave a long, lugubrious, and carefully worded eulogy—which, not surprisingly, made no mention of Hu's ouster in 1987—Deng stood with his hands clasped in front of him staring grimly off into space. The entire room seemed leaden with conflicted feeling. The ceremony was like a drama in which, with the exception of Hu's family, all the players had been miscast. Many of these "mourners" had not only questioned Hu's ideological convictions, but had helped orchestrate his downfall. Deng had forced Hu to resign; Zhao Ziyang had taken his place as general secretary; and Li Peng had never seen eye-to-eye with Hu's brand of politics. But here they all were, "like assassins attending the funeral of one of their victims," as one scornful Chinese friend character- ized them.

When a dirge finally signaled that it was time for this gallery of poseurs to file, hobble, or be wheeled past Hu's sarcophagus and bow three times, many must have sighed with relief. But there was still one more agonizing wicket through which to pass before liberation from this awkward ritual. Custom called for all mourners to pay their re- spects to Li Zhao, Hu's widow. To say that many of the handshakes were chilly and abrupt would be an understatement. When Deng's turn came, Li woodenly accepted his hand.

Although television cameras broadcast no images of the crowds in the Square to viewers across the country, those inside the Great Hall were not unaware of what was going on outside. They could hear the distant roar of the crowd, and some sympathetic insiders sought out places near windows where they could peek out through the curtains to glimpse the tumult in the Square below. One of these was Ge Yang, a seventy-year-old veteran revolutionary and editor of the freethinking journal *New Observer*. When she saw how the students had been cordoned off by squads of police, she was reminded of her own days as a young Communist protester.

"Many people of my age took part in the student movement in our youth," she remembered afterward. "The students in the Square were demanding democracy; the same democracy for which we [Commu- nists] once asked the Nationalist Party. . . . [I wondered to myself] how come we've turned into a party which is against the people and against the students? Since I knew that the Communist Party I once joined was not this party, I felt very emotional."

The fact that Hu's true supporters had been kept out of the service while his detractors had been let in inspired Ge to begin composing a poem: "This Side and That Side."

A single land split
By a wall of brute force.
On one side lies an iceberg,
    chilling those who dwell therein.
On the other, a warm sea.
Here lies Yaobang's body,
And there his soul.
From there we all came;
If there was no "there,"
    there would be no "here."

By the time the ceremony ended, singing and chanting outside had risen to a steady din. With Wu'er Kaixi as drillmaster, demonstrators had begun chanting, "Dialogue! Dialogue! Dialogue!" and "Li Peng come out! Li Peng come out!" When by 1:30 P.M. they had still received no response, three student representatives ascended the Great Hall's stone steps, and after falling to their knees, one proffered a scroll over his head, beseeching Li Peng to emerge and accept it. For half an hour these three supplicants remained in this position, pointedly reminiscent of imperial underlings prostrating themselves before the emperor, and still no official emerged to receive their petition.

"When people kneel down in China, there are two meanings," Wu'er Kaixi later explained to me. "One is to acknowledge that you have been defeated, in which case your kneeling down suggests a kind of spiritual collapse. But by kneeling down you may also be showing that you still harbor some bit of hope that your grievances can be worked out." Wu'er went on to describe the historical significance of the Chinese word *guijian,* which means "to kneel in order to memorialize the throne." "This is a very old term which was used when loyal ministers memorialized the emperor," he said. "When those three students knelt on the steps of the Great Hall, they were making such a plea. We just wanted 'the emperor' to consent to a dialogue with us."

While the students had chosen a form of supplication that was traditional and submissive enough that it could effectively shield them from accusations of disrespect, they were also giving the government a backhanded slap in the face. By resorting to this archaic form of petitioning, they were implying that despite Party assertions that their revolution had freed China from the fetters of the "feudal past," its leaders were actually no different from the autocratic emperors of old.

Of course, Li Peng never emerged. When the three petitioners finally descended the steps again with their scroll calling for a free press and better conditions for students still in hand, some bystanders burst into tears for what the author of one subsequent wall poster deplored as "this tragic country" in which "the title of the people's premier was given to such a faithless and incompetent man."

Although some students disapproved of such an obsequious gesture, others, including many ordinary Chinese, were deeply moved by its sincerity and filial deference to authority. "Fellow students who participated in the April 22 protest will be unable to forget this scene," read a wall poster written by Beida geology students shortly after the funeral. "They sacrificed their own self-respect and human dignity to fulfill a mission entrusted to them by tens of thousands of students. . . . After the petition had been ignored over and over again, what else could they do but use this most provocative, most feudal method—kneeling? What self-mockery to use a feudal method of expression in a struggle for democracy in present-day China! And what powerlessness and impotence it implies!"

In the war of symbols the government's refusal to accept the petition created a new wave of sympathy for the student movement. "The prime minister didn't heed the students at all!" complained Lü Jinghua, the manager of a privately owned dress shop who later joined worker activists in the Square to help organize China's first independent labor federation. "He was supposed to be the servant of the people, but Li Peng stood there with the attitude of a master. . . . It made us feel very strange . . . and very sad."

Perhaps the most tragic part of the government's refusal to respond decisively to the demands of students was that they missed a critical opportunity to defuse the confrontation at a time when modest concessions might well have mollified the demonstrators. Even after Hu's funeral, student demands remained couched in the language of moderation rather than extremism and were still very much within the century-old Chinese tradition of progressive intellectuals seeking reform within the context of the existing political system. "We did not want to overthrow the Communist Party," insisted student activist Feng Congde. "All that we said was that one-party dictatorship is no good."

A wall poster that appeared at the People's University caught this reformist, and sometimes even playful, tone perfectly. "The government is, in fact, a type of donkey," the poster declared, spoofing the traditional tale of Bai Le, an ancient folk hero renowned for his talents for appraising donkeys and horses. "Originally, we used it to pull the cart, but now it has changed into a lazy ill-tempered beast of burden that loves to eat and sleep and that lashes out at will. It is, however, impractical to sell it and buy another because there is no other donkey on the market. To kill it for its meat is even more unacceptable, and besides, the meat tastes awful. The only alternative we have is to train [the donkey] with a carrot and a big stick! The 'carrot' is the support of the people; the 'stick' is the resistance and protest of the people."

The goal of the student movement should not be to "overthrow the government," insisted the poster, but rather to "supervise and prod it'' like one of Bai Le's proverbial donkeys. ''Of course, this donkey is awfully difficult to train, so we must have patience. At the very least, [we must] show more patience than the donkey itself. Don't forget, after all, a donkey is a donkey, and you can't expect it to behave and think like a person! . . . And one last thing, pay attention not to get kicked by the donkey—it is really fat and strong!''

In failing to recognize the still basically reformist bent of the students and by refusing to make even modest concessions, Party leaders assured that the standoff with protesters would become more intractable than ever. But still smarting from the humiliation of watching student demonstrators march with impunity into their sacred Square again and again, the Party leaders were unable to bring themselves to make compromises. While they had not immediately lashed out to suppress the demonstrations as once they might have, their inability to see beyond their loss of face made it impossible for them to yield at a time when it might have served them to do so.

Nor were the students immune to their own kind of political blindness. Amid the whirlwind of successive demonstrations, they had forgotten that every attempt at radical political reform since the Emperor Guangxu's failed Hundred Days Reform in 1898 had been defeated as much by the innate conservatism of Chinese culture and society as by the machinations of autocratic and inflexible leaders, and that, more often than not, well-intentioned pushes for high-speed reform only provoked violent reaction. But with their expectations fueled by their initial successes, students were in no mood for the kind of compromise that they, too, would have had to make in order to end the standoff. ''There are two possibilities,'' declared a statement by an independent Beishida teachers' group. ''One is to die halfway and leave China the same. The other is to push forward, to develop [the movement] in depth until a major step is made toward democratization in China.''

The day after Hu's funeral, student leaders met to formalize a new independent student organization that would press their cause forward. They called it the Provisional Students' Federation of Capital Universities. In addition to Wu'er Kaixi and Wang Dan, a twenty-three-year-old woman named Chai Ling, a psychology student at Beishida, was elected to the new steering committee. The next day, April 24, they called for the resignation of Premier Li Peng and a boycott of classes at all Beijing universities.

Smarting all the more from the effrontery of this latest challenge, Party hard-liners moved to counterattack. But there was both paradox and tragedy in their efforts. Although student rhetoric sounded dangerously inflammatory, the truth was that after Hu's funeral the movement had actually begun to fall into the doldrums. If Deng had not provided it with new provocation, the protest movement might very well have fizzled out there and then.

3

Deng Speaks and the Students Defy

On April 26 the *People's Daily* published a damning attack on the students under the headline "Take a Clear-cut Stand Against the Instigation of Turmoil." As was the custom with such important declarations of official policy, it was featured on the front page beneath a logo that depicted sunbeams radiating from a line drawing of Tiananmen Gate. As it turned out, Deng Xiaoping was responsible for the editorial's general content. The day before, while Zhao Ziyang was on an official visit to North Korea, Deng had delivered an unyielding speech to Party elders behind closed doors. "An extremely small number of people with ulterior motives," he warned, were seeking "to poison people's minds" and "sabotage the nation's political stability and unity." He ominously called upon the government to launch a two-pronged counterattack against the students, first by publishing a "forceful editorial," and if that proved insufficient, by using military force.

Quoting much of Deng's speech verbatim, the editorial labeled the student demonstrations a "well-planned conspiracy" calculated "to negate the leadership of the Communist Party and the socialist system." Referring pointedly to the Party's "tolerant, restrained attitude toward certain inappropriate words and actions of emotionally excited students," the editorial warned that if the government continued to "take a lenient attitude toward this turmoil and just let it go, a situation of real chaos will emerge . . . and hope for reform and opening up . . . will be reduced to nothing.'' Then it put student activists directly on notice: ''Those who deliberately create rumors and spread slander must be held criminally responsible in accordance with law.'' For good measure, the editorial reminded worker activists who had begun to support the students that ''unauthorized use of names of workers' organizations'' and their distribution of ''reactionary leaflets'' had not gone unnoticed.

While preserving the Party's grip on political power was undoubtedly Deng's paramount concern, other considerations also helped produce his uncompromising view of the student movement. Foremost among these was a visceral fear of *luan*, or chaos. Deng and his fellow gerontocrats had come of age when China was so hopelessly divided by warlordism and racked by chronic social disorder that Sun Yat-sen had disparagingly referred to it as being like a ''dish of loose sand.'' Fear of falling back into such a state of humiliating disunity was deep in the bones of these senior leaders. In addition, the experience of the Cultural Revolution—now euphemistically referred to as the ''ten years of chaos''—when most had suffered at the hands of zealous Red Guards, left them deeply suspicious of any spontaneous youth movement taken to the streets. Deng himself would never forget how he had been cashiered and forced to make an embarrassing self-criticism, and how his eldest son, Deng Pufang, had been thrown from a window in an incident that left him paralyzed from the waist down. Fear of losing political control once more was a recurring theme in many of Deng's post–Cultural Revolution speeches. So elemental was this fear that Deng seemed to have little capacity to distinguish between constructive forms of debate and outright chaos. When Deng cracked down on the Democracy Wall Movement in 1979 and sent Wei Jingsheng to prison, he warned that if such public demonstrations of dissent were allowed to continue, they would ''inevitably lead to the unchecked spread of big-democracy and anarchism, to the complete disruption of political stability and unity, and to the total failure of our modernization campaign.'' During the 1986 student demonstrations, he again warned, ''If our country were plunged into disorder and our nation reduced to a heap of loose sand, how could we ever prosper?''

The April 26 editorial made it likely that the government would brand student activists as ''counterrevolutionaries''—the ultimate political damnation in the Party's lexicon—if they did not desist. Since such threats had usually been enough to stifle unrest in the past, Deng may have imagined that another blast of stern rhetoric would cow this new generation of rebellious students into submission.

"In 1986 when the Central Committee issued a document or an editorial in the papers, it immediately frightened students and the movement stopped," said Xiang Xiaoji, an activist student from the Chinese University of Politics and Law. "It had been like this throughout the forty years of Communist rule. But this time it was different. . . . When the Government issued an editorial, we were not only not frightened, we became even stronger and fought right back."

"With one death blow the editorial has vilified the present patriotic movement," a Beida student wrote in a wall poster. "The extremely negative tone of the editorial has caused deep shock, disappointment, and anger among the nation's citizens. Since the government has not taken any constructive action, our movement must continue to the very end!"

On the night of April 26 student leaders met and formulated three new composite demands. First, they called on the government to meet with student representatives on an equal footing for an open dialogue. Second, they demanded an apology for the police attack outside of Xinhuamen. Finally, they demanded that the government allow journalists to cover the student movement in an unbiased manner. If they did not receive an immediate response, said the leaders, students would march again on the Square.

Deng's reaction was swift and uncompromising. "We are not afraid to shed a little blood, or to lose face, since this will not seriously harm China's image in the world," he was reported to have told Party leaders.

Although they were aware that now rather than commemorating a dead leader they would be challenging the country's paramount leader himself, protesters refused to be cowed. Ren Wanding, a Democracy Wall activist who had served four years in prison and chided China's "feudal leaders" at Wang Dan's Democracy Forum for the way their "intolerance of opposition has resulted in minor policy differences repeatedly escalating into life-or-death struggles for power," now warned: "If there are people who force us to shed blood, then let our blood flow." If the democracy movement was "strangled in its cradle," said Ren, it would only help "propel the birth of a new political party and a new social organization."

Deng's intolerance of political dissent had changed little during the ten years since the Democracy Wall Movement, when he had unabashedly declared that "so long as class struggle exists, it is inconceivable that the dictatorial functions of the state should wither away, that the standing army, public security organs, courts, and prisons should wither away." Wei Jingsheng's critique of Deng, made just before his arrest in 1979, was as germane now as ever. "The people must maintain vigilance against Deng Xiaoping's metamorphosis into an autocrat," he wrote. "We believe that normal order does not mean everyone marching in lockstep, especially in politics. Only if different kinds of ideas exist side by side can a situation be called normal."

The next day Party cadres on every university campus tried frantically to convince faculty and influential students to oppose the march. "This is a warning! Do not leave the university gates! Go back to class!" blared loudspeakers at People's University. Many students were so afraid violence would erupt that they hesitated to commit themselves to marching. In fact, so alarmed were leaders at Qinghua University, the country's foremost engineering school, that they even tried to call off the demonstration. Many who finally joined were so fearful of what might happen that they wrote out wills to leave behind in their dorm rooms. As accustomed to success as they had become, the students were aware that if the full force of the government's constabulary was turned against them, they would be defenseless. "We began to accept that it might end in death," remembered Wu'er Kaixi, head of the Beishida Autonomous Student Union. Fearing detention by the PSB, Wang Dan and several other prominent activists went into hiding. But student leaders were also determined not to back down.

The next morning students at forty different universities surged out of their campus gates and, with banners announcing their colleges and academic departments flying, poured into the streets. Thousands of homemade placards gave expression to the uneasy mixture of defiance and uncertainty that prevailed. "Willing to Die!" proclaimed the banner of one Qinghua student. "Patriotism Is No Crime," asserted another, rebuking Deng's editorial. A contingent from the University of Politics and Law carried an enormous placard inscribed with Articles 35 and 37 of the Chinese Constitution, which respectively guarantee Chinese citizens freedom of speech, press, assembly, association, and procession, and freedom from unlawful search and seizure. One marcher held aloft a quotation from Chairman Mao: "Whoever Suppresses the Student Movement Is Doomed." Another carried a citation from Deng: "If the Old Does Not Get Out of the Way, the New Cannot Come In." And as a reminder that most students still did not see themselves as revolutionaries, there was a plethora of placards and banners bearing such inscriptions as "Support the Correct Leadership of the Communist Party of China" and "Support Socialism and Reform."

To prevent troublemakers or provocateurs from infiltrating their ranks and starting fights, student monitors held hands to form a protective chain on either side of the long column of marchers. "This was our first really organized march and everyone was in a very serious frame of mind," remembered Wu'er Kaixi. "We were all ready to be confronted with severe repression, and most students brought wet towels with them in case tear gas was used. Some of the girls even carried packets of powdered lime, which they imagined they could throw into the eyes of police to immobilize them if they were attacked. But many were still so unnerved by what might happen, they wept as we set out."

Almost 90 percent of the student body at Beishida ended up participating. But as soon as the marchers got off campus, they ran headlong into a phalanx of police who were armed with electric cattle prods and had locked arms to block the way. So immense was the crowd pushing from behind, that even if the students in the lead had decided to turn back, it was impossible to do so. Fortunately, the troops carried no guns, and to everyone's surprise and relief, as the mass of marchers pushed forward, the line of police stretched like an oversized rubber band until it finally snapped, allowing students to surge triumphantly through the crossing.

When Beishida marchers met another phalanx of police at the next intersection, student leaders called for a sudden detour, and masterfully maneuvered the procession around it. When further down the road they found an even larger human barricade, Wu'er Kaixi hastily beckoned a contingent of strapping young men from the university's physical education department to the front and used them like the hardened tip of a spear to ram their way through.

When Beida students left the safety of their campus, they were just as frightened as their Beishida counterparts. And once out of the main gate, they, too, ran into a huge blockade. But just as at Beishida, their sheer numbers left police with little choice but to break ranks or be trampled by the surging crowd.

Similar scenes took place outside campuses all over Haidian. When all the tributary marches finally merged on Baishiqiao Road in a grand rendezvous, they comprised a human river miles long with more than 150,000 participants. Each time marchers breached another police barrier, a new roar of triumph went up. At some intersections crowds of local workers and unemployed youths surrounded blockades and neutralized the police before the first student marchers even arrived.

As surprised as observers were by the numbers and by the ease with which police were overwhelmed, they were even more astonished by the enthusiasm of the onlookers who greeted marchers along their seven-mile route. Unlike 1986, when ordinary people had been extremely standoffish in their support, on this April morning in 1989 they turned out by the hundreds of thousands to watch and cheer. Construction workers beat on their aluminum lunch boxes with chopsticks; vendors handed out free drinks, Popsicles, and steamed buns; bystanders thrust out cash contributions; and all along the way supporters clapped, whistled, and cried out, "We love the students."

Hou Dejian, the well-known rock singer—who created a sensation when he defected to the Mainland from Taiwan in 1981 and who lived along the march route—remembered feeling electrified by what he saw. "Ordinary people were standing along the streets just cheering and clapping," recalled Hou, who at that point had no inkling of the important role he would later play in the finale of this protest movement. "Everyone's good side, their kind side, had a chance to show itself. . . . I felt a sense of relief, as if a kind of repressed feeling had all of a sudden been released."

As the protesters passed Xinhuamen on the Avenue of Eternal Peace, where police had beaten students the week before, marchers began chanting, "We are not afraid! We are not afraid!" When without suffering a single casualty they victoriously entered the Square itself, their sense of exhilaration and confidence was soaring. And when they burst out singing the "Internationale," it did seem as if the Square had been repossessed by the heirs of the May Fourth Movement.

While marchers could easily have occupied the Square for the night, leaders sensibly decided not to force a confrontation. Some students returned to their dorms, while others kept on going to complete a great meandering loop through the city like a conquering army returning from a victorious foreign campaign. Along the way they were greeted by thousands of additional well-wishers. When weary Beida students finally reached their campus that night, they found a long white banner hanging out a dorm window proclaiming, "History Will Never Forget April 27." The day had been one of Beijing's most cathartic since Mao Zedong rode into the city in 1949.

Months later, after the movement had been crushed and he himself had fled into exile, Wu'er made a wistful confession to me. "The only time I ever thought that we might actually succeed was on April 27. It was a great moment and a great victory." The next day Wu'er was elected chairman of the new Beijing Autonomous Student Federation (BASF).

Several factors contributed to the student movement's stunning April victories. Rampant official corruption and the country's troubled economy had made ordinary Chinese citizens willing to listen to anyone

courageous enough to challenge the government in public. Deep political divisions within the Party leadership prevented the government
from reacting with the sort of resolve that many hard-liners called for.
And the skill with which the students organized themselves and the
symbols they succeeded in appending to their movement lent them a
powerful aura of moral conscience and integrity. In concert, these
factors helped create a feeling among a broad spectrum of Chinese that
the "mandate of heaven" was, indeed, slipping from the hands of
China's older Communist generation, and that the traditional virtues of
righteousness, sincerity, loyalty, conscientiousness, and compassion
that Chinese once considered to be the sine qua non of good rule were
passing irrevocably into the hands of a younger generation.

4

Fissures at the Top

The April 27 march was a stinging rebuke to Deng Xiaoping and his allies. "It was as if hundreds of thousands of people in Beijing had thrown cold water in the faces of the leaders and woken them up," crowed Wu'er Kaixi. Never before had such a large group of protesters voiced opposition to the Party in such a brazenly defiant and public fashion.

But the truth was that the Party itself was deeply divided by a factionalism that defied simple categorization with terms such as "conservative" or "liberal." While all leaders were dedicated to maintaining Party power, and most were in favor of certain kinds of economic and even political reform, some stubbornly resisted any changes that fundamentally altered the status quo. Throughout the 1980s, the balance of power within the Central Committee shifted back and forth between these two blocs, one composed of leaders who tended to favor central economic planning, proletarian isolationism, and rigid authoritarian political control, and the other that tended to favor moving ahead more boldly with marketization and privatization, greater openness toward the outside world, and a program of cautious political liberalization. Although there were factions within these two broad political groupings, journalists began to refer to them in shorthand as "hard-liners" and "reformers." As the demonstrations of 1989 progressed, battle lines between these two groups became more distinct and fraught with tension than ever.

Hoping to gain some advantage over the hard-liners by bringing the protest movement to heel through negotiation, on April 27 reform-minded officials consented to hold "dialogue meetings" with student representatives. However, because hard-liners feared that formal acknowledgment of an "autonomous" student group would only encourage other elements of society such as workers to establish their own independent organizations, these reform-minded officials were blocked from meeting with leaders of the new Beijing Autonomous Student Federation (BASF). Indeed, the appearance in the Square of disaffected workers was already sparking fears in the Party that China was about to contract "the Polish disease," an allusion to the Polish workers' union, Solidarity. In fact, in March just a month before the 1989 demonstrations erupted in the Square, Wang Dan had written an article in his *New May Fourth* frankly extolling Solidarity as a model for China. On April 20, five days after Hu Yaobang's death, a nascent independent organization calling itself the Beijing Autonomous Workers' Federation (BAWF) had already issued an open letter appealing to "people from all walks of life to come together to fight for truth and the future of China."

Although Deng was evidently bent on taking severe measures to quell the students, two upcoming dates made it inauspicious for him to launch an immediate crackdown. The first was the anniversary of the May Fourth Incident. The second was the arrival of President Mikhail Gorbachev on May 15, coming to normalize relations between the USSR and China after three decades of animosity.

The May Fourth anniversary was important to Party leaders because it was from this movement that they traced much of their own anti-imperialist revolutionary lineage. If the students were successful in marching to the Square again on May 4, they would be able to challenge the Party's claim to its legacy. And with the glare of world attention on Gorbachev's visit, the last thing Deng wanted was to be fighting in the streets, much less in the Square itself, with protesting students.

Still, the government stubbornly refused to recognize the Autonomous Student Federation led by Wu'er Kaixi, Wang Dan, and Chai Ling, or to make concessions to resolve the impasse. As a result, "dialogue meetings" between students and officials on April 29 and 30 came to naught, and on May 4 tens of thousands of students again broke through police blockades to raise their blue and white standard in front of the Monument and to hear Wu'er herald them for reviving the "May Fourth spirit of science and democracy."

As this drama was being acted out in the Square, another more shadowy play was unfolding behind the scenes between warring Party factions. Even though Zhao Ziyang had been handpicked by Deng to replace the ousted Hu Yaobang in 1987, he nonetheless shared many of his predecessor's relatively liberal views. Along with his supporters—who included Hu Qili, Politburo Standing Committee member and head of the Party Central Committee's Propaganda Department; Li Ruihuan, mayor of Tianjin and Politburo member; Tian Jiyun, Politburo member and vice-premier; and Yan Mingfu, member of the Central Committee Secretariat and director of the United Front Department—Zhao wanted to continue to marketize China's centralized economy and expand foreign trade and overseas investment in order to pull the country out of its doldrums. While Zhao retained a belief in China's need for an authoritarian one-party system, and even espoused a theory of "new authoritarianism," he differed from hardliners in believing that a certain amount of political liberalization or *toumingdu* (transparency) must go hand in hand with economic reform.

Although Zhao was hardly a libertarian, he held that the only way to get China's intelligentsia fully behind the country's modernization drive was to allow intellectuals to think, exchange ideas, speak out, and to write without undue fear of censorship or political recrimination. Although Zhao was more cautious than Hu Yaobang and his cohorts when it came to endorsing the free flow of political ideas, he tended to view doctrinaire Marxism as an impediment to the country's development. Instead, he argued in favor of a more practical and technocratic approach to raising people's living standards. Thus it was not surprising that in response to student demands Zhao advocated patience and negotiation rather than obduracy and confrontation.

In opposition was a loose coterie of mostly elder leaders, many of whom were veterans of the Long March. Although most of them, like Deng, had suffered political persecution during the Cultural Revolution and thus recognized the need for some reform, they tended to be as concerned about resisting influences that undermined China's socialist principles and centralized system of political control as they were about stimulating economic production. This faction, known as the "Council of Elders," was most visibly represented by Premier Li Peng, but included a host of Party elders such as eighty-one-year-old Vice-President Wang Zhen, a Long March veteran and former head of the Central Party School; eighty-four-year-old Chen Yun, chairman of the Central Advisory Commission and former Politburo member; eighty-year-old Li Xiannian, former president; eighty-two-year-old President Yang Shangkun, a Long March veteran, permanent vice-chairman of the Military Affairs Commission, and Politburo member; seventy-four-year-old Deng Liqun, former Secretariat of the Central Committee member and member of the Central Advisory Commission; and eighty-seven-year-old Peng Zhen, ex-mayor of Beijing, former Politburo Standing Committee member, and ex-chairman of the National People's Congress. These so-called "hard-liners" took a much more cautious view of reform. "A planned economy must remain our primary goal; a market economy can only be a supplementary measure for temporary adjustment," warned Chen Yun at a Party conference in 1986. It was his view that "everything for money is a decadent capitalist idea that has gradually prevailed in our Party and society."

Hard-liners were even more wary of putative reforms of China's political structure that might undermine the Party's hegemony over politics or subvert the Marxist-Leninist-Maoist ideology on which it rested. For them, diversity and pluralism were the road to ruin. Whatever changes were to occur in the People's Republic would be initiated at the top by the Party leadership in response to an assessment of its own needs, not in response to outside forces from below demanding more freedom and democracy.

Most notably, hard-liners were wary of the kind of subversive foreign influences and values whose uncontrolled propagation within China had become a major menace to social and political stability. They had a tendency to demonize things imported from abroad and to condemn any public protest as both an assault by a foreign ideology on their prerogative to rule in the name of the proletariat and as an embarrassing affront to the dignity of the Party they had spent their lives defending.

Straddling these tectonic political plates was Deng Xiaoping, who was capable of great flexibility, particularly when it came to economic development. When push came to shove, however, and economic matters began to have political consequences, he could become as unyielding as any doctrinaire hard-liner. Although by 1989 his only official position was chairman of the Military Affairs Commission, Deng remained China's unofficial "paramount leader" and the final arbiter of all political disputes. Although twice celebrated by *Time* magazine as "Man of the Year" for his economic reforms, Deng believed political reform meant making the Leninist state function more efficiently and prosperously.

One of the students' main criticisms was that while China had a constitution and a codified political system, leaders continued to rule like warlords with their tenure dependent on behind-the-scenes deal making rather than on open elections. "The fundamental defect of socialist countries is that the political structure makes officials, not people, into masters," complained one wall poster put up at Beishida in late April. "The leader enjoys lifelong tenure of office and becomes an autocrat who even possesses the power to appoint his own successor. Such a practice violates the basic principle of a republic."

Such power could only be attenuated by a purge, coup, or putsch, which meant that the process of governing went on in a climate of almost constant paranoia. "You overthrow one bad person and then another bad person comes along," complained rock singer Hou Dejian. "When we criticize the rule of personalities, and at the same time declare this leader as a good or bad person, we are making the mistake of rule by personality. . . . Chinese history is a history of driving away the tiger and inviting in the wolf."

Deng's role as a grand manipulator was crucial to managing all the competing factions and maintaining China's stability. What allowed him to be effective was the web of highly personalized connections he had cultivated in both the Party and the military over fifty years of involvement. Using this informal power, Deng was able to mediate disputes between competing cliques of leaders to keep the ship of state on a relatively even keel. Where Mao had made extreme ideological pronunciamentos to "arouse the masses," Deng spoke pragmatically and worked quietly behind the scenes to build coalitions. And where Mao actively sought out contradictions in a way that generated disagreement and antagonism, Deng sought to build consensus. Deng's may have been "a dynasty of personal dictatorship," as one 1989 wall poster alleged, but by making the Chinese body politic dependent on him for stability, he made himself indispensable.

At eighty-five, however, he clearly would not be able to perform this role much longer. To prevent the delicate political balance from degenerating into outright warfare after his death, it was essential that he designate a *jiebanren* (successor apparent), who might take over the helm without major political upheaval. Unfortunately, like many of their imperial predecessors, Communist *jiebanren* rarely fared well. All of Mao's chosen successors—Liu Shaoqi, Lin Biao, and Hua Guofeng—met ignominious ends. Deng's heir apparent, Hu Yaobang, had not fared much better; and now much to Deng's chagrin, his second candidate, Zhao Ziyang, also seemed headed for recall.

When China's political situation appeared stable, Deng frequently sided with moderates like Hu and Zhao, pushing hard to transform

China into a modern, technocratic society in which economics rather than radical politics were the main focus. But whenever upheaval threatened, he invariably tilted toward the hard-liners. As vice-premier in 1978 when the Democracy Wall Movement arose, Deng had at first supported it. However, when his own position within the Party leadership had been consolidated and the protest movement began to expand its political critique so that it no longer served his personal political interests, he unapologetically arrested the movement's leaders. In late 1983, after joining hard-liners in a movement against "spiritual pollution" from the West, he suddenly called off the whole campaign and championed another interregnum of reform. But after the student demonstrations in 1986, Deng once again sided with the hard-liners by sacking Hu Yaobang. "When necessary we must deal severely with those who defy orders, and we can afford to shed some blood," he said with chilling pragmatism. "Just try as much as possible not to kill anyone." When students took to the streets in 1989, they not only exacerbated these long-standing intra-Party tensions, but also set Deng in motion again. As the unrest grew, he predictably tilted toward the hard-line coalition.

Lurking backstage during each of these internecine Party struggles was the Chinese military. As far as most foreigners were concerned, China's 3-million-man People's Liberation Army (PLA) remained as shrouded from public view as China itself had once been under Mao. But the political importance of the military was inescapable. Few Chinese had forgotten that after a leadership struggle brought the country to the brink of total chaos during the Cultural Revolution, it had been the PLA that finally succeeded in restoring order.

Just as in the government, where political power was transmitted through a set of leadership cliques bound together by a web of highly personalized relations, the military's relationship to the state lacked codified form. Instead of being under the command of a system of elected civilian authority, the army remained loyal to a pantheon of elderly ex-generals in the leadership hierarchy whose long military careers enabled them to command feudal allegiance from high-ranking field officers. Thus, even though Zhao Ziyang had been appointed vice-chairman of the Military Affairs Commission in 1987, he lacked the network of close personal ties that elders like Deng, the chairman, and Yang Shangkun, another vice-chairman, could rely on if push ever came to shove. As long as Deng, a respected soldier, remained alive, he could expect to command the loyalty of key PLA commanders. It was his trump card, and it gave significant weight to whatever political position he chose to take.

Although it was often difficult for ordinary Chinese to discern exactly what was taking place in the Byzantine corridors of Party power, by the beginning of the second week of May it was clear that the call for reprisals against the students implicit in Deng's April 26 editorial was meeting substantial resistance from Zhao Ziyang and his moderate allies. This split at the top helped account for the government's schizophrenic behavior—heaping vitriol on the protesting students and calling for harsh reprisals at one moment, and then issuing statements urging negotiation and dialogue the next. It also helped explain why the security units in the streets had allowed themselves to be pushed aside by marchers rather than resist with the kind of ferocity the Party had previously shown itself quite prepared to use.

But the contradiction went far deeper. Behind the disagreement over how to confront the student protesters lay the still-unresolved question of whether or not it was possible to reform China economically without also reforming it politically. Although in May 1989 few Party leaders were bothering to debate this fundamental point, the question lay at the very heart of almost everything that had happened since Deng returned to power a decade earlier. Through the April 26 editorial Deng had announced not only his tilt to the side of the hard-liners, but his opposition to the notion that major changes in the political structure were essential for China's ongoing economic well-being.

For the students, the factional division at the top of the Party had two practical consequences. First of all, it made it difficult for them to be sure if those government officials with whom they were negotiating actually had the power to effect the kinds of compromise solutions that were, from time to time, dangled as incentives to get them to call off their marches and strikes. Even though many protesters wanted to have nothing to do with Party factionalism—"You support one person and then he turns into a dictator again," warned Feng Congde—at the same time, the fissure at the top presented them with an irresistible opportunity to play leadership factions off against each other. By throwing their weight behind Zhao, it was tempting to imagine that they might help him prevail in his struggle with the hard-liners. Likewise, Zhao and his allies were tempted to hope that in keeping lines open to the students, their position within the leadership might be shored up by insinuating that only they could deal with prodemocracy demonstrators filling the streets in ever greater numbers. In fact, by currying favor with the students through expressions of leniency and sympathy, Zhao and his reformist allies sought to create an impression within the Party that not only could they help control the students, but they could also unleash more demonstrations if hard-liners ignored them.

Zhao widened the breech between reformers and hard-liners on May 3, when in a gesture clearly designed to appease the students, he argued in a speech commemorating the May Fourth Movement that "in our building of socialist modernization and in the course of all-around reform, we must study and develop democracy, and study and respect science." By emphasizing that the promotion of democracy and science was an "extremely important task" both for the Party and "the people and the youth of the whole country," Zhao was not only playing to the students, but upping the ante with his hard-line opponents.

The next day, while addressing a gathering of the Asian Development Bank in Beijing, Zhao went one step further. Not only did he fail to vet his speech with Deng and the Politburo but he insisted that what was needed was "calm, reason, restraint, order, and a solution to the problem" arrived at in a way that was "consistent with democracy and the rule of law." Moreover, in a gesture that was most certainly meant to signal his disagreement with Deng's militant editorial, Zhao went so far as to add that the majority of the students were "by no means opposed to [China's] basic system," and that "responsible demands from the students must be met through democratic and legal means."

By the second week in May the intra-Party struggle had heated up to such a degree that Politburo meetings were punctuated with acrimonious shouting matches between leaders. Behind each faction were irreconcilable views about political dynamics. Whereas Zhao was receptive to viewing political adversaries as loyal opposition, Deng and the hard-liners viewed anyone who challenged the Party's dictums as traitorous and their movements as rebellious. And where Zhao saw discussion and negotiation as a way of resolving differences, Deng and the hard-liners saw surrender, humiliation, and defeat. As Yang Shangkun then warned, "Retreating would be our downfall, the downfall of the People's Republic of China."

By mid-May, hard-liners were accusing reformers of "splitism," breaking "Party discipline," and of trying to set up a "second headquarters" within the Party. To a certain extent such allegations were accurate, but the "two headquarters" were hardly equal in terms of either political or military clout. The "headquarters" that Deng figuratively ruled was by far the more powerful. With little chance of winning military backing in a showdown, Zhao tried to convey to the students how important it was that they temper their demands. Deng, meanwhile, was busy consolidating his political and military support, both to show Zhao that Party elders were still in control and to crush the "planned conspiracy" of the students. As early as the end of April,

Deng ordered the 38th Group Army headquartered in Baoding, in nearby Hebei Province, to take up positions around Beijing. It was an intimidating reminder that if political power did indeed grow out of the barrel of a gun, as Mao had insisted, it was Deng and the hard-liners and not Zhao and the reformers who had their fingers on the trigger.

Holding out the hope that their grievances would be heard in high places within the Party, Zhao's moderation did, in one sense, allay the dissatisfaction of the students. But in another sense, it encouraged them to press on with their struggle. After all, many reasoned, if they were powerful enough to convince mid-level government officials to meet for a dialogue, why not push a little harder for real concessions—to meet with Li Peng or Deng himself?

The growing sense of student indomitability made it all the more difficult for protest leaders to justify offering any concessions until the government made a few dramatic gestures of its own. Wu'er Kaixi and Wang Dan, both of whom had a realistic awareness of the stakes involved, found it difficult to argue in favor of yielding when the best that Zhao's allies could offer were vague promises that student demands would be addressed—later. The Party's forty years of perfidy and mendacity had left a miasma of mistrust so deep that it was almost impossible for student leaders to accept anything but actual quid pro quo deals, which Zhao was in no position to offer. They seemed to concur with Karl Marx's 1852 admonition "Never play with insurrection, but once it is begun, remember that it must be carried through to the end."

5

"What Are We to Do?"

When students marched to the Square on May 4, onlookers were surprised to see that several hundred journalists carrying banners proclaiming "Newspapers Should Speak the Truth" and "Reinstate Qin Benli" had joined their ranks. It was a sign that the protest movement was broadening to include other segments of society. And with the exception of the military, there was no segment of society that hardliners needed to control more urgently than the press. At the center of their struggle to keep the press muzzled was a small but influential weekly paper called the *World Economic Herald,* which was put out in Shanghai by its diminutive and feisty septuagenarian editor, Qin Benli. Founded in 1980, the paper initially devoted itself to reportage and analysis of economic reform. It was not long, however, before it began straying into such taboo subjects as the need for political reform, raising questions about human rights abuses and the probing PSB's network of informants and collection of personal dossiers.

The *Herald*'s outspoken editorial policy was dependent both on its unusual editor and its curious institutional status. The paper was a *guakao* publication, meaning that instead of being an integral part of any official organization, it was "hung from" the Shanghai Academy of Social Sciences and the Association of World Economics as a satellite operation, enjoying the kind of tangential institutional affiliation that Deng's reforms had for the first time made possible. And, instead of relying on state subsidies for survival, the *Herald* was one of the first serious publications in China to support itself with revenues from circulation and advertising. Not being dependent on the state economically or directly answerable to the Party politically, its editors were able to get out pieces that never would have passed muster at publications under more direct official control.

Nonetheless, the paper was often accused of having adopted a "bourgeois liberal" line, and only through the patronage of prominent Party liberals did Qin manage to keep it open. Editing an honest newspaper in China, he once said, was as tricky as playing Ping-Pong. "If the ball doesn't hit the table, you lose a point, but hitting the middle of the table is too easy. The really difficult thing is just to graze the edge."

The *Herald*'s problems came to a head just after Hu Yaobang's death when Qin teamed up with Ge Yang, the plucky editor of the Shanghai-based *New Observer* (who after Hu's funeral had written the poem "This Side and That Side"), and organized a conference to honor the memory of the ex–Party chief. And when officials in Shanghai learned the paper planned to publish a special issue that would include five pages of largely adulatory comments from the conference, they immediately demanded that Qin make certain deletions. He countered by offering two alternative courses: either the text would be published in its entirety, or wherever lines were censored, notes would be inserted reading "Deletions made per order of the Chinese Communist Party." Qin also impishly insisted that before he would do any editing, Deng Xiaoping himself should examine the text.

When Shanghai Party chief Jiang Zemin learned of Qin's defiance, he was reported to have angrily called for his suspension, ordered the *Herald*'s entire press run impounded, and sent a Party "work team" into the paper's office to "oversee" future editorial policy. However, by chance, several hundred copies of the issue had already been shipped to Beijing, where they promptly found their way into the hands of protesting students and foreign journalists who immediately made a cause célèbre out of Jiang's action.

Instead of meekly accepting the crackdown, journalists rallied to defend the embattled paper. Colleagues at the *China Daily* wrote a couplet in the style of a mourning poem, got seventy colleagues to sign their names to it, and then telegrammed it to Qin.

The Truth never dies.
The *Herald* pioneered ten years of reform.
Men of nobility do not bow to force.
Editor Qin is the moral example of a whole generation of journalists.

On May 9, just as Beijing's streets had returned to calm again for the first time in almost a month, a crowd of several thousand people materialized near Mao's mausoleum. In it were representatives from thirty major news organizations bearing a petition protesting Qin Ben-li's ouster that had been drafted by a *China Youth News* editor, Li Datong, and signed by over a thousand other writers and reporters.

The procession marched with much fanfare to the All-China Journalists' Association headquarters for a press conference before a throng of reporters from both local and foreign media. As Li stood before a bank of cameras answering questions and criticizing the official press for having "failed to be comprehensive and fair in its coverage" of the students, he was repeatedly drowned out by applause.

One of the most striking changes evident in the room was the openness and camaraderie that now seemed to exist between the assembled journalists. Whereas in the past Chinese reporters had only warily mixed with their foreign counterparts, now they seemed to view themselves as part of an international fraternity of like-minded professionals. There was no clearer manifestation of this than the way in which they bantered with members of the foreign press corps, and even consented to interviews, something that not so long ago would have meant an instant loss of job and possibly arrest.

"The students had begun to accuse journalists of not doing anything," *Guangming Daily* investigative journalist Dai Qing told me a few days later. "Even though our exposure as professionals is much greater than that of the students, most journalists wanted to do something to support them. Besides, we are also fed up. We, too, want to break out of the old pattern, to throw away the old straight-jacket."

Their participation in the May 4 march and their rally on May 9 also suggested that support for the students might be growing among professional circles. To encourage this support, leaders of the BASF decided to organize a solidarity demonstration of their own. On May 10, over 10,000 activists rode bicycles and pedicarts into downtown Beijing, stopping to rally at the headquarters of each of Beijing's major media outlets. I met up with one segment of this long procession near the Central Academy of Music on Fuxingmen South Road, where, to everyone's great delight, a brass ensemble on the roof of the Academy's new high-rise building was pealing forth a series of fanfares and military-style cavalry charges. The marchers, who had just come from the Central People's Radio Station and were headed to the New China News Agency (NCNA), were in a mood that seemed almost suicidally relaxed and convivial. One young man had a paper sign pinned on the front of his shirt that proclaimed, "Resolutely Support Journalists: A Righteous Profession." A girl wearing a foam-rubber Statue of Liberty crown held hands with a young man in a jacket covered with hundreds of variations on the characters *huangyan* (lies) magic markered onto it. Another young man wore a headband inscribed with the characters "We Are Willing to Die for Freedom." When I asked him if he was really ready to die, he replied, "Of course!" Then his face broke into a sly smile that made it impossible to tell whether he was serious or putting me on. Having protested for over three weeks without any real police retaliation, the students now seemed to presume the right to demonstrate as if it were an entitlement. Although the only police in evidence were a few overwhelmed traffic cops trying to keep intersections open, it was hard to imagine how the Party could long allow this kind of brazen challenge to go unjoined.

When we arrived in front of the NCNA headquarters, the students started chanting:

The *People's Daily* speaks nothing but nonsense!
Central Broadcasting turns truth into lies!
The *Guangming Daily* does nothing but manufacture rumors and
concoct falsehoods!

When several employees inside responded by opening a window and throwing out a cloth banner declaring support for the *World Economic Herald,* the crowd let out a delirious roar.

Moving from site to site like strolling Christmas carolers, the crowd stopped next to serenade the Central Committee's Propaganda Department, and then finally the *People's Daily.* "Where's your conscience?" chanted the students. "Journalism needs freedom! Newspapers should speak the truth!" Then, sticking a bullhorn through the steel latticework of the paper's locked gate, Wu'er Kaixi began lecturing the police and officials gathered anxiously inside. "A billion Chinese people have only one mouth with which to speak," he chided. "You are violating the Constitution. The *People's Daily* should side with the people." Then he began reading their April 26 editorial out loud. When he finished, he turned back to the crowd. "Are we makers of turmoil?" he cried out. "No!" roared the crowd. "Are we a patriotic movement?" "Yes!" they shouted.

Then the crowd broke into a ditty sung to the tune of "Frère Jacques":

People's Daily, People's Daily,
Truly strange! Truly strange!
They are always printing lies, they are always printing lies,
Oh how strange! Oh how strange!

By May 12 the Party still had not yielded to any of the students' major demands. But by then many protesters had grown weary of marching, and with final exams and graduation approaching, most students seemed relieved when things appeared to be quieting down. What Wu'er Kaixi, Wang Dan, Chai Ling, and other student leaders feared was that, despite their impressive successes, their movement might now disintegrate. Chai Ling observed to one interviewer that this moment when students might actually expect to extract real concessions from the government was one that "not even several hundred million American dollars could buy." By turning the media eyes of the world on Beijing, Gorbachev's imminent arrival presented a new opportunity—if only student leaders could come up with a compelling new way to use his visit to highlight their grievances.

As it happened, shortly after Hu Yaobang's death, an open letter had begun circulating around Beijing campuses calling on students to consider a hunger strike as a nonviolent protest tactic. The idea had languished until the second week in May when Chai and her husband, Feng Congde, began promoting it again. As the only woman in the student leadership, Chai occupied a unique position. Intelligent and articulate, she could also be determined and tough, qualities that led some to stereotype her as yet another in a long tradition of female Chinese leaders—from the Tang Dynasty's Empress Wu to Mao's wife, Jiang Qing—who were commonly perceived as matriarchal usurpers and archconnivers. But Chai's physical slightness, her pageboy haircut, her breathless way of speaking, and her penchant for tears also lent her an air of vulnerability that was heightened by her passionate conviction and her proclivity for speaking about sacrifice in almost mystical terms. Such qualities made her an instant favorite of foreign reporters, if not always of fellow student leaders.

Chai seemed entranced by the symbolism inherent in a voluntary fast that would turn self-denial into a form of political commitment. Speaking to an enthralled crowd of students at Beida on the evening of May 12, she argued that a hunger strike would be a way to force the government to show its "true face," to "talk with us," and to acknowledge that student protestors "are not traitors." To reemphasize her belief that only through sacrifice, even bloodletting, could students prove their patriotic intentions, Chai proclaimed: "We, the children, are ready to die! We, the children, are ready to use our lives to pursue truth! We, the children, are ready to sacrifice ourselves!'' She seemed to suggest that only through death could students really expect to influence China's future.

Wu'er Kaixi and Wang Dan had expressed some initial skepticism about the efficacy of a hunger strike, but on May 12 the BASF issued a statement declaring that if Party leaders did not quickly engage in a serious dialogue, students would begin a fast. "History asks this of us," declared a student handbill. "Our purest feelings of patriotism, our simple and complete innocence have been called 'turmoil.' We have been described as having 'ulterior motives,' and alleged to have been 'exploited by a small handful of people' . . . But what crimes have we committed? . . . Our demands for dialogue as equals have been repeatedly put off. Student leaders face danger. What are we to do?"

Many responded by signing a pledge in blood to renounce food before preparing to march to the Square. It was fitting that they planned to congregate at the base of the Monument to the Martyrs of the People, built by Mao to venerate earlier generations of idealistic Chinese who had given their lives to build the "New China."

While the ideal of sacrifice was deeply rooted in the culture of Chinese patriotism, the notion of using a mass hunger strike as a form of protest was not. Around the time of the December Ninth Movement in 1935 a group of university students petitioning Chiang Kai-shek to resist the Japanese had traveled from Beijing to Nanjing to stage a fast in front of the presidential palace. Chiang ultimately did come out and promised to consider their demands. But otherwise, political hunger strikes had little precedent in China, and not without good reason. Not only was Chinese history replete with countless instances of drought, flood, and famine, thus making the issue of starvation a central theme in people's historical consciousness, but for centuries food has played an important ritual function in Chinese life. During imperial times, no lesser personage than the emperor himself was obliged by tradition to make an annual pilgrimage to the Temple of Heaven before the winter solstice. There, after making a series of ceremonial offerings to heaven at the Hall of Prayer for Good Harvests, he visited the Temple of Agriculture to plow a ritual furrow. This symbolic act allowed the Son of Heaven to demonstrate concern for the livelihood of his subjects and for the cosmic balance between heaven and earth on which all natural things, as well as his mandate to rule, depended.

The notion that the right balance of foods and their proper presentation were fundamental to human harmony occurs again and again as a theme in classic works of Chinese philosophy and literature. And in no culture is the act of eating more ritualized. The Qing Dynasty literary masterpiece *The Dream of the Red Chamber* is filled with elaborate descriptions of ritual food preparation and ceremonial banqueting that were commonplace among the ruling scholar-official class at the time, and which continued on in mutated form during the Communist era as any recent visitor to China who has been endlessly wined and dined at Party banquets well knows. As Arthur Smith, an observant if condescending American missionary, insightfully noted near the turn of the century, "If there is anything which the Chinese have reduced to an exact science, it is the business of eating." Even today when famine is less common, one of the most common greetings among Chinese is, *"Ni chifanle meiyou?"* ("Have you eaten yet?")

Food is also among the most elemental components of traditional Chinese medicine as well. Rather than simply dispensing remedies, practitioners of Chinese pharmacology are more likely to prescribe a dietary change designed to rebalance fluctuating forces of *yin* and *yang*. "A good doctor makes the diagnosis, and having found out the cause of the disease, first tries to cure it by food," advises one sixth-century medical text. According to an ancient saying, "Food and medicine come from the same source."

Doubtless it was precisely because of the important role that food has played in Chinese culture that the notion of fasting for political reasons initially seemed so alien to many students. But as several of them later acknowledged to me, after they really thought about it, a hunger strike finally struck them as a perfect stratagem for remonstrating with their government. The kind of passive resistance implicit in a fast was congruent with one other deeply ingrained aspect of traditional Chinese culture, the notion that when an upright official disagrees with a ruler, he should express his displeasure and then withdraw from direct action rather than form an opposition party to foment overt rebellion. This tradition dates back at least to the Warring States period in the fourth century B.C. when legend has it that the long-suffering official Qu Yuan chose to go into exile, and then drown himself in grief, rather than openly defy his sovereign, who had refused to heed his advice.

In a system where might still made right and dissenters had virtually no prospect of winning open confrontational struggles against established authority, a strategy of nonviolent mass demonstration through fasting had an undeniable, if desperate, logic. "We have petitioned through a series of peaceful actions . . . for direct and open dialogue with the government on the basis of full equality," proclaimed a handbill that circulated around Beijing campuses. "The government delayed answering our petition . . . [and] we can no longer tolerate such a deceitful attitude of one delay after another. To make a determined and forceful protest, we have decided to hold a hunger strike."

At noon on May 13, the four hundred students who had signed up to join the fast under the aegis of the Students' Hunger Strike Committee trooped off to local restaurants for what wags glibly called "the Last Lunch."

When an American TV reporter asked one earnest young head-banded student from Beida how long the hunger strike would last, he replied: "We don't know. Until whenever we get satisfactory answers from our government; until they talk with us as equals. We are just doing something guaranteed by the Constitution. We have the right."

Then, chanting, "This is our country! Its people are our people! The government is our government! If we do not speak out, who will?" students once more set out for the Square. "I Love Life, I Need Food, but I'd Rather Die Than Go Without Democracy," read one banner. "Sacrifice Ourselves to Rejuvenate the National Spirit," proclaimed another. "In the spirit of sacrificing our lives, we fight for life," Chai Ling melodramatically proclaimed. "Death is not what we seek, but we are willing to contemplate death knowing that the eternal broad echoes of our cries and of the cause we write with our lives will suffuse throughout the Republic."

When they reached the Monument at the center of the Square, marchers hoisted a crude banner inscribed with the characters for *jueshi* (fast) between flagpoles where the national flag normally flew. Then, with Wu'er Kaixi presiding over the gathering like a clergyman administering communion, each hunger striker vowed to refuse all food until Party leaders agreed to start a "substantive, concrete, and equal dialogue" and to acknowledge the student movement as "patriotic and democratic."

Once more, student protesters had taken over the center of Beijing, but by adopting what proved to be one of the most symbolically potent forms of protest ever seen in the Square, they upped the ante. Although exhilarated by the apparent ease with which they had again captured this hallowed place, many fluctuated manically between confidence that the government would not dare harm them, and a dark sense of foreboding that this protest would ultimately be no more immune to the Party's repressiveness than all the others that had been crushed before it. Yet this very sense of risk also had a strangely seductive allure, evident in the hunger-strike declaration:

In this bright, sunny month of May, we are on a hunger strike. In the finest moment of our youth, we must leave behind everything beautiful about life, no matter how reluctant or unwilling we are! The country has reached an impasse. . . . When history demands it, we have no choice but to die.

Then in a passionate adieu, the statement concluded:

Farewell mothers, farewell fathers! Please, forgive us, if your children cannot remain loyal to their country and act in a filial manner at the same time. Farewell, people! Please allow us to use these means, however reluctantly, to demonstrate our loyalty. The vows written with our lives will brighten the Republic's skies!

That night the students held their first press conference in the Square, and revealed just how far they had moved from those earlier times when virtually no Chinese dared make unauthorized contact with foreigners, especially journalists. Bathed in a protective halo of light from flashing cameras and TV sun-guns, their leaders forthrightly answered questions from the hundreds of fascinated foreign reporters who gathered to watch. The students had astutely begun making their movement more accessible to its new overseas audience by providing English translation and borrowing images from protest movements elsewhere in the world. Their white headbands inscribed with political slogans came from South Korean students who had adopted them from Japan, where they once signified a samurai's willingness to fight to the death. They flashed the V-for-victory sign from the American peace movement. They wore T-shirts scrawled with political maxims, autographs, and cartoon art that helped declare Chinese protesters part of a larger common pop culture of international political dissent. Some even waved banners inscribed with Patrick Henry's "Give Me Liberty or Give Me Death."

By adopting internationally recognizable symbols that the overseas press corps—and particularly American television viewers—could recognize as familiar, the students showed a new understanding of the power of the global media and the ways in which it could sometimes exercise leverage, even on their own government. With Chinese in distant Heilongjiang and Xinjiang provinces now part of the global electronic village through the shortwave broadcasts of the BBC and the VOA, they were now able to hear what their own country's protest leaders were saying in Beijing by listening to broadcasts from London or Washington.

It was one of the many paradoxes of the movement that the students' newfound media savvy was largely a result of the reform program initiated by the very man with whom they now found themselves locked in struggle, Deng Xiaoping. For it was through his "open door" that they had caught their first seductive glimpses of life in the outside world. Now they were in the process of using this knowledge against his *ancien régime*. Like the scientist who clones a monster he cannot control, it now seemed possible that Deng might be unhorsed by forces that he himself had created. As Wu'er Kaixi noted several months later, "Deng Xiaoping's greatest contribution to China is that he raised a generation of people who would oppose Deng Xiaoping and bury his dynasty."

Throughout the first night of the hunger strike, the Square hummed with excitement and expectation. Like an army of hastily bivouacked soldiers, fasters sprawled around the base of the Monument on pieces of cardboard, newspapers, and anything else they could get their hands on to insulate themselves from the cold cement paving stones. Soon such large crowds of onlookers gathered that student supporters had to form a protective human ring to protect the fasters from being trampled.

The sense of drama was only heightened that first night when dozing students were aroused by a commotion around 2:30 A.M. They learned, to their astonishment, that Beijing's hard-line mayor, Chen Xitong, had come to the Square in a last-minute effort to persuade them to leave before Gorbachev arrived the next day. This time it was the government that found itself playing the role of supplicant. Chen was quickly hooted and jeered into a humiliating retreat by students who were now less than ever in the mood for unilateral compromise.

6

Hunger Artists

May 14 was a beautiful sunny Sunday, and word of the student fast spread like wildfire throughout Beijing. When I reached the Square around 8 A.M., curious onlookers were already arriving from every direction. Strolling amid the multitude of hunger strikers, protesters, supporters, onlookers, and reporters, it was almost impossible not to be swept up by the heady good cheer of it all. As though en route to a fair, whole families arrived with small children riding on their fathers' shoulders gazing in wonder at all the hubbub, as packs of older kids dodged and weaved through the crowd, young lovers strolled arm-in-arm amid the protesters, and elders looked on with perplexed fascination.

Still desperate to find a way to end the fast before Gorbachev's plane touched down, that afternoon moderate reformers Yan Mingfu, director of the United Front Department, and Li Tieying, head of the State Education Commission, made another last-minute effort to bring the government and the students together to talk. Although he was still unauthorized to meet officially with members of the BASF, Yan did apologize for "not taking measures that should have been taken" much earlier, and promised student representatives that any further "dialogue" would be televised. Yan also warned that if the Square was not cleared, it would precipitate dire consequences that were "not hard to predict."

"Although he couldn't come right out and say that there was a big split among Party leaders, it was obvious that Yan felt the situation was pretty desperate—that if we students continued with the hunger strike it would not be good for Zhao and reform,'' remembered Wu'er Kaixi, who was allowed to attend the discussions only as an observer. ''At that point it had become clear to me how divided the government was, and I began to think that probably the best thing we students could do was just have a big celebration, declare victory, and leave the Square.''

But neither side was any more willing than before to make the kinds of formal concessions necessary to bring the impasse to a resolution. Deng was evidently not prepared to retract the April 26 editorial, and it was doubtful that Yan had enough authority to cut a real deal with the students, even if they had been willing to compromise. Likewise, since the student ''representatives'' to the ''dialogue'' were chosen by neither the newly formed Hunger Strike Committee nor the BASF, they were unable to speak authoritatively for the protesters as a whole. And with support for the hunger strike growing by leaps and bounds both in China and around the world, the protesters were hardly inclined to abandon their fast, even if their putative leaders had counseled such a move. What is more, by this time the student leadership was becoming badly divided. Under such circumstances it was hardly surprising that the May 14 ''dialogue'' foundered.

Party propaganda organs had long been heralding the Sino-Soviet summit between Deng Xiaoping and Mikhail Gorbachev as a watershed in Chinese diplomatic history. The dramatic reconciliation was scheduled to begin with a grand ceremony in Tiananmen Square at 4 P.M. on May 15, when Gorbachev was to be greeted by a Chinese honor guard and a twenty-one-gun salute, and then to lay a wreath at the foot of the Monument. But since thousands of student protesters stood their ground in the Square, waving placards emblazoned with pictures of Gorbachev and slogans such as ''We Salute the Ambassador of Democracy!'' and ''In the Soviet Union They Have a Gorbachev, But What Do We Have in China?'' the welcoming ceremony had to be moved to the airport with such haste that there was not even time to arrange for a red carpet. Then a scheduled meeting between President Yang Shangkun and Gorbachev in the Great Hall of the People not only had to be delayed two hours, but Gorbachev had to be hustled into the building through a back door. It was a humiliating beginning to what was supposed to be a crowning moment of Deng's long political career.

By then, the Square had taken on such a life of its own that anything happening outside its boundaries seemed completely epiphenomenal. The conspicuous absence of any governmental presence there made the place seem all the more unreal—like a scene from a child's fairy tale in which a mysterious force has banished all dyspeptic adults, leaving only lighthearted children free to play to their heart's content. The students had established an island of freedom in the midst of the very citadel of Party control. Although people took it for granted that plain-clothes PSB operatives were circulating, most were so infected by the buoyant mood that they threw caution to the wind. Upon entering, everyone seemed to lose their fear about acting out in public. This sense of being inside a protected neutral zone was only heightened by the endless columns of new supporters of every conceivable age and occupation who kept arriving under banners openly proclaiming the names of their official "work units" and such sentiments as "Down with Li Peng" or "Deng Xiaoping Must Resign." The whole city appeared to be converging on this one central spot.

Such euphoria made it difficult to ask oneself such questions as, "What will happen when Gorbachev leaves?" or "What if Deng orders the 38th Group Army into the city?" much less, "Who will rule the country if the Communist Party falls?" Even outsiders found it tempting to believe that maybe China was on the cusp of some great and hopeful, but still undetermined, change.

Walking through the Square was like roaming a huge bazaar filled not with merchants selling goods but with people trading ideas, giving speeches, debating, and arguing politics with one another. By May 15 the Square was so inundated with people that it looked like the live set of a Hollywood epic being filmed with a "cast of thousands." Students were sprawled everywhere. Makeshift shelters had sprung up all around the Monument. A clinic set up under a canvas tentfly was overflowing with semicomatose students on IVs. Out of the din of chanted political slogans, songs, drums, and raucous orations delivered through handheld bullhorns came the sound of government spokesmen over their own loudspeakers ordering people to leave the Square. And rising and falling over this whole cacophony was a wail of sirens as ambulances manned by Red Cross volunteers ferried unconscious fasters off to nearby hospitals.

As of May 18 more than 3,500 students had collapsed. As soon as they were revived with intravenous fluids in the hospital, most of them returned to resume their fasts. Some claimed to have made numerous round-trips from the Square to the hospital and back again. By May 24, Beijing doctors were reporting that they had handled more than 9,000 admittances.

Few things contributed more to the popular groundswell of sympathy and support for the students than rumors that some of them were either close to death or had already died from refusing liquids. An even more alarming piece of hearsay had it that several protesters planned to publicly immolate themselves if the government did not respond to student demands. Such rumors played on one of the government's greatest fears—that if a protester actually died, the volatile situation might explode into violence.

As the number of people in the Square grew, students found themselves forced to become traffic policemen, hospital orderlies, communications experts, sound technicians, printers, commissary specialists, accountants, and logistical coordinators. With a skill that amazed everyone, these amateur urban planners succeeded in organizing the Square into what amounted to a primitive city-within-a-city. In many respects it was like a small principality surrounded by a larger state. One friend referred to it as a "Chinese Liechtenstein."

As this principality's homegrown rulers—the cool Wang Dan, the emotional Chai Ling, and the charismatic Wu'er Kaixi—became more familiar to outsiders via the media, people laughingly noted that "leaders emerge from under the scrutiny of the camera lens." One of Wu'er's theatrical hallmarks was periodic fainting spells. Whether these episodes came from the physically debilitating effects of his fast, a rumored heart condition, or a flare for the dramatic, nobody quite knew. But they provided moments of excitement and helped put Wu'er all the more in the spotlight, a place where he seemed to thrive. In fact, he gravitated to the spotlight so easily that he quickly acquired a reputation for self-promotion. When the *Independent*'s Andrew Higgins asked him what made the 1989 demonstrations so different from previous prodemocracy movements, he pointed at himself and replied, *"Wo!"* ("Me!")

As the days progressed, the leaders of this insurrection-born minirepublic had to find ways to imbue it with a semblance of infrastructure. Rolls of plastic packing string held by rows of human monitors were used to demarcate "lifeline" access roads through the crowds so that the ambulances could reach the first-aid tents. The area around the Monument was divided into zones resembling neighborhoods and designated for each of Beijing's major institutions of higher learning. Special areas were also set up for a communications center from which the main loudspeaker system was operated; a print-shop area equipped with silk-screen machines for duplicating leaflets; a financial district where cash contributions were tallied; a commissary section where the huge volume of food, drink, and clothing donated by supporters was received and distributed; and a hospital quarter where weakened hunger strikers could receive medical care. The sanctum sanctorum of this rudimentary community was the command center at the foot of the Monument where the leadership met to discuss strategy for their amorphous movement. Entry into this privileged sanctuary was strictly controlled by a network of student-run security guards and an elaborate system of access passes.

As the scale of the protest movement grew and security consciousness increased, complaints arose that student leaders themselves were becoming undemocratic and "isolated from the masses" by relying on their newly formed security system to keep gawkers, autograph seekers, provocateurs, and especially the press, at bay.

The area immediately around the student "command center" was almost always teeming with foreign journalists scrawling in notebooks, firing the automatic drives of their Nikons like machine guns, and thrusting tape recorders into the faces of any young Chinese wearing a headband who was willing to speak. Everywhere there were sweating TV cameramen in their regimental fishnet vests towing big-bellied sound-men along behind them. Even Dan Rather was there, bounding around the Square in a Banana Republic safari jacket. When it came to making a worldwide media splash, the students had hit the jackpot. Coinciding as it did with the armies of news-hungry foreign reporters who arrived to cover Gorbachev's visit, the fast soon became the best-covered and most eagerly watched political event in the history of the People's Republic. What made the presence of the augmented foreign press corps so catalytic was that this time TV producers were instantly able to beam images of students defying their Communist government around the world via satellite uplink dishes that the Chinese government had improvidently approved for the Sino-Soviet summit. And so just when the Party found itself most in need of controlling the foreign press, it was unable to staunch the hemorrhage of images that were being transmitted abroad and creating a groundswell of foreign support for the students.

"It was not possible to be dispassionate," admitted Charles Kuralt, who was in Beijing for CBS News. "The most cynical journalists could not help but be caught up." It was almost impossible to walk more than ten yards without a smiling young Chinese approaching to ask a flood of questions. Did Americans know what was happening here in Beijing? Did the people of America support the students' demands? Since the United States was viewed as the Holy See of freedom and democracy, it was important to these neophyte democrats that they receive America's blessing. The pride that registered on students' faces when they heard of the interest that their protest movement had generated abroad was unmistakable.

"When [we saw] these very appealing young people with their ideology that seemed to speak directly to our history—remembering us as a revolutionary country—it made us feel good, good towards them," Richard Wald, vice-president of ABC News, was reported to have said. "It made us feel invincible, so we thought they were [invincible] too."

Many young Chinese were as deeply affected by the oblique but poignant lyrics of rock music as they were by the political rhetoric about freedom and democracy. Rock songs such as Hou Dejian's "Children of the Dragon" and Cui Jian's "Nothing to My Name"—both of which conveyed a sense of gnawing dissatisfaction with the status quo and a yearning for some inner dimension of life that politics could not provide—played the same role for this generation of Chinese as did Bob Dylan's "The Times They Are A-Changin' " in the United States during the 1960s. As Cui observed, Chinese rock did not aspire to change the political system but to make people "feel freedom," which was in a sense precisely what many of the students in Tiananmen Square sought most eagerly. Soon Cui, Hou, and numerous other rock musicians were giving impromptu miniconcerts in the Square. Even the youthful proto-punker He Yong and his band, Mayday, performed in the shadow of the Monument before a homemade banner reading, "Willing to Become Martyrs."

The combination of youthful elation, commitment to nonviolence, and fascination with rock music led some foreigners to compare the scene in the Square to the Free Speech Movement and Woodstock in America. "In the past people had felt individual spirits oppressed," remembered rock star Hou. "But now as things opened up, individuals felt a sense of liberation." As one worker put it, "There was a feeling of bent backs being straightened and standing tall."

As the number of people living in the Square continued to rise and the logistics of feeding, caring, organizing, and controlling them grew ever more daunting, student leaders were increasingly criticized by some for their arrogant and peremptory manner. Wu'er's cocky, at times imperious, attitude made some compare him to Li Peng and the urge for hierarchical order within the movement to that of the Party.

"Left to their own devices, the students created an overly bureaucratic, highly policed system which, like the old [one], operated on personal credentials, or *guanxi*," Sarah Lubman, a young American student, wrote in the *Washington Post*. "What began as an efficient and necessary security system degenerated into a petty abuse of power."

Even Feng Congde acknowledged that most students, himself included, "didn't understand exactly what democracy was and how it should be organized. As decision makers in directing roles, we tried our best to make all our actions and decisions known to the general student body, but many students couldn't get any information about us and there ended up being no effective channels for them to express their wishes."

The fact that there was a certain murkiness to their understanding of how democratic systems function, or how such imported ideas might be fashioned into a new Chinese system, was perhaps understandable. After all, Chinese students had only recently been able to start reading about Western politics. When pressed to be more precise about their vision of political reform or their notions of democratic process, many protesters became vague, even flustered. As one student only half-facetiously told me, "I don't know exactly what we want, but we want more of it."

One principle that most student activists did understand, however, was freedom of speech. "In this new Chinese Enlightenment, intellectuals must make freedom of speech the priority," Wang Dan had written. "Although freedom of speech is proclaimed as an important principle in the Chinese Constitution, it has clearly been violated in an authoritarian manner. This is shown by the illegal and violent suppression of opposition voices by the political authorities. . . . Without critical voices, those consumed by ambition could fearlessly pursue their ends by distortion of the truth."

Rather than trying to overthrow their government, protesters seemed more intent on overthrowing passivity in the face of political repression. What was happening in the Square was less a political insurrection than a psychological catharsis that fed on the sense of exhilaration people felt at no longer being forced to submit to the Party's authority. "At the time, I simply felt, 'I'm speaking the truth and feel great—I feel like a human being now!' " said worker Zhao Hongliang about the appeal of this movement that was for many more emotional than cerebral.

Despite criticisms like Lubman's, one still could not but be impressed by the fact that the student leadership was able to hold the movement together at all. Given that few of these students were out of their early twenties, that they had been forced to build a functioning political organization from the ground up on extremely short notice, and that they had only the most primitive means of communication at their disposal, it sometimes seemed a small miracle that they had succeeded in establishing any coherent control over the Square whatsoever.

By midafternoon on May 17, the crowd in the Square approached a million people, and was growing steadily by the hour. Providing such services as drinking water and toilet facilities for so many people was a daunting task. Although there were some public bathrooms on the Square's peripheries, they were far too few. Chinese public-toilet hygiene standards have never been very high, but these latrines quickly became so overloaded and foul-smelling that even those desperately in need of relief were reluctant to go near them. In an effort to solve the problem, the students jerry-rigged a new bank of latrines on the east side of the Square by opening an underground drainage ditch that had been used to create squat toilets for Red Guard rallies during the Cultural Revolution and then curtaining off the area with opaque plastic sheeting. Almost immediately, however, these primitive alternatives also began to overflow, and a fetid swill of urine and excrement spilled out across the sidewalk, causing volunteer doctors at first-aid stations to fret about their health consequences.

To make the sanitation problem even worse, there was soon so much garbage and trash strewn around, that parts of the Square had begun to look like a landfill. But such disarray did little to dampen people's sense of euphoria. With all the banners, colorful hats, strange clothing, and the effusion of gaudy umbrellas many used to shield themselves from the sun's glare, from afar the Square appeared as if it were blossoming with a ground cover of wildflowers. After sympathizers in Hong Kong air-freighted thousands of pounds of camping equipment to Beijing and whole colonies of colorful mountain tents sprouted up, it became all the more difficult to imagine the Square ever returning to its previous state of drab emptiness.

7

A Hundred Flowers Bloom

To lose control of students was one thing, but to lose control of the media quite another. The best chance Party leaders had to confine growing support for the protest movement was to keep the press muzzled. Although for years the government compiled special compendia of "restricted access" news for use by select officials, daily media fare for ordinary Chinese came in the form of a strictly controlled diet of state-run newspapers, periodicals, and radio and television programs whose function was not so much to keep people informed as to disseminate the Party line. Except for occasional interludes of liberalization, there were few muckraking articles on government corruption and no behind-the-scenes reports on leadership struggles or probing portraits of the private lives of Party bigwigs.

While Mao was alive, it was extremely difficult for most Chinese to circumvent the government's monopolistic grip on news and information. During Deng's era of reform in the 1980s, the situation began to change. Chinese-language publications from overseas, television broadcasts from Hong Kong that could be received in the Canton area, and shortwave broadcasts by the VOA and the BBC began to penetrate the Chinese vacuum and provide a less monochromatic picture of the world. In fact, during the first four weeks of demonstrations the students relied far more on these outside sources than on the Chinese press to find out what was happening within China. Sometimes they even copied down VOA broadcasts by hand and then distributed the transcripts like newspapers around the Square.

The other main source of "unofficial" information came from the *xiaodao xiaoxi* (back alley news), which was a highly efficient vehicle for spreading hearsay about events taking place in the capital and within the Party hierarchy. Tidbits about which leaders were on the way up in the leadership pecking order; hints about which gerontocrats were in the hospital; rumors about children of ministers who were squirreling away fortunes in foreign banks or using their parents' influence to quietly slip out of the country to study were the specialty of the "back alley news." This underground news service quickly became a leading source of scuttlebutt about the hunger strike and the reactions of top Party leaders. But like messages sent in a game of "telephone," facts sometimes became garbled or exaggerated as they were transmitted from person to person. But often such reports contained nuggets of truth that could be learned no place else.

Although numerous Chinese reporters filed stories about the beatings police had given protesters in front of Xinhuamen in April and about Hu Yaobang's funeral, no official media source had dared to publish them. After the April 27 march, only a few audacious specialized papers—Ge Yang's *New Observer,* the *Science and Technology Daily* and the *Farmer's Daily*—risked printing factual accounts of what had happened. When higher-visibility papers finally got around to making mention of the protest movement, they did so only in the most cursory way via brief and often misleading NCNA *tonggao* (general reports). After the triumphant April 27 march, for example, the *Beijing Daily* ran a headline declaring, "The Working Class in the Capital Firmly Opposes Social Disturbances."

This absence of accurate reporting had became one of the main sources of contention between the students and the government. Indeed, reading the Chinese press during April was a very strange experience. Whereas foreign papers were festooned with headlines, photos, and front-page articles about what was happening in distant Beijing, papers published right in China gave almost no hint that anything historic was in the making. "It is not that we news reporters lack a conscience, but that we are not the real masters of the newspapers," explained an unsigned statement from reporters at the *People's Daily* and the *Guangming Daily* that was circulated in the Square near the end of April. "The vast majority of news reporters at the *People's Daily* firmly support the students . . . but we have no power!"

Since the reformers still exercised preponderant control over the media, they had one trump card left to play. As the Party's factional struggle began to heat up in late April, Hu Qili, the Politburo Standing Committee member in charge of press and propaganda and a supporter of Zhao Ziyang, began meeting with the editors and telling them that it was now permissible to "open up a bit" and to begin reporting on the "actual state of affairs." Like a split-image in a camera's viewfinder that merges when the lens is finally twisted into focus, the glaring division between official press accounts and reality now began to align. When on May 5 the *People's Daily* carried both a photograph and an article about the previous day's demonstration on its front page, it sent a signal to others that they, too, could begin reporting on the student movement. Not until the hunger strike actually began, however, did China's press really slip the harness of Party control.

On May 14, a group of CCTV editors and reporters who were sensitive about their earlier silence circulated a mimeographed sheet around the Square acknowledging that they had been "stand[ing] facts on their heads." Saying that their "throats had been cut," they declared that "any news reporter with a conscience must feel sad at being a propaganda tool." Then they proclaimed, "We can keep silent no longer! We firmly support the students, and we strongly demand a dialogue between students and the government!"

Two days later the *People's Daily* broke forth in an uncharacteristically elegiac manner to publish a poem entitled "Looking Forward to Spring":

Standing on the edge of winter,
Looking forward to spring,
I feel spring so close to me.
Reaching out I can touch it,
Its fragrant aroma intoxicates me and compels belief
That this vast life of ours can suddenly turn many-splendored. . . .

The citizenry of Beijing took this new openness in the press as a sign that an ax had finally broken through China's frozen sea within, and that it was no longer taboo for them to take to the streets, even to support the students. Encouraged by what they read in papers and saw on TV, Chinese in other large cities such as Changsha, Xian, Nanjing, and Shanghai also took to the streets to march in sympathy demonstrations. In a way that elderly leaders must have found terrifying, the press now seemed to be aiding and abetting the "turmoil." It was hardly surprising that Deng concluded the protest was aimed at overthrowing him and the Party.

On May 18, the *People's Daily* relegated Gorbachev's visit to an

THE SQUARE / 95

insignificant item at the bottom and ran six front-page stories about the student protest. "One Million from All Walks of Life Demonstrate in Support of Hunger-Striking Students," proclaimed a large headline. "Save the Students! Save the Children!" pleaded another, using words that had great resonance among educated Chinese because they comprised the final chilling line of writer Lu Xun's classic short story, "Diary of a Madman." Editors even ran a photo of their own staff members marching under a *People's Daily* banner. That same day the *Guangming Daily* exploded with no less than seven front-page stories about the demonstrations. "The conditions of the students and the future of the country touch the heart of every Chinese who has a conscience," proclaimed one of them.

"They not only demanded but actually achieved freedom of the press," said former *People's Daily* investigative journalist Liu Binyan. "This had never happened before. It was what I had fought for, what I longed for, all my life."

Although during these spring days it seemed as if the Chinese press had abruptly come to life, its flowering was actually the culmination of a long process that began during the period of relaxation and liberalization in the mid-1980s. Ever since 1984, when several representatives from the Chinese Academy of Social Sciences' Institute of Journalism were commissioned to draft proposals for promulgating a formal press law to protect Chinese reporters from political intimidation, the subject of "press reform" had been continuously debated. The debate was between those who believed that the press should continue to serve as the mouthpiece of the government and the Party, as Mao had insisted, and those who argued that China needed more independent outlets for "providing people with a safe channel for expressing dissatisfaction," as Hu Jiwei, the outspoken former editor in chief of the *People's Daily* who had been forced out of his post during the 1983 Anti–Spiritual Pollution Campaign, put it. Despite his fall, however, under the protection of liberalizers like Hu Yaobang, Hu Jiwei continued to be a member of the National People's Congress Standing Committee and to lobby for a press law, insisting that "more openness" was a "crucial element in modernization."

By May 1989, Zhao Ziyang had concluded that fuller coverage of the protest movement would help his cause by generating mass support for him in his increasingly intense struggle against hard-liners. The weaker Zhao's position became within the Party hierarchy, the more he seemed to urge the press, one of the last institutions still indirectly under his control, to open up. On May 8 an article by Hu Jiwei entitled "Without Freedom of the Press There Will Be No Real Stability" enthusiastically welcomed the media thaw precipitated by Zhao. Originally, "even freedom to talk about freedom of the press was restricted," wrote Hu. "Now, at least, we can bring the subject up and discuss it." In Hu's view, the greatest threat to the government was "not democracy, but the absence of freedom." When the press is restricted, argued Hu, people may become passive and silent, which creates no more than "a false impression of stability and unity" that in the end is "superficial" and "pregnant with risks." Hu pragmatically argued that press freedom was important not only because it was a right guaranteed by the Chinese Constitution, but because it was universally regarded "as a very good 'release for anger' " that provided a "safe channel for expressing dissatisfaction."

But what Hu had viewed as a healthy "release for anger" Party hard-liners viewed as a dangerous form of ideological insubordination. As the protest movement progressed, they deemed the media to be not only a dangerous political catalyst in Beijing, but the main vector for transmitting the destabilizing demands of protesters across the country.

8

The Citizens of Beijing Join In

In the middle of May, almost everyone in Beijing wanted to come to the Square to *kan renao,* a Chinese expression that literally translates "to watch the heat and noise." In socialist China, where spontaneous forms of entertainment had long been at a premium, gawking—whether at an auto crash, an argument in the street, a marital squabble, or a drunken brawl—provided much-welcomed diversion from the dull routine of daily life. On the Richter scale of excitement, the hunger strike was a veritable earthquake—a bonanza of around-the-clock divertissement. For younger Chinese, the crowded Square provided a chance to hang out and ogle members of the opposite sex; for middle-aged intellectuals it offered an unexpected opportunity to mix and become reacquainted with colleagues; and for older Chinese it provided a reason to get out of the house. Once there, few remained unmoved by the fasting students sprawled out around the base of the Monument and the enthusiastic crowds.

Noticeably absent was the sullen, cynical, and solipsistic attitude so evident when the demonstrations began. In a startling metamorphosis, Beijingers had become models of civility and politeness. There was noticeably less pushing and shoving in lines. People said "Excuse me" after bumping into someone on the street, or "Thank you" in return for small gestures of deference. Cabdrivers, normally among the most unpleasant members of Beijing society, were seen with pennants affixed to their radio antennas and placards in their windows proclaiming their support for the protest and shuttling students gratis between the Square and their distant campuses. Even *liumang* (street hooligans) had declared a moratorium on petty crime. "Don't Fight! Don't Make Trouble!" read the banner of one *liumang* seen parading through the Square.

"When we heard them sing their songs, and when we heard them speak to the crowds, their voices growing hoarse, our hearts beat faster and our eyes filled with tears," remembered Zhang Langlang, a graduate of the Central Academy of Fine Arts and the son of a well-known artist, who made frequent sorties into the Square from his family's nearby home. Zhang had spent ten horrific years in jail as a political prisoner—and at one point was even sentenced to death—during the Cultural Revolution, and so was particularly moved by the way in which this younger generation of students had at last begun to speak out. "We felt sick at heart when we heard they were going on a hunger strike," he wrote. "What did they want? Actually, they wanted something for all of us. Each of us might judge them in our own hearts, but none of us could deny the justness of their cause. We thought that they would certainly win. Our fathers and grandfathers had always been so submissive, they never had the courage of the students, even though they wanted the same things."

After so many years of intimidation the sweet sensation of finally having turned the tables on their tormentors made students, supporters, and onlookers alike savor this moment of freedom. "Party leaders have no alternative," one student from the Beijing Aeronautical Institute told me. "You don't think they'd try to take this Square with force now, do you? If they did, they would have everyone in the city against them."

Such comments highlighted the kind of overconfidence that prevailed during the first few days of the fast, especially among younger Chinese who had grown up during Deng's reforms and were thus less acquainted than their elders with the Party's repressive power. Although at first fearful of the consequences of this unprecedented upheaval, as the hunger strike progressed, many older citizens, too, soon lost their timorousness and became openly supportive of their children's bold challenge to authority.

"There was only one authority in the capital and it was not the Party Central Committee, it was not the government, it was not even the BASF," remembered Yan Jiaqi, former director of the Institute of Political Science at the Chinese Academy of Social Sciences and a key supporter of Zhao Ziyang. "It was the hunger strikers at the Square.

They were the supreme authority, at least in Beijing. Whatever they said, the people would comply with.'' Whatever their shortcomings in democratic procedures or their failings in developing long-term political strategies, the students had for the moment succeeded in establishing a new moral center for China.

Everywhere in the city one saw the characters *shengyuan* (support) inscribed on homemade placards, banners, headbands, and clothing. Some youths drew the characters right on their skin like tattoos. Ordinary workers brought cartloads of drinks and food as testaments of their support. Private vendors contributed free sun visors and umbrellas from their stands. Peasants bicycled in from the countryside with steamed buns. Anxious teachers appeared to make sure their students were alright. Doctors and nurses flocked to care for those fasting.

On May 15, I watched as one father bathed his daughter's face with a damp cloth and fed her broth from a thermos bottle, all the while begging her to return home. She steadfastly refused to go, and eventually her father departed in tears. He was so overcome with emotion that as he walked away, he dropped his thermos bottle. Helping him pick it up, I tried to console him, only to find that he was weeping not because he had failed to convince his daughter to abandon her fast, but because he felt so proud of her determination to risk her life for the sake of her country. "My generation never dared to speak out, much less to act out what we really believed," he told me, half-sobbing, half-laughing. "Now my daughter is doing it for me. How can I not thank her?"

The paradox was that even as the events in the Square filled so many ordinary people with a sense of pride and optimism, they humiliated Deng and hard-line Party leaders, making them more obdurate and the impasse more intractable and dangerous than ever.

On May 16 an increasingly desperate Zhao Ziyang sent a message to the Square acknowledging the patriotic spirit of the protesters and promising that if given a chance the government would "work out concrete measures to enhance democracy and law, oppose corruption, build an honest and clean government, and expand openness." Although Wu'er Kaixi and Wang Dan viewed the offer as an important opening, they could not convince other hunger-strike leaders to relent, and thus Zhao's effort failed. The students' reluctance to yield unless the government made more tangible concessions was fortified by the waves of new supporters, who, having seen what was happening on television, had begun arriving in Beijing from the provinces. One large contingent from Tianjin even came on bicycles after having been prevented by authorities from boarding trains for the ninety-mile trip.

Beijing Mayor Chen Xitong later claimed that over 200,000 outsiders flooded the city in support of the students. For this generation, coming to Tiananmen Square to join the protest movement was the equivalent of the trips their parents had made to the capital as Red Guards in order to *chuanlian* (link up) with others during the Cultural Revolution.

It was on May 16 that it became evident that the social base of the protest movement was again beginning to expand. While walking in the Square just after dark that evening, I heard an unexpected clamor over in front of the museums. Working my way through the dense crowd, I arrived on the east side of the Square, where I found a throng of about a thousand young men gathered beneath a crudely lettered burlap banner proclaiming them as *shimin* (citizens). Some wore flashy Western clothing, modish mustaches, and studied coiffures, while others sported rumpled Mao jackets, unshaven faces, and tousled hair. As I watched, these self-appointed "citizens" rallied around their standard, and then with a great roar, surged off in the direction of Tiananmen Gate. Out of curiosity, I followed in their wake to see who they were and what they would do. As it turned out, they were a ragtag group of *daiye* (unemployed youths "waiting for work"), *geti hu* (private entrepreneurs), *liumang* (street hooligans) and an assortment of miscellaneous day laborers, migrant workers, and taxi drivers, all of whom felt somehow short-changed by China's economic situation.

Although I had been hearing rumors of an "autonomous labor union," this was the first obvious sign I had seen that urban support for the hunger strike extended beyond the rarefied sphere of student activists, outspoken journalists, and liberal intellectuals. Indeed, there was no mistaking the members of this raucous procession for the refined student elite. As the *shimin* circumambulated the Square, they had no monitors keeping order, no carefully calligraphed placards, no prearranged slogans about freedom and democracy to chant, or any evident leader. Instead, they boiled forward chaotically, yelling out vulgar epithets against Party elders with a lumpen wildness that had a distinctly menacing aspect to it. For the first time since arriving in Beijing, I had the sense that events might soon outpace leaders on either side of the struggle. Fate, rather than conscious design, seemed to be taking over. Deng would later call it "a storm" that seemed "bound to happen sooner or later . . . independent of man's will." The appearance of these *shimin* raised the question of how long it would be before other, more crucial social groups cast their lot in with the students, creating a rolling snowball of antigovernment disaffection. After all, there were plenty of other groups with grievances, and what the students were saying and doing made many who had never questioned the status quo become far more skeptical.

"At the time I thought, 'Well, am I not free? If I'm not free, how can I come to Tiananmen Square and go in and out of my house,' " transportation worker Zhao Hongliang explained about the evolution of his own political consciouness during those days. "But after the students began explaining things to me, and after the PSB arrested some of our members, I suddenly realized that I was not free. Why wasn't I free? Well, look at the police. They can arrest people at will!"

In many ways May 17 divided the first four halcyon days of the hunger strike from the more complex, darker period that followed. On May 17 more than a million people massed in the Square, forcing Gorbachev's tour of the Forbidden City to be canceled. That afternoon I went to the Square and stood for several hours on the elevated traffic island immediately in front of Mao's famous portrait and watched as hundreds of thousands of banner-waving protesters surged down the Avenue of Eternal Peace. An obvious sign of the radicalization of the crowd was the personal insults that were now being leveled against Deng himself. "Xiaoping, Xiaoping is over eighty,/His body's all there but his head's gone batty!" chanted one group of workers. A contingent from a Ministry of Aviation and Aerospace factory carried a poster advising Deng to "Retire and Enjoy Life!" And alluding to Deng's favorite pastime, students from Qinghua University chanted, "Step down and go play bridge!"

Tiananmen Square was awash in a roiling torrent of people: workers in Mao jackets, Buddhist monks in saffron robes, children in school uniforms, hip youths in acid-washed jeans, intellectuals in drip-dry white shirts and slacks, hotel bellhops in puce-colored waistcoats, and entrepreneurs in three-piece suits. They seemed to come from every echelon of society and almost every imaginable walk of life. There were groups from the Foreign Ministry, the Party Central Committee's Cadre School, Central Radio and Chinese Central Television, the People's Courts, the National Men's Volleyball Team, and even the People's Liberation Army's General Logistics Staff. As if this were not shock enough, there was even a contingent from the People's Public Security Bureau Academy. And holding up the rear of this unlikely contingent was a young man carrying a placard announcing, "We Have Arrived!"

More significant were the hundreds of thousands of workers marching under banners inscribed with the names of some of the best-known factories and state enterprises in Beijing: the Civil Aviation Administration of China, the Capital Iron and Steel Works, the Bank of China, the Beijing Boiler Factory.

Whereas previous demonstrators had entered the Square on foot, some of these workers now arrived on motorcycles with two and three people sitting astride them, in public buses commandeered from their routes, and in off-duty taxis so crammed that they looked like those vehicles at the circus from which scores of clowns somehow manage to emerge. Construction workers arrived in the backs of dump trucks or sitting in the hydraulic buckets of giant pieces of heavy earth-moving equipment. There was even a cortege of "night-soil" collectors in their motorized "honey trucks" and a Red Flag limousine, driven by two soldiers spoofing the Party leadership's addiction to foreign limos, with a handmade placard taped onto the mammoth car's radiator grill reading, "Don't Take a Benz!"

It was the largest and most diverse urban protest demonstration in Chinese history. To have rebelling students hijack the May Fourth Movement tradition from the Party was embarrassing enough, but to have the proletariat, the very social force that Marx had designated as the vanguard of Communist revolution, rebelling against the Party was utter ignominy. More ominous from the Party's point of view was the news that some of these alienated workers were, indeed, organizing an independent labor union, the Beijing Autonomous Workers' Federation (BAWF). In fact, that very day the federation had issued an open to letter to all "compatriots of the nation" saying that "the lawlessness and brutality of corrupt officials" has become so extreme that there was "no longer any place for truth." Belittling Deng's reforms as "false and superficial," federation organizers called on fellow workers to "push the democratic movement to new heights" by supporting the students in yet another march to the Square on May 22. Now it seemed as if China, too, had contracted "the Polish disease."

For weeks protesters had blithely relied on the Sino-Soviet summit meeting as a bulwark against governmental repression. However, on May 18 when Mikhail Gorbachev left Beijing, this protection was lost. When I asked a young protester wearing a grimy headband inscribed with the words "Democracy or Death" how long he thought the students could hold their redoubt now that Gorbachev was gone, he replied, "We will never be silent again! Just look!" He gestured at the mass of humanity around us. "How will they ever succeed in intimidating us back into silence?"

That same day the *Beijing Youth News* published the results of a poll showing that 95 percent of those surveyed felt that the student movement was "patriotic" and that over 80 percent believed that demonstrators would ultimately "compel the government to give in and initiate democracy." What was telling about this survey was that it showed how many Chinese believed the students might actually triumph and how few worried about a crackdown. Yet if it was hard to imagine banishing such a crowd from the Square, now that Gorbachev was gone, it was harder to imagine the Party doing nothing.

Around noon on May 18 the sky suddenly darkened and a torrential rain began to pour down, creating an atmosphere of almost apocalyptic eeriness. Even in this deluge, tens of thousands of workers continued to flow toward the Square. When the downpour finally subsided, and I walked back to the Square myself, all along the way I encountered slogan-screaming workers, their clothes drenched, their hair plastered to their heads, speeding along the city streets in convoys of vehicles commandeered from their factories. As they went, they honked their horns and yelled out slogans and epithets. On street corners workers gave impromptu speeches to anyone who would listen. "In this movement to fight for democracy and freedom, all we proletarians have to lose is our chains!" one impassioned worker declared in an oration that borrowed heavily from the *Communist Manifesto*. "We have the entire world to gain. Arise! Let us be slaves no more!" Long gone were the placards of April written by students insisting they had no wish to overthrow the government or socialism. In their place were scurrilous caricatures of Deng with blood dripping from his mouth or with red *X*'s slashed across his face as if he were a common criminal sentenced to death. Others portrayed Li Peng with devil's horns and Nazi swastikas etched onto his cheeks.

The heavy rain had turned the area in front of Tiananmen Gate into a fetid swamp of soggy, stinking rubbish. Despite the Red Cross having brought in a fleet of city buses as shelter for the hunger strikers, most of the students looked puffy and sick. Not only were they wet, but they had not taken a shower, had a shave, brushed their teeth, or changed their clothes, much less had a good night's sleep, in days. When I asked a weary-looking doctor in a white smock splattered with the black muck how things were going, he sighed and said that many of the remaining hunger strikers were experiencing regular fainting spells.

Feeling a sudden need to escape this squalor, I walked over to Tiananmen Gate. Surprisingly, the ancient gate was still open to tourists, and for about five dollars I was able to buy a ticket that admitted me up to its rostrum. Climbing the stairway on one side, I soon found myself just above Chairman Mao's portrait in exactly the same spot where he himself had stood on October 1, 1949, to greet the "broad masses" after founding his New China.

"Imperialists and domestic reactionaries will certainly not take their defeat lying down and they will struggle to the last," he prophetically warned just a week before the People's Republic of China celebrated its first National Day. "After there is peace and order throughout the country, they will still engage in sabotage and create disturbances in various ways and will try every day and every minute to stage a comeback. This is inevitable, and under no circumstances must we relax our vigilance."

What was now taking place in front of his portrait surely exceeded even Mao's worst nightmares of sabotage. Not only had the main principles of his "great" and "glorious" revolution been nullified by a decade of crypto-capitalist reforms enacted by a coterie of Communist Party revisionists, but now even his beloved Square was awash in mobs of "domestic reactionaries" demonstrating in support of heretical, bourgeois, Western values. The spectacle before me was so fantastic and unbelievable that without thinking I raised my camera to take a photograph. Like a striking snake, an agitated attendant suddenly appeared at my side and seized my arm. "It is not permitted!" he cried out. "Photographs are not permitted!"

At a time when the Square was without any official constabulary, it was stunning to find that this lone government sentinel still manned his post atop the Gate. As the city drifted toward chaos, this single guard's continued vigilance seemed as absurd as the behavior of those imperial eunuchs who struggled to maintain their old way of life inside the Forbidden City after China's last dynasty fell in 1911. But his tenacity was also a reminder that in spite of all that had happened, Party leaders had still not relinquished their grip on the Square—much less on China itself.

9

"Not to Have a Correct Political Point of View Is Like Having No Soul"

"The habit of submitting to the group or leader is too deep within us," one young historian complained to China scholar Perry Link just before the 1989 upheaval. "The problem is that deference to the *leader* is ingrained in us. . . . We need to recover [our] independence; it was the most precious legacy of May Fourth."

For centuries before the 1919 protest movement, the state was the only organized institution through which men of learning could gain status, power, and prestige. This situation left scholars inextricably bound to the government through a system of official examinations that provided the gateway to imperial service and personal fulfillment. Despite all its revolutionary rhetoric, in this respect at least, Mao's New China was hardly any different. If anything, there was less latitude for mavericks and independent-minded scholars under Mao than under the emperors, when nonconformists could at least take to the hills as Daoist recluses. In the People's Republic the state was the only employer of intellectuals and Party authorities were the only dispensers of life's necessities; everything from decent housing for one's family to preferred schooling for children, from career advancement to the use of cars and permission to travel abroad. By choosing a path of dissent, an intellectual had almost everything to lose and nothing to gain. With rare exceptions, being an educated person in China consequently meant becoming an establishment intellectual and accepting all the obligations, restrictions, self-censorship, and compromises that such dependency entailed.

Whereas in the West diversity, individualism, independence, and autonomy have long been esteemed, in traditional China opposite traits such as harmony, orthodoxy, loyalty, and submission to authority were those acclaimed as most worthy of emulation by intellectuals. Moreover, their patriotism and concern for their country's "wealth and power," which many viewed as the prerequisite to China once again becoming strong and proud, made them reluctant to raise criticisms that might undermine the process of *jianguo* (nation building). All of these traditional values tended to predispose intellectuals to being much more accommodating to the established political system than their Western counterparts.

As far as Mao was concerned, embracing intellectuals was always a risky political proposition. "Not to have a correct political point of view is like having no soul," Mao wrote in his 1957 essay "On the Correct Handling of Contradictions Among the People." According to Mao, one of China's most potentially "soulless" groups was the intelligentsia, whom he appraised as being just as capable of opposing the revolution as supporting it.

"Intellectuals often tend to be subjective and individualistic, impractical in their thinking and irresolute in action until they have thrown themselves heart and soul into mass revolutionary struggle, or made up their minds to serve the interest of the masses and become one of them," he wrote in 1939. Warning that some intellectuals will "drop out of the revolutionary ranks at critical moments and become passive," while others "may even become enemies of the revolution," Mao, in effect, put China's intelligentsia on political probation. As far as he was concerned, they needed to be watched and sometimes even forced to do their revolutionary duty.

Although he sometimes spoke admiringly of "the revolutionary spirit" of the May Fourth Movement, what Mao really sought from his subjects was unfailing obedience. Educated Chinese who venerated the May Fourth tradition of opposition learned through bitter experience that to espouse any "incorrect" political points of view in Mao's China meant putting themselves and their families in extreme jeopardy. Surviving as an intellectual in the Mao era meant winning and cultivating official favor, which often entailed publicly repudiating one's own beliefs in the form of self-criticisms and confessions. Political criticism of the Party, when it was called for at all, was expected to be made gently and obliquely—by "pointing to the mulberry bush to disparage the ash tree"—so as not to disturb the all-important appearance of consensus and unity. Those who were more explicit were immediately tagged as troublemakers, and paid a grave price for their forthrightness.

In this chronically repressive atmosphere, many intellectuals came to believe that it was "unpatriotic" to voice opinions that clashed with the Party's official line, and that silence was a higher form of patriotism than speaking out. Most intellectuals simply endured their hardships without complaining until China had become more like a vast colony of long-suffering mutes than a civilization of cultivated, free-thinking individuals. Even when in the late 1980s Chinese found themselves allowed an unprecedented degree of openness, many continued to evince a deep fear of rocking the boat. Compliance had become such a deeply rooted habit that even the profound alienation rampant at the time was insufficient to move more than a handful of them to outright dissidence. With few exceptions, intellectuals accepted the dominance of the Communist Party, hoping only to temper its authoritarianism with piecemeal reforms. Given this context, it is easier to understand why most intellectuals initially remained aloof from the student protest.

The term "dissident"—translated into Chinese as *chibutong zhengjian zhe* (someone who holds different political views)—was deemed unutterable in the same breath as the vaunted term "intellectual," as if it somehow besmirched the honor of the title. In fact, even those intellectuals who had been quite courageous in what they said or wrote usually waved off any suggestion that they were "dissidents" as if the term carried with it a bad smell. Although the Western press often referred to Fang Lizhi as "China's Andrei Sakharov," even he was sensitive about the term "political dissident," and not surprisingly never quite succeeded in occupying the same place on the Chinese political stage that Sakharov or Alexander Solzhenitsyn did in the USSR. Whereas these two Russians unfailingly articulated their independent convictions, no matter how they thought the Party would react, and embraced their "dissident" status, even after the Chinese students began breaking away from the political establishment in 1989, most of their elders still found it difficult to speak out with complete candor, much less take a lead in such an anti-establishment protest.

"Chinese intellectuals are weak," acknowledged Liu Binyan. "They were that way decades ago and they are still weak now. Why? Because they don't really believe that if they stand up and fight there is a possibility of major change. This mentality includes me."

Before the hunger strike began, I was surprised by how few of the Beijing intellectuals whom I knew personally joined the marches. It was not until May that some of them began to feel troubled by their collective silence and inactivity. Other than the journalists' petition in support of the *World Economic Herald* on May 9, it was only on May 13, when a group of twelve prominent liberal intellectuals, all members of China's "democratic elite," put up a wall poster at Beida entitled "We Can No Longer Remain Silent," and then the following day went to the Square, that this group began to galvanize publicly. But the purpose of their trip was not so much to express solidarity with the students as to make an "urgent appeal" for them to "temporarily" leave the Square in order to protect the "long-term interests of reform." Although their appeal also demanded that the Central Committee acknowledge that the student protest was a "patriotic democracy movement," recognize the new autonomous student union, and renounce any intention of seeking retribution against those who were demonstrating, these intellectuals seemed more concerned with strengthening the position of Zhao by ending the hunger strike than with bolstering the students' cause.

This appeal did bring welcome attention to the protest movement when it was reported in the press as being supported by such prominent figures as Dai Qing, the well-known investigative reporter for the *Guangming Daily;* Yan Jiaqi, the former director of the Chinese Academy of Social Sciences' Institute of Political Science and an advisor to Zhao Ziyang; Yu Haocheng, a legal scholar and former editor of the Masses Publishing House; Bao Zunxin, an associate at the Chinese Academy of Social Sciences' Institute of History, editor of a series of books on Western political philosophy, and political confidant of Zhao; and Su Xiaokang, investigative journalist and scriptwriter for the controversial television series about China and reform, "River Elegy." But many student and worker activists were offended by the thought of these middle-aged intellectuals deigning to demand that they give up everything for which they had been struggling and quit the Square in order to save the reforms and Zhao Ziyang.

"I believe that the quality of people in the younger generation is higher than those of the older generation," Wu'er Kaixi later said with his usual disregard for tact. "Young people are purer. Due to all the restrictions of their political environment and of the feudal system that has lasted for thousands of years, Chinese intellectuals are generally weak and prone to compromise."

It was not surprising that when these intellectuals read their "urgent appeal" at the Monument they were greeted with a torrent of booing and hissing from the hunger strikers. Having already gathered their own political momentum, students—especially those now led by the militant new "Hunger Strike Group"—spurned the May 14 appeal, jeering at Dai Qing as she tried to reason with them. As the literary critic Liu Xiaobo, who had been Wu'er's political advisor, put it in a subsequent book, "Dai didn't understand the students' state of mind, much less how strong was their willingness to actually die."

Most protesters felt that it was way overdue for the Party to respond to them, rather than vice versa. And while many had sympathy for the reformers, they wanted to stay free of intra-Party factional struggles. "The way I see it, the Communist Party is all one faction—the 'harm-the-people faction,' " said one activist worker. "The reformers and Deng Xiaoping both breathe out of the same nostril."

It was clear to militant students that their strength lay outside the Party. This left them at odds with older intellectuals who, at best, were still deeply ambivalent about falling into outright opposition. Curiously, it was the factional rifts within the Party that presented these intellectuals with an opportunity to enter the political fray without completely cutting themselves off from all official patronage. By attempting to bridge the gap between the students and the government, they could manifest their loyalty to Zhao. So even while their efforts at reconciliation conferred a certain aura of independence on the signatories of the May 14 appeal, it also underscored how difficult it still was for them to break completely free from the state as the students had done by occupying the Square.

What the students did not appreciate as fully as their older counterparts was how their protest movement was strengthening the hand of the hard-liners within the Party leadership. The failure of liberal intellectuals to persuade the students to leave was proof to fence-sitters as well as hard-liners that reformers were unable to control the protest through negotiation. Without quite realizing what they had done, the students had dealt the efforts of Zhao's faction to find a peaceful settlement a fatal blow. But the students were certainly not entirely to blame. Because hard-liners would not allow those negotiating on Zhao's behalf to make the kinds of concessions that might have broken the impasse, they had precious little leverage. The more Zhao's supporters got involved in the factional struggle, the more they seemed to grasp the hopelessness of their situation. When some of them finally overcame their ambivalence and moved into outright opposition, it was because there were no longer other real choices.

On May 15, Yan Jiaqi and Bao Zunxin marched to the Square under a banner reading "The Students Love the Country, and We Love the

Students.'' Behind them an endless procession of writers, reporters, schoolteachers, professors, scientists, musicians, and artists surged down the Avenue of Eternal Peace. When on the following day more than a thousand intellectuals signed the ''May 16 Statement'' urging the Government to yield to student demands and warning that ''those who suppress student movements will come to no good end,'' it did seem as if the broadly based coalition reminiscent of the May Fourth Movement might once again be coalescing.

On May 17 a group of twelve intellectuals—again led by Yan Jiaqi and Bao Zunxin—released another, far harsher declaration that proclaimed unreserved support for the students and blamed their refusal to stop fasting on the government's intransigent attitude. What was significant about the May 17 Declaration was that it unabashedly asserted that China's problems were due to ''the absolute power enjoyed by a dictator.'' Asserting that China's leaders had ''lost all sense of responsibility and humanity,'' it claimed that the government was being run from behind the scenes by ''an emperor without a crown—by a senile and fatuous autocrat.'' It ended by proclaiming, ''Rule by old men must end! The dictator must resign! Long live the university students! Long live the people! Long live democracy! Long live freedom!''

On May 18 a veritable chorus of incensed older intellectuals began speaking out. One of the last living members of the May Fourth Movement generation, Bing Xin, penned an emotional appeal to Party leaders: ''I believe that if right now one or two top leaders . . . would just show up at Tiananmen Square, speak to the huge crowd of hundreds of thousands, and say one or two sentences with sincere sympathy and understanding, this would move the present state of affairs toward reason and order,'' she imploringly wrote. ''Then our sons and grandsons will not have to pay an unnecessarily grievous price.''

This was followed by an open letter from the eighty-five-year-old Ba Jin, another May Fourth veteran, and perhaps the country's most venerated living writer. ''Seventy years ago, during the May Fourth Movement, a group of patriotic students [demonstrated] for the cause of science and democracy in our motherland,'' he wrote. ''Seventy years have passed, and we are still a backward country. I believe the students' demands are completely reasonable. What they are doing today is completing the task we were unable to finish. They are the hope of China. I am now a sickly and decrepit old man, but I feel deeply encouraged by the example of these young people.''

While this upsurge of support took a long time in coming, when it finally materialized, it had important consequences not only for the students, but for the intellectual community itself. By speaking out against the Party in such an unambiguous way, intellectuals took an important step toward breaking the taboo against political opposition that had for decades prevented them from becoming a coherent and autonomous political force.

10

The Leadership
Takes to the
Airwaves

While the bruising factional struggle raged behind the scenes that spring, the leadership sought to maintain an outward appearance of unity. But on May 16 even this facade was marred when Zhao Ziyang stunned Party elders and ordinary citizens alike by telling Gorbachev on a nationwide television broadcast that although Deng had stepped down from the Central Committee and the Standing Committee of the Politburo in 1987, he nonetheless remained "supreme leader," and continued to call the shots. What made Zhao's statement such a breach of Party discipline was not just that it denied the carefully cultivated fiction that Deng had yielded the reins of power to younger leaders such as Zhao himself, but that it confirmed that Deng was still the final arbiter of all important intra-Party disputes. In this not so subtle way, Zhao laid responsibility for the mishandling of the student protest movement directly at Deng's feet. Deng was furious.

Accustomed to watching their leaders deliver predigested speeches regurgitating the Party line, this moment of cinema verité jolted television viewers. For the first time in memory, a high Party official had not only publicly broken ranks with China's paramount leader, but had used the medium of live television to take his appeal directly to the people. The effect was like seeing two actors engaged in a backstage brawl suddenly tumble out from behind a curtain into full view of the audience.

On May 17 the leadership struggle erupted again at a late-night emergency session of the Politburo at Deng's house where Zhao was accused of sowing division within the Party and an appeal made by him to visit the students was voted down. When a declaration of martial law was formally endorsed, Deng was reported to have told Zhao, "I have the army behind me."

"But I have the people behind me," countered Zhao.

"In that case, you have nothing," Deng replied.

Zhao refused to announce the declaration to the public and then attempted to resign. Even though he was in outright opposition to the other four members of the Politburo's Standing Committee, his resignation was refused. The last thing these leaders wanted was another ex–Party chief like Hu Yaobang drifting around as a symbol for protesters to appropriate as their own.

Isolated and besieged, Zhao tried once more to take his case directly to the people. In the early-morning hours of May 18, after another tumultuous Politburo meeting, he went to Beijing and Tongren hospitals to visit convalescing hunger strikers. Awkwardly, he found himself accompanied by Premier Li Peng and Standing Committee members Hu Qili and Qiao Shi, as well as the secretary of the Central Committee Secretariat, Rui Xingwen. Whether they were wary of letting Zhao out of their sight after his defiant refusal to endorse martial law, or whether they, too, hoped that a last-minute appeal might convince the students to leave the Square, is not clear. But only Zhao seemed to really belong among these students. For days he had been prevented from visiting the Square by hard-liners who feared that he would use the occasion to cement an alliance with the demonstrators. Still not enough of a rebel to defy them outright, Zhao had waited obediently until this night.

When Chinese turned on their television sets that morning, they saw their leaders in yet another unscripted TV appearance—this time trooping through a hospital ward full of bedridden students like generals reviewing wounded troops. Indeed, it was the kind of real-life television drama that would have astonished any viewing audience, particularly one that had been fed nothing but carefully sanitized and edited news stories for forty years. Clearly, no one was more surprised to see this wayward scrum of feuding Party bigwigs than the patients themselves, awakened in the middle of the night by blinding klieg lights.

Zhao was clearly reaching out to the students in sympathy. But Li seemed only to be going through the motions. Knowing that martial law would soon be declared, he seemed more intent on laying down an evidential trail of simulated sympathy so that history would perhaps not be able to accuse him of being completely insensitive to the plight of China's youth.

That evening, when at last Party leaders acceded to the students' demands for a televised face-to-face dialogue, CCTV broadcast an even more riveting real-life drama. Again, it was unclear whether the government viewed the meeting as a last-ditch attempt to come to terms or as a public relations move designed to portray them as having left no stone unturned before unleashing a crackdown. During this third teleplay Zhao Ziyang was nowhere to be seen. Instead, Li played the lead role, supported by Beijing's hard-line mayor, Chen Xitong; the city's equally conservative Party chief, Li Ximing; and liberal Secretariat member Yan Mingfu, who more than anyone had been identified with negotiation efforts. The *dramatis personae* of students starred Wu'er Kaixi and Wang Dan, and the *mise en scène* was ironically the Great Hall of the People's Xinjiang Room, Xinjiang being Wu'er's native province. The performance was taped on the morning of May 18, and when it was shown that evening, left viewers agog.

People all across China had been watching the mass demonstrations on television and hearing the names Wu'er Kaixi and Wang Dan for some time, but these young renegades had as yet not been interviewed by CCTV, much less on a Ted Koppel–style "Nightline" format. So when they finally appeared on Chinese television with a ragtag band of other student representatives sitting opposite Premier Li Peng, for many viewers the occasion was a bit like having the Eight Immortals of Daoist legend materialize on their TV screens.

Few contrasts were more emblematic of the gulf that divided the Party and the students than the sartorial styles that distinguished the protagonists at this meeting. Li Peng sat stony-faced in an overstuffed armchair with lace antimacassars. His hands hung awkwardly at his sides. Buttoned up in a gray Mao suit that was accessorized with nothing but nerdish gray Hush Puppies, his colorless and rigidly orthodox manner clashed starkly with the disheveled, irreverent students. Wang Dan wore a dark leather jacket, a dirty blue T-shirt, traditional cotton-soled Chinese shoes, and a headband; Wu'er, who came straight from the hospital where he had been convalescing from his fast, was wearing a pair of striped pajamas and clutched a khaki-colored oxygen bag that trailed plastic tubes, which he indelicately stuck up his nose during the meeting in order to fortify himself against fainting spells. While the idea of wearing pajamas in the Great Hall during an audience with the premier left some viewers aghast and others squirming with delight, the gesture perfectly captured Wu'er's studied disregard for authority and the students' mounting impatience with the rituals of deference that supplicants were expected to display when petitioning their rulers. In case viewers missed the message implicit in his fashion statement, Wu'er very pointedly slighted Li by refusing to get up as the premier approached to shake hands with each of the other students. Not until he was almost face-to-face with the premier did Wu'er finally rise, and then only for a moment before plunking himself back down again in his chair. "I was really very upset, thinking that for too long China's leaders have continued to behave as emperors who could lord over us," he later explained.

"I am delighted to meet you all," Li Peng began awkwardly, as if greeting yet another group of model workers. Perhaps fearing he might appear too solicitous and weak before a nationwide audience, Li immediately began laying down ground rules for the discussion. "In today's conversation we are going to talk about only one subject, and that is, how to get the hunger strikers out of their present plight," he said. "The Party and the government are very concerned about this matter. We are deeply disturbed by the situation and concerned over the health of the students."

Then Li began to discuss his own three children—none of whom, he pointedly insisted, were "involved in profiteering." This was a not-so-subtle dig at Zhao's sons, several of whom were rumored to have capitalized on their father's name and position by making lucrative overseas arms deals. In a way that might have been well intentioned but appeared condescending, Li then surveyed the students slouched around him and declared, "We look on you as if you were our own children."

Wu'er, who was in no mood to be Li's figurative child, interrupted the premier with a dismissive wave of his hand. "We don't have much time," he said, his voice filled with impatience and irritation. "While we are sitting comfortably here, students outside are suffering from hunger." Without giving the premier a chance to regain the initiative, the intrepid Wu'er continued. "Now, I would like to tell you what we have to say. Just now you said that we were going to talk about only one subject. But the actual situation is not that *you* invited *us* to this discussion, but that *we*—all those people in the Square—asked *you* to come and talk!" Therefore, he said, wagging an admonishing forefinger, "how many topics will be discussed ought to be up to us!"

With his jaw clenched Li called his interlocutor impolite. "Impolite?" Wu'er shot back. "You've got a million people on the streets, and you're calling me impolite? Premier Li, I don't think we have enough time for this kind of talk!"

When this confrontation was first broadcast, I happened to be with some friends in a Beijing hotel room, and the unprecedented spectacle of a twenty-one-year-old student in a pair of pajamas dressing down the premier of China drew a collective gasp from us all. Even the way Wu'er sat screamed hauteur and defiance. Whereas most Chinese granted an audience with the premier sat nervously on the edge of their chairs bent slightly forward with obsequiousness, Wu'er sprawled back in his seat like a junior gangland boss holding court. The realization that hundreds of millions of Chinese were watching this free-form encounter was enough to take one's breath away.

Getting to the heart of the matter, a hoarse Wang Dan reiterated student demands, which by now had been simplified to three: repudiate the April 26 editorial, recognize the Beijing Autonomous Student Federation, and begin negotiations.

"Up to the present, no one has yet declared that the student movement is not, in fact, a form of turmoil," reminded Wu'er. "The nature of this movement must be properly redefined. . . . Either Comrade Zhao Ziyang or Comrade Li Peng—Zhao Ziyang would be best—should go to the Square and speak directly to the students, or the *People's Daily* should print another editorial repudiating the one published on April 26, one that apologizes to the people across the country and acknowledges the great significance of the current student movement." Only then, insisted Wu'er, would student leaders be in a position to urge protesters to cease fasting and quit the Square. But even then, cautioned Wu'er, "we cannot say for sure that we will succeed."

"The student movement has already become a people's movement," Beida student Shao Jiang warned. "The students are relatively reasonable, but we cannot be so sure that this people's movement will also be reasonable."

"Neither the government nor the Party has ever stated that the masses of students were creating turmoil," Li argued. "We have always regarded the patriotic enthusiasm and wishes of the students as positive and good." This was an important admission, and it might have helped answer student demands if Li could have assured them that he was speaking officially on behalf of the Party as a whole. But, alas, since the editorial was an expression of Deng's own sentiments, it was unthinkable to retract it, and so what might have served as an avenue for further discussion came to nothing, and soon Li Peng was again chiding the assembled students.

"In the past few days Beijing has basically fallen into a state of anarchy," continued Li. "We must protect the safety of our students, protect our factories, protect the achievements of socialism, and protect our capital. . . . Creating turmoil may not have been the original intent of most people, but in the end, turmoil is what has occurred."

"It seems to me that some of you leading comrades still do not understand me," rebutted Wu'er, as it became clear that Li was going to make no major concessions. "Let's avoid this endless quibbling. . . . If this meeting leads nowhere and we continue to disagree on this question, then we cannot but conclude that the government is not sincere—that it does not have the slightest sincerity in trying to solve the problem. In that case, there is no need for us student representatives to remain sitting here any longer."

The tantalizing drama ended with Wu'er diving for his oxygen bag as five white-smocked medical personnel jumped to attend him. "They've been inside their offices too long," said Wu'er contemptuously once he was back in the hospital. "They don't comprehend the power of this movement."

"Chinese sometimes say, 'To be met by the premier is the happiest moment in one's life,' " Wu'er commented later. "It's so difficult for Chinese to give up their habit of thanking the 'emperor' for his noblesse oblige. [But] I didn't feel thankful to Li Peng. I felt that our respect for him should depend on his abilities. People throughout the country were able to see for themselves how a twenty-one-year-old man spoke critically to the premier of the nation as an equal and without hesitation. We had the guts to do so because we had truth on our side, and people liked what we said because in it they heard an expression of their own anger at the government."

"Even now I sometimes can't distinguish one day from another during that period, but I will always remember with perfect clarity the date and the images of those students confronting Li Peng," one student activist later told me. "For us, Li Peng was the incarnation of everything wrong with China, and when Wu'er stood up to him, we felt he was speaking for all of us."

By confronting Li openly on a nationwide stage, Wu'er and the other student representatives gave expression to one of the most deep-seated and forbidden fantasies in the Chinese psyche—challenging arbitrary authority under the threat of retaliation without flinching. The sight of these young students facing down the unpopular premier represented an important step in breaking the stranglehold of fear and intimidation that had immobilized generations of Chinese for so long. Like the young boy in Hans Christian Andersen's cautionary tale "The Emperor's New Clothes," Wu'er's effrontery helped puncture the image of Li's invulnerability. Having not only occupied the Square but then penetrated the inner sanctums of Party power to challenge the premier within the throne room of the Royal Palace itself, the students had doubly breached the government's mystique of omnipotence.

Before most viewers had had a chance to fully digest what they had just seen, the next morning TV sets exploded with yet another episode of what was becoming an almost daily leadership soap opera. Shortly before dawn on the morning of May 19, Zhao Ziyang, who for so many years had faithfully followed the dictates of the Party, decided to break Party discipline and make a swan-song pilgrimage to the Square. What he expected to accomplish by this impetuous move is still not completely clear, but confidants report that, with five children of his own, the knowledge that the government was now committed to bringing in troops had left Zhao conscience-stricken about the plight of the fasting students. He also appears to have wanted to make one final gesture of solidarity with them for posterity's sake, so that when the dynastic histories of Deng's reign were written, Zhao would not go down as having favored suppression.

Without permission from either the Politburo or Deng, at around 4 A.M., Zhao left for the Square. He was so fatigued from the travails of the previous days that when he finally got there, he hardly seemed to know what to do. As he stepped from his chauffeur-driven car, his face had no more color in it than his somber gray Mao suit or his ashen hair. To his annoyance, he was once again followed by his political nemesis, Li Peng. Given that Li was so thoroughly despised by the students, his appearance in the Square seemed even more anomalous than at the hospital the night before. The only explanation for his presence was that he was tracking Zhao in an attempt to blunt whatever effect this eleventh-hour sympathy mission might have on the volatile situation.

With Li behind him like a shadow, Zhao walked toward the fleet of city buses in which hunger-striking students were living. When they groggily sat up to see what the commotion was and realized that both the Party's general secretary and the premier were outside, some assumed that the government had at last yielded to their demands, and began applauding and reaching out of windows to shake Zhao's hand.

Zhao boarded one of the trash-strewn buses and began to talk with several of the surprised students inside. Awkwardly, Li also tried to make small talk, inquiring about such banalities as where the students went to school and how they were feeling. But perhaps sensing how unwelcome he was, or fearful that he would be compromised on camera by whatever breach of Party discipline Zhao was preparing to commit, Li mysteriously departed after only a few minutes. Moving to the doorway of the bus as a throng of astonished but excited students crowded around, Zhao began to speak through a small orange-colored battery-powered bullhorn. "I just want to say a few words to you students. I have come too late. Too late," he said as tears welled up in his eyes.

"But you have finally come," insisted one student.

"I am sorry, fellow students, I do not come to ask you to excuse us. All I want to say is that because your fast has entered the seventh day, students are now physically very weak, and this situation simply cannot go on." As Zhao spoke, a video cameraman caught the faces of several headbanded hunger strikers flanking him. Like Zhao, their faces looked gray, their eyes were hooded with exhaustion, and their lips chapped from lack of sleep. "I know that your fasting is aimed at winning satisfactory answers to the demands you have put forward to the government and the Party," Zhao continued wearily. "And I think that satisfactory answers are obtainable. . . . You should understand, however, that resolution of such problems is complicated, and more time is needed. But since your hunger strike is reaching the seventh day, you must not persist in it until satisfactory answers are given." Then he made one final appeal for them to leave the Square. "I know that you comrades all have the best of intentions to do something beneficial for the country, but if this strike continues and gets out of control, the consequences could be very serious."

It was obvious that Zhao knew this was his final farewell. His tone was made all the more desperate by his awareness that, whatever happened to him, if the students did not relent, they would soon confront troops. "Are you going to give up your lives?" he finally asked. "Please think about this in a rational way."

Despite their exhaustion, as soon as Zhao finished speaking, students crowded around him proffering notebooks, umbrellas, T-shirts, and in one case a bare arm for him to autograph. Despite Zhao's lifetime as a Party apologist, his appearance in the Square did win him popular sympathy. But it was clear that this pilgrimage ended any chance he still had of surviving within the Party leadership. Indeed, it was the last time Zhao was seen in public before being put under house arrest.

With Zhao shunted aside, and the possibility of a negotiated settlement more remote than ever, hard-liners were now able to effect their own solution to the problem without obstruction. Later that morning, when Li Peng met Richard Woolcott, a diplomat from the Australian Foreign Ministry who had arrived at this most improbable time to discuss economic cooperation, he hinted darkly at what was soon to come. "Turmoil has occurred in Beijing," warned Li. "The Chinese government will, with a responsible attitude, take measures to stop the chaos so as to restore order."

11

"We Have Won a Great Victory Because the People Support Us"

Although the citizenry of Beijing did not know it, at dusk on the evening of May 19 an "extraordinary" joint meeting of officials from the Central Committee, the State Council, the Beijing municipal government, and key military commanders was convened in the cloistered confines of the Beijing Military Region headquarters. With the exception of Zhao Ziyang, every ambulatory ranking Party, government, and military leader was there. When their deliberations finally concluded around 10 P.M., loudspeakers in the Square crackled to life, and the shrill voice of Li Peng reverberated out to the fasting students. At the same time, regular television programming was interrupted and a grim-faced Li flickered onto Beijing screens. "Comrades, anarchy is becoming more and more serious; law and discipline are being violated" he began. "If we do not promptly bring this standoff to an end, and instead just let things go on, a situation that no one wants to see develop will very likely emerge." Shaking a fist in the air, Li asserted, "It is becoming clearer and clearer that an extremely small handful of people want to achieve their political goal of negating the socialist system . . . undermining the leadership of the Chinese Communist Party, overthrowing the government . . . [and] totally negating the people's democratic dictatorship through turmoil. . . . If they should achieve their goals, reform and the open-door policy, our democratic legal system, and socialist modernization will go up in smoke, and

China will undergo a historical reversal.'' As a result, said Li, the government had decided to ''take decisive and firm measures in order to put a swift end to the turmoil, to protect the leadership of the Party, and to protect the socialist system.'' The next morning, May 20, Beijing was to be placed under martial law. All forms of public protest would be banned, all journalists prohibited from entering the martial-law area of jurisdiction, and troops would be authorized to handle the situation ''forcefully.'' Li's statement was met by choruses of booing, catcalling, and chanting in the Square: ''Down with government by hooliganism!'' ''Down with Li Peng!''

Ironically, just hours before Li's declaration, students had voted to call off their hunger strike. They were exhausted, and no doubt Zhao's *cri de coeur* had influenced them. ''We have won a great victory because the people support us,'' Chai Ling, a key figure in the Hunger Strike Committee and spokesperson for the most die-hard faction of protesters, had announced. But plans to vacate the Square were hastily abandoned when word that martial law would be declared was leaked through Zhao's supporters. In fact, it was because of this leak, which immediately caused people to flood back into the Square, that Party leaders had called the ''extraordinary'' joint meeting. Hoping to catch the protest movement off guard, they moved formal announcement of martial law up by one day.

From the Party's perspective the situation was dire. Not only were students and intellectuals in a state of rebellion, but that very day, a young railroad worker, Han Dongfang, who was from the nascent Beijing Autonomous Workers' Federation (BAWF), called for a general strike. Fearing that a powerful coalition might be forged between renegade workers, dissident students, alienated intellectuals, and partisans of Zhao, Li Peng and other hard-liners saw potential conspiracies almost everywhere.

Actually, the whole protest might well have fizzled out if the government had not chosen to act so precipitously. For anyone still hoping for a peaceful resolution, Li's declaration of martial law came at precisely the wrong time; but from the standpoint of the hard-liners the timing contained its own cynical logic. Many of them felt that an early showdown was the only way to prevent the entire population of the capital from rising up in outright opposition. Blood might be shed, as Deng had already acknowledged, but with decisive action, the hard-liners might in a single blow yet rid themselves of the Beijing Autonomous Student Federation, the Autonomous Workers' Federation, and Zhao's traitorous faction.

Rumors swept the capital that troops bivouacked on its outskirts would soon move in. Nobody was sure what to expect. Although it was impossible to know how troops would actually respond if ordered to take the Square by force, there was still such a mythology about the PLA being at "one with the people," few could imagine that soldiers would ever fire on unarmed citizens. It was true that a younger and more professional core of commanders had gained key field positions during Deng's modernization drive over the last decade, but a coterie of octogenarian leaders known as the Gang of Elders, whose ties to one another dated back to the Long March, still made all major military-policy decisions. This "gang" was led by Deng Xiaoping, who was still chairman of the powerful Military Affairs Commission, and included Yang Shangkun, state president and vice-chairman of the Military Affairs Commission; Wang Zhen, state vice-president and a former general with strong ties to China's westernmost military region; Chen Yun, a veteran state planner, Politburo Standing Committee member and chairman of the powerful Central Advisory Commission; Bo Yibo, deputy chairman of the Central Advisory Commission; and Li Xiannian, former general and president, and current chairman of the Chinese People's Political Consultative Congress. All were born before 1910, and despite there being an elaborate bureaucratic apparatus formally charged with overseeing the military, these men effectively controlled the country's seven military regions and twenty-four group armies through networks of personal loyalties.

Sympathy for the students had become so widespread by May 19 that Beijing was rife with hearsay about disaffection in the military. Several high-ranking commanders who had children fasting in the Square were said to be opposing any use of force. General Xu Qinxian, commander of the 38th Group Army, was said to have refused to follow orders to position his men around Beijing and been imprisoned. "The people's army has a history of never having suppressed the people," he was reported as saying. "I cannot sully that history." Although seven months later Yang Shangkun revealed in a classified speech that twenty-one officers and cadres with ranks of division commander or higher, thirty-six officers with ranks of regimental or battalion commander, and fifty-four officers with ranks of company commander had, in fact, "breached discipline in a serious manner," at the moment it was difficult to assess how such rumors of insubordination might impede the implementation of martial law.

General Xu notwithstanding, elements of the 150,000-man 38th Group Army and units of China's twenty-five other group armies had, in fact, already encircled Beijing long before martial law was actually declared. But the citizenry of Beijing were being kept alerted to troop movements through a group of hastily organized messengers known as the Flying Tigers, a motley collection of some several hundred private entrepreneurs and *liumang* who happened to own motorcycles and had deputized themselves to serve as the eyes and ears of the resistance movement. On the evening of May 19 as troops in the suburbs began moving in, the Flying Tigers sped around Beijing sounding the alarm. Given the absence of a real communications network, their warnings were crucial in turning out tens of thousands of people of all ages and from all walks of life to block major arteries leading into the Square. Some observers estimate that by dawn on May 20 as many as 2 million citizens had taken to the streets.

Before troop transports could clear the outskirts of the city, commanders found themselves confronted by barricades constructed out of traffic-lane dividers, public buses, booths from street markets, Dumpsters, and concrete sewer pipes, as well as throngs of ordinary people. Pajama-clad patients from one hospital were reported to have risen from their sickbeds in order to form human blockades. Some people went so far as to lie down in the middle of the street to prevent convoys from passing. Columns of troop trucks and supply vehicles were soon halted and backed-up for miles.

Meanwhile, thousands of Beijingers returned to the Square itself to provide psychological support, and to bring food, drink, clean clothing, wet gauze for face masks in case the troops fired tear gas, and even a new generator for the students' sound system. As the night progressed, crowds in the Square waited anxiously for news.

Just after midnight student loudspeakers came to life: "Students! The people of Beijing have stopped the advance of the PLA at the Hujialou intersection!" exclaimed an excited voice. "A few seconds elapsed as the true impact of this momentous news began to dawn on the exhausted students in the Square," remembered Robin Munro, an observer monitoring the demonstrations for the U.S. human rights group Asia Watch. "And then a joyous roar of triumph went up all around."

About half an hour later another breathless announcement reported that troops had also been blocked at Wukesong in the west. Yet another claimed that units had also been halted at Fengtai and Liuliqiao in the southwest, and Donggaodi in the southeast. To the astonishment of everyone, it appeared that the advance of all initial columns of martial-law troops had been stopped on the city's outskirts.

To its credit, the government had not equipped this first wave of troops with firearms, but while the decision most certainly helped prevent the outbreak of violence, it also made the soldiers virtual prisoners of encircling crowds. For many advancing soldiers the experience of being trapped in their trucks by a sea of agitated civilians was bewildering and terrifying. To prevent trucks from attempting to break loose from obstructing crowds, tires were punctured, distributor caps removed, and cartloads of gravel and rubble were dumped behind the wheels to make sure that they could not back up.

Mao Zedong had once described the relationship that should exist between "the people" and a "people's army" as being one in which "the former may be likened to the water, and the latter to the fish that swim in it." Bogged down in the streets of Beijing by thousands of ordinary citizens, these latter-day Maoist "fish" now seemed to be drowning in, rather than sustained by, the water of "the people." As one redecorated traffic sign near the Square proclaimed, "Forty years ago, [when] the PLA entered Beijing, our fathers rushed into the streets to welcome it. Today, forty years later, the PLA is again entering Beijing, but the people are opposing it. Such is the difference between winning and losing the hearts of the masses."

When these citizen-resisters realized that their primitive people-power tactics of flooding streets with human bodies could actually bring whole columns of military vehicles to a grinding halt, many grew less frightened and began talking sympathetically to their captives. They were surprised to discover that soldiers had been forbidden to listen to the radio or read anything but the *People's Daily,* and thus had very little idea why the students were in Tiananmen Square, much less why they themselves were being prevented from carrying out their orders. As one Beida handbill was soon advising, "The soldiers are not our real enemies. They are the people's brothers. They have been tricked into coming here, and they do not understand the situation. . . . We understand that soldiers are required to obey orders, but we should try to make it clear to them that they also have the right to reject orders that run counter to the people's wishes." Another appeal by Beishida students melodramatically declared, "Soldiers, we love you! The people love you! Your hands must not be stained with the people's blood."

Bewildered troops were soon also being proffered tea, cigarettes, and food. Lü Jinghua recalled how small children began smiling and saluting the soldiers, while elderly women brought them things to eat and drink. "You had a real sense of people supporting troops on the front lines during wartime," Lü said. "You could see the relationship between the soldiers and the people deepen until many soldiers seemed really moved." Such efforts at persuasion were surprisingly effective, and caused many soldiers to apologize, and even to weep openly over the trouble they were causing. Others shed their uniforms and melted into the crowds.

"We'd like to say: Compatriots, please do not abandon us, treat us coldly, or reject us," one soldier of the Central Security Guard's 3rd Battalion was reported to have said. "Our hearts are linked with yours. We are also common people who are suffering."

Needless to say, military commanders viewed such insubordination as calamitous. Shi Renquan, a frustrated officer, described such citizens' tactics as "poisonous, bewitching, and inciting." "Between the orders and decisions coming from the Party Central Committee and the abuses hurled by these people," he lamented, "how can a soldier think clearly?"

Incredibly, foreign television had until now continued live coverage via satellite uplinks that had been approved for the Gorbachev summit. But with martial law in effect, Chinese officials now moved to pull the plug on "live TV feeds." "You are here to report on Gorbachev," the Chinese Foreign Ministry curtly told CNN. "Gorbachev is gone. Your task is over." In a dramatic telecast, Americans watched as CNN's live coverage vanished into a static haze of white noise.

Li Peng's declaration of martial law was also a signal for China's domestic press to fall silent. The Ministry of Radio, Film, and Television ordered all branches of the Chinese broadcast media to become once again "mouthpieces of the Party, government, and people," to "publicize the brilliant decisions of the Party Central Committee on ending the turmoil."

May 20 was a hot, sultry spring day. Despite their great triumph the previous night, people in Beijing stayed at the barricades lest troops make a second attempt to reach the Square. Rumors were rife of soldiers trying to infiltrate the city disguised as civilians. There were even reports of troops stealing into the city via the vast network of air-raid tunnels dug at the height of the Sino-Soviet rift and then regrouping at staging areas in the Forbidden City and the Great Hall of the People. The sense of paranoia grew when it was discovered that whole units were, in fact, trying to reach the Square through the subway system. In one instance, a crowd of civilians rushed down into the subway tunnel and succeeded in forcing some soldiers to turn back. When word reached the Square that freight trains loaded with troops were also trying to enter Beijing, another army of resisters raced to the railroad station, where they succeeded in bottling up the new arrivals before they could unload and leave the terminal. However, a detachment of soldiers wearing white surgical smocks did get through the city's zealously guarded defenses in ambulances and reached the *People's Daily* building. After the previous night's debacle, the government had evidently decided to try a more surreptitious, Maoist strategy of guerrilla warfare.

It was clear by Sunday, May 21, however, that most troops had been prevented from reaching the heart of the city, and this engendered an even greater sense of euphoria. Just before dawn students played Schiller's "Ode to Joy" from Beethoven's Ninth Symphony over their public address system at the Monument. When day broke, hundreds of thousands of festive people spilled into the streets and milled joyfully through the Square congratulating each other, trading news, passing out leaflets, and listening to impromptu curbside speeches.

"At the call of college students, a great and unprecedented patriotic mass movement is now taking place in Beijing and throughout the country," effused an open letter to Deng from student organizations in the Square. "How this part of history is written has much to do with you. We sincerely hope that with your intervention the process of democratization in China will be advanced nonviolently."

Hopes for such a nonviolent ending were heightened when it was revealed that seven senior military figures had written Deng a letter pleading that the PLA not be used to deal with the situation. Then on May 21 a delegation of students from the University of Science and Technology visited retired Marshals Xu Xiangqian and Nie Rongzhen, and they both expressed opposition to using soldiers to suppress the protest. Such news made it more tempting than ever for resisters to believe that "people power" might actually succeed in bringing about a "peaceful revolution" against the armed might of the Party.

As the week progressed, however, there were more and more hints that the government had not given up hope of militarily reoccupying the city. On May 22, Deng Xiaoping's son Deng Pufang was rumored to have dispatched representatives to the Square to warn of another military assault and counsel protesters to retreat quickly if they wished to avoid bloodshed. Such ominous signals left the student leadership more divided than ever. Fearing that the hard-liners would be harsher than ever after their embarrassing failure, Wu'er Kaixi and Wang Dan urged the students to declare victory and stage a tactical retreat. However, Chai Ling, who had been "elected" to the grandiose position of commander in chief of Tiananmen Square Unified Action Headquarters, remained committed to "defending the Square" at all costs. "Each day and hour that we stay here, we make more people around the country aware that there are people in China who still dare to resist and to cry out that they are no longer willing to be slaves,'' was the way Chai's husband, Feng Congde, put it.

''The Square was a symbol that should not fall,'' Li Lu, Chai's twenty-three-year-old lieutenant, insisted in his autobiography, *Moving the Mountain*. ''Those of us who were at the forefront of the struggle knew what was in store for us, and that moderation could not be expected.'' After a vociferous debate, Wu'er and Wang's position was rejected, and the students decided to remain in the Square. When troops did not immediately make an effort to reenter the city, Wu'er stood down from his position as BASF chairman: Wu'er claims that he resigned; others claim that he was sacked.

Since many students wanted to get back to their classes and normal lives, student leaders had an increasingly difficult time maintaining enthusiasm among supporters. They were also plagued by increasingly vitriolic factional splits. The situation was made even more uncertain by the fact that no one could be sure whether the government's inaction was a temporary delaying tactic taken to allow the army to regroup, or an artful pause calculated to allow the protest movement to slowly implode on its own.

In fact, beneath the surface appearance of inactivity, the army was busy. Having learned how difficult it would be for unarmed troops to reach Tiananmen Square by way of a frontal assault, but having some experience infiltrating small groups of soldiers into the city, military commanders began covertly funneling bands of ununiformed soldiers into key locations. At the same time, undercover operatives were dispatched around Beijing to gather intelligence about the students' morale, the locations of barricades, the activities of the new workers' federation, and the general mood among the populace. Meanwhile, Deng, who had made no public appearances since Gorbachev's departure, was reported to have flown to Wuhan to gather up 200,000 fresh troops and set up a command center in Central China just in case control of Beijing was lost. His new strategy was to mobilize detachments from all of China's seven military regions, thereby reducing his reliance on any one group army in which an insubordinate commander like Xu Qinxian might complicate his plans.

As the waiting game dragged on toward the end of May, morale plummeted, and a growing number of students abandoned the Square. After six weeks of occupation, its hundred acres were heaped with deepening piles of trash and garbage, its makeshift shelters tattered, the buses in which students had been living filthy and inhospitable, and in the ninety-degree heat the latrine situation had gone from bad to worse. The Square looked and smelled more like a squalid squatters' camp than the headquarters of an idealistic political movement.

On May 27, in a summit meeting of movement leaders held outside the Square, Chai Ling finally relented and agreed that the students' cause would be best served by leaving. It was decided that before making their strategic retreat back to their university campuses to continue a struggle in "a new form," protesters should hold one last face-saving rally on May 30. As soon as news of this agreement reached the Square, however, out-of-town militants wedded to the idea of defending this symbolic seat of protest charged that the plan was a "sellout." Not only had the students failed as yet to win any substantive government concessions, they argued, but if the students lost their leverage as an organized movement by abandoning the Square, there would be little to prevent the government from wreaking retribution on them later on. They urged protesters to remain until the Standing Committee of the National People's Congress met on June 20.

Pressured by Li Lu and other militants, Chai Ling began to reconsider. Rumors that blacklists were being prepared by the government and the threat of long prison terms made many students reluctant to give up the protection, however illusory, that their togetherness in the Square afforded. Li Lu later remembered wondering: "I'm twenty-three—how many years will I be in prison now? Most probably they would sentence us to five or ten years in prison, but perhaps for leaders like us it would be as much as fifteen or twenty. We would be over forty years old when we came out." By the morning of May 28 such worries, as well as concerns over the dwindling numbers in the Square, had so confused and upset Chai Ling that she relented and then threatened to resign as "commander in chief." It was a faithful decision.

Tension levels heightened on the night of May 29 when three BAWF workers were arrested by the PSB. It was a sign that if the government had a chance to "settle accounts after the harvest," it would be those insubordinate proletarians who had deigned to call a general workers' strike and set up a "Dare-to-Die Corps" to resist future military incursions into the city rather than students who would bear the greatest burden. Despite his fears about his own future, Han Dongfang promptly organized a demonstration in front of the Beijing PSB headquarters situated just off the Square. Next to a banner proclaiming "Secret Kidnapping," he delivered a speech to several thousand supporters in which he denounced the illegality of the arrests. To everyone's surprise, the three detainees were soon released.

For the final May 30 rally, students from the Central Academy of Fine Arts had been asked by protest leaders to make a statue that could be erected in the Square as a symbol of the movement that would remain after demonstrators dispersed. "At this critical moment. . . . We need a powerful cementing force to strengthen our resolve, and this force is the Goddess of Democracy," declared a statement by the arts institutes that sponsored the project with the Central Academy. The statement went on to say that the statue should "declare to the world that the great awakening of the Chinese people to democratic ideas has reached a new stage."

The thirty-seven-foot-high foam-and-plaster monument arrived in the Square in three sections on a procession of flatbed bicycle carts. As a tinny loudspeaker played Bach's "A Mighty Fortress Is Our God" over and over, students from the Central Academy erected their new icon, directly in front of Tiananmen Gate. "It was on the great axis, heavy with symbolism both cosmological and political, that extended from the main entrance of the Forbidden City with the huge portrait of Mao Zedong over it, through the Monument to the Martyrs of the People, which had become the command headquarters of the student movement," recalled Cao Xingyuan, a former student at the Central Academy and wife of the American art historian James Cahill, who was in Beijing at the time and chronicled each stage of the project. The object of such placement, explained Cao, was to make it "confront the Great Leader face-to-face."

When it came time for the official unveiling of the Goddess, a man and a woman were chosen from the crowd to come forward and pull the ropes that held a shroud over the statue's head. "As these veils fell, the crowd burst into cheers, and there were shouts of 'Long live democracy!' " remembered Cao. Revealed was a figure of a woman holding a torch of freedom aloft.

"The statue of the Goddess is made of plaster, and, of course, cannot stand forever," explained a statement read out over a P.A. system in the Square. "But as the symbol of the people's hearts, she is divine and inviolate. Let those who would sully her beware: The people will not permit this!"

The sight of this pristine white statue being erected to the accompaniment of Western music allowed educated Chinese in the crowd to hope that their country was, at last, breaking out of its Communist provincialism and merging with cosmopolitan political currents that would bring more openness, tolerance, and democracy. For older intellectuals who had been trained abroad before 1949, it had been a long and agonizing wait. When the shroud fell, some openly wept.

Enormous crowds immediately gathered to gaze up at the towering Goddess and to enjoy the nonstop carnival of musicians, martial-arts experts, storytellers, comedy teams, dancers, and dramatic troupes that began performing at her base. For a moment it almost seemed as if the first halcyon days of the hunger strike had returned. Some foreign correspondents began to write about signs of a "deadlock" in the confrontation, as if the government had been permanently paralyzed. In fact, the foreign press treated the unveiling of the Goddess as a kind of coronation ceremony for what most were now unabashedly calling the "Chinese democracy movement." For Americans, in particular, the Goddess's striking resemblance to the Statue of Liberty made it a TV image with which everyone could instantly identify.

In a devastatingly simple, visual way, the Goddess again challenged the Party's claim of being rightful heir to the Square. Facing Tiananmen Gate, the Goddess looked almost as if at any moment she might swing her torch of freedom like a club and blasphemously strike out at Mao's portrait. Understandably, Party hard-liners found everything about the statue an abomination.

As the presence of the Goddess in the Square fanned the protest movement back to life, Party propagandists mobilized to nullify its influence. "Your movement is bound to fail! It is foreign. This is China, not the United States," a voice boomed out over speakers in the Square. "All citizens have the duty to cherish and protect Tiananmen Square, which is equal to cherishing and protecting our motherland and our nation," fumed the *People's Daily*. "The Square is sacred. No one should have the right to add any permanent memorial or to remove anything from the Square."

Because once again the students had successfully occupied the Square with their powerful visual symbols, Party propagandists were forced to the peripheries to create retaliatory images. By comparison, however, their efforts were lackluster. A massive banner proclaiming "Oppose Bourgeois Liberalization" was unfurled down the side of the state-owned Beijing Hotel at the northeast corner of the Square. At the new Kentucky Fried Chicken franchise at the south end of the Square, a banner proclaiming "Maintain Unity and Stability" hung down over a plastic statue of Colonel Sanders. To create competing images of popular support for television, Party officials staged "spontaneous displays of anger against bad elements" by busing thousands of school-children and peasants to suburban stadiums for progovernment demonstrations. At one such rally held in suburban Daxing County, a lackadaisical crowd of peasants was paid 10 yuan ($1.50) each to wave government-issued picket signs saying "Smash the Traitors to Smithereens" and "Resolutely Uphold Li Peng." A climax of sorts was contrived when three men outfitted in Uncle Sam suits, oversized noses, and top hats proffered fake dollar bills to an effigy of Fang Lizhi that was promptly burned. The immolation was a clue that Party leaders had already decided on a list of scapegoats, or "black hands," upon whom this monumental debacle could ultimately be blamed.

Actually, Fang had not come near the Square. He had, however, continued to give interviews to the foreign press corps. "From the short-term perspective of realism, what has happened may seem like a tragedy of historical development," he told the Taiwan-based *United Daily News* on June 2. "But from a long-term perspective, just like the May Fourth Movement this movement will certainly be advantageous to the development of democracy in China. . . . The success of today's student movement does not depend on whether it achieves its proposed aims, rather it lies in the fact that it has made intellectuals, students, and ordinary people understand that they have a right to make their own choice; that if they don't like certain leaders, they have the right not only to demand that they step down, but to do so openly."

On the afternoon of June 2, as student resolve was again weakening, events in the Square took another unexpected turn when four prominent middle-aged intellectuals presented themselves at the Monument and announced that they would begin a hunger strike of their own. The participants in this eleventh-hour mini-fast were Hou Dejian, the well-known pop singer; Liu Xiaobo, the maverick literary critic from Beishida who had served as Wu'er Kaixi's behind-the-scenes advisor; Zhou Duo, an economist with the privately owned and highly successful Stone Corporation; and Gao Xin, a former editor. Although Hou was by far the best known because of his hit song "Children of the Dragon," it was Liu who best articulated the reasons why the four decided to undertake this belated fast.

"In the face of the high-handed military violence of the irrational Li Peng government, Chinese intellectuals must bring to an end their age-old propensity—handed down over the millennia—of being spineless and merely speaking while never acting," said a statement largely penned by Liu. What China needed, said the statement, was "not a perfect savior, but a sound democratic system." "We would rather have ten devils who check and balance each other than an angel who holds absolute power." Refusing to criticize only the government, they also appealed to the students "to examine their own actions" and make "democratic reorganization" of the student movement a priority. "Mistakes by both the government and the people are inevitable," they said. "The key is to admit mistakes when they become evident, and to correct them after they appear."

Although theirs was one of the most thoughtful manifestos to come out of the protest movement, at the time few people on either side were inclined to pay it much heed. However, rock star Hou Dejian's arrival in the Square did attract a good deal of attention. On the evening of June 2, when word got around that he would lead a sing-along with his guitar, thousands of youths showed up for what amounted to a Chinese hootenanny. Later that night, while sitting in his tent, Hou managed to pen a new song that included the surprisingly rose-tinted lines: "Ugly Chinese though we've been, how beautiful we are today! Everything is possible. Nothing too far away."

Meanwhile, Deng and his military allies were marshaling their forces. "In Chinese tradition there is no such notion as compromise," lamented Xiang Xiaoji. "Either you die or I die. . . . The philosophy of the Chinese Communist Party is the philosophy of struggle."

"If the turmoil created by this small handful of people is not resolutely put down, then there will be no peace in either the Party or the country," eighty-four-year-old Chen Yun, chairman of the Central Advisory Commission, a bastion of the Gang of Elders, had warned at an emergency Standing Committee meeting the week before. "Not only is there a danger of losing the achievements of ten years of reform, but there is also a danger of losing all the fruits of the revolution, and all the achievements of socialist construction. . . . We must never make concessions. There should not be the slightest amount of vagueness on this point."

"There is no way for us to retreat," President Yang Shangkun warned a short while later. "To retreat means our downfall. To retreat means the downfall of the People's Republic of China and the restoration of capitalism."

12

"Recover the Square at Any Cost"

Having endured seven weeks of humiliation and frustration, by the end of May hard-line leaders had more than reached the limits of their tolerance. "Recover the Square at any cost," Deng Xiaoping was said to have commanded the fresh troops that he had been assembling in preparation for another assault.

As rumors flew and tension in the capital once again mounted, many of the Party's key leaders withdrew from the city to the walled Jade Spring Mountain leadership compound nestled in the Fragrant Hills northwest of Beijing. There they pored over reports from intelligence operatives scouting the streets. Yang Shangkun, president of China and vice-chairman of the Military Affairs Commission, and his brother Yang Baibing, chairman of the army's General Political Department, were among Deng's most crucial allies. Their strategy for retaking the city called for troops from the Military Armed Police and the People's Liberation Army serving under loyal commanders to launch a pincer movement that would converge on the Square from all points of the compass at once. What they feared most was not just that another advance might be halted, but that a new military operation might ignite a full-scale proletarian insurrection.

On the night of June 2–3, a succession of events took place which suggested that the final act of this protracted drama was about to begin. Around 11 P.M. a military jeep on loan to CCTV ran down three civilian cyclists near the Yanjing Hotel at Muxidi, killing all three and sparking an angry response from local residents. At around 2 A.M. citizens who had deputized themselves to keep an all-night watch over the eastern reaches of the Avenue of Eternal Peace were baffled when several thousand men wearing white shirts, green pants, and running shoes came jogging toward them like an oversized sports team on an early morning workout. As it turned out, they were soldiers from the 24th Group Army who were part of a Trojan-horse strategy to infiltrate troops "behind enemy lines" prior to launching a main assault. Army tacticians evidently hoped that under the cover of darkness these jogging foot soldiers would be able to penetrate the barricades that were again being constructed to halt the advance of transport vehicles. Civilian pickets were, in fact, so bewildered by the sight of this improbable mass jogathon, that the soldiers almost did succeed in reaching the Square to muster with other troops already waiting in the Great Hall and the Forbidden City. But as they passed the Jianguomenwai diplomatic compound, several suspicious citizen sentries pedaled out in front of them on bicycles, and like Paul Reveres, began shouting, "The army is coming! The army is coming!"

When the soldiers were confronted with barricades, as army tacticians had hoped, they simply ran around them. However, when they reached Wangfujing—Beijing's main shopping street, which lies near the northeastern entrance to the Square—they encountered a large crowd that had managed to form a blockade across the street in front of the Beijing Hotel just as they approached. "Go back! Go back! The people don't need you here!" the crowd taunted. "We are all patriots. . . . We have no power! We have no guns!"

The soldiers tried to break into small groups to evade the taunting crowd, but they were quickly surrounded and immobilized by angry resisters. "They simply gave up," wrote Higgins and Fathers. "Bewildered, and sometimes even weeping, the soldiers sank back on their haunches, staring blankly up at their lecturers. . . . The students rejoiced in near disbelief at the ease of their victory over what looked to be the army's best efforts."

Near dawn one contingent of these ersatz joggers did manage to get to a subway station, through which they evidently hoped to escape. But at the next station they found themselves barricaded inside by yet another crowd. And there they remained until the next day, ingloriously trapped underground like animals in a burrow that has been sealed off at both ends.

As other units were found trying to steal into the city from different directions, Flying Tigers sped through Beijing spreading the word. It soon became obvious that other military units were also trying to insinuate troops into Beijing by using various disguises. Suspicious vans were promptly surrounded by crowds, and using skills that they had honed during the May 19–20 assault, they set about demobilizing them by deflating tires, cutting fuel lines, smashing windshields, and ripping out ignition wires.

Some vehicles were found to be carrying not only soldiers disguised as civilians, but caches of weapons and ammunition. As the crowds became increasingly indignant, many began calling the soldiers *guizi* ("devils"), a derogatory epithet that had not been used in Beijing since the Japanese occupation, when the invaders were derided as *riben guizi* ("Japanese devils").

One cache of automatic rifles, helmets, and uniforms was intercepted near the Liubukou intersection on the Avenue of Eternal Peace while another was stopped at Xidan and displayed with a banner reading, "Look at the Gifts the Li Peng Government Presents to the People of Beijing!"

A hint of how gravely the government viewed the prospect of confronting an armed citizenry was revealed when detachments of security forces emerged from the Great Hall and the Zhongnanhai leadership compound to try to retrieve these weapons. Because student leaders knew that possession of arms would only provide the government with a pretext to open fire, they quickly announced a policy of prompt repatriation to the PSB of all weapons that fell into their hands.

Although a number of people were beaten in the melees that ensued, instead of trying to fight troops in pitched battles, the crowds did what they had learned to do best—surround and engulf them in a sea of humanity. One group of almost a thousand well-equipped soldiers was encircled behind the Great Hall and left with no alternative but to sit down on the hot pavement and wait. As the hours passed, an unexpected camaraderie developed between them and the crowds as soldiers began chatting with students, workers, and *liumang* until they were laughing and offering cigarettes to one another. The climax of this unlikely convergence came when an officer began directing the troops and the crowd in a collective chorus of "Without the Communist Party, There Would Be No New China" and "The Eight Disciplines and Three Awarenesses," an old PLA song extolling fraternity between soldiers and the masses. This moment of fraternity notwithstanding, the appearance of so many security forces around the Square made it clear that in spite of all the citizen checkpoints and barricades, many soldiers had, in fact, nonetheless reached the heart of the city.

As the afternoon of June 3 progressed, the acoustic battle between the government's broadcasting station in the Great Hall of the People and the students' far weaker sound systems around the Monument raged on in the Square. The din of government invective thundering forth from speakers on light poles dotting the Square was so unrelenting that volunteers finally shinnied up and cut the wires. The silence was short-lived, however, because the government also had a bank of powerful speakers perched on the roof of the Great Hall, and by early evening they had sprung to life.

"Lawless acts . . . have infuriated the officers and men of our units, and cannot be tolerated anymore," proclaimed one warning from the Martial Law Headquarters. Henceforth, anyone using "any pretext to illegally intercept military vehicles, impede or speak against the PLA, or obstruct troops imposing martial law from carrying out their duty" would be held responsible for the consequences.

By 8 P.M. the warnings, now being broadcast all over the city, had become even more dire. "The situation has become very serious. . . . There should be absolutely no softness in dealing with thugs."

"You will fail," came another warning. "You are not behaving in the correct Chinese manner. This is not the West, it is China. You should behave like good Chinese. Go home and save your life."

Although such injunctions were intended to frighten people into staying home, they served as tocsins instead, signaling that it was once again time to take to the streets. At Beishida, Wu'er Kaixi gave a speech before an anxious gathering of 20,000 students. "Today, every Chinese faces a choice. Chinese history is about to turn a new page. Tiananmen Square is ours—the people's—and we will not allow butchers to tread on it! We will defend Tiananmen Square, defend the students in the Square, and defend the future of China!"

Like so many others who had only days before advocated quitting the Square, Wu'er now returned to rejoin his colleagues there. Around 9 P.M. they gathered to take a ceremonial pledge of allegiance. Raising their right hands they swore: "For the sake of our country's democratization, for the sake of our country's real prosperity, for the sake of preventing our country from being usurped by a small band of conspirators, for the sake of preventing 1.1 billion people from dying on the altar of a White Terror, I will devote my young life to protect Tiananmen and the Republic. I may be decapitated, my blood may flow, but the people's Square will not be lost. We are willing to lose our young lives to fight to the very last person."

Martial-law troops massing in the suburbs had also just taken a vow. But whereas the students were willing to make the ultimate sacrifice to promote freedom and democracy, military commanders were urging their troops to sacrifice themselves to prevent "turmoil." "If I can wake up the people with my blood, then I am willing to let my blood run dry," they swore. "If by giving my life the people will awake, then happily I go to my death."

That evening was moonless; the muggy heat was relieved only by a soft spring breeze that rippled through the handmade protest banners around the Monument. As they waited, protesters listened to speeches, sang songs, talked among themselves, prepared face masks in case tear gas was used, and composed farewell letters home. Some wrote wills.

"Most of the students simply sat near the Monument or inside their tattered tents, waiting," wrote Scott Simmie and Bob Nixon, two Canadians who had worked as "foreign experts" in China for CCTV and who later chronicled the 1989 movement in their book, *Tiananmen Square*. "The soft sound of guitar music issued forth from a few canvas shelters where classmates huddled together and sang. Their voices sounded different that night; the youthful enthusiasm, the sense of invincibility which had characterized the democracy camp for the previous three weeks was gone. In its place was a grave, almost suicidal sense of commitment."

Although a palpable sense of foreboding hung over the Square, few could bring themselves to believe that the People's Liberation Army might actually harm "the people." Not even under the vindictive Gang of Four had troops opened fire when tens of thousands of demonstrators had spontaneously occupied the Square to mourn the death of Zhou Enlai in 1976. So many ominous-sounding government threats had come to naught since April 15 that most ordinary Chinese were now inclined to view this latest salvo of warnings as more overinflated rhetoric. The triumphs, symbolic and otherwise, of the preceding weeks had given many, especially protesters, an exaggerated sense of their own invincibility.

But there were some Chinese who understood that when threatened, the Party would ultimately stop at nothing to preserve its grip on power. They understood the old adage "When scholars confront soldiers, it is impossible to speak with reason." Most of these pessimists were from the older generation of educated Chinese who had learned through bitter experience that the Party rarely allowed such challenges to go unconfronted. "The Day the Soldiers Enter the City, Then the Blood of the People Will Flow," declared one banner flying outside of Zhongnanhai.

As ever, Commander in Chief Chai Ling remained possessed by her vision of grim and bloody apocalypse as if any sacrifice less than death demeaned the cause. "The next step is bloodshed," she had said shortly before the Goddess of Democracy was erected. "Only when the Square is washed in blood will the people of the whole country wake up."

Around dusk the Flying Tigers began bringing back reports that soldiers equipped with automatic weapons and backed up by armored vehicles were moving toward the city center from several directions at once. In response, the strengthening of barricades reached fever pitch. By the time the first troops neared key intersections on the city's outskirts, an estimated 2 million people were again in the streets. At first, these citizens' brigades continued to rely on the same defensive techniques that they had used two weeks earlier, and by dark, many unarmed units were again bottled up around the city. "We have the soldiers surrounded," crowed one elderly bystander on the Jianguomenwai Overpass in the East City District. "They can't even piss without permission." In the western outskirts, however, the rules of the game were about to change as troops armed with tear gas, stun grenades, and AK-47s, and supported by armored vehicles, were readied for action.

Around 9 P.M. two motorized infantry divisions, an armored division, an artillery brigade, and an engineering regiment set out to establish a forward position at the Military Museum in Muxidi, west of the Square. As a convoy neared a traffic circle on the 3rd Ring Road at Gongzhufen, they ran into a barricade of buses blocking the intersection. With crowds of people throwing debris, soldiers opened fire, and the motorized column smashed its way through, killing and wounding a number of people and further enraging the crowd.

A horrified Finnish journalist at the scene watched as, at one point, two soldiers armed with AK-47s made the miscalculation of jumping off one of the trucks and were immediately set upon by the crowd. "They were torn to pieces," she said. "It was a horrible sight." Before the night was over the same sequence of events would repeat itself over and over: jumpy troops under nervous commanders determined not to be stopped as they had been two weeks before would drive into or fire at obstructing crowds, who counterattacked with sticks, rocks, and steel pipes.

By 10 P.M. the assault from the west was in full swing. As several infantry and armored divisions pushed toward the Military Museum, they soon found their way blocked by a wall of angry citizens and Dare-to-Die squads of workers pledged to defend the students and the Square until death. The juggernaut of military vehicles ground to a halt, allowing government propaganda to cite these instances of hesitation as evidence that the army had exercised a "high degree of restraint'' while entering the city. Such ''restraint'' did not last long.

The next volley of gunfire was aimed over the heads of the resisters. The crowd refused to disperse. Finally, an officer in a jeep was reported to have yelled out through a megaphone, ''Charge, you bunch of cowards! Sweep away this trash!'' A volley of concussion grenades was lobbed into the crowd. Only when steel-helmeted soldiers carrying truncheons and riot shields were ordered to charge did those resisting give way.

It was around 11 P.M. before advancing troops approached Muxidi Bridge near the Diaoyutai state guesthouse. By then the order to ''go ahead at any cost'' and to shoot at anyone obstructing the soldiers' path had been given. Before soldiers had even arrived at the giant barricade constructed out of articulated city buses, large earthmoving trucks, commandeered minivans, and tons of urban detritus, the first wounded were being rushed on bicycle carts to hospitals. As troops approached the bridge, someone torched the fuel tank of a bus, turning the barricade into a raging wall of fire. The column had no choice but to halt. With Gallic flair, Pierre Hurel, a French journalist writing for *Paris Match,* described the scene:

> In front of the flaming barricade, facing the soldiers alone, four students with their feet planted wide apart make the heavy air snap with the sound of the waving scarlet banners. In an unbelievable gesture of defiance, they are naked martyrs before a sea of soldiers in brown combat helmets and tense with anger. The silk of their university banners gleams in the fire's light, and behind them a crowd, waiting for the worst, applauds. It is 11:30 P.M., and for the first time tonight, the soldiers have had to pull back.

As the convoy began pushing forward again a short while later, a noise resembling the sound of popcorn popping was suddenly heard over the din of the crowd. Out of the smoky darkness, troops armed with AK-47s charged the barricades, shooting as they advanced.

''Live fire! Live fire!'' people began to scream as scores of civilians crumpled to the ground. ''The opening volley, single shots, claimed few victims,'' wrote Higgins and Fathers. ''Most were shielded by busses. But within seconds the troops reached and passed the barricades. Their backs to the burning buses, and facing forward into the crowd, they fired at close range onto unarmed, unshielded civilians. Panic took over. Some tried to flee, others threw themselves to the ground. . . . They howled abuse: 'Fascists!' 'Animals!' 'Motherfuckers!,' every filthy insult they knew. Many were hit in the back as they ran.''

"Soldiers were shooting indiscriminately; there were bullets flying everywhere; dead bodies and injured people were lying in the streets," reported one anonymous foreign journalist cited in a subsequent Amnesty International report. "Crowds of residents from the neighboring lanes had left their houses and stood unprotected in the streets. They did not try to hide because they did not seem to realize what was going on. They were in a state of shock and disbelief."

Pierre Hurel, who was wounded at Muxidi but was fortunate enough to have his own car and driver waiting nearby, described his escape. "I got into the front and three young men climbed into the back," he recalled. "The fingers of one of them had been torn off. Another, an adolescent, helped his brother, whose stomach had been opened by a bullet." As his terrified driver struggled to force his way through the panicked crowds and reach a hospital, Hurel saw numerous wounded, including a frantic woman "carrying her unconscious husband on a three-wheeled bicycle cart. Jostled by the fleeing crowd, she overturns it by the curb. The young man in the seat behind her vomits blood."

As troops forced their way toward the Square, the violence escalated. "Old men and women, young girls and boys who tried as they had in the past to sit in nonviolently in front of the tanks, were brutally run over," recalled Lee Feigon, an American professor from Colby College doing research in China at the time. "Others who kneeled down in front of individual soldiers, pleading for mercy, were machine-gunned. . . . Troops raked the crowds with stun grenades, automatic weapons, and armor piercing bullets. Men, women, and children sitting on their balconies, and sometimes deep in their apartments were slaughtered by the random and uncontrolled gunfire of soldiers."

It was bitterly ironic that the apartment blocks overlooking the battleground farther down toward the Avenue of Eternal Peace at Fuxingmenwai were inhabited by senior government officials and were known as the "Towers of the Ministers." Throughout that spring many of these families had become deeply divided as children joined the protest movement while parents struggled to rationalize the government's intransigence. Now, with their children in the Square and the streets below, parents found themselves not just watching with horror from above, but suddenly under fire themselves.

At Fuxingmen Bridge the slaughter was repeated. Jasper Becker of the London *Guardian* reported that only after he arrived at the bridge around midnight and heard what he described as "the steady crackle-crackle of small arms fire and the intermittent thud-thud of heavy machine guns'' did he begin to appreciate the gravity of what was happening.

All along the Avenue of Eternal Peace, at the Minzu Hotel, at Xidan, and Liubukou, equally ferocious battles broke out as citizens stood their ground with an almost religious fanaticism before advancing troops. Bystanders who ran into surrounding alleyways for safety were chased down and sprayed with automatic-weapons fire. Those who tried to rescue the wounded were shot in cold blood. The slaughter was so merciless that rumors began circulating that the soldiers had been administered some kind of drug as a stimulant. A more likely explanation was that all the frustration, embarrassment, humiliation, and anger that had been building within the military during the preceding two weeks was now finally finding its awful release.

By 1 A.M. soldiers had neared the intersection where Xidan crosses the Avenue of Eternal Peace and began lobbing tear-gas canisters into the crowds. Moments later several buses serving as barricades burst into flames. Then another order to fire was given. "Several lines of students and residents instantly fell," claimed one BASF eyewitness. "Dozens were killed, and several hundred were wounded."

"The Avenue of Eternal Peace was packed with angry people and everyone was weeping," recalled eyewitness Hou Tianming of the scene near Xidan, a major commercial intersection about a mile from the Square. "They followed the troops, and shouted, 'Bandits! Bandits!' ''

Yang Jianli, a Ph.D. candidate in mathematics from the University of California at Berkeley who was back in China on a visit, watched in horror as these shock troops advanced, firing their automatic weapons as if they were assaulting a heavily armed enemy position. "Tanks and truckloads of soldiers armed with machine guns were rolling in, one after another, toward the Square," he remembered. "At the intersection we heard perhaps a thousand people shouting, 'Down with Fascism!' . . . [Then] flashes spouted from the muzzles of soldiers' rifles. We ran back a bit and threw ourselves on the pavement. 'Did they really fire?' I asked H. 'I still can't believe it!' Some people continued to stand up, saying nonchalantly, 'Don't be frightened, they're only using rubber bullets.' But before they had finished speaking I heard someone scream, 'Look out! There's a cart coming through!' Two men with gunshot wounds were being carried away. . . . Suddenly, there was more gunfire, and we dropped to the ground again, my heart jumping from sheer fright.''

"His blue T-shirt was soaked with blood, and his eyes were bloodred,'' recalled Yang of one outraged citizen. "With a hoarse voice he shouted to the soldiers, 'You have killed more than one hundred twenty people at Muxidi! Four of my best friends died in my arms! Fire on me, I don't care anymore!' Several students went to drag him away, telling him not to give up his life like that. At this point gunfire erupted again, sounding like firecrackers, and we all sprawled on the ground.

"A moment later a jeep sped toward us from between two trucks," Yang continued. "Over a hundred people rushed the jeep, breaking glass and shouting slogans. Five seconds later soldiers on a truck thirty meters away opened fire. Dozens of people were killed on the spot. As citizens rushed to take the bodies away, an old man . . . screamed at the soldiers, calling them fascists. With my own eyes, I watched as an officer took out his pistol and shot the old man, who crumpled immediately on the ground."

Farther down the Avenue at Liubukou where the last major barricade before the Square had been set up, an even more grisly scene of slaughter was enacted. "As the army reached the intersection, an angry crowd of over ten thousand surged forward to surround the troops," wrote a Chinese student of the final march to the Square in an account later published by the Yale-China Association's *China Update*. "This time the soldiers turned on the people with even greater brutality. The fusillades from machine guns were loud and clear. Because some of the bullets used were of the kind that explode within the body, when they struck, the victims' intestines and brains spilled out. I saw five such bodies. They looked like disemboweled animal carcasses. . . . A man with a Chinese journalist's identity card all covered with blood rushed toward the troops screaming, 'Kill me! Kill me! You've already killed three of my colleagues!' Then I saw them shoot him, and when he fell, several soldiers rushed over to kick him and slash at him with their bayonets."

"Troops have been firing indiscriminately and still people would not move back," BBC News Chief Correspondent Kate Adie reported in a television broadcast after visiting both the western and eastern reaches of the Avenue of Eternal Peace. "Indeed, it was hard at the time to grasp that this army was launching into an unarmed civilian population as if charging into battle. . . . There was not one voice on the streets that did not express despair and rage. 'Tell the world!' they said to us."

The magnitude of the slaughter was far beyond anything that Chai Ling had predicted. As Michael Fathers of the *Independent* wrote, "If this is the People's Liberation Army, God spare China!"

As these horrific scenes began to unfold, those who turned on their TV sets to see what was happening were treated to one of the most surreal sideshows of this macabre night. Premier Li Peng, who had not been heard from in nine days, was giving a taped speech about government strategy to combat environmental pollution.

At the same time, other PLA units were trying to move into the city from the north, east, and south. But all afternoon and evening convoys rolling in from Shahe Airfield in Beijing's northern suburbs had been getting bogged down in huge crowds blocking access roads. The more troops that commanders deployed, the more massive the occlusions became, until finally the stalled convoys themselves became barricades. On two overpasses across the 2nd Ring Road at Jianguomenwai and Chaoyangmen, convoys of troop trucks were trapped and their marooned soldiers forced to listen to rebukes and lectures by irate citizens.

The government's strategy for breaking this stalemate on the "Eastern Front" was to send cleat-track armored personnel carriers, or APCs, down the Avenue like high-speed bulldozers. But instead of reaming out a viable passageway, these rampaging APCs only provoked bystanders all the more. When several pedestrians were run over and killed, mobs of infuriated youths began attacking the vehicles, jabbing steel pipes in their clanking treads and hurling bricks and firebombs at their turrets. Some resisters soaked blankets and garments in gasoline, and then cast them like fishing nets onto the passing APCs. When later that evening several vehicles were finally immobilized and furious crowds had a chance to wreak vengeance on their crews, the scenes that followed were every bit as ghoulish as the soldiers' attacks on the people.

"They screamed with anger and hate as the vehicle swung randomly in different directions threatening to knock down people as it made its way through the Square," recounted BBC correspondent John Simpson of an incident involving APC #003. "The Molotov cocktails arched above our heads, spinning over and over, exploding on the thin shell of armor that protected the men inside. A pause, and it charged head-on, straight into a block of concrete—and then stuck, its engine whirring wildly. A terrible shout of triumph came from the crowd: primitive and dark, its prey finally caught.

"[As] the screaming around me rose even louder, the handle at the door of the rear of the vehicle turned a little, and the door began to open," continued Simpson. "A soldier pushed the barrel of a gun out, but it was snatched from his hands, and then everyone started grabbing his arms, pulling and wrenching until finally he came free, and then he was gone: I saw arms of the mob flailing, raised above their heads as they fought to get their blows in. He was dead within seconds, and his body was dragged away in triumph.''

When a second soldier appeared, the mob hauled him out, too. "His eyes were rolling, his mouth was open, and he was covered with blood where the skin had been ripped off. Only his eyes remained—white and clear—but then someone was trying to get at them as well, and someone else began beating his skull until the skull came apart, and there was blood all over the ground, and his brains, and still they kept beating and beating what was left.''

Then Simpson spotted a third soldier inside. "I could see his face in the light of the flames, and some of the crowd could, too. They pulled him out, screaming wild at having missed killing the other soldiers. It was his blood they wanted, I was certain, it was to feel the blood running over their hands. Their mouths were open and panting, like dogs, and their eyes were expressionless. They were shouting that the soldier they were about to kill wasn't human—that he was just another thing, an object, which had to be destroyed. . . . I saw the soldier's face, expressing only horror and pain as he sank under blows of the people around him.'' At this penultimate moment a group of students who had remained faithful to their vows of nonviolence appeared in a bus. Somehow they waded through the enraged crowd, dragged the half-senseless soldier away, and pulled him onto their bus.

Another gruesome attack against a soldier took place in the Chong-wenmen area southeast of the Square, where an infantryman named Cui Guozheng was bludgeoned to death by an angry mob, his body doused with gasoline, hung by a rope from a concrete pedestrian overpass, and then set on fire. Lurid video footage of his charred corpse was meticulously collected by government cameramen and broadcast again and again as part of the Party's subsequent propaganda efforts to convince its subjects that the violence in the streets that night was perpetrated by "counterrevolutionary rioters" bent on creating "turmoil," not soldiers.

Actually, the true story of Cui Guozheng's death bore little resemblance to the government's version of him as an innocent victim of mob violence. It so happened that two foreign witnesses observed Cui's demise from the nearby Hadamen Hotel, and made a subsequent report to Amnesty International. According to them, Cui's army truck stalled that night. When he and several other soldiers tried to leave the vehicle, an altercation broke out with taunting bystanders. In response, Cui fired into the crowd, killing an elderly woman, a man, and a young girl, and then tried to protect himself by locking himself in the cab.

"The crowd was incensed and stormed into the truck," Amnesty reported the two witnesses as saying. "The soldier re-emerged from the cab, his clothes half-torn. He ran toward the Chongwenmen Hotel, managed to reach the sidewalk, but was dragged away to the left. . . . The next thing they saw was a fire burning."

As of 2 A.M. the troops advancing from the west had finally reached the edge of the Square. But all along the Avenue of Eternal Peace they had left a wake of blood-drenched pavement, crushed barricades, overturned buses, burning armored vehicles, and corpses. Nowhere, however, was the human carnage worse than at hospitals.

"There was blood everywhere, not just in the emergency room— but everywhere," American journalist Margaret Herbst recalled after she visited Capital Hospital, located only several long blocks from the Square. "Doctors took me down a corridor that was filled with injured people lying on blood-soaked mattresses. The mattresses were on the floor because all the operating rooms were already full. These were the cases which were less serious, but they included people who had been shot in the head."

"It looked like an abattoir," Jasper Becker wrote after visiting People's Hospital near Xidan. "There were bodies on benches and beds or on blood-soaked mattresses on the floor. Many had gaping bullet wounds to the chest, legs, or head. A doctor told us that three hundred wounded had come in."

Kate Adie had her car commandeered to rush a young woman with a severe head wound to Children's Hospital near Fuxingmen where she found herself caught in a crush of people frantically trying to arrange medical care for wounded friends. "Casualties were arriving every few seconds, on bicycles, on park benches, on tricycle rickshaws, all with gunshot wounds—housewives, elderly residents, people shot while sitting in their homes," she said in one of her BBC reports. "The operating theater was overflowing, and many of the staff were in tears."

"I looked at my watch: it was 3 A.M. and the wounded were still coming in," remembered one Beijing doctor who requested anonymity. "There were college students, teachers, local residents, children, elderly people. Two students were brought in. Their friends had torn off their shirts and pants to tie up their bleeding thighs. Then there were five students from Beijing and Nanjing universities who were stuck together with their own blood when we pulled them out of the ambulance. Three of them were already dead, but we managed to save the other two. In tears, the nurses sent the bodies to the morgue. The emergency room was a mess; the floor was stained with blood, everyone was cursing and sobbing."

"The hospitals could not cope," wrote Higgins and Fathers. "Hundreds of friends and relatives jammed entrances and roamed corridors. Inside the morgues they found bodies with faces so disfigured by bullet wounds that they were only identifiable by scars and birth marks."

As the night went on, wounds became progressively severe, making many doctors speculate that soldiers had started firing explosive shells that are outlawed by the Geneva Convention because of the massive internal injuries they cause on impact. It was not long before hospitals began running out of dressings, medicines, blood, and plasma. Harried doctors also had to deal with the expectation that soldiers would soon enter the hospitals and probably use wounds as evidence of guilt to arrest patients. Consequently, they reluctantly discharged all but those who could not survive without continuous care.

When Margaret Herbst returned to Capital Hospital several hours after her first visit, she found that the number of dead and wounded had doubled. Because of the combination of shock and fatigue, doctors and nurses were openly weeping. "They didn't have enough drawers for the bodies, so they had to stack them," she recounted after a harrowing visit to the morgue. "All of the victims were young men. . . . They were just piled up in there halfway to the ceiling."

13

The Eye of
the Storm

As troops on the outskirts of Beijing began their bloody march to Tiananmen Square, the scene around the Monument to the Martyrs of the People remained as eerily quiet as the eye of a raging hurricane. Only when the first eyewitnesses made their way back to the Square with horrifying tales of slaughter did a sense of impending doom settle over the encampment. By midnight most of the four-to-five thousand remaining student protesters had abandoned their tents for the huge stepped plinth of the Monument. There they huddled close to one another like survivors of a shipwreck marooned on an island while government loudspeakers continued to thunder warnings. "Tonight a serious counterrevolutionary rebellion has taken place. Thugs frenziedly attack PLA troops, seizing weapons, erecting barricades, beating soldiers and officers in an attempt to overthrow the government of the People's Republic of China. For many days now the PLA has exercised restraint, and now it must resolutely counteract the rebellion."

Around midnight armored vehicles and the first soldiers began arriving on the peripheries of the Square to prepare for a final assault. Her voice infused with dark fatalism, Chai Ling rose to give her final speech. "There is a story about a clan of a billion ants who lived on a mountain," she began. "One day there was a terrible fire on the mountain. The only way for any of them to escape was by holding each other tight in a ball and rolling down the mountainside—even though the ants on the outside of the ball would be burned to death. We are now standing at such a moment. We stand on the outer edge of our nation. Only our sacrifice can save it. Only our blood can open the eyes of our people and the world.''

Her peroration contained a certain element of unintended irony. While the student elite listened as yet unharmed to Chai's grandiloquent oration about self-sacrifice, working-class Chinese were being killed and wounded by the hundreds in the streets as they tried to prevent the army from reaching the Square.

By 1 A.M. students at the Monument could hear the distant crackle of automatic weapons fire. Numerous eyewitness accounts describe soldiers at the northwest and northeast corners of the Square along the Avenue of Eternal Peace shooting indiscriminately into crowds of people who, at first, did not seek protection because they believed troops were firing rubber bullets.

A Canadian Broadcasting Corporation journalist found herself dragged into the killing ground by a group of bystanders frantic for an outsider to bear witness to what was happening. Stretched out just in front of Mao's portrait on Tiananmen, she saw four casualties, all shot in the neck, head, and chest. As another volley of fire erupted from the vicinity of the Forbidden City, ''a man came running up,'' she remembered. ''He pulled his jacket open: his shoulder had been blown away. Then the crowd parted like the sea, and a girl who had been shot right between the eyes was brought through. There wasn't much left of her face. Not even two minutes after she was dragged [away], a man was brought out. He had no head.''

By 2:30 A.M. soldiers had established a cordon across the Avenue of Eternal Peace where it enters the Square, not far from the Beijing Hotel. They remained there for the rest of the night, periodically shooting into crowds to warn them against approaching. ''You could see guns firing, and people ran like crazy,'' Timothy Brook in his book *Quelling the People* quoted one eyewitness as saying. ''Bullets ricocheted off the wall. . . . Some people went down.''

Around two-thirty the crowd linked arms and began singing the ''Internationale,'' as if this anthem of socialist solidarity could somehow shield them from death. Then they began marching toward the cordon of soldiers. ''We kept trying to tell the soldiers that no one wanted to start a revolt, that we were demonstrating against official corruption,'' remembered Cao Xingyuan, the art student who had chronicled the birth of the Goddess of Democracy. ''We hoped that their consciences would be awakened and that they would retreat. We were naive. They suddenly opened fire on us, unarmed civilians, with machine guns! The whole front row fell. I was paralyzed with fear. Everybody ran toward the Beijing Hotel, and I ran with them. When I tripped and fell, I was sure it was the end.''

Instead of fleeing the hail of fire, many, including a number of courageous pedicab drivers, tried to help those who had fallen. "The only thing on our minds was to rescue the wounded," Cao recalled. "Several rescue vehicles tried to enter the area, but they failed. Then a No. 38 bus, which we later called the 'heroic bus,' succeeded in getting some of the wounded out. It had already lost three drivers; as the fourth drove up to Xiehe Hospital with the wounded, he too slumped over the steering wheel and died."

"We had never imagined that the government could be so cruel and so barbarous," said Wu'er Kaixi. "We heard the first news that a student from my university was hit in the head at Liubukou . . . this was the first time I cried uncontrollably."

Once the Square was finally sealed off, troops turned their attention toward the real object of their operation—the students still waiting unscathed around the Monument. "All citizens and students in Tiananmen Square must leave immediately so that martial-law enforcement troops can carry out their duties," blared speakers on the Great Hall. "The safety of those who do not heed this warning cannot be guaranteed, and they themselves will bear all responsibility for what happens."

Students at the Monument knew that their final reckoning was upon them. Troops had already set fire to the BAWF's tent headquarters at the Square's northwest corner. Flares were being fired into the dark night sky, and to the south behind Mao's mausoleum tracer bullets arced into the air like so many fireflies. Not far from where the Goddess of Democracy shimmered with a ghostly whiteness in the flickering light of burning tents and APCs, phalanxes of troops massed to carry out their final order. As the assault neared, a strange lull fell over the Square.

By 3 A.M. rock singer and faster Hou Dejian had heard enough reports about the savagery of the assaulting troops to be deeply alarmed. He knew that many workers had been arming themselves because several had appeared at the Monument with captured guns. "What we saw on their faces was hatred, a new hatred to kill," Hou recalled. "They pulled off their clothes to show me how their bodies were covered with wounds caused by the fighting with troops at Xidan and other places. And they told me that many of their brothers had died, and that they wanted revenge."

What alarmed Hou and Liu Xiaobo was the awful certainty that if a single weapon was fired from the Monument, thousands of students would be killed and wounded. Only after Hou and Liu made personal appeals to these militants did they finally cool down. Even then, it was probably not their arguments but Hou's status as a pop star that convinced them to relinquish their weapons, one of which Liu smashed to pieces on the balustrade of the Monument.

Equally alarming to Hou was the fatalism he detected among student leaders. Chai Ling appeared paralyzed by the gravity of the approaching cataclysm. "The students held each other's hands tightly and began to sing the 'Internationale,' " she tearfully recounted the next day. "We knew that the purification of the Republic could only be achieved by our sacrifice." Not wanting to be responsible for deciding the fates of her classmates, Chai took the position that each person must decide for himself whether to leave the Square. She herself would remain. "We were ready to receive the butchers' knives in peace. We knew that the moment had come for us to lay down our lives for the nation."

Such passionate declarations of willingness to sacrifice made it psychologically extremely difficult for others to discuss tactical retreat without appearing to advocate capitulation. Thirty-six years old, famous, and far more self-assured than most of the students, Hou felt no such conflict. When he heard Chai's decision, he feared that if some students left while others stayed, things would become confused, creating a situation that was "bound to give the soldiers reason to kill." He felt strongly that "no one had the right to gamble with the lives of thousands of students in the Square" and decided that someone must act.

By 3 A.M. troops were in the final stages of forming up for their assault. As tracer bullets sliced through the sky, the four older hunger strikers gathered in their tent, desperate to figure out some move. It was at this point that two doctors from Xiehe Hospital appeared and proposed that they drive in an ambulance toward the troops' mustering point and try to obtain permission from the military command for a peaceful withdrawal. Hou and Zhou Duo, one of his fellow hunger strikers, decided that the plan was worth the gamble.

"When our ambulance abruptly halted and the troops saw us running toward them," remembered Hou, "they all began to load their guns and shouted at us to stop." Somehow Hou managed to attract the attention of Colonel Ji Xingguo, political commissar of the 27th Group Army. To Hou and Zhou's great relief, he was both civil and receptive to their proposal for a planned student withdrawal. Before Colonel Ji could definitively agree, however, he had to secure approval from the Beijing Military Region Command.

When at 4 A.M. the streetlights suddenly blinked out plunging the Square into darkness, Hou and Zhou's hearts sank in despair. They surmised—correctly, it turned out—that the extinguished lights were a signal for the units poised around the Square to ready themselves to advance. "We were extremely frightened," remembered Hou, "because at this point the soldiers were getting angry again, and beginning to load their guns and shout loudly."

Moments later Colonel Ji appeared out of the darkness to announce that his superiors had agreed to postpone their sweep for a short while, and to leave a small breach in their cordon at the southeast corner of the Square through which the students could make an orderly withdrawal. "If you leave now, we can guarantee your safety," Colonel Ji said. "Otherwise, we can guarantee nothing. Our time is already up." Party elders had ordered that, one way or another, the Square was to be cleared by dawn.

Hou and Zhou sped back to the Monument with less than an hour remaining, and no idea whether they could convince the students to leave. "My head was spinning," recalled Hou. But when the lights flickered back on and a voice over the loudspeakers acknowledged the agreement that he and Zhou had just worked out, Hou felt a glimmer of encouragement. "Martial Law Headquarters accepts the request of the students to be allowed to withdraw. All the people within the Square should leave at once after hearing this broadcast. If anyone refuses to abide by the decree and stays in the Square, troops will enforce martial law by any means possible."

Back at the Monument, Hou tried to gather the students together. A tape made by a German journalist of the chaotic debate that ensued recorded the following: "We cannot remain here anymore!" pleaded Hou. "Students and citizens, I dare to say that our movement has succeeded and has won a great victory, but now we must leave this place! . . . None of us fears death, but our deaths must serve some purpose!"

"No! No!" voices countered.

"Students! If we can save even one more drop of blood now, there will be much more hope for the future of our march forward," Zhou implored. "We cannot use fists against soldiers armed with rifles and bayonets! We must now try to save ourselves!"

"If you want to achieve democracy, we must start now with ourselves—the minority should listen to the majority!" interjected Liu Xiaobo, who only a short time earlier had been urging people to remain in the Square as a form of sacrificial atonement.

As five o'clock neared, Hou was close to despair. Columns of troops and rows of APCs were approaching the Monument and rifle fire, aimed at student loudspeakers, was growing intense, and he feared the students would take the advance as a sign that the Military Command had gone back on its promise to allow a retreat.

"Please blame me for this if you want! Please blame the four of us!" Hou cried out over the students' feeble sound system. "As long as you leave the Square safely, you can do whatever you want to us!"

A feverish last-minute effort to take a voice vote followed, during which militant students who had already resigned themselves to dying strenuously opposed Hou's last-minute appeal.

"If we must die, let's die together!"

"You fascist running dogs!"

"They're shooting at the loudspeakers!"

"Frankly, I couldn't tell which side was louder," Hou admitted afterwards. "It was the kind of situation where those who wanted to leave were not speaking up, and those who didn't want to leave were quite loud. . . . Finally, I didn't bother with the vote, and simply told everyone to leave!"

By now the gunfire was intense, and bullets were ricocheting off the upper part of the Monument near the inscription in Mao's hand that fittingly read, "Eternal Glory to the People's Heroes." In desperation, Hou and Zhou drove their ambulance out toward the advancing army. By sheer happenstance they ran into Colonel Ji again, who was by then in no mood to hear excuses. The time was up, he said angrily, and now his troops "had to finish their task." Panicked by the momentum of events, Hou and Zhou sped back to the Monument as loudspeakers on the Great Hall thundered, "Tiananmen is the heart of Beijing and capital of our great motherland. It is an important place for political assemblies and receiving foreign dignitaries. It is the symbol of New China. But now it has become a market for a tiny handful of people to create turmoil and disseminate rumors. In order to restore order in Tiananmen Square as soon as possible, we have decided to immediately carry out the responsibility of clearing the Square."

Like a purse seine drawing tighter and tighter around a school of hapless fish, troops closed inexorably in on the Monument. "Tanks and APCs were simply crushing everything in their paths—tents, railings, boxes, provisions, bicycles—all were knocked over and squashed flat in a slow-motion display of military might," remembered Asia Watch's Robin Munro. But faithful to their word, the military did leave a narrow avenue of egress to the southeast.

In was not until just before 5:00 A.M. that Hou and his colleagues, aided by Li Lu's declaration that those voting in favor of evacuation were in the majority, finally managed to convince the frightened, confused, and divided students to leave. Though exhausted and anguished, they still carried their tattered banners, and several managed to flash the V-for-victory sign or to shout hoarsely, "We will return!" to Televisión Española of Spain, whose team was the only Western crew to document the retreat.

Now it was the frightened students' turn to endure the humiliation of defeat and retreat. They had to pass through a gauntlet of taunting troops, some of whom aimed weapons at them or fired menacingly into the air. According to the writer Lao Gui, who was part of this final exodus, several APCs added to their ordeal by charging full-speed at defiles of retreating students, then stopping just before hitting them.

"They had tears rolling down their cheeks, men and women alike," wrote Munro, one of the last to leave the Monument. "All looked shaken, and many were trembling badly or walking unsteadily—but all looked proud and unbeaten."

As they straggled out of the Square, an armored vehicle rammed the Goddess of Democracy, knocked it to the ground, and crushed it beneath its steel treads. Seeing her so ignominiously destroyed was for many students almost as agonizing as abandoning the Square itself.

According to Hou Dejian, Munro, and a number of Western journalists such as Nicholas Kristof of the *New York Times* and reporters from Televisión Española, most, if not all, of the students were able to withdraw from the Square unharmed. In this respect, at least, their reports corroborate the Chinese government's claim that "no one fired at any citizens or students," and that there were "no deaths in the Square." Nonetheless, a large number of contrary eyewitness accounts quickly appeared in the world press, presaging a debate over whether "a Tiananmen Square Massacre" had actually taken place.

Although Hou acknowledged that he did not see any killing "with his own eyes" in Tiananmen Square, his description of the retreat was suggestively violent. "Before the last group of students rose, troops pressed us from the west in a human wall. They moved in quickly and squeezed us like water in the neck of a bottle, [so that we were] barely able to move. I could hardly breathe. All around me antiriot police were waving wooden sticks and beating people on the heads and bodies. Students were bleeding. The crowd stumbled over railings that had been scattered on the ground. A whole row of people fell. Those behind fell over them, and [then] the next wave fell over them."

One of the most widely circulated of the massacre-in-the-Square accounts was by a putative student from Qinghua University. Published in the Hong Kong newspaper *Wen Wei Po,* and subsequently translated and reprinted in both the *New York Times* and the *Washington Post,* this version of events claimed that soldiers in the Square had crouched on the ground and shot right at the "chests and heads" of students, and that while the evacuation was in process, "over thirty APCs came crushing into the crowd" causing "some students to die under their wheels." However, since the account was written pseudonymously, there was no way to check its veracity.

This was not the only eyewitness reports chronicling casualties in the Square. "Some students did not leave, either because they were too weak [from fasting] to walk, were strong-willed, seriously wounded, or could not crawl out of their tents in time," a medical worker alleged in a leaflet released at Beida the next day. "Behind them armored vehicles were catching up with them at a very fast pace. Brutal police began beating everyone, and many students were beaten unconscious and fell to the ground. The military even attacked medical workers who had risked their own safety to dash ahead to rescue the students. . . . A student was awakened just as an armored vehicle ran over his tent. Instantly, a youth full of patriotic zeal became a mixture of flesh and blood."

The BBC's John Simpson claimed in the quarterly *Granta* to have "filmed the tanks as they drove over tents where some of the students had taken refuge," and that "dozens of people seemed to have died in that way, and those who saw it said they could hear the screams of people inside the tents over the noise of the tanks." He then described how "the troops moved toward the Monument itself, shooting first in the air and then, again, directly at students themselves, so that the steps of the Monument and the heroic reliefs which decorated it were smashed by bullets."

In a taped message made on June 8 and smuggled out to Hong Kong, Chai Ling maintained that some Dare-to-Die Corps workers had remained behind in the tents, and that as armored troops advanced toward the Monument "at least two hundred students in tents were rolled over by tanks and crushed to death." She also claimed that soldiers subsequently used gasoline to set fire to the crushed bodies in order to "clean up every trace" of what had happened.

An Australian student who retreated back to the university district with the hunger strikers on the morning of June 4, and claimed to have tape-recorded their descriptions of what had just happened as they walked, detailed the following account: "I was at the edge of the column, trailing behind. There were also lots of female students at the back. Their heads had been beaten bloody and they were screaming and crying. . . . I started running alongside a huge fellow from Beida.

He stopped to pull some students to their feet so they wouldn't get squashed. This was because in front of us a lot of students had already fallen to the ground, and the ones at the back were stomping on them. Many were already dead. From the sides, soldiers were shooting. A lot of students fell with the shots.''

In such a chaotic situation, eyewitness accounts are, of course, not always reliable. However, in the absence of army videotapes or hospital records, which the government refused to release, they are all that is presently available to help reconstruct the events of that night. After sifting through all available accounts, it seems safe to say that while some casualties were sustained during the withdrawal, there were probably not many. This is not to say, however, that there was little or no killing during the overall process of "clearing the Square," as the Chinese government later claimed. Between the hours of about midnight and 2 A.M., many skirmishes broke out between troops and crowds of angry citizens around the Square's periphery, and it was in these confrontations that numerous *laobaixing*, or ordinary people, appear to have been killed or wounded. In fact, during a briefing with reporters twelve days after June 4, the chief political commissar of the 38th Group Army acknowledged that because "thugs" provoked them, "some of the soldiers in our units directed fire into the Square."

The government's insistence that nobody was killed "in the Square" seems to have been a ploy to diminish the import of those atrocities that *were* committed around its outer reaches and throughout the rest of the city. Much of the confusion—which the government certainly augmented and exploited—appears to have arisen over differing interpretations of what constitutes Tiananmen Square proper. For example, does it include the Avenue of Eternal Peace, which runs through the Square's north end, or the enormous area behind Mao's mausoleum that extends all the way around the old Front Gate? Both of these were places where government troops regrouped prior to their final push toward the Monument, and where numerous fusillades of gunfire were directed against citizens.

By defining "the Square" in the narrowest terms possible—namely, the area immediately around the Monument but excluding the wide boulevards that bound it—the Chinese government felt more able to insist that no killing took place "inside the Square." It was a purely semantic point, but a crucial one, because it allowed those who had ordered or implemented the assault to maintain that the blood of unarmed Chinese had not been spilled by the PLA on the sacred ground of Tiananmen Square itself.

As of 1994 there was still insufficient evidence to support the contention that a full-scale massacre of students took place "within the Square"—even if broadly defined—or that armored vehicles had squashed students inside their tents. Such reports appear to have originated in the "back-alley news" rumor mill, which understandably ran wild for some time after the night of June 3–4. In the heat of the moment, it was all too easy for everyone, even members of the foreign press, to accept hearsay as fact and to exaggerate the scope of bloodshed. John Simpson, for example, later acknowledged that although he afterward "felt guilty about the decision," he and his BBC crew had already left the Square by the time the final assault on the Monument took place, and thus would have had a difficult time seeing (much less filming) tanks driving over tents. A careful reading of Chai Ling's accusation that students were crushed in their tents reveals that she prefaced her statement with the caveat "It was said," implying that she had not actually seen students crushed with her own eyes.

Are we then to believe the Party's claims that soldiers searched all the tents carefully before bulldozing and burning them? Robin Munro, who watched the advance, saw no evidence of such a search. He did note, however, that tanks advanced toward the Monument extremely slowly. At about 5:30 A.M., after the student evacuation was completed, "CBS Evening News" reporter Richard Roth and cameraman Derek Williams, both of whom had been detained by Chinese authorities earlier in the evening, were driven across the Square in a jeep. Williams later reported that he saw "no bodies in the Square."

So many imponderables remain that it will probably not be possible to determine the real magnitude of the slaughter anywhere in the city that night before official Chinese archives on the incident are opened to historians. Until then, arguments about whether or not a "massacre" took place in the Square, or even whether anyone at all was actually killed there, will only serve to distract attention from the undeniable slaughter that took place elsewhere in the city. Only within the perverted logic of the Party's own self-serving propaganda are such distinctions as "inside" or "outside" the Square meaningful.

Whatever the number of dead, and wherever they died, the state-sponsored terror in the streets of Beijing on the night of June 3–4 not only ended the lives of untold hundreds, possibly thousands, but also put a violent end to the beguiling fantasy of many Chinese that their country was finally on the verge of becoming a democratic state. Before leaving the Monument to the Martyrs of the People that night, one student scrawled a final farewell on the bas reliefs of righteous "insurrections" carved around its pedestal: "June 4, 1989, the Chinese People Shed Blood for Democracy. Written at 4 o'clock in the Morning."

By noon this inscription had disappeared, expunged by military clean-up crews that were immediately put to work restoring the Square to a semblance of its pre–April 15 orderliness. The ragged "Hunger Strike" banner that hung in front of the Monument was quickly hauled down, and in a ceremony that was televised repeatedly, the state's crimson flag with five gold stars was raised once again in its stead.

14

"To Right a Wrong It Is Necessary to Exceed a Proper Limit"

In his 1927 report on the peasant movement in Hunan Province, Mao wrote that "to right a wrong it is necessary to exceed a proper limit." In dispatching fully armed detachments of the PLA to reclaim Tiananmen Square from a few thousand unarmed students, Deng Xiaoping carried Mao's admonition to a gruesome extreme. The Square had been "returned to the people," but at an awful cost.

When daylight broke on June 4, the streets revealed scenes of desolation and ruin. Main thoroughfares leading toward the Square were strewn with wreckage and trash. Bicycles lay twisted like mangled coat hangers where they had been run over by APCs and tanks. Windows had been shot out in many apartment buildings and several hotels along the western reaches of the Avenue of Eternal Peace. Tattered and bloody clothing, spent shells, broken bricks, shattered glass, twisted steel road dividers, charred wreckage, and disfigured bodies littered the streets. Intersections were clogged with the hulks of burned-out cars and buses. Whole military convoys stood in ghostlike smoldering columns, the steel cleat tracks of armored vehicles strewn about like broken parts of childrens' toys. The government was to claim that 120 public buses, over 1,000 military trucks, 60 APCs, and 30 police cars had been torched or otherwise damaged. On one disabled tank someone had emblazoned a swastika. On the scorched side of a bus, someone else had scrawled in blood, "Li Peng! You will never be at peace!"

By dawn Tiananmen Square had been sealed off on all sides by a cordon of armored vehicles and infantry. Military helicopters clattered overhead through clouds of black smoke billowing up from around the Monument, fueling rumors that soldiers were incinerating student bodies as Chai Ling claimed.

"Ordinary people were stunned by the army's savagery," recalled Higgins and Fathers. "They gathered in doorways and *hutong* [alleys] to assemble details of the night's violence, or ventured out to set fire to the few trucks and buses not already incinerated." In several places around the city, crowds of people gathered to gaze at the charred and dismembered bodies of lynched soldiers left dangling from ropes.

Marching slowly across this bleak landscape, the defeated students wearily made their way back to their campuses. Trudging down the same streets that had brought them into the Square with banners flying so triumphantly in April, the students now found themselves not only in retreat, but confronting resentful and heavily armed troops along the way. Though numb with horror, fatigue, and disbelief, many in this defeated procession were still enraged. At the southwest corner of the Square a round of epithets screamed at soldiers prompted a fusillade of automatic-weapons fire. No one was hit, but as one student told me, "At that point, many of us didn't really care what happened—whether we lived or died."

As the procession passed Liubukou just to the west of Tiananmen, the students encountered a motorized PLA unit. While they made their way around the remains of a smoldering barricade of burned-out buses and crushed bicycles, several tank crews responded to insults by charging the sluggishly moving column with their armored vehicles. "The students began to run in panic," remembered Qinghua University student Liu Tang. "The tanks kept gaining on us. I remember someone screaming at me to hurry up. Another student helped me drag my bike up on the curb. The tank missed me by a few yards. As it passed, the soldiers inside opened up the hatch and tossed out four gas canisters." When some students hurled rocks and bricks in retaliation, one of the tanks spun around to make another pass, and this time ran down and crushed eleven students as they frantically tried to scatter. "The first body I saw was a girl dressed neatly in a white blouse and red skirt," remembered Liu. "She lay face down on the avenue, one of her legs was completely twisted around, the foot pointing up toward the sky. Another, a male student, had his right arm completely severed from his shoulder, leaving a gaping black hole. The last body in the line of students was a young man on top of a flattened bicycle. He had been trying to climb over the bicycles to get away from the tank. His head was crushed: a pool of blood and brains lay on the pavement a few feet away.''

At about 10 A.M. a large crowd gathered to taunt and shout at soldiers positioned at the eastern entrance to the Square. "Don't shoot! You are one of us! You are one of the people, not a tool of the government!" Then, growing bold, the crowd began inching forward into the no-man's zone that divided them from troops and scores of tanks and APCs. "Without warning the soldiers' guns exploded," wrote Higgins and Fathers. "For one endless minute, the bullets poured out. The soldiers seemed to have no idea if they were shooting to kill or simply to frighten.''

One headbanded young man had become so incensed by the slaughter that he commandeered a Red Cross ambulance and set it afire for a kamikaze run at the firing soldiers. Bystanders managed to pull him out of the cab at the very last moment, leaving the driverless vehicle careening toward the soldiers to finally collide with a police traffic box and burst into flames.

The troops crouched, and continued firing, killing and wounding scores. Then, as if a *coup de grâce* were needed, several APCs opened up with their machine guns. "For the moment the Avenue was still," wrote Higgins and Fathers, "a hundred-yard length of corpses, abandoned bicycles, and prone, terrified survivors.''

Beijing was a madhouse of uncertainty and grief. Families had no way of knowing whether loved ones had been killed, wounded, or had gone into hiding to avoid arrest. Parents searched frantically for their children in hospitals and in the makeshift morgues hastily set up amid the chaos of the night before. One friend told me of seeing a woman tripping through the streets near the Institute of Metallurgy in Haidian with the bullet-riddled body of her child in her arms. British journalist Jonathan Annells recalled a man standing in the street near a long convoy of military vehicles waving a broom handle with his child's torn and blood-soaked dress affixed to the end in the faces of a group of soldiers. "Look what you've done!" he cried out. "You've killed my daughter!''

Having received no authorization to broadcast any real news from the Party, over and over again programmers at Beijing Television aired a traditional Chinese opera in which the hero of the Ming Dynasty novel *The Romance of the Three Kingdoms,* Liu Bei, mourns the death of his comrades-in-arms Zhang Fei and Guan Gong. Hung above the stage was the character for *dian* (to make offerings to the spirits of the departed), the same character that adorned so many wreaths in Tiananmen Square after Hu Yaobang's death.

On college campuses students were trying both to come to terms with all that had happened and prepare for an anticipated military occupation. Outside Beishida's main gate hung a funeral banner reading, "A Generation of Young Heroes Has Gone to an Early Death." Inside, white funeral flowers had been hung on trees. On Beida's front gate was a poster emblazoned with crimson characters proclaiming, "We Promise That We Will Repay This Blood Debt." And from a dorm window hung bloody shirts punctured with bullet holes. At the University of Politics and Law, whose students had been among the first to join the catalytic April 17 protest march, the shrouded corpses of five protesters were laid out on ice, surrounded by a black and white banner that read, "China's Soil Has Been Cruelly Fertilized by the Blood of Its Youth."

As they learned more details about what had happened that night, some students became racked with guilt for having survived by abandoning the Square. "Although I didn't die, I feel terribly bad," one student told Canadian professor Michael Duke. "I feel like the others died in my place. . . . I hope that I will be able to die because I want to use my blood to awaken even more people."

In the weeks that followed, many who had participated in the protest movement sank into an almost catatonic state of depression in which guilt, fear, anger, despair, and loss mixed together in a crippling combination recognized as "survivors' syndrome."

Shortly after the massacre, Australian China specialists Geremie Barmé and Linda Jaivin received an audiotape smuggled out of China containing a recording of a poem by the Sichuanese poet Liao Yiwo who was shortly sentenced to four years in prison for making a documentary film about June 4 called *The Massacre*. The poem captured the feelings of agony and the derangement that many young Chinese suffered. Punctuated by the sound of shrill screams and desperate sobbing, the poem gave harrowing voice to the anguish experienced by many former protesters.

. . . In the name of the citizens, blow up cities! OPEN FIRE! FIRE! FIRE! FIRE! Upon the elderly! Upon the children! Open Fire on women! On students! Workers! Teachers! OPEN FIRE! Blast away! Take aim at those angry faces. Horrified faces. Convulsing faces. Empty all barrels at despairing and peaceful faces. FIRE AWAY to your hearts' content! . . . Do away with all beauty! Do away with flowers! Forests! Campuses! Love! Guitars and pure clean air! Do away with flights of folly! OPEN FIRE! BLAST AWAY! IT FEELS SO GOOD! SOOOO GOOD! . . . Crycrycrycrycrycrycrycrycrycry!

For several days after June 4 jumpy troops continued firing at buildings and sometimes at crowds as people gathered to survey the ruin, commiserate with one another, and hurl insults at the soldiers. Even as reinforcements rolled into the city, bands of angry citizens continued to resist by pushing disabled vehicles into intersections or throwing rocks and bricks.

On June 5, as a column of tanks rumbled eastward down the Avenue of Eternal Peace, several western cameramen in the Beijing Hotel captured what was perhaps the most enduring image of the whole seven weeks. A young man holding nothing more than a jacket in one hand and a small satchel in the other stepped out in front of the oncoming tanks. For one quintessential moment, the entire armored column came to a grinding halt. When the lead tank jerked to the right to circumvent this unexpected obstruction, the young man stepped into its path and stretched out his arms, as if he were trying to corral a stubborn animal. Then he climbed atop the halted tank and began banging on its turret. When the head of a surprised crew member peeked out of the hatch, this lone Horatio-at-the-bridge was reported to have shouted, "Turn around! Stop killing my people!" When he finally jumped down onto the pavement again, several agitated friends ran out and dragged their comrade to safety.

Other youths engaged in different kinds of hit-and-run protests. They burned stray military vehicles and attacked any "green devils," as soldiers in their olive-drab fatigues came to be known, whose misfortune it was to become separated from their units. According to the government's own statistics, during the three months immediately following the massacre, 170 assaults against martial-law troops led to 21 deaths. In the end, soldiers were almost as traumatized as civilians.

Meanwhile, the city had come to a halt. Stores had closed, postal service and sanitation services had ceased, and most people stayed home from work. Nobody knew what to believe amid all the rumors about imminent civil war, the assassination of leaders, and workers' strikes.

By June 6, the reoccupation of Beijing was essentially complete. Although reports from the provinces told of continuing unrest in such cities as Shanghai, Chengdu, Wuhan, Qingdao, Canton, Changsha, Tianjin, Nanjing, and Xian, Beijing had essentially been cowed into submission. It had fallen into a period that one People's University law professor described as "utter darkness without light."

15

"We Should Not Have One Bit of Forgiveness for Them"

On June 5 as television showed soldiers benignly sweeping up debris on the streets of Beijing, the Central Committee and the State Council issued a proclamation declaring that the "quelling" of this "horrifying counterrevolutionary rebellion" is a "totally righteous action that is in keeping with the desire and basic interest of the people in Beijing and all over the country." It extravagantly claimed that the real aim of the protesters was to "take up arms" in order to overthrow the government and ultimately kill the Party's 47 million members. "The plotters and organizers of the counterrevolutionary rebellion are mainly a handful of people who have for a long time obstinately persisted in bourgeois liberalization, engaged in political scheming, collaborated with hostile forces overseas, and provided illegal organizations with top secrets of the Party and state," the proclamation charged. "Those who committed the atrocities of beating, smashing, looting and burning are mainly unreformed elements released after serving prison sentences, hordes of political hooligans, remnants of the Gang of Four, and other dregs of society. In brief, they are reactionary elements who harbor a deep hatred for the Communist Party and the socialist system."

By accusing demonstrators of collaborating "with hostile forces from overseas," Party leaders were, in effect, charging them with espionage. By labeling them "reactionary elements," they equated them with class enemies. Such language suggested that the assault on the Square was intended not only to silence the students, but as Chen Yizi said, to serve "as a coup against a decade of reform."

At a June 6 press conference that contrasted sharply with the kinds of freewheeling public appearances Party leaders had been making before martial law was declared, State Council spokesman Yuan Mu and Director of the Political Department for Martial Law Forces Zhang Gong elaborated on the official version of events. Denying that a "bloodbath" had taken place while the army was "cleaning up the Square," Zhang insisted that reports of corpses burned in Tiananmen Square were "sheer rumor." Praising the "great self-restraint" exercised by troops, Yuan Mu maintained that "the basic situation of the students' withdrawal from Tiananmen Square was peaceful." In fact, he argued, it was the army rather than protesters who were the main victims of violence. A "handful of lawless ruffians and bystanders" had launched a brutal and unprovoked attack on the army, he asserted. Yuan's prescription for dealing with the political alienation that was now so rampant was to "isolate the thugs," and under no circumstances "be softhearted in dealing with them."

Yuan then offered a disturbing discourse on neo-Maoist pop sociology. "For a time, class struggle was not stressed at all, while even political struggle was underemphasized," he said, smiling nervously. "It was said that classes were all gone, that people were all brothers and sisters, and that the world was full of love." But the "objective fact" remained, continued Yuan, that Chinese society still harbored "a number of bad people," and that because the contradictions "between them and us are of an antagonistic nature," the government should now "show no mercy." Such language was for many taken as an ominous sign that the political climate was on the brink of regressing, rhetorically if not in fact, to the Mao era.

Most Chinese still understood that even though more than a decade had passed since the end of the Cultural Revolution, once a social or political group was identified by the Party as part of an "antagonistic contradiction"—which Mao had defined as resolvable only through prolonged struggle, even violence—they ipso facto became part of the "enemy." Chinese also knew that since the Communist Party had come to power in 1949, the fate of those relegated to this category of political damnation had invariably been bitter. Yuan was essentially hanging scarlet letters on all protest leaders, and on anyone else who had played more than a passive role in the demonstrations.

Equally unsettling for political activists was Yuan's declaration that the military occupation of Beijing was only the beginning of a larger campaign to stamp out political dissent. "We have achieved an initial victory —or, shall we say, taken a first step—in crushing the rebellion," he said. Despite Li Peng's April promise not to seek vengeance against those who took part in the protest movement, Yuan made it clear that the hard-line coterie of leaders now in control did, indeed, intend "to settle accounts." For those thousands anxiously waiting for clues about the Party's post–June 4 attitude before deciding whether to go into hiding or to flee the country, Yuan's statement was discouraging. The way media organs all over the country quickly began grinding out propaganda to reinforce these themes only augmented their pessimism. "The reason why the students landed in such a predicament is extremely complicated," echoed the hard-line *Liberation Army Daily,* "but one key point is that the concept of class struggle has completely vanished from the minds of the broad masses of students."

While Chinese waited to see how hard the political winds of repression would begin blowing, and as the Party insisted, "There was no bloodshed in Tiananmen Square!" foreign observers began debating the body count. Early on June 4, the Chinese Red Cross told foreign news agencies that a survey of Beijing hospitals revealed that 2,600 people had died in the government assault. According to Yuan Mu, however, no more than 300 people had died, only 23 of whom were students. He also insisted that military casualties far outnumbered civilian casualties, with the army suffering 5,000 dead and wounded, while the citizens of Beijing suffered only 2,000. Although he did admit that some civilians had been "killed by mistake," Yuan dismissed them as "bad elements who deserved this because of their crimes."

There was something about the unfathomable depth of people's anguish over the event that made almost everyone crave concrete statistics as a way of giving the tragedy finite dimensions. If the government's fear of fueling popular outrage led them to issue low (and constantly changing) casualty figures, others were only too willing to exaggerate the scope of the bloodshed. One Russian report put the death toll at around 10,000. *Time* magazine estimated 5,000. Amnesty International estimated between 700 and 3,000. The *New York Times* put the figure between 400 and 800. It did not help, of course, that the Chinese government refused to release the names of the dead, claiming that loved ones and family members of the deceased refused to authorize such action. Since it was difficult to extract meaningful counter-statistics from eyewitness accounts, the government's figures were impossible to refute.

Another of the Party's concerns was controlling the terminology that would henceforth be used to describe the protest movement and the bloodletting. Now that the organs of propaganda were firmly back in Party hands, the demonstrations were never to be referred to in the official press as part of a "democracy movement," but as a part of a *fan geming dongluan* (counterrevolutionary rebellion) or a *baoluan* (violent turmoil). And the bloodletting was never to be referred to as the *Beijing tusha* (Beijing massacre), a term that was quickly adopted by Chinese abroad, but as *pingxi baoluan* (the quelling of violent turmoil). But even with such sanitizing of official language, it was no easy task to airbrush away the memory of what had happened, particularly when each day the government was being forced to take increasingly harsh measures to hunt down and punish those who had participated in the protest.

On June 8 the municipal government and Martial Law Headquarters declared the nationwide Federation of Autonomous Student Unions and the Federation of Autonomous Labor Unions illegal, and warned union members that they should turn themselves in to the police or risk being arrested and "punished severely." The Headquarters also called on Chinese citizens to strike back by "exposing and denouncing the criminal activities of counterrevolutionaries." To facilitate what it hoped would be an outpouring of denunciations from informants, seventeen special telephone hot lines were set up to receive tips. Contrary to the Party's hopes, however, irate citizens began telephoning the hot lines with bogus information, so that they quickly became jammed up and virtually useless.

On June 9, Deng Xiaoping reemerged from seclusion in a coming-out ceremony held inside Zhongnanhai in Huairen Hall (Cherishing Humanity Hall). He entered the room dressed in an ordinary gray-blue Mao suit flanked by President Yang Shangkun and Vice-President Wang Zhen. In spite of his eighty-five years, Deng looked remarkably fit and in control as he greeted members of the Standing Committee and military commanders who had "quelled the turmoil." He may not have been very popular among Beijing's ordinary people just then, but among these officers his popularity appeared undiminished. They smiled, clapped spiritedly, and reached out enthusiastically to shake his hand as if he were a politician on the campaign trail.

After paying a moment of silent tribute to the military "martyrs" who had lost their lives on the streets, Deng sat down at a circular table with an ashtray and a cup of tea before him and launched into an extemporaneous talk that hailed the PLA as "a truly Great Wall of iron and steel around the Party and country." Using the first person plural to create the impression that army and Party were fused in unalloyed solidarity, he said that "no matter how heavy the losses we suffered and no matter how generations change, this army is forever an army under the leadership of the Party, forever the defender of the country, forever the defender of socialism, forever the defender of the public interest, and the most beloved of the people." The assault on the capital had been "a test," he said, which PLA troops "passed" with flying colors, and thus "they fully deserve to have it said of them that they were resolute in death."

Under normal circumstances few Chinese would have bothered to pay attention to such pontifications, but on this occasion they sat spellbound before their TVs, eager to hear how the "paramount leader" would assess what had just happened. Many were perplexed by Deng's declaration that the protest movement was a "storm that was bound to happen independent of man's will," and took it to mean that Deng looked upon the whole imbroglio as a form of cosmic bad luck that even the most virtuous and astute leader could not have avoided. Others viewed it as a veiled acknowledgment that Deng knew all along that a showdown with advocates of more rapid political reform was inevitable.

Reformers were relieved, however, when Deng did not call for a hard-line economic rollback. "Is our basic concept of reform and openness wrong?" he asked rhetorically. "No," came the emphatic reply. "Without reform, how could we have what we do today? . . . Our basic proposals, ranging from our development strategy to principles and policies, including reform and opening to the outside world, are correct." At the same time, however, Deng also declared that "we should never forget how cruel our enemies are. We should have not one bit of forgiveness for them."

Almost immediately, Beijing Television news began showing film clips of frightened and often badly beaten detainees being taken into custody. "Some had ribs broken," reported one woman who refused to allow her name to be used for fear of reprisals. "They were beaten to such a horrifying state that when they were turned over to the PSB, they took pictures of them so as not to be blamed—to have proof that these people arrived in their hands in this state." Viewers understood the intended message of the video images all too well: Those perceived to have been among the "very small handful of troublemakers" would now pay dearly for the trouble they had caused, especially young workers, who had none of the protective status of elite students. By June 11 municipal authorities had already detained some four hundred "looters, vagrants, rumormongers, individual entrepreneurs, and recidivist criminals."

On June 13, fear levels among protesters-in-hiding rose precipitously when the government issued its "21 Most Wanted List" of student activists. At the top of the list was Wang Dan, who only days before had told Sheryl WuDunn of the *New York Times*, "I have nothing to be afraid of. I don't think that they will be able to imprison me as long as Wei Jingsheng." Also included on the list were Wu'er Kaixi, Chai Ling, Li Lu, and Feng Congde. Photos of each were now broadcast repeatedly on nationwide television along with their "criminal activities" and appeals for information on their whereabouts. The PSB began a massive search of homes, spied on suspects at work, and pressured people to inform on friends. Surveillance was stepped up at stations, airports, and docks to prevent those who were "wanted" from escaping.

Among the first prominent Chinese to be arrested was thirty-four-year-old Liu Xiaobo, one of the four older intellectuals who began their hunger strike on June 2. Only a year earlier Liu had sarcastically declared that "all of China's tragedies are authored, directed, performed, and appreciated by the Chinese themselves, so there's no need to blame anyone else." Now Liu found himself the object of just such blame—accused by the government of being one of the "black hands" behind the turmoil. On June 6, Liu was picked up by police while bicycling in the street, pushed into a van, and packed off to Qincheng Prison.

Three days later, on June 9, public security police raided the apartment of forty-one-year-old human rights activist Ren Wanding. Ren, who had already been imprisoned for his activities during the Democracy Wall Movement, was accused of having delivered "slanderous and inflammatory speeches" constituting illegal "counterrevolutionary incitement," and sentenced to seven more years in prison. Just days before, he had tried to seek sanctuary in the American embassy but was turned away by U.S. diplomats fearful that sheltering him might presage a flood of other desperate asylum seekers.

On June 12, Li Jinjin, a legal scholar who had advised Han Dongfang on how to legally set up his workers' federation, was arrested in his home at gunpoint.

These were just a few of the thousands of detainees, most of whom the outside world never came to know by name. Yet despite the government's dragnet, as of June 26 only half a dozen students on the "21 Most Wanted List" had actually been taken into custody.

It was not until early July that the government caught its first big fish, Wang Dan, the Beijing University history student whose role in the student leadership triumvirate had landed him right at the top of the list. He was picked up on July 2 while meeting with a Taiwanese journalist who was allegedly helping him flee. Like Wu'er Kaixi and many others, Wang had fled south in hopes of escaping to Hong Kong. But after failing to connect with anyone in the underground, Wang was forced to return to Beijing. After seventeen months' detention in solitary confinement, he was tried on charges of "counterrevolutionary propaganda and incitement" and sentenced to four years in prison.

The government continued to exhort those who had participated in the demonstrations to turn themselves in and to entrust their fates to the magnanimity of the Party, but most Chinese were understandably loath to rely on the mercy of China's judicial and penal system. After all, millions of political victims had disappeared into its network of prisons and labor camps during the preceding forty years. It was for this reason that so many set off on the perilous trek to Canton in hopes of finding a way to cross the border to Hong Kong. Since provincial PSB offices and border officials had been given photos of those being sought, reaching one of China's international frontiers was not easy, and actually crossing one even more difficult.

When Lü Jinghua, a twenty-six-year-old private dress-shop owner in Beijing found herself included on a most wanted list of worker activists because of the role she had played in Han's Autonomous Workers' Federation, she tried to hide in a friend's apartment. When it became clear that sooner or later she would be found, she was forced to confront the most painful decision of her life: stay and be arrested, or flee and leave behind her young daughter, her husband, and her elderly mother. In the end, she decided to flee. "I knew that even though I might never see my daughter again, I still had to run for my life or be arrested. If they caught me, I could only imagine their cruelty."

"We always have to give up our children because of poverty or political persecution," lamented Xiang Xiaoji who also had to leave his young daughter to escape. "This is our lot for being Chinese."

"The psychological strain of hiding was almost too much to bear," remembered Feng Congde, Chai Ling's husband, who spent ten months on the run before finally reaching Hong Kong. "I spent three whole months alone in a forest without a single other human being around me. Once while listening to the VOA, I heard that in one jail eight students were thrown in a single cell, and I was envious of them! At least, I thought, there were eight of them together, while I was all alone trying to hide." In spite of his loneliness, however, Feng says that he found "great inspiration and encouragement" in all the sympathy and support offered by the ordinary people along the way who put themselves at great risk to help him and other fleeing students.

Zhao Hongliang, a worker who had helped organize the Autonomous Workers Federation, described how as he was fleeing south on a train, an assault rifle–toting policeman suddenly pulled him into the conductor's office. He thought he was done for. But to his surprise, the policeman whispered, "If you are lucky enough to escape alive, young man, tell the outside world what has happened. We are all friends, but don't ask my name." Then the policeman shook Zhao's hand and pressed a fifty-yuan note into his palm. "Tears ran down my face," recounted Zhao. "I cannot describe how I felt."

As the campaign of mass arrests gathered momentum, the Chinese Supreme People's Court issued a bulletin calling on lower courts to "promptly try, according to the law, serious criminal offenders and counterrevolutionaries who staged the counterrevolutionary rebellion and created social turmoil." "According to the law" was a standard refrain appended to almost every announcement made about the detention of dissidents. In actual practice, however, "the law" afforded defendants virtually no due process and precious little protection from arbitrary arrest and long sentences whose length had more to do with the whims of Party leaders than with criminal statutes.

On June 8, for instance, the PSB issued warrants for the arrest of thirteen young workers in Shanghai accused of setting fire to a train that had run over six demonstrators holding a nonviolent sit-in on a railroad track to protest the Beijing massacre. With fearsome swiftness that made allowance for neither adequate legal defense nor appeals, all eleven were put on trial ten days later. On June 18 three were sentenced to death for sabotage. Three days later they were summarily executed.

Meanwhile, on June 17 eight more people were found guilty of "rioting" and setting fire to army vehicles, and were sentenced to death in Beijing. On June 22 the government announced that twenty-four more executions had taken place. An official source insisted that only seven of those shot in the back of the head had participated in antigovernment protests. But who could say? Even after a decade of legal reform, the distinctions between *zhengzhifan* (political criminals) and *xingshifan* (ordinary criminals) remained extremely murky.

Of the forty-nine publicly announced executions carried out in connection with crimes committed on or around June 4—and many more certainly went unreported—none of them were of students. What seemed to have inhibited Party leaders from taking such draconian measures against students was their awareness that because of the sympathy their protest had evoked, executions would only fuel a backlash at home and abroad.

Decades earlier during an official banquet, when Mao's one-time heir apparent Lin Biao made an allusion to China's tyrannical first emperor Qin Shihuang, his mentor contemptuously replied: "So what's the big deal about Qin Shihuang? He buried only 460 Confucians alive; well, we've buried 46,000! When we suppressed counter-revolutionaries, we also killed some intellectuals, didn't we? We've debated with the democrats: They attack us for being another Qin Shihuang. Well, they're wrong. We're a hundred times greater than Qin Shihuang!"

But things in China had changed considerably since Mao's time. Deng's economic reforms had made China increasingly dependent on the expertise of its intellectual elite, so that their persecution now had real economic consequences. In addition, because Deng's "open door" policy allowed much greater foreign scrutiny, mass political campaigns against educated Chinese had a negative effect on efforts to project an image of stability that would reassure foreign businessmen and investors. It was one thing to execute unknown working-class Chinese, but quite another to kill articulate young intellectuals from prestigious universities where faculty members maintained extensive contacts with academic colleagues abroad. Moreover, Mao notwithstanding, the traditional respect that most Chinese still reserved for scholars made the Party leadership all the more hesitant to act more forcefully. It was telling that when proclaiming martial law on May 19, Li Peng had said, "We regard them [students] as our own children and the future of China. We do not want to hurt good people, especially young students." Students lived within what Robin Munro called a "charmed circle," and just as they had been spared in the Square on June 4, they once again found themselves exempted from the most extreme kinds of government retribution.

It had not taken the government long to figure out that while executions were a successful tool for silencing protest on the home front, they created storms of protest overseas. Thus it was not surprising that around the beginning of July the Party forbade any further mention in the press of death-penalty cases, much less of aggregate statistics on the number of executions. As a result, outside observers found it virtually impossible to gain anything but the most cursory information about capital cases. Even information about the number of people detained or arrested remained sketchy. From time to time, the Chinese press hinted at the scope of the government's campaign against dissenters by publishing a few random local statistics. The *Beijing Youth News* reported that by July 4 some 578 arrests had been made in the city of Beijing, but this figure did not include detentions of people who had been jailed but not charged. The NCNA reported that during a three-day period in mid-July over 3,000 people were detained in Jiangsu Province alone. Such fragmentary reports provided only the most incomplete picture of the widespread campaign of repression that was under way.

The Party also moved to stifle political opposition within its own ranks. A June 25 statement from the Central Commission for Discipline and Inspection, charged with the task of "rectifying" violations of Party rules, advised all branches that those "who deviated from the correct political stand and violated the Party's discipline during the turmoil and the counterrevolutionary rebellion" would be "strictly punished." The purge was directed primarily against the supporters of deposed Party General Secretary Zhao Ziyang. The day before, Li Peng had officially consigned Zhao to political oblivion, charging that "at the critical juncture involving the destiny of the Party and the state," he had "made the mistake of supporting the turmoil and splitting the Party." Consequently, said Li, he must bear an "unshakable responsibility for the way the subsequent turmoil shaped up." Zhao was unceremoniously stripped of all official positions and put under house arrest, ironically in the same walled compound where Hu Yaobang had been left to languish after his "resignation" in 1987. In Zhao's stead Jiang Zemin, Shanghai's bland but uncontroversial former mayor and Party chief, was elevated to general secretary of the Party. "Toward these cruel enemies there must not be even one percent of forgiveness," he was quoted as saying on June 29 on the front page of the *People's Daily*. "If we go easy on them, we shall commit an error of historic proportions."

On June 30, Beijing's hard-line mayor Chen Xitong issued an exhaustive and accusatory report on the protest movement to the National People's Congress. It overflowed with so many facts and quotations that it was obvious that the PSB had hardly been idle during the seven weeks of demonstrations. For those who had been involved, the report's most frightening aspect was that it made it clear that hard-liners were now in the ascendancy within the Party and that they were prepared to go to almost any length to win what Chen called a "struggle involving the life and death of the Party."

"I don't think I'd ever felt such despair about China," a senior Beijing intellectual who had not been active in the demonstrations told me. "When I watched television and heard our leaders speak, or saw what was happening to the young people who had participated in the demonstrations, I could only weep helplessly. It was all so terribly familiar and depressing. For a few short years we had allowed ourselves to believe that perhaps China had finally broken free from its terrible revolutionary conservatism. Now we were once again hurtling backward into the past with no idea where this latest regression was taking us.''

16

A Hundred Flowers Fade

The morning after the massacre an announcer on Radio Beijing's English-language service somberly began his news report: "Remember June 3, 1989. A most tragic event happened in the Chinese capital, Beijing. Thousands of people, most of them innocent civilians, were killed by fully armed soldiers when they forced their way into Beijing. Among the killed are our colleagues at Radio Beijing. The soldiers were riding in armored vehicles and used machine guns against thousands of local residents and students who tried to block their way. . . . Radio Beijing deeply mourns those [who] died in the tragic incident and appeals to all its listeners to join our protest against this gross violation of human rights and this most barbarous suppression of the people." The announcer was Wu Xiaoyong, the son of former Foreign Minister Wu Xueqian. Wu Xiaoyong had been so horrified by what he saw while bicycling to work that he decided to risk everything to make this bold broadcast.

The same day, staff members at the *People's Daily* managed to print a brief report that alluded to the enormous number of civilian casualties resulting from the army's rampage. Acknowledging that "martial-law troops have already stormed Tiananmen Square," the report said that "local hospitals have been calling our newspaper nonstop to report the injuries and fatalities of people receiving treatment."

Such efforts did not last long, however. By June 6 papers had become virtually devoid of any news about the massacre or the military crackdown. The only way that writers and editors could express their true feelings was by using Aesopian obliqueness. For example, on June 5 a headline appeared in the *People's Daily* over a story about a handicapped person winning an athletic medal that read, "The People's Hearts Will Not Be Conquered." On June 7, above an irrelevant and dated story about the illegal poaching of deer in Inner Mongolia, the headline "Guileless Fawns Brutally Slaughtered" appeared. And the following day over a story concerning South Korean dissident Kim Dae Jung's call for his own government to punish authorities who had bloodily suppressed the 1980 Kwangju student uprising, editors managed to insinuate the headline, "Fascist Clique Wantonly Kills Students and Civilians."

Almost immediately, however, the Party moved to suppress even these indirect expressions of dissent. In every official organization a *gingcha* (ferreting out) campaign to root out those who had taken part in any kinds of activities considered counterrevolutionary was launched. The editorial staff of the *People's Daily* was particularly hard-hit. The editor in chief, Tan Wenrui; the director, Qian Liren; three deputy chief editors, Yu Huanchun, Fan Rongkang, and Lu Chaoqi; and forty-six reporters were replaced. Shao Huaze, a hard-line propaganda chief of the PLA, became editor in chief, and Gao Di, the conservative vice-president of the Central Communist Party School, became director. As the crackdown deepened, nearly six hundred of the paper's seven-hundred-person staff of writers and editors were subject to some kind of disciplinary action.

An article in the August 7 issue of the reorganized daily set the tone for all future press coverage in China. Accusing certain reporters of "flaunting the banner of press freedom" and of "confusing black and white, fabricating rumors, slandering, confusing and poisoning people's minds," the paper called on everyone in the media to "shoulder the important task of propagating the line, the guiding principles, and the policies of the Party and state."

The purge at the *People's Daily* was only the tip of the iceberg. In Shanghai alone some twenty-eight publications were forced to close their doors. Of the 536 registered book-publishing houses throughout China, 41 were reported to have been shut, while numerous fly-by-night independent printers were closed. At the same time, the General Press and Publishing Administration went into high gear blacklisting books and authors. In a directive issued to all its local branches, this watchdog organ listed the works of fourteen well-known writers— including Fang Lizhi, Bei Dao, Dai Qing, Liu Xiaobo, Ge Yang, Ren

Wanding, and Wang Ruowang—for suppression. According to the NCNA, some 65,000 inspectors searched through over 40,000 private bookstalls and video outlets, closing many of them while confiscating over 11 million publications and almost 100,000 "pornographic" tapes. Even VOA Chinese-language broadcasts were jammed, and the sale of foreign newspapers and magazines in tourist hotels forbidden.

But even these measures told only the most incomplete story about government efforts to defoliate the media. Those publications that continued to appear were quickly shorn of all independence by Party "work teams" dispatched to editorial offices. Lacking any means of protest, most writers retreated into double lives, expressing their real thoughts only to close friends while continuing to do the state's bidding at work.

Instead of the demonstrators that had momentarily blossomed on Chinese television screens, there was now nothing but images of the "beating, smashing, looting, and burning" that "hoodlums" were alleged to have perpetrated on innocent troops. With lightning speed the Party cobbled together a series of "documentaries" to propagandize for their new line. The four-part *Fluttering Flag of the Republic: An On-the-Spot Report on the Suppression of the Counterrevolutionary Rebellion* showed grisly footage of wounded troops and of the scorched corpses of slain soldiers. The editors of these hastily made and overbearingly didactic films frequently altered the chronology of events or doctored soundtracks to conform to the official version of what happened. Video sequences were reversed so it appeared as if troops had used their weapons only after demonstrators had turned violent rather than vice versa, and scenes of enraged crowds assaulting soldiers with bottles and bricks were shown while the sound of automatic-weapons fire was muted on the soundtrack so that it seemed as if the attacks were unprovoked. One sequence showing crowds clapping as troops passed was actually shot of troops retreating on June 3 after being trapped by street crowds.

A glossy government-published coffee-table–style volume, *The Truth About the Beijing Turmoil,* was jam-packed with lurid color photos of knife-wielding protesters, frenzied citizens attacking troops, blood-drenched soldiers, and incinerated trucks and tanks. It also featured many shots of the two charred soldiers who by that time had appeared in so much government propaganda that they seemed more like PLA mascots than martyrs. Extolling the restraint of the troops, the book's introduction asserted that "although they had their weapons in hand, they preferred to endure humiliation and even death unflinchingly out of fear of injuring civilians by accident. . . . It can be said that there is no army in the world that can exercise restraint to such an extent.'' The book ended with a wide-angle shot of Tiananmen Gate silhouetted against a rare smogless blue sky as orderly queues of bicycles, cars, and buses flowed along the Avenue of Eternal Peace. ''Tiananmen Square has again regained its solemnity and magnificence after the quelling of the rebellion,'' read the accompanying caption.

Such rationalizations notwithstanding, events of the spring of 1989 and their bloody finale had left China's leaders more humiliated than at any other time in the history of the Communist Party. What made the situation all the more unbearable was that their ignominy had been inflicted not by Western imperialists as in the past, but by themselves. But since the Party could admit no wrong, explanations needed to be found and alibis created. Most of all, ways to export some of the blame had to be invented. Conspiracies between domestic and foreign enemies became the essence of the Party's explanation for why things had gone so awry. And nowhere was their belief in such a conspiracy made clearer than in an incident that occurred on June 5. When interviewed by ABC-TV reporter James Laurie, an outraged Chinese factory worker named Xiao Bin erroneously claimed that he had heard the Voice of America report that 20,000 people had been killed and wounded during the massacre. Unfortunately for Xiao, Chinese authorities intercepted ABC's satellite feed from Tokyo to the United States, and within hours his photograph was being broadcast across China by CCTV with an appeal for information regarding his whereabouts. With the help of informants who saw these broadcasts, Xiao was apprehended for ''rumormongering'' several days later in the Manchurian city of Dalian, forced to ''confess'' his crime, and after a speedy trial, sentenced to ten years in prison.

Although such attacks against Chinese alleged to have sold out to foreigners was nothing new, what was unprecedented was how little real substance actually lay behind these imagined conspiracies. What did lie behind them, however, was a deeply felt sense of having been shamed in the eyes—or perhaps it would be more accurate to say on the screens—of the world; a feeling that something intangible—as hard to pin down as a poem or a rock lyric, as difficult to ignore as the need for foreign capital, and as impossible to destroy as an idea—had crept into China during the previous decade of reform and corroded everything Party hard-liners valued. Once, such sensitivity to things foreign and to foreigners had been as obvious as gunboats on the Yangtze River, as observable as ''foreign concessions'' in China's great cities, as tangible as China's customs revenues once controlled by Westerners, and as horrifyingly graphic as the "rape of Nanjing" by Japanese soldiers.

For more than a century and a half, technologically advanced Western powers and then Japan had encroached again and again on a China too weak to defend itself. Chinese stood by helpless as foreigners heaped scorn on their country as the "poor man of Asia" and threatened to "carve it up like a melon." Wars were launched, and expeditionary forces seized Chinese coastal cities and even took the national capital as a prelude to extracting economic concessions, while spheres of influence, reparations, and special privileges were wrested first from a collapsing imperial government, then from weak regional warlords. This bitter history of Western and Japanese domination was encoded on the mental genes of China's leaders, most of whom had been born before the last dynasty fell in 1911. It was this hostility toward interlopers and the humiliation they experienced from their inability to control their country's fate that made Chinese leaders so susceptible to Lenin's notion of imperialist exploitation as an explanation for China's failures. The great promise of Mao's revolution had been that it would deliver China from poverty and backwardness, and raise it up as a powerful, unified, and respected sovereign country that could no longer be pushed around and belittled. Now, however, in a single night without one foreign power occupying a single inch of Chinese territory, China's international reputation had been besmirched and its government condemned around the world in a way that made its leaders once again feel besieged.

In a desperate effort to find face-saving explanations for this sudden ignominy, the Party resurrected twin shibboleths from the past— "bourgeois liberalization" and "peaceful evolution." Each of these notions echoed back to actual perils China had once suffered at Western and Japanese hands, and each in its own way implied that, just as before, China's problems were not caused by itself or its leaders, but by hostile outsiders with alien and subversive values gratuitously stirring up trouble among Chinese.

"Bourgeois liberalization" was a code word for such varied internal manifestations of Western culture as multiparty systems, free expression, private ownership, ideological pluralism, and art for art's sake that were deemed to threaten Chinese socialism. As early as 1937, Mao Zedong had written an essay, "Combat Liberalism," in which he warned that the spirit of liberalism was "a corrosive which eats away at unity, undermines solidarity, induces inactivity, and creates dissension." Since the capitalist West was typically identified as the seedbed of such degenerate bourgeois thought, foreigners were seen as the carriers of this dangerous contagion and China's own urban bourgeoisie as its most vulnerable receptors. Thus, it was hardly surprising that in the grand scheme of "building Chinese socialism," the expulsion of Westerners and the extermination of the urban bourgeoisie were given the highest priority.

But even after China had been expunged of its own middle class so that the idea of "bourgeois liberalization" remained little more than a label without an actual class basis, Chinese leaders continued to find it a useful handle for vilifying supposed "enemies." Throughout the 1980s, Deng made repeated allusion to its menace, even launching several full-fledged Party-sponsored campaigns against its wages. But what was so contradictory and confusing about his concern was that at the same time he railed against the embourgeoisement of Chinese society, his own policies aggressively promoted the phenomenon.

The rampant spread of "bourgeois liberalization" during the late 1980s, explained Chen Muqi in his Party-sponsored polemic "Beijing Turmoil: More Than Meets the Eye," was "like a voracious sea that swept across various fields, including politics, economics, art, literature, and the social sciences." Equating the trend with "individualism and money worship," Chen warned that if these phenomena were allowed to "run wild, they will inevitably become the spiritual force which will shake and crush socialism and make people infatuated with capitalism."

"Peaceful evolution" was the twin of "bourgeois liberalization" and the second main ideological theme in the Party's 1989 propaganda campaign. Although the notion of foreigners corrupting China's socialist virtue was everywhere implicit in the idea of "bourgeois liberalization," it was made explicit in the notion of "peaceful evolution," which, according to Party theorists, was the process whereby foreign enemies were covertly but "peacefully" conspiring to transform China from a socialist state into a "bourgeois democracy." The notion was a product of the Cold War, a time when China was, in fact, under siege by militant anti-Communists in the West. According to Party theorists, "peaceful evolution" as a strategy was first articulated by U.S. Secretary of State John Foster Dulles in 1953 when he told the U.S. Congress that "the liberation" of "enslaved" Chinese could be achieved "with methods other than war," namely, "peaceful methods." Such statements only aroused Mao's already deeply suspicious feelings about the Western powers. "The imperialists and their domestic reactionaries will certainly not take their defeat lying down; they will fight to the last ditch," he wrote of his victory in China.

"After there is peace and order throughout the country, they are sure to engage in sabotage and create disturbances by one means or another."

So after June 4, Party elders reached back into this historical reservoir of suspicion and hostility toward foreigners for explanations of their debacle and for ways of rallying the Chinese people to their side. In a speech made on September 29, 1989, to mark the fortieth anniversary of the founding of the People's Republic, the newly ensconced Party General Secretary, Jiang Zemin, sketched out a paranoid vision of domestic and foreign enemies as conspiring to "support and buy over so-called dissidents through whom they foster blind worship of the Western world and propagate the political patterns, sense of values, decadent traits, and lifestyle of the Western capitalist world." Whenever these foreign conspirators "feel there is an opportunity to be seized," warned Jiang, "they fabricate rumors, provoke incidents, plot turmoil, and engage in subversive activities against socialist countries."

It was a measure of how deeply rooted these two concepts had become in the psyches of elderly leaders that when cataclysm befell them, their almost autonomic response was to blame everything on foreign bogeymen as if they were still China's foremost threat. What gave their efforts such a tragicomic cast was the fact that the strident rhetoric they exhumed from the past was so out of sync with all the changes that they themselves had initiated in China. Their paranoia was hardly soothed when the people of every country in Eastern Europe suddenly began overthrowing their socialist governments, so that once again they felt surrounded by a sea of ideologically hostile yet strangely invisible and indefinable enemies.

The collapse of so many fraternal states raised an awkward question: If socialism was so superior to capitalism, why was it so much on the run? But what was even more distressing was the fact that the countries of the socialist bloc were succumbing to capitalism and democracy without any overt military action being taken against them. They did, indeed, seem to be getting subverted from within in precisely the way that Party leaders warned in their tirades about the menace of "peaceful evolution." For China's Gang of Elders, "bourgeois liberalization" was like a mysterious pathogenic vapor infiltrating through every nook and cranny and causing dangerous infections. In fact, propagandists often depicted it as insidiously plague-like and highly contagious to anyone not inoculated with the requisite ideological resistance.

In October 1989, for instance, a telling commentary in the *Economic Daily* even compared the spread of "bourgeois liberalization" and the creeping process of "peaceful evolution" to the transmission of the AIDS virus. The transliteration in Chinese for AIDS is *aizibing*, literally "AIDS sickness." However, *aizibing* also happens to be a homophone for the Chinese characters which mean "the sickness of loving capitalism." It was a perfectly ambiguous term for Party hardliners to latch on to in their efforts to equate the contamination of Chinese society by Western bourgeois values with contracting this deadly and alien biological disease.

Aizibing is a sickness that "destroys a person's ability to distinguish, remember, and compare," the dire commentary warned. This "infectious disease" makes people believe that if "something is called capitalism, everything will be good; that commodities from foreign countries are good; that white skin is smarter than yellow skin; and that individualism that ignores national interest should be called freedom and human rights. . . . The turbulence that has just passed can be said to show the enormous impact of *aizibing*, the 'sickness of loving capitalism.' "

Part II

Three
Routes to
Exile

17

Imprisonment

During the protest movement foreign journalists were so captivated with student demonstrators that few of us bothered to investigate the extent to which workers had also become an independent and organized political force. In fact, until workers had proved themselves a crucial element in stopping the first advance of troops on the night of May 19, the students had also dismissed them, refusing even to allow leaders such as Han Dongfang to enter their command post at the Monument. They had many rationalizations: they feared that government spies and provocateurs would pose as workers to infiltrate their ranks, that workers would refuse to accept student leadership, and that uneducated workers might not be fully committed to nonviolence.

The irony was that Party leaders were far more fearful of the working class rising up against them than of students demonstrating. Students were de facto members of the elite, and accounted for only one-fifth of 1 percent of Chinese society, whereas workers were one of China's most underprivileged classes and constituted almost 15 percent of the population. Moreover, since the Party purported to have come to power through a Marxist revolution, the idea of disgruntled workers was a deep embarrassment.

"The working class is the vanguard class, and we in the democratic movement should be prepared to demonstrate its great power," the Beijing Autonomous Workers' Federation (BAWF) declared in a manifesto on May 21. "The People's Republic is supposedly led by the working class, thus we have every right to drive out all dictators." Such proletarian rhetoric disturbed Party leaders because they were aware that if workers united in opposition as they had in Poland, the problem of protesting students would seem trivial. Thus it was not surprising that Han Dongfang, an electrical machinist from the Fengtai Locomotive Maintenance Yard who had won the sobriquet of "China's Lech Walesa" by founding the BAWF, ended up at the top of a workers most wanted list.

I was nonetheless unprepared for what I found when I finally met Han Dongfang in New York in 1992. Twenty-nine years old, tall, handsome, and dapperly dressed, he looked far more like a member of China's intelligentsia than a proletarian agitator. Moroever, the clarity of his thought and the directness with which he answered questions left the impression of someone accustomed to repairing systems of political philosophy rather than electrical generators on trains, which was his actual métier. Appearances aside, Han was the model of an ordinary worker. He had grown up in a penurious Beijing family in which his mother, who worked in the household of a relative as a domestic, was the sole provider for her two children. After graduating from high school and doing a stint as a soldier, Han was assigned by the government to work in the Fengtai yard. His keen political sense seems to have grown out of his attempt to idealize the Party while teachers and officials, the Party's representatives, ignored or even scorned him because he had no status. "What you must understand is that when I was growing up even the Chinese proletariat had its oppressive aristocracy," Han laughingly told me, even though at the time the experience of being snubbed because of his family's poverty and low social position had been no laughing matter.

Like millions whose passage from socialist romanticism to cynicism and dissent advanced slowly, Han's odyssey began in the early 1980s when as an idealistic young man he was assigned to serve in the People's Armed Military Police. It was not long before he found himself deeply offended by all the favoritism and privilege that even in the military lay behind the facade of China's purportedly classless society.

The most critical moment of his disillusionment came in late 1986 when university students made their first organized protest march into Tiananmen Square. "My family's house is quite near there. From where I stood with a friend on the northeast corner of the Square near the gate to the PSB headquarters, I was able to watch as about a hundred policemen rushed out of the compound and began beating

student marchers ferociously with clubs. If the students had been chanting 'Down with the Communist Party!' that would have been one
thing. Even I would have opposed them. But their slogans could hardly
be counted as opposition, and yet they were beaten to the ground! And
then some of them were dragged off toward police vans and thrown
inside as if they were hogs being sent to market! As I went home from
the Square that night, I felt terribly upset. However, since I'd never
had any education, I really had no idea of what to make of all I had
seen, much less what could be done about it."

When Hu Yaobang died, Han was one of the first Chinese to head
back into the Square. "Although I had never encountered the kinds of
things that were starting to go on there, I immediately knew that they
were important. What people were saying about there being no rights
in China and about how the country would never develop without
political change was exactly what was in my own heart!"

As it turned out, not only did Han begin speaking out in the Square
himself, but he publicly held up his I.D. card so that everyone could
see his name and work unit. "I felt I had crossed a line—as if the
Party's legitimate right to rule had been somehow shaken," he told me
of this experience. "As an ordinary worker, I naturally had serious
doubts about whether I could actually accomplish anything. But finally
I decided that if I could be just successful in setting up some kind of
organization for workers—even one that didn't survive—I would at
least have established some sort of precedent for people to take action
on their own in the future."

The result was the BAWF, which all workers with a Beijing residence certificate were entitled to join. Han hoped that the new union
would help guarantee workers the basic necessities of life, as well as
negotiate grievances between labor and management. From its first
modest public declarations when Han's group consisted of just a few
fellow activists with barely enough funds to buy paper for leaflets, the
federation evolved through the next few weeks into an organization
that claimed a membership of 20,000 "members" and a loudspeaker
station on the northwest corner of the Square from which they broadcast lists of workers' complaints, slogans, and instances of corruption
among officials. Needless to say, exhortations such as "Sweep Deng
Xiaoping from the historical stage!" did not escape the attention of the
Party.

After dispatching teams of workers to key street intersections to help
stop the advancing troops on the night of the massacre, Han waited in
the federation's new tent headquarters in the Square. During an interview with a Dutch journalist, Heleen Paalvast, Han said that he was

sure that the government would "take action" against him and his
fledgling union, but he insisted, "we are prepared to go to prison, and
we are not afraid to die." Han was well aware of the dangers that now
lay ahead. When union members had gotten together during the demonstrations to elect its leadership, Han had warned that the vote would
not only decide who would lead, but also "who would go to jail first,
and perhaps even who would be executed first." But he was also able
to derive a certain sense of satisfaction from the Martial Law Headquarters' condemnation of the federation as a "counterrevolutionary"
organization. "I knew we were in grave danger, but I also knew that
this condemnation meant that our activities had actually been successful."

So exhausted was Han from the previous weeks that even as troops
battled their way toward the Square on the night of June 3, he fell
asleep. By the time he woke up, the sound of automatic-weapons fire
was clearly audible. "I was struck dumb," he recalls. "For anyone
who had grown up in China thinking of the PLA as the people's savior
as we had, what was happening came as a total shock." Despite the
gravity of the situation, even as troops approached the very edge of the
Square, Han refused to leave the federation's tent. "Somehow I felt
that it was wrong, lacking in dignity, just to give up and leave at that
point."

Stubbornly holding his ground even as tracer bullets creased the
night sky overhead, Han left only when a group of concerned and very
agitated supporters physically carried him out of the Square. Unable to
return home to his wife for fear of arrest, for several days Han hid out
in friends' houses. When he realized that there would be no refuge for
the likes of him in Beijing he reluctantly decided to flee.

On the night of June 8, he got on his bike and headed out of the city.
His intention was to disappear into the Manchurian countryside and at
the same time try and educate himself about how ordinary people lived
in rural China. He hoped that he might someday write a summary of
his findings—something like Mao's 1927 "Report on an Investigation
of the Peasant Movement in Hunan"—that he could submit to the
government.

Only as he began pedaling on his solitary journey did Han realize
how deeply upset he really was by what had happened. In fact, he
remembers being suddenly overcome by a primal urge "to repay blood
debts with blood."

Once he was in the countryside, however, far more immediate
concerns quickly closed in on him. The first difficulty he encountered

was finding a place to sleep. Since he had not dared bring along any identification papers, which were a strict PSB requirement for registering at all hotels, managers would not rent him a room. The best he could do was to pay something to watermelon vendors or other small-time entrepreneurs along the roadside to sleep on the ground in their lean-tos. "It was a pretty crude existence, but listening to these guys describe their lives each night was fascinating. And living like that did give me a real sense of what the *laobaixing* (ordinary people) outside of Beijing had heard about the Tiananmen Square demonstrations."

After being on the road for several days, Han stopped at a small shop. A radio was playing and to his surprise he heard his name spoken over the airwaves. His was the first on the PSB's most wanted list of workers. "Never in my wildest imagination did I think I would end up as a most-wanted criminal and hear my name broadcast over national radio!" he said. Then something quite strange happened to him. "As I stood there listening, my mind went absolutely numb, and I suddenly began to feel as if everyone knew who I was and was staring at me."

In panic, Han retreated to some isolated woods, lay down on the grass, and in his typically methodical way, tried to analyze the situation now before him. "I knew that whatever I did, sooner or later I would be captured, and I didn't want to become known as someone who had run away. I also knew what Chinese police were like, and I figured that if I was arrested on the run, I would probably be killed." Han finally decided it was safest to turn himself in, but to do so while refusing to acknowledge any guilt.

On June 19 he arrived back in front of the PSB compound where ironically he had first seen student demonstrators beaten in 1986. What followed caught him completely off-balance. Far from being pounced on by police and taken into custody as an archcriminal, as he had imagined, Han found it difficult to get anyone to heed him. "I'm Han Dongfang, the Security Bureau is after me, and I would like to turn myself in," he told several helmeted guards at the gate. Each time, however, he was either ignored or shunted aside like a bothersome vagrant, a misapprehension that was perhaps understandable given his unlaundered and unbarbered appearance. He began wondering if he had not misjudged the seriousness of the government's accusations against him, and was just beginning to reconsider his plan to turn himself in, when a police official with whom he had negotiated the fate of three workers arrested at the end of May stepped out of the PSB compound. It was only when Han introduced himself and explained why he was there that it dawned on this police official who the bedraggled stranger before him was.

"I could see it slowly occurring to him that he had a very big fish on the line," Han remembered. The policeman solicitously ushered Han into a reception room, seated him on a sofa, and even served tea. Soon several higher-ups had congregated in the room, where, as is the custom with Chinese receiving someone who has just arrived after a long journey, they expressed sympathy for how *ku* (difficult) Han's trip through the countryside must have been.

"So, you've decided to surrender and acknowledge your guilt," one policeman finally said, dropping all pretense at cordiality.

"No. Those in the democracy movement are not guilty," Han replied. "I'm simply here to clarify what I did and what I did not do."

Shortly thereafter, Han was locked into a van and taken to the Paoju Lane Detention Center and held for *shourong shencha* (shelter and investigation), a vague category of administrative detention that permits the authorities to detain a suspect almost indefinitely without filing charges. He was thrown into a cell with two ordinary criminals whose task as "trusties" was to pry information out of him and guard against suicide. Soon he was transferred to solitary confinement. After several months he was moved again, this time to a twelve-by-twelve-foot-square cell with nothing but a sink and a toilet that contained twenty-eight inmates. In the summer heat with the only air and light coming through a single small window overhead, the cramped cell was unbearably claustrophobic and fetid. Without cots, the inmates were forced to sleep side by side on filthy and lice-infested quilts on the wet floor. Except during two daily meals, when inmates were fed vegetable soup and coarse cornmeal flatbread, Han and his fellow cellmates were forced to sit in rows without talking or moving. Anyone who disobeyed was denied his daily rations, and often beaten or shackled as well. Han's wife and sister still did not know if he was dead or alive. And even after they were finally informed of his detention, they were not allowed to write, much less visit.

Han's main activity during these first months of incarceration was being interrogated, sometimes all day and all night long. The intent of these exhausting sessions was to goad him into admitting his "guilt" and signing a "confession." "They told me that the only reason I was still alive was that I had turned myself in. Of course, I was scared, but the last thing I wanted to do was to let them know it."

Han stubbornly refused to make any admission of guilt. By demanding that he be given legal explanations and justifications for everything that was being done to him, he forced his captors into dueling with him in an intellectual struggle, the only field of combat where he was not completely disarmed.

"But to survive, I finally had to reconcile myself to the idea of dying," he explained. "And you know, I found that accepting death had a strangely calming effect. A person who imagines that he is hanging precariously between life and death will grab at any hope of staying alive. But once he resigns himself to the idea and knows that nothing worse than death can happen, everything changes. In fact, because I no longer felt any ambiguity or doubt about dying, I actually became quite arrogant, a trait that the guards really detested."

At one point Han's interrogators showed him a copy of a newspaper article about the three workers accused of torching the train in Shanghai who had been executed. "We blew out their brains, and we can blow out yours just as easily," they warned. "All it takes is a single bullet to put a hole in your head. We hope you'll be wise enough to cooperate before it's too late."

For months Han expected that he would either be put to death or would die from mistreatment. The thought that he might perish in prison, where his death would have no political effect, bothered him deeply. "If you're killed demonstrating in the Square, your death has some meaning because it at least serves as a public lesson. But if you die of neglect or torture, forgotten in prison, so that authorities can just say you got sick and passed away. . . . What value is there in a death like that?"

Nevertheless, Han continued to infuriate his interrogators by refusing to evince any sign of contrition, which they considered essential to a detainee's "rehabilitation." Unable to break Han's stubborn will, prison officials moved to break down his physical resistance. When he developed an enigmatic but agonizing stomach condition, they dismissed his symptoms as fake and refused to provide him with medical treatment. When they belatedly responded to his complaints, they sent him for involuntary acupuncture, where he was forced to endure a "treatment" that felt like a form of torture. One of his hands was pierced with an enormous needle that caused him excruciating pain. He was then thrown into a *xiaohao* (punishment cell), a standard feature in Chinese prisons. But far from becoming more willing to confess, Han began a hunger strike in protest. The reponse of the Paoju warden was to order prison trusties to restrain Han while a tube was rammed down his nose and he was force-fed. Unfortunately, the tube became lodged in his trachea, and when an attempt was made to pump liquid nourishment into his stomach, he nearly suffocated.

One mistake Han had made was to tell his guards of his deep fear of becoming sick. Although Han's stomach ailment showed no signs of being infectious, he was soon transferred to a prison wing where inmates plagued by contagious diseases, including tuberculosis, were confined. Here Han languished for four bitterly cold winter months, so sick that he frequently had to be put on intravenous fluids.

Not until March 1990 when charges of having engaged in counter-revolutionary activity were finally preferred against him was Han transferred. His next stop was the Banbuqiao Detention Center, the prison where Democracy Wall activist Wei Jingsheng had been held a decade before. According to Han, internment in Banbuqiao felt "like entering the gates of hell." It was not long before he began running high fevers, having fits of violent coughing, and experiencing episodes of severe lung congestion. Over the next nine months Han's physical condition worsened steadily. When he was again moved—this time to China's most infamous place of detention, Qincheng Prison outside of Beijing—Han was so weak that he could hardly walk or speak. Depite his almost complete incapacitation, he was shackled to a bed with leg irons. Worse still, no medical diagnosis of his respiratory condition had been made.

There was, however, one cryptic bright spot. "In spite of my physical condition, I began to feel a little more hopeful because I surmised that since I had survived this long, I was probably not going to be executed. But on the other hand, I knew that while the government might release students to mollify world opinion, they would not readily release a worker, especially one who had been the head of an upstart trade union. So at that point I imagined that I would still probably get fifteen years."

Although Chinese authorities probably looked upon Han's deteriorating physical condition as just punishment for his unrepentant attitude, by the beginning of 1991 his illnesses started to become a public relations problem. Because of the lobbying efforts that human rights groups such as Asia Watch and Amnesty International had launched on Han's behalf, his case was being closely watched by certain members of the U.S. Congress calling for conditions on renewal of China's much-desired most-favored-nation (MFN) trade status. With Han unable to walk, it was almost impossible for the Chinese government to hold a show trial and wrap up his case.

By April 1991, Han's health had so deteriorated that the prison officials were forced to transfer him again, this time to Military Hospital No. 261. "When I entered the hospital, I was in such bad shape that the nurses and doctors didn't think I would survive more than two or three more days," Han said. "When I begged to be able to see my family one more time before I died, there was one kindhearted guard who promised to make a report to his superiors."

The last thing Chinese officials wanted at that moment was for "China's Lech Walesa" to die in jail after two years of illegal detention. On April 10 his wife and his sister were stunned when a Qincheng Prison official showed up at their home to inform them that they could visit Han. What impressed them as so strange about this sudden change of heart was the urgency with which, after twenty-one months of refusing all visitation rights, officials now pressed for a reunion. It was not until the next day when the two women arrived at the hospital and saw Han's emaciated figure lying in an isolation ward with an IV drip dangling overhead that they understood what had brought about this sudden change in attitude. Han was near death. He was barely able to move, and could speak only in whispers.

As it happened, the following week former U.S. President Jimmy Carter arrived in China, and in a speech before the Beijing Foreign Affairs College called for the release of several specific political prisoners, including Wei Jingsheng, Wang Juntao, Chen Ziming, Lobsang Tenzing (a Tibetan student), and Han. Han's wife and sister were subsequently allowed another visit, and were gratified to find that not only was Han responding to hospital care, but a diagnosis had finally been made. Bizarre as it sounded, he was listed as having Legionnaires' disease. Then on April 28, 1991, prison authorities surprised Han's wife by announcing that after almost two years of waiting, her husband was being released on a medical discharge. Even though such expenses were far beyond their meager means, his family was forced to sign a document agreeing to cover all future medical bills.

Alarmed by his continuing high fevers, fits of uncontrollable coughing, and gravely diminished physical strength, and with virtually no financial means, Han's family turned abroad in desperation. Physicians for Human Rights and Asia Watch arranged to have Dr. David Fedson of the University of Virginia Medical Center fly to Beijing to treat Han. Since Han had been forbidden to meet with all foreigners, Fedson was forced to work through an elaborate network of covert go-betweens and friendly Chinese doctors before he could make a diagnosis. As it turned out, Han had tuberculosis. "It was a classic case of TB, one that even a second-year medical student should have been able to diagnose,'' said Fedson.

It was not until November 1991, when U.S. Secretary of State James Baker visited Beijing and took up Han's case with counterparts in the Foreign Ministry that the Chinese government finally agreed to drop charges against him and, in principle, allow him and his wife to go abroad. After Baker's return to Washington, however, months passed and still Han's passport failed to materialize. In the meanwhile, he was slowly regaining his strength, and in his dogged way, he once again began making plans to take up the cudgel for Chinese workers.

By March 1992 as the National People's Congress was considering a new draft of China's labor law (which Han opposed because it contained no provisions for workers to set up their own independent unions), he filed for permission to hold a one-man demonstration. His application was carefully designed to comply with all guidelines of China's new "Law on Assemblies, Marches, and Demonstrations," which had been hastily promulgated in the wake of the 1989 protest movement to make it bureaucratically impossible for anyone to gain legal permission to hold a street demonstration. "In view of the [Party-run] All-China Federation of Trade Unions' proven inability to effectively protect the vital interests of the working masses," Han wrote in his application, "I request that the National People's Congress add a clause to the new Trade Union Law permitting workers to freely organize and choose their own unions." Where he was required to describe the "form" that his proposed demonstration would take, Han glibly wrote, "Myself riding a bicycle." Han's plan was to go by bike (with "eye-catching placards attached to it to differentiate it from other vehicles") from his house in Xibiaobei Hutong to the Beijing Railway Bureau (the parent organization of his own work unit), and then to the Square itself. Here he proposed to circle the Great Hall in a clockwise direction so that pedestrians would be able to read the placards on his bike and understand the "aims of the demonstration." His application assured authorities that there would be "no shouting of slogans or use of amplification equipment."

The idea that a lone bicycle rider, who had just been released after almost two years in prison, whose lungs were ravaged with tuberculosis, and who had absolutely no money or organization behind him, might pose a threat to the state by riding through the streets with a couple of signs tied to his bike seemed absurd. Han was like the proverbial mouse who frightens the elephant, and in this case, the elephant was not going to take any chances. Han's application was summarily, if comically, rejected on the grounds that under the new law, a single person did not qualify as a "demonstration." When, tongue in cheek, Han inquired as to whether his application might be accepted if it called for more people, the authorities replied that they might "accept" the application, but that they still would not give permission for the demonstration unless he could somehow guarantee that no one would "take notice" of it.

Undeterred, Han next infuriated the PSB by ignoring their order against meeting with foreigners by giving a series of candid interviews to members of the overseas press corps. On April 16, 1992, after recounting his prison travails to the *New York Times,* an article appeared on the front page of the paper along with a smiling photo of Han decked out in a tweed jacket and necktie. "If the law allows me to do something, I'll do it," Han was quoted as saying. "If it doesn't allow me to do it, then I'll press for a new law. . . . Sure, there'll be plenty of misery ahead, but that's OK. It's bearable."

Indeed, more misery was not long in arriving. A month after Han's interview, Chinese authorities delivered a notice evicting him from his family's shabby state-owned courtyard house. Since his mother, to whom the house had been assigned, had recently died, the government now felt entitled to repossess it. Despite a lingering high fever, Han appeared at the Dongcheng District People's Court on May 14 to attend a hearing on the matter. When it became evident that officials were not about to offer any dispensation, Han informed them that he had retained an attorney. When court officials derided the idea of such counsel as nothing more than "dog farts," Han indignantly got up to leave. When court bailiffs moved to restrain him, a scuffle broke out. Before the brouhaha was over, Han had been seized, kicked, beaten, jabbed with an electric prod, handcuffed, and thrown back into a holding cell for several hours.

"This incident was something that we do not like to see," said the director of the court, Jia Zhiyun, after news of the incident was picked up by foreign media outlets. Nevertheless, Chinese officials insisted that the eviction of the family was "legitimate" and that "Han should take blame for the entire episode."

By this time, outside pressure on the Chinese government had grown to a point where officials felt compelled, perhaps even relieved, to allow this obstreperous labor organizer and his wife to leave the country. After almost two years in prison and nine months of waiting, Han was finally issued a passport, and in August 1992, with Han's wife six

months pregnant, they boarded a plane. But no sooner had he undergone an operation on his prison-infected lungs in New York than Han
announced that as soon as he recovered he would return to China and
continue to work toward the establishment of an independent labor
union.

18

Internment in Limbo

On the morning of June 4, 1989, Princeton University professor
Perry Link, deeply concerned that his friends astrophysicist Fang Lizhi
and his physicist wife Li Shuxian might be arrested, had hurried by
bicycle through the streets of Beijing to the Fangs' apartment. Although he found Fang and Li very agitated, Link was relieved to learn
that they were safe. However, fearing that they might be picked up at
any moment, before he left, Link set up an emergency telephone code
in case something suddenly happened. If Li phoned Link and said,
"Bring your children over to play," Link was to return to the apartment as quickly as possible.

At about 5 P.M. the call came. Friends with close connections to the
central leadership had called Fang to alert him that the Party had just
issued a classified directive ordering a wave of arrests. "Some of those
who called were rather important personages," Fang said. "And they
all warned us that we were in great danger."

After a hasty discussion, Fang, Li, and their son Fang Zhe agreed to
leave with Link for the Shangri-La Hotel, where CBS News had rented
an entire floor to cover Gorbachev's visit and then stayed on to cover
the ensuing protest movement. Link hoped that if his friends were
lodged in a joint-venture hotel with access to members of the American
press, the Chinese government would be less inclined to intrude and
arrest them.

When Link returned to the hotel the next morning, Fang and Li had decided that the situation was so unstable that they should risk the trip across the embattled city and seek refuge in the American embassy. By taking back streets, they managed to reach the diplomatic quarter in the Jianguomenwai district without incident. Once at the embassy, however, they had to get past the PLA soldiers guarding the main gate. Link jumped out, flashed his American passport, and succeeded in distracting the guards with his excellent Chinese long enough to allow the Fangs to slip into the compound.

Link and the Fangs were immediately ushered into a meeting with Ray Burghardt, the deputy chief of mission, and McKinney Russell from the embassy's press and cultural section. During the discussions everyone's state of alarm was raised when Chinese troops outside suddenly began firing their weapons in the street. "We asked if we could stay until things quieted down, hoping that in one or two days, when the government had become more rational and order had been restored, we could come out again," said Fang. "Above all, we told them that we did not want our presence in the embassy made known to the Chinese government."

The Americans indicated it would be possible to obtain "temporary refuge" if the Fangs were willing to officially request it, but that hidden eavesdropping devices throughout the embassy had probably already alerted Chinese authorities to what was happening. All agreed that the Fangs would be pilloried as traitors, the United States denounced for interfering in China's internal affairs, and the Chinese democracy movement impugned as being covertly in league with "hostile foreign forces."

"Finally, Fang turned to me, eyebrows lifted high as if to suggest, 'I guess there's no choice,' and said, 'We'd better not stay. Let's go,' " Link later wrote. "His casual manner belied the palpable danger to him of simply walking back out on the street. But that is what he did."

Since the Fangs were still fearful of returning to their apartment, Link succeeded in borrowing a room at the nearby Jianguo Hotel that his former classmate, *Washington Post* reporter Jay Mathews, was not then using. At about 11 P.M. the phone rang. A male voice speaking in English introduced himself to Fang by saying that he was "one of the two people you met with this afternoon," and then announced that he wished to come over immediately to speak with them in person.

A short while later there was a knock on the door and Russell and Burghardt stepped inside. They told the Fangs that they had been in touch with Washington, and had been authorized to escort the family in a bulletproof car back to the embassy as the "personal guests" of the president. They accepted. Although it was difficult to predict how China's political situation would unfold, the Fangs still hoped that things would settle down enough to allow them to leave the embassy in a few days. Unfortunately, the secret of their whereabouts was revealed on June 6 when White House press spokesman Marlin Fitzwater announced that Fang and Li had formally requested sanctuary. The following day President Bush himself alluded to the couple in a way that made it difficult to determine whether he was trying to justify his decision to offer them shelter or capitalize on his largesse at a time when he was coming under greater fire for not having demonstrated American displeasure over the Chinese crackdown more forcefully.

When Fang heard about these announcements in Washington, he wanted to leave the embassy, before an official Chinese Foreign Ministry protest could be issued. Li begged her husband to stay. And embassy officials, worried that their arrest would make it appear as if the United States had put the couple out in the cold, also urged them to stay. Eventually, Fang relented.

As expected, an angry protest charging the United States with "wanton interference in China's internal affairs" and with violating "both international law and the relevant laws of China" soon followed. For a week Fang and Li waited anxiously inside the embassy. On June 12, the Ministry of Public Security issued warrants for their arrest on charges of "counterrevolutionary propaganda and incitement." Though Fang had not gone near the Square during the demonstrations, he was branded a "traitor" and vilified as one of the "black hands" behind the "counterrevolutionary rebellion." A commentary in the *People's Daily* scorned him for "degrading his position to that of a beggar" by "hiding himself" in the American embassy, while the *Beijing Daily* called him "scum" for "taking refuge under the protective wings of foreigners."

So while thousands of other political activists were trying to escape China or being jailed, Fang and Li found themselves neither imprisoned nor free, neither inside China nor out, but suspended in a twilight zone. As one wag put it, they were in "the five-star wing of the Chinese gulag."

Over the previous few years my wife and I had become good friends of the Fangs, and we had just seen them on a picnic to the Ming Tombs before the student hunger strike began that May. Naturally, we watched with concern as their confinement in the American embassy stretched on into fall. Because the State Department had not allowed anyone to visit them, they seemed to have fallen off the edge of the world. That

October, however, the board of the Robert F. Kennedy Memorial Center for Human Rights decided to make Fang the 1989 recipient of the center's annual award. Since Fang's quarantine prevented the Kennedys from meeting or speaking with him, they asked me if I would go to Beijing and try to see him.

The rationale that the State Department and American Ambassador James Lilley had used for isolating Fang and Li from visitors was twofold: They feared disclosing their hiding place in the embassy and wanted to avoid complicating the sensitive negotiations being conducted with the Chinese to secure their release. U.S. diplomats in Washington argued that if Fang began using the U.S. embassy as a platform for making controversial public statements, hard-liners in the Chinese government would seize upon on such activity as an excuse to delay his release. But since a dissident voice speaking out from the sanctuary of the American embassy would certainly also have hampered the process of reestablishing normal Sino-U.S. relations, a goal that lay at the heart of the president's policy toward China of "constructive engagement," critics suspected that the Bush administration also had a vested interest in keeping Fang silent. The Kennedy family hoped I could find out if Fang shared the State Department's concerns about the publicity the award would create, or whether he would welcome the chance it would afford him to publicize his case.

I was not optimistic about getting in to see Fang. An initial conversation with Richard Solomon, assistant secretary of state for East Asian and Pacific affairs, was not very encouraging. But when I spoke to him once more just before leaving, he told me that he had notified Ambassador Lilley and that when I arrived in Beijing, I should wait in my hotel room for a phone call.

No sooner had I set my suitcase down inside my room at the Palace Hotel than the phone rang. Offering no salutation and giving no name, a voice said, "I am waiting for you downstairs by the marble column just inside the front entrance." Then the line went dead.

I took the elevator down to the lobby, where I immediately spotted a young Caucasian man in a dark suit standing near the designated column. As I approached, he glanced furtively around before proffering his hand. Then, without saying a word, he ushered me through the revolving door and out into the chilly fall night. Only after we were halfway down one of the dark *hutong* that surround the hotel did this mysterious figure introduce himself as the Foreign Service officer (although he was probably from the CIA) to whom Ambassador Lilley had assigned the task of looking after the Fangs. Clements, as I shall call him, told me that besides the ambassador and himself, who brought the Fangs all their necessities, no one else had been allowed in to visit them. In fact, no one else among the embassy staff even knew where they were sequestered.

"I don't know whether you'll actually be able to see him," Clements whispered, evidently reluctant even to mention Fang's name out loud. He said that U.S. diplomats were fearful that if the couple's whereabouts within the three sprawling compounds of the American legation became known, xenophobic Chinese hard-liners might be tempted to storm the embassy and seize them by force. Given that Beijing was still under martial law and that each of the American embassy compounds was surrounded by armed soldiers, the idea of such intervention was not entirely fanciful. Hard-line General Wang Zhen, who had been intimately involved in the assault on the Square, was even reported to have made such threats. Nonetheless, Clements told me that Ambassador Lilley wanted to meet with me at the embassy the next morning at 10 A.M.

To avoid being followed to the embassy, I left my hotel the next morning on a rented bicycle, transferred to a taxi halfway there, and then walked the final few blocks through a crowded street market. I had absolutely no idea whether or not my presence in China had been noticed by the authorities, but as far as I could tell, I had not been tailed by the PSB. When I arrived at the embassy (two of its compounds contain offices; the third is the ambassadorial residence), I found it surrounded by unsmiling Chinese soldiers armed with assault rifles. As I approached the embassy gate, one of the soldiers menacingly clicked the magazine of his weapon.

No sooner had I entered Lilley's inner office than he rose from his desk and gestured for me to follow him. Opening a small door in the wall behind his desk, he led me into a cavernous, windowless room in which there was a smaller, freestanding, clear-plastic-walled room glowing in the dark. This was the embassy's bugproof and soundproof safe room. As we approached the door, Clements reached over and threw a switch, activating a noise-making ventilator fan. It was not until we were safely locked inside the transparent inner chamber that Lilley finally greeted me.

James Lilley is a tall, gray-haired man in his early sixties who grew up in China where his father worked for Standard Oil in Qingdao and in Tianjin. He returned to China in 1974 to serve as the CIA station chief during George Bush's tenure as head of the U.S. Liaison Mission a few years before formal diplomatic relations were established. Since then he had served in Taiwan as chief of the U.S. unofficial mission there and then as ambassador to Korea. He arrived back in China during the spring of 1989 just as the protest movement was beginning.

Having gotten to know Lilley during previous trips to the Far East, and having corresponded with him during the preceding months, I knew that he had become friendly with his new guests and was dedicated to seeking their release as soon as possible. However, despite his obvious outrage over the Chinese government's brutality on June 4 and their belligerent and xenophobic posturing since, he remained wary of taking provocative steps that might antagonize officials and jeopardize current U.S. policy or his relationship to President Bush. It was this latter concern that made him uneasy with the Kennedy award. Not only would it remind people of Fang's continued presence in the embassy, but would invite the question: Why had he not been visited or spoken out earlier? After all, Fang was one of the few dissidents still in China who was still able to say what he wished, and the fact that he had not done so struck some critics as a sign of faintheartedness. Because it was not in the interest of either side to have him speaking out at the moment, Fang's silence in the American embassy could be construed as serving both Chinese and U.S. purposes.

When I asked Lilley what my prospects were for a visit, he pursed his lips together and fell silent. "Does anyone else here know that you are in Beijing?" he finally asked. "Do you have any reason to believe that you were followed here?" I told him that I didn't think so. Lilley pensively twiddled a pencil in one hand. Then, turning to Clements, who had been jotting down notes as we talked, he asked, "Does Fang want to see Orville?"

"Yes, he does," Clements replied.

"Why don't you drop by the house for an informal dinner tonight and we can chat some more then," he said noncommittally.

A little before seven that night, Clements picked me up in his car at a street corner where we had agreed to meet. I was surprised to find that even in a moving vehicle he did not feel free to talk openly, telling me that it was quite possible for the PSB to bug an embassy car. At the ambassadorial residence there were more soldiers, but with Clements's diplomatic badge, we were not challenged. Since Lilley's wife was abroad, the two of us sat down alone for dinner. As we ate, Lilley said nothing about Fang.

After dinner we retired to the library for coffee and to watch a CNN satellite newscast. Quite unexpectedly, we found ourselves looking at a news report about a raid that radical Korean students had just launched on the American ambassador's residence in Seoul—the very house Lilley had lived in as ambassador to Korea prior to being posted in Beijing. The news served as an unnerving reminder of how defenseless an embassy is against mob attack.

When the kitchen staff finally bid Lilley goodnight and still he had not said anything about Fang, I was on the verge of taking my leave when he suddenly stood up, put on a parka, and with the same hand gesture he had used to summon me into the safe room at his office, motioned to me to follow him. I trailed him through the kitchen, down a flight of back stairs, and out across a small courtyard. Upon reaching a low-lying building against the north wall of the compound, Lilley knocked softly on a door. It opened, and I saw Clements waiting in the shadows. Leading me by the sleeve through the darkness like a blind man, he tapped on an inside door in what seemed to be a code. I heard a latch click, saw a crack of dim light emerge from the darkness before us as the door opened, and then suddenly, there were Fang Lizhi and Li Shuxian.

After the door was shut, we greeted each other in the shadowy half-light of their hiding place. Fang looked much smaller than I remembered him. Given to wearing zip-up windbreakers and nondescript trousers, he is a short, unathletic man with a shock of dark hair that falls over his brow toward a pair of owlish, horn-rimmed glasses. He does have one flamboyant feature, however, and that is a disarming, whinnying laugh. Now his hair was much longer and his clothes were baggy and rumpled, giving him the air of a hibernating animal just awakened from brumal slumber. Yet in his characteristic way he was smiling broadly. Li, who looked more haggard and gray, stood beside him, grinning. It was the first time in almost five months that either had met with an outsider.

We sat together in the minuscule room that now served as his office. When I asked him how he was, Fang sighed. The first weeks of their ordeal, especially the first few days, had been tense and frightening, he said. They had heard stories about Cardinal Joseph Mindszenty, the dissident cleric who spent fifteen years confined to the American embassy in Budapest, and about the group of Pentecostals whose request for refuge left them confined in the basement of the American embassy in Moscow for five years. "We haven't imagined that our time here will be very short," Fang whispered, intimating that he feared they might have to stay until the older generation of leaders died off. "It couldn't be longer than that!" Fang said trying to laugh. "Nonetheless, we feel well and have been working hard."

Their hiding place consisted of a few tiny rooms that had comprised part of a clinic. The windows had been covered up so that no one could see in or out, special doors had been hung to deaden sound, and the entire complex had been wired with a security system that included alarm buttons located beside the places where Fang and Li worked and slept. Cramped and claustrophobic though they were, compared with the cells in which many other political prisoners were being held, their quarters were positively luxurious. Actually, few people could have been better equipped for the rigors of such a monastic existence than Fang. As a theoretical astrophysicist with an interest in history and politics, Fang possessed precisely the sort of intellectual resources that enable a person to put slack time to good use. In fact, he had been busy keeping abreast of world events, including the status of the overseas Chinese democracy movement and the protest movements that had been shaking Eastern Europe. In the absence of visitors, his lifelines to the outside were the books, newspapers, magazines, and scholarly journals that he received through the embassy's diplomatic mail system. Fang seemed to take particular delight in the small library that had been accumulating on a set of shelves beside his desk. But his most important possession was a Chinese-English word processor, which enabled him to write scientific articles, work on his memoirs, and correspond with friends and colleagues abroad.

To support this Anne Frank–like existence, there were myriad behind-the-scenes details that had to be taken care of. Most of these tasks fell to Clements. Everything that was brought in to them, including food, clothing, mail, and reading material, had to be apportioned into small packets and then stuffed into Clements's briefcase so that neither soldiers at the gate nor Chinese embassy employees—most of whom were assumed to be working for their government—would become suspicious, much less deduce where Fang and Li were secreted. Likewise, all the garbage and wastepaper the couple generated had to be surreptitiously carried out and disposed of, which was no small feat considering the mass of effluvial pulp generated by a man given to reading as much as Fang Lizhi. When the Fangs needed new clothing, the problem was solved with old-fashioned American ingenuity—the Sears mail-order catalogue. Cooking was accomplished with the help of a microwave oven that Fang called his "high-tech Chinese restaurant." Fang had humorously nicknamed his new living quarters the "black hole." "I am an astrophysicist who cannot see the stars," he remarked with an ironic laugh.

As we talked, it became apparent that what constrained Fang from publicly speaking out against his government's repressive policies was both a concern over the effect such statements would have on the negotiations for his release and the possibility of upsetting his American hosts. Like a typical Confucian *junzi*, or gentleman, Fang did not wish to seem ungrateful by doing anything that might embarrass Lilley. But when I mentioned the topic of the Kennedy award, Fang expressed not only a keen desire to accept it, but a willingness to write a speech that could be read publicly during the televised award presentation ceremony.

Before I knew it, it was after eleven o'clock, and Clements was warning that if we left too late, the guards outside the residence might become suspicious. For a brief instant we had all managed to forget where we were. But taking his cue without further ado, Fang stood up and disarmed the security system. In whispers the three of us bid each other good-bye, and I slipped back out the door of the clinic. Moments later I was out on the street where the soldiers in full battle gear stretched all the way around the compound. From the inside the compound wall had seemed massive and tall. But as I looked at it now from the outside it seemed frighteningly insubstantial. It would be almost eight more months before the Chinese government would allow Fang and Li to pass out onto this same street.

I continued to correspond with Fang via the diplomatic pouch for the next seven months. By the spring of 1990 moderate Chinese leaders were worried enough about China's MFN status to have coaxed out a few reciprocal gestures from their government as repayment to President Bush for his concessionary diplomatic stance. That June, President Bush announced that he would again unconditionally renew China's MFN status. As Congress moved to countermand the president's decision, Lilley found himself invited to lunch at the Chinese Foreign Ministry, which led to the reopening of negotiations over Fang and Li's release. When the two sides finally sat down together, Lilley's Chinese counterparts asked for reassurances that the president would support China's MFN status. Lilley countered by demanding Fang's release and the lifting of martial law.

There was one problem, however. If after having so stridently vilified Fang, the Chinese government was going to release him, Party leaders required some face-saving device allowing them to justify their reversal. As it happened, a short time before, Fang had reported experiencing some minor heart palpitations. Although it turned out that they were not due to any serious medical problem—Fang later blamed the chest pains on "too much coffee"—Lilley raised them during his negotiations. Such information provided the Chinese with exactly the kind of pretext they needed. Now they could claim that they were releasing Fang as a humanitarian gesture so that he could go abroad for medical treatment.

On June 23, 1990, Fang and Li were flown to England, where Fang had been offered a position as a Royal Society Guest Professor at the University of Cambridge's Institute of Astronomy. After a bizarre year in limbo Fang and Li joined those hundreds of other Chinese political dissidents who had left home to go into exile.

19

Escape

"Yeah, I think I am quite different," declared Wu'er Kaixi, mixing indifference and satisfaction with a shrug when I spoke with him in Boston in August 1989 just after his arrival in the United States. "I come from a younger generation that didn't experience all the political terror that our parents did, and then I'm not Han Chinese, but Uighur."

The Turkic Uighurs are a Muslim minority from China's western-most province of Xinjiang. Known in Uighur as Uerkesh Daolet, Wu'er Kaixi's family came from the desert capital Ürümqi, and moved to Beijing when Wu'er's father, a mid-ranking Communist Party cadre, was posted to the capital at the Minorities Institute in the late 1970s. Since Wu'er's father was both an official and a Uighur, the members of his family were treated with that special deference reserved for select representatives of minority groups who serve as window dress-ing for the Party's efforts to build the appearance of "socialist soli-darity" between central China and its non-Han regions. In Beijing, Wu'er was sent to one of the special "experimental" schools reserved for the children of the Party elite that soon became incubators for the kind of privileged youthful rebelliousness that would erupt all over urban China during the late 1980s.

"As a young boy, I was always surrounded by people who admired me, doted on me, even spoiled me," Wu'er said. "Because of my father's position, I was also automatically deferred to by teachers and other kids at school, so I got accustomed to the feeling of leading.''

While it is true that parental Party rank played just as important a role in establishing a child's social status in Communist China as official rank had in the imperial system of traditional China, Wu'er also showed natural leadership abilities at an early age. In almost everything he did, he was ambitious, assertive, and self-assured, often to the point of appearing flamboyantly confrontational. Indeed, as a teenager, he often chafed against authority figures whom he considered arbitrary or unjust. By age fifteen this antiauthoritarian bent had already led him into a series of bitter confrontations with his disciplinarian father that came to a head in 1984 when his parents were reassigned back to Xinjiang and Wu'er was uprooted from his school, his circle of friends, and the relatively sophisticated world he had come to enjoy in Beijing.

"Leaving Beijing made me feel that I was falling from grace,'' he recalled. "From then on, my problems were almost continuous. First, I fought with my parents over whether as a Uighur I could date a Han Chinese girl with whom I had fallen in love. And then, to make matters worse, I got kicked out of school.'' Looking back on it, Wu'er admitted that in many ways his expulsion was a warm-up act for the events that would later overtake him in Tiananmen Square.

It was as a sixteen-year-old high-school student in Ürümqi that Wu'er first discovered his interest in student activities and his talent for political organization. He also discovered what he impishly calls his interest in ''making trouble.''

"We had an election at school for student union president. Since I liked one of the candidates very much, I asked him if he would let me help him manage his campaign. He agreed, and we ended up winning ninety-five percent of the vote!''

In appreciation, the victorious new president appointed Wu'er to run the school paper. Having become interested in literature and writing in Beijing, Wu'er set out to transform the paper from a mouthpiece of the school administration into an unpredictable independent voice.

"School papers were usually just mimeographed throwaways, but we started having ours printed with movable lead type like a real newspaper,'' he told me with evident pride. ''We started drumming up advertising and expanded it into an eight-page weekly, and before long we were making money. Then we even started paying our staff and began writing some pretty bold articles!'' He paused for a moment. "You have to remember that in the mid-1980s the idea of a student paper making money and publishing critical articles was a very . . . well, a very modern one—unheard of in China!''

Wu'er described an editorial that he himself had written criticizing a teacher who had beaten a female student during a disciplinary action. ''The eye of the student who had been beaten was seriously injured, and my editorial criticized the lack of respect for human dignity that this teacher had shown. Because of its antiauthoritarian tone, it created quite a stir.''

Because Wu'er's editorial was viewed as a challenge to the faculty as a whole, it led to his expulsion. It was only through his father's Party connections that he was able to gain admittance to another high school where he did well enough to finally gain admission to Beishida.

After moving back to the capital, like many other bright young members of his generation, Wu'er was quickly swept up in the intellectual subculture that was emerging as a result of Deng's reforms. Because they felt that China's official culture was a ''kind of poison,'' Wu'er and his classmates reached out to embrace almost any new idea or trend, from so-called ''misty poetry'' and pop music to Western fashions and libertine sexual mores. Their willingness to explore intellectually and artistically—even when doing so put them at odds with official Party culture—quickly became the hallmark of their generation. Whereas their parents had come of age in the 1960s and 1970s, when the high tide of Maoism had made such experimentation unthinkable, Wu'er and his cohorts were growing up during a period in which, for the first time in the history of the People's Republic, it was possible to defect from at least part of collective life and to focus on the self without risking serious reprisals. Wu'er himself spent many hours alone composing verse and writing songs, and at one point even aspired to become a rock singer. What he enjoyed about poetry and music, he explained, was that by emphasizing ''the validity of individual feelings,'' they helped young people create an oasis where individualism and personal creativity could prevail over the Party's mind-numbing version of culture.

''When something this appealing appears in the midst of such a cultural desert, you of course hold on to it for dear life,'' Wu'er told me. ''The shame of it is that most people in Chinese politics don't have any artistic sense at all. To be a really successful politician, in my view one must have *some* artistic side. But the only Chinese leader who ever qualified in this sense is Mao. He was an autocrat, but he did have artistic sensibilities. So while we may dislike him, we must also respect him. What is so twisted is that with more than a billion people, China is today led by men like Li Peng.''

What seemed to draw Wu'er toward Beijing's proto-bohemian life was not so much a desire to become an artist as the fact that, in the absence of any political opposition, the antiestablishment bent of this subculture provided some outlet for his own antiauthoritarian impulses. And when Hu Yaobang died and young Chinese began taking to the streets in hopes of creating a political alternative, it was not long before Wu'er emerged as a leader on the campus of his university.

On the night of April 17 thousands of Beishida students gathered for a spontaneous rally at the center of their campus. Nobody quite knew what the meeting was meant to accomplish, but everyone was charged with the same urge to memorialize Hu's death. However, because university officials were posted nearby and plainclothes security police were taping everything with video cameras, no students dared come forward to lead.

''Everyone wanted something to happen, but because we all knew how dangerous it would be to step forward, everyone just milled around, grousing about the fact that no one dared stand up,'' Wu'er later recalled. Then Wu'er himself did something that stunned everyone. Not only did he step forward and address the crowd, but the first thing he said was, ''Since we all know there are people here tonight who will immediately want to find out the name and identity of any student who dares speak out, I'm going to save them some time and effort. My name is Wu'er Kaixi. I am a Beishida education management student in the entering class of 1988 and I live in dorm room no. 339.''

As with Han Dongfang when he first spoke in the Square, Wu'er's declaration was an attempt to step beyond the psychological intimidation that the government had used so successfully for decades to silence students and intellectuals. Of course, Wu'er's speech also helped galvanize Beishida into playing a key role in what would become the largest student movement in China's history.

Two days later Wu'er was back in the middle of the action when he again stepped forward and succeeded in persuading an unruly crowd in front of Xinhuamen Gate to sit down and maintain order. During the next month he played a public role in almost every aspect of the growing movement. He was elected president of the Beishida Autonomous Student Union and soon thereafter also became president of the entire Beijing Autonomous Student Federation. But it was his role in the hunger strike and his dramatic confrontation with Li Peng that conferred an almost legendary status on him.

By then he had become convinced that the student movement would end in catastrophe if protesters did not withdraw from the Square. His inability to persuade hunger strikers to leave led to his removal from the leadership. Nonetheless, Wu'er returned to the Square on the night of June 3. When troops began mustering for a final assault on the Monument, Wu'er was rushed to safety in the back of an ambulance with several gravely wounded victims. But no sooner had they started to leave, than a group of hysterical students carrying yet another wounded student flagged them down. "Even though the ambulance was already carrying four other people, the doctors and nurses crammed this guy into the back with me [so that] he lay almost right on top of me," Wu'er remembered. "He was bloody all over, with brains and blood coming out of his head. . . . I didn't know whether the student was dead or alive."

After arriving at the hospital, Wu'er discovered that two of his fellow passengers had died. "I will never forget that I left Tiananmen Square holding on to a dead body," he recalled grimly.

For several days after the massacre, Wu'er hid out in a succession of friends' houses. As the crackdown intensified and it became obvious that sooner or later he would be found and arrested, he and his nineteen-year-old girlfriend, Liu Yan, set off like so many others on a cross-country trek to Canton in hopes of escaping to Hong Kong. Because almost everyone in China had seen Wu'er during his televised contretemps with Li Peng, he was in constant danger of being recognized. To make matters worse, halfway through their trip south, the PSB released its "21 Most Wanted List" and Wu'er's picture was again televised throughout the country. Living in constant fear of being recognized, he and Liu never stayed in one place for more than a night, and wherever possible allowed a friend who had agreed to accompany them to rent hotel rooms, book train and bus tickets, buy food and drink, and contact sympathizers for them along the way.

Despite the government dragnet and several close calls when police moved in on places from which they had just departed, Wu'er and Liu finally reached the Zhuhai Special Economic Zone across the border from the Portuguese territory of Macao. There they succeeded in making contact with the "underground railway"—an informal network of Chinese who had volunteered to secretly help protesters escape. At this point their go-between returned to Beijing, where he was soon arrested and sentenced to four years in prison.

In Zhuhai, Wu'er and Liu were hidden in a safe house while members of the underground completed arrangements for their escape. The government was well aware that many of those on its most wanted lists were in the Canton area and trying to make it across the frontier. As a result, border patrols had been stepped up on both land and sea, making efforts to escape extremely risky.

After they had waited almost a week, a contact finally appeared with a car, drove them out of the city, and left them at an isolated oyster farm on the coast. They were told that if things went according to plan, at 7:50 P.M. they could expect two long flashes of light on the water, toward which they were to swim. A high-powered speedboat from Hong Kong was to be awaiting them. They were warned that if no signal appeared, they were on their own. Wu'er did not need to be told that if the rescue boat failed to appear, arrest was a foregone conclusion.

It was a moonless night as they sat down on the bank to wait for the providential flashes of light to blink out of the inky darkness. After two months of the protest movement, the massacre, and several weeks of travel and dodging the police, Wu'er and Liu were both bone-weary. "I had no idea where we were," Wu'er remembered. "All that I knew was that we were somewhere along the coast by a clump of trees."

By eight o'clock, they had seen no signal. When eight-thirty came and went, Wu'er became fatalistic. Because the price of a Hong Kong citizen getting caught while engaging in such rescue activities was extremely high, he knew that the boat's captain would only attempt to make one rendezvous, and he feared they had somehow missed it.

"I lay down in the grass looking up at the stars," Wu'er told me. "I knew how difficult it had always been for people to escape from China! And now that things were tighter than ever, I really doubted we would make it."

By nine o'clock, Wu'er said, he had begun to almost want to be arrested. "I was getting prepared just to walk away from there, find our way to some hotel, get a room, have a nice meal, and simply wait for the police to come and take us away. By then part of me would have been relieved just to get the whole ordeal resolved."

At nine-thirty, just as they were on the verge of giving up, Wu'er saw two flashes of light out in the darkness. Quickly, they clambered to the shore and waded into the water. The shoreline was encrusted with sharp oysters whose shells sliced at their legs as they stumbled through the shallows. "But it didn't matter, because as we started swimming, I knew we would be saved," Wu'er said, giving a hearty laugh.

A short time later Wu'er remembers being seized by an unexpected emotion. "As we sped toward Hong Kong, I could not help feeling responsibility for all that had happened and everyone who had died, and I felt the first pangs of guilt about surviving."

Wu'er and Liu had imagined that in Hong Kong they would be greeted as heroes by cheering crowds. Instead, they found themselves sequestered by British officials nervous about antagonizing Beijing. Wu'er was allowed to make only one public statement, an impassioned address over Hong Kong television on June 28. After lashing out at the "bestial fascists" who fired upon the students, he said, "As survivors, our lives no longer belong to us alone. Our lives must now embrace those of our fellow students and compatriots who gave their lives for democracy, freedom, our beautiful motherland, and for her strength and prosperity. Their lives have now been melded together with ours."

Shortly thereafter, Wu'er was put on a flight to France. It was not until reaching Paris that he began to fully appreciate the magnitude and tragedy of the events in which he had just participated. "I began to realize that things were now out of my hands, and I felt overwhelmed by a deep sense of loss." Not only had his hopes that China might somehow break free from its authoritarian past been dashed, but, like others who had succeeded in escaping the crackdown, Wu'er now found himself in a world with which he had little familiarity and whose languages he did not speak. Moreover, he had no means of support, much less a permanent place to live. For him and other political refugees, escape began not so much a chapter of liberation as an agonizing interregnum that left most of them exhausted, deeply confused, and depressed.

Before these wounds had a chance to heal, however, Wu'er was swept up by plans to organize an overseas Chinese opposition movement. In Paris he was elected vice-president of the newly formed Federation for Democracy in China (FDC), and thrust into a new political maelstrom, this time a factional struggle among members of the defeated and exiled democracy movement. Although he was greeted as a hero of democracy everywhere he went on behalf of the FDC over the next few months, this was actually a time of painful disassembly.

Upon arriving in the United States that August, Wu'er was plunged into a cyclotron of media hype. Because he had been seen so often on foreign television during the demonstrations in the Square, Americans viewed him as a superstar, and everywhere he went he was besieged by reporters, well-wishers, autograph hounds, and people eager to make contributions to the cause of Chinese democracy. At one banquet in Los Angeles's Chinatown, he auctioned off a handwritten note pledging his allegiance to the democracy movement in exchange for a $3,000 contribution to the FDC. Such celebrityhood and power was heady stuff for a twenty-one-year-old, even one who had grown wiser to the ways of the world.

There are few places more dissimilar than Tiananmen Square and Los Angeles's Federal Plaza. The plaza is centered around an ivory high-rise office building festooned with American flags that looks out over a panorama of manicured lawns, palm trees, and a cascade of gleaming cars speeding along Wilshire Boulevard. One August day in 1989 an expectant crowd of several thousand had gathered in the plaza to hear Wu'er speak. When walkie-talkie–toting security guards rounded the corner of the Federal Building, heads jerked around and photographers and TV crews jumped to their feet like fighter pilots scrambling in response to an air-raid siren. As the entourage approached the microphone and Wu'er himself appeared, a hush fell over the crowd. This was hardly the dynamic superhero they remembered in broadcasts from the Square. Wu'er's face looked puffy and contorted with a mixture of pain, sourness, and fatigue. He was in such discomfort that he was almost doubled over, held up by two acolytes like a wounded soldier being carried out of combat by buddies. Whether his incapacity was due to fatigue, psychological trauma, his mysterious heart condition, or his love of theatrics was impossible to know. Whatever its cause, Wu'er seemed spent and lost. It was not until he stepped up to the microphone and the cameras began rolling that he regained any suggestion of his old Tiananmen Square swagger.

"We want to say that we Chinese have hope and a future," Wu'er said through a grimace of apparent pain. "Our wish is to allow people to have a choice." He squinted out over the crowd into a haze of sun-infused smog. A concerned adjutant proffered him a straw hat to shield his eyes from the blinding brightness. He looked at it for an instant and then skeptically rejected it. Even in this state of near collapse he had evidently not lost his concern for appearances. He began speaking again, but perfunctorily. After only a few minutes he grabbed his midriff again and was then hastily ushered away by his retinue. He left a stunned and bewildered crowd behind.

"I was just a young, naive guy," Wu'er recalled when I later reminded him of the event. "At that time I was completely and absolutely lost. I had just been jumping from one thing to another, and after everything that had happened, I was basically dysfunctional, incapable of making any major decisions at all."

20

Verdict First, Trial Second

"Once upon a time, there was a country whose rulers succeeded in completely crushing the people, and yet they still believed the people to be their most dangerous enemy." These words were written by Lu Xun nearly half a century ago, but they described the situation in China during the 1989 crackdown with macabre perfection. Having forcibly ended the protest movement in Tiananmen Square and having restored order to Beijing, Party leaders ironically felt more vulnerable than ever. In a way that eerily repeated their own experience of persecution, arrest, and torture by Nationalist police during the thirties and forties, China's Communist leaders set about brutalizing yet another generation of dissidents.

The organs of the Ministry of Public Security, the People's Courts, and the Reform Through Labor Bureau, comprise a system of repressive institutions with which outsiders rarely have much contact. Even foreigners who have spent long periods of time in China and have become familiar with other aspects of Chinese society still rarely have much awareness of the impact the judicial and penal systems have on everyday life. The reason is that except for those few "model prisons" and carefully scripted judicial proceedings that foreigners are sometimes permitted to see, these institutions are kept shrouded behind an almost impenetrable veil of secrecy.

Only occasionally is this veil unintentionally drawn back for a moment, allowing outsiders to catch a glimpse of what lies behind. One such occasion occurred in the winter of 1984 when I was traveling in South China during the nationwide anticrime campaign against "spiritual pollution." While I was walking through the seat of Taishan County in Guangdong Province early one morning, a phalanx of motorcycle police suddenly roared down the main street. At first, I thought some visiting dignitary's motorcade was approaching. But instead of Red Flag limousines, the procession consisted of a convoy of khaki-colored flatbed trucks loaded with handcuffed prisoners, each with a white placard around his neck inscribed with his name and crime. Several placards had large red X's slashed across them, a traditional indication that an offender has committed a capital crime and been sentenced to death.

Curious to know what was happening, I followed this cortege to a nearby sports field where, before a crowd of thousands of young students, a rally was just beginning. Heads bowed, the prisoners stood in the back of the trucks while local officials delivered exhortatory speeches about the perils of criminal activity. As the rally concluded with a burst of martial music and static, those with crimson X's on their placards were marched by white-uniformed police down to the river that flowed alongside the sports field. While hundreds of morbid onlookers gawked, these prisoners were blindfolded, forced to kneel on the stones, and then shot in the back of the head. As a form of familial ostracism, the spent shell casings were then delivered to the families of the executed, who were required to reimburse the state for the cost of the bullets.

When the local PSB discovered that I and several other "foreign friends" in our group had managed not only to witness but to photograph the procession and rally, they informed us with great agitation that we would not be allowed to leave Taishan until we handed over all undeveloped film.

The rally and executions were a reminder that even as Deng's reforms were advancing, a Stalinist public security apparatus, a judicial system beholden to the Party, and a penal system that operated without the niceties of due process continued to detain, imprison, and execute thousands every year. (Needless to say, statistics on the number of executions carried out each year have always been a closely guarded state secret, but Amnesty International estimated that some 20,000 were executed in this 1983–84 crackdown.) About the only way those accused could protest was to write songs and sing them in their cells. Some were bitter and mocking, others sad and fatalistic. "Ma Polin Road Is Broad and Long" was written by a prisoner from Changsha, the capital of Hunan Province.

> As I arrive at East Wind Square this clear morn,
> Thousands of people are already here to see me.
> My fate has come.
> See the motorcycles on the street,
> The machine guns are at the ready on army trucks.
> Ma Polin Road is broad and long.
> A black and white placard hangs on my back.
> Then I hear the rifle shots and I fall to the ground.
> Good-bye, Mother, Father, and loved ones.
> For eighteen years Mother raised me.
> Then one shot through my heart . . .

By the time I saw the Taishan anticrime rally in 1984, the NCNA was acknowledging that some 20 million "bad elements" had already undergone "labor reform"; many believed the figure to be much higher. A classified document issued at the time said that "active counterrevolutionary elements" as well as six different classes of common criminals had been targeted for arrest. All "should be dealt resolute blows," the document declared, "and those who deserve to die must be executed." Since I had caught only a fleeting glimpse of the placards, I did not know if the prisoners were all *xingshifan* (ordinary criminals) or *zhengzhifan* (political criminals), people accused of crimes of "counterrevolution." In fact, like most other foreigners, I knew very little at the time about the Chinese system of criminal justice and what someone detained by the state might expect by way of treatment.

In 1989, sections of China's 1979 Criminal Law still allowed the state to arrest citizens for political crimes. Article 90 states that "all acts endangering the PRC committed with the goal of overthrowing the political power of the dictatorship of the proletariat and the socialist system are crimes of counterrevolution." Article 102 defines "counterrevolution" as any activities that "incite the masses to resist or to sabotage the implementation of the state's laws or decrees . . . through counterrevolutionary slogans, leaflets, or other means, propagandizing for and inciting the overthrow of the political power of the dictatorship of the proletariat and the socialist system." The vagueness of these provisions, the conception of which China inherited from Stalin's "legal system," allowed the government to arrest "according to law" almost anyone with whom it politically disagreed. And frequent "anticrime campaigns" provided opportunities for the PSB to round up political dissidents along with other antisocial elements.

However, as China opened up to the outside world, a small group of legal scholars gingerly began to challenge the notion of "counterrevolutionary crimes," claiming that such offenses should be abandoned because there was no objective way to define them. The January 1989 issue of the *Law Review* asserted that because the term "counterrevolutionary" had been "imbued with different political significances at different historical periods by those in control," the definition was "unstable and imprecise." A motion was even drafted to bring the subject before the National People's Congress. However, this cautious debate came to an abrupt halt after June 4 when the Supreme People's Court declared that the demonstrations had been "counterrevolutionary" in nature, and the Party's Propaganda Department ordered publications to desist from any future discussions of the subject.

By 1992 there was once again muted discussion of dropping "counterrevolution" as a legal definition. But rather than discussing the abolishment of the whole notion of political crimes, proposals centered around cosmetic changes, substituting, for instance, "offenses endangering state security" for crimes of "counterrevolutionary propaganda and incitement" which were punishable under the State Security Law.

An accused person's travails in the Chinese criminal justice system hardly end with being charged. Even though the Criminal Procedure Law carefully spells out regulations on arrest, notification of kin, limits on time of detention without charges being preferred, and the right to counsel, open trial, and appeal, the fact that the legal system has never been independent of the Party has made every politically sensitive trial subject to extrajudicial interference. As a 1991 Amnesty International report stated, "In practice, the Communist Party of the PRC has an extraordinary influence over the functions and procedures of each institution, and is often in a position to dictate a complete course of action." For example, although detainees are not legally supposed to be held over ten days without being charged, under Party pressure many, like Han Dongfang, are regularly detained much longer. What is more, although by statute the state may not hold anyone after being charged for more than five months of pretrial investigation, many detainees have spent several years in jail before being tried. Moreover, since China does not allow for habeas corpus proceedings, the accused are unable to challenge their custody in the courts.

Once an accused person is finally brought to trial, he finds himself confronting an even more Kafkaesque situation. To be arrested in China is considered prima facie evidence of guilt. The notion of "verdict first, trial second'' has rendered pretrial procuratorial investigations little more than conclusions in search of scripts. Once written, these scripts are virtually invulnerable to challenges by the defense. As the Shanghai Municipal Lawyers' Association reminded its members in a post–1989 report, ''Defense is not a matter of victory or defeat, and the [defense] lawyer is not competing with the procuratorial and court personnel to see who comes out on top.'' Instead, said the report, trials are ''propaganda effort[s] directed at citizens to condemn vice and praise justice.''

In such a system the function of a defense attorney is not to plead the accused's innocence but, by demonstrating his contrition, to win some modest reduction in sentence. And since trials are usually closed, there can be no playing to public sympathy or the press. The law guarantees ''public trials,'' but almost all politically sensitive cases are tried in camera or before carefully selected audiences from which even family members are often excluded. Needless to say, outside observers, and especially foreign journalists or human rights monitors, have not been welcome.

Once a case is decided, a defendant has between three and ten days to appeal before being sent off either to a prison or one of China's *laodong gaizao dui* (reform-through-labor camps). However, since refusal to acknowledge guilt has always been viewed as a judicial affront, fear of receiving a higher sentence is usually enough to dissuade a defendant from making appeals. The hazards of exercising one's right of appeal were graphically brought home to me by a chance acquaintance in Shanghai who told me of a case in which one defendant had dared appeal a long prison sentence only to have his efforts rewarded with the death penalty.

While courts are, at least, theoretically obligated to heed China's Constitution and its various legal codes, there is another, parallel system of criminal justice that lies completely outside of the law and the judicial system. If authorities do not wish to bother with formal charges, arrests, and the potentially adverse publicity that may come from staging a show trial, they may avail themselves of a wide variety of extrajudicial or ''administrative'' sanctions to put offenders away. Such convenient punitive measures were widely used after both the Democracy Wall Movement in 1979 and the 1989 demonstrations in Tiananmen Square.

The most common administrative sanction is *shourong shencha* (sheltering for investigation), a procedure which allows the PSB to hold suspects almost indefinitely without according them any due process. The basis for such extralegal forms of detention are found in a series of classified regulations issued over the past four decades that provide the Party and the government a way to silence political opponents without having to give any legal justification or explanation. Millions have been "administratively detained" and not reappeared until it has pleased the state. The classified journal *People's Public Security* reported that in 1988 alone some 1.5 million people had undergone such detention.

Those whom the government wishes to put away "administratively" with more institutional finality are remanded from "shelter and investigation" centers to a *laodong jiaoyang dui* (reeducation-through-labor camp). Although technically such detainees can be held for no more than three years in such camps, they are frequently kept much longer. The objective of such "reeducation" is to "redeem" persons whom authorities view as criminal. As the Chinese government told the International Labor Organization, the process is "an effective measure suited to the situation in China, pertinent to its social needs and beneficial in maintaining social stability."

Liuchang jiuye (forced job placement), more a form of post-imprisonment internal exile than outright incarceration, is another category of extralegal detention unique to China. Prisoners who have completed their sentences in labor camps but are not considered to have ideologically reeducated themselves are often denied permission to return home and must continue to work in the labor-camp enterprises. Although they are paid small salaries and allowed to live outside of the prison walls, if they try to leave the area, they are arrested and returned to camp. The mechanism for extending their detention is indirect: The state simply refuses to transfer their *hukou* (residency permits), needed by all Chinese citizens to reside legally outside a prison, back to their hometown or city.

What has always made imprisonment in China doubly terrifying are the abysmal conditions existing in most penal institutions. Inmates must not only endure overcrowded cells, primitive sanitary conditions, barely edible food, long political study sessions, and scant medical care, but must suffer psychological abuse and physical torture as well. For example, most prisons contain a bank of *xiaohao* (small numbers). Barely larger than coffins, these "isolation cells" have only small apertures in their steel trap doors for light and air. Although refractory prisoners are thrown into them for long periods of time, most "small numbers" are so cramped that it is impossible to stand up inside. To make matters worse, most are not even equipped with cots, forcing prisoners to lie down on concrete, which during the winter becomes numbingly cold. The object of the confinement chambers is to break down the resistance of prisoners to the point where they welcome a chance to confess, even when no crime has been committed. One recent Chinese account describes the *xiaohao* as an "operating room" for uncooperative inmates in which "loneliness is the scalpel used for performing surgery on the soul."

Such surgery is calculated to induce acknowledgments of guilt so that the process of repentance can begin. As a 1992 State Council *White Paper on Criminal Reform* asserted, "the legal and moral education of criminals emphasizes the need to plead guilty." And so, a defendant's best hope of obtaining early release is to surrender all pretension of innocence. As the commonly used slogan puts it, "Leniency for those who confess, severity for those who resist."

Given this emphasis, those in prison awaiting trial have been regularly subjected to enormous pressure to admit to whatever crime they are accused of, and the techniques used to force confessions are often brutal. "Some law enforcement officials just don't care whether a criminal lives or dies," wrote a court employee in an article that appeared in a 1992 issue of the *Yunnan Legal News*. "Use of torture to extort confessions is not a chance phenomenon, but is the consequence of long-standing problems in law enforcement. Some law enforcement officers think, 'No beatings, no confessions.'"

In 1992, Amnesty International reported that torture was "endemic in many places of detention in China," and that abuses suffered by prisoners were "now far more severe than they were ten years ago." Tang Boqiao, a 1989 democracy-movement activist, had firsthand experience with such treatment when he spent more than eighteen months in over ten Hunan Province jails and prisons. After finally escaping abroad, he charged that "torture and ill-treatment are rampant in Chinese jails" because prison officials "know that so long as they don't actually beat a prisoner to death they have nothing to worry about, for there will be no repercussions."

Even when inmates are murdered, measures are rarely taken against offending prison officials. According to Guo Peiqi, a former lieutenant commander of the Shenzhen Public Security Bureau Criminal Division who defected to Hong Kong in 1990, eight inmates in his jurisdiction alone were tortured to death in the first three months of 1989. One of the victims, a seventeen-year-old boy who "was beaten to death within two hours of being brought in," should not have been detained at all.

Beatings are only one of the many forms of torture visited on Chinese prisoners. *Dianji* (electric batons) are regularly applied to sensitive parts of the body such as the face, abdomen, genitals, and even the inside of the mouth, and *jieju* (fettering of prisoners with shackles) on *menbanliao* (shackle boards—slabs of wood on which a victim is splayed out as if on a rack, with ankles and wrists tightly secured for days at a time) are two other common forms of physical abuse.

"Prisoners who regularly break camp rules are dealt with by committal to *yanguandui* (strict regime), a highly punitive regime where a host of imaginative abuses and indignities lie waiting in store," explained Tang Boqiao in an Asia Watch report. One trio of punishment techniques is known as Playing The Three Games. It includes the "Clinging Gecko," in which a prisoner is forced to kneel down on the ground with his hands raised above his head and pressed against the wall for hours at a time until "the strain on muscles becomes so excruciating that eventually the prisoner collapses on the ground in a state of shock"; the "Golden Chicken Standing On One Leg," in which a prisoner's right arm is handcuffed to his left leg while his left hand is shackled to the wall forcing him to put the full weight of his body on one leg and arm; and the "Pillar Standing Feat," in which a prisoner is perched on a narrow column with his hands chained behind his back to a wall so that when he falls asleep and topples from the pillar, his arms are wrenched out of his shoulder sockets. So horrific is treatment in many Chinese penal institutions that untold thousands of inmates have tried to commit suicide or to injure themselves deliberately by eating nails or poison in hopes of being transferred to a medical facility.

Of all the forms of abuse inflicted on prisoners, the most systematized is forced labor. Almost all inmates are compelled to work in one of the thousands of factories, farms, and mines that make up China's vast "reform through labor" gulag. The rationalization for forced labor was spelled out by Mao Zedong in his 1957 essay "On the Correct Handling of Contradictions Among the People": "Towards enemies, the people's democratic dictatorship uses methods of dictatorship . . . [that] compels them to engage in labor, and, through such labor, to be transformed into new men." But if the original justification for compelling prisoners to "participate in labor" was to ideologically remold them, it did not take long before officials realized that the production facilities attached to detention centers, jails, reeducation-through-labor camps, prisons, and reform-through-labor camps were also a potentially important source of state income. As China's first minister of public security, Luo Ruiqing, noted in 1951 when the forced-labor system was first borrowed from the Soviet Union, "Labor reform production . . . directly aids the development of the nation's industries, and also saves the nation a great deal of expense." With authorities estimating China's camp population at 10 to 20 million people during peak periods, the Chinese penal colony offered an almost inexhaustible fund of low-cost labor. Not only were inmates unpaid, but they always showed up for work, never engaged in stoppages or strikes, and could always be counted on to put in whatever overtime was needed to meet production targets. From the perspective of factory managers, prisoners were a dream workforce come true.

As of 1989 when the latest generation of political prisoners began matriculating through this system, the state began putting more emphasis on prison labor as a productive force than as a tool for ideological reeducation. Just as Deng's economic reforms aimed at weaning state enterprises from the dole by making them more responsible for their own profits and losses, so prisons and their attendant enterprises were also nudged into becoming more self-sufficient. In this new entrepreneurial world where factory managers of successful enterprises could win large bonuses, prison officials became suddenly eager to make prisons profitable. The best way of accomplishing profitability was more efficient utilization of their unique labor force.

Typical of production-oriented prisons is the sprawling Lingyuan Motor Vehicle Industrial Corporation (also known as the Lingyuan Labor Reform Sub-Bureau). It is situated in Manchuria's Liaoning Province and includes six labor-reform detachments with more than 160,000 square meters of factory floor space, fixed assets worth almost $25 million, and manufacturing units producing everything from tractor-trailers to trucks, and metering devices to engine parts. So many political prisoners were processed into this facility during the 1989 crackdown that in 1990 the Ministry of Justice bestowed the honorific title of "Outstanding Collective in Curbing Turmoil and Suppressing the Counterrevolutionary Rebellion" on the complex.

At Lingyuan, fourteen-hour days of forced labor, the use of diminished rations as a form of punishment, beatings, and torture have been everyday facts of life. One police commander was quoted by Asia Watch as explaining away such physical abuse of inmates this way: "It is my duty to beat you. It is your duty to reform. So you want to stage a hunger strike? Go ahead. Labor reform detachments aren't afraid of deaths. When one does [dies], we'll bury one. When two die, we'll bury two."

Conditions in the prison were so bad that in 1991 inmates confined in the Lingyuan No. 2 Reform Detachment, a number of whom had participated in the 1989 demonstrations, began a series of hunger strikes. In a letter smuggled out, one inmate described how officials reacted when a prisoner named Li Jie tried to stage a one-day fast in protest: "The brigade commander, Yang Guoping, assembled all the prisoners of the training brigade for a meeting. They dragged Li Jie to the front of the stage, stripped him naked, and had several common criminals ('trusties') hold him down on the floor. Yang then repeatedly applied a huge 5,000-volt electric baton to the inside of Li's leg. Then two guards used four 5,000-volt batons on his head, neck, shoulder, armpit, chest, belly, and fingers. Li Jie sweated profusely, went into spasms, and then became motionless. . . . Yang Guoping blustered, 'So you want to pay homage to those who died on June 4? They died as they deserved. If you are tired of living, just say so. . . . As long as you keep up your counterrevolutionary actions, we will never relent.' "

Another way to maximize prison profits was to manufacture for export. As Liu Dehao, the general manager of one of the Lingyuan prison factories proclaimed in a letter of solicitation to outside investors, "Our factory welcomes foreign businessmen to come and invest in the factory on a joint venture basis in order to further develop [China's] mighty car-making industry." (The Japanese company Isuzu is reported to have concluded an agreement with the Liaoning Lingyuan Vehicle Company to assemble vans.) According to the sales catalogue of another Liaoning prison, the Shenyang New Life Rubber Plant, because of "excellent" quality, their rubber boots and shoes "sell very well" not only throughout China and elsewhere in Asia, but in the United States, Latin America, and Europe.

Since most Western countries have a sensitivity to buying Chinese goods made with so-called slave labor—especially when some of those laborers may have been students and workers arrested and imprisoned for their roles in the 1989 demonstrations—such exports posed problems. In the case of the United States, China's foremost trading partner, a law, the 1930 Smoot-Hawley Tariff Act, banned the importation of goods made abroad with prison labor. Nonetheless eager to try and tap lucrative U.S. markets with their goods, prison factory managers hid behind a series of subterfuges. Conveniently, all Chinese prison enterprises already operated under two separate names, one for their designation in China's penal system, and the other their plant name used for commercial purposes. Thus the Shanghai No. 1 Reform Through Labor Detachment was known to the outside world as the Shanghai Laodong Machinery Plant.

A second ruse was to cloud the origin of prison-made goods by laundering them through state-run import-export corporations so that foreign buyers would have no way of knowing where they were made. Those foreign businessmen who requested to visit production lines in order to assure themselves about quality control before signing contracts presented a real problem for prison enterprises. As one classified Ministry of Public Security bulletin issued in 1979 declared, foreign trade departments at prisons "may in principle" approve requests for visits, but they "must be done under strict control." In fact, many prison-enterprise managers have gone to elaborate ends to deceive businessmen into believing that they were in normal factories rather than jails. "We made an explicit rule that whenever foreign businessmen come to the workshop to inspect product samples for quality, they must be accompanied by a special person, [and] prisoners are not allowed to have direct contact or talks with foreign businessmen," wrote Qin Guishan in a classified journal called *Theoretical Studies in Labor Reform and Labor Reeducation* about such visits to his own prison-run New Life Cotton Textile Mill.

Sometimes prisoners were removed from their normal work stations and replaced by substitutes; and telltale political slogans were taken down; hats were put on prisoner-workers sitting at production lines to hide their shaven heads; and prison uniforms were swapped for civilian garb. So successful were these efforts that Qin was able to boast, "No secret has ever been leaked and thus other incidents involving foreign contacts have been prevented from happening."

Even after a number of Chinese enterprises were caught red-handed engaging in illegal trade with the United States, the Chinese government continued to make denials. "Labor reform departments are not allowed to engage in foreign economic and trade activities, and China has never granted any labor reform department a permit to engage in foreign trade," maintained Chinese embassy Press Counselor Chen Defu in a 1990 letter to the editor of the *New York Times*.

Such denials were difficult to accept, particularly in view of a letter that the Volvo Company in Sweden received in 1989 from a Chinese trader with offices in Belgium. He claimed to represent the Chinese Reform Through Labor Bureau and offered to "provide large numbers of criminals who received already [sic] basic technical training as very cheap labor on a lease basis" if Volvo wished to manufacture parts in China. With such brazen solicitations being made public, it was not long before Americans concerned over China's human rights record were lobbying the U.S. government to put conditions on recertification of China's MFN trading status.

In a way that few could have foreseen as they watched China's 1989 protest movement unfold, Americans once again found themselves linked to the students and workers they had rooted for in Tiananmen Square. This time it was not through a shared interest in democracy, but a shared global market system into which Chinese prisons were feeding plastic toys, garments, fabric, shoes, tools, steel pipe, diesel engines, and other products—part of what some critics started to refer to as a system of ''gulag capitalism.''

Part III

Dead Time

21

Back to the Square

By late September 1989 after the situation in Beijing had stabilized somewhat, China's new hard-line leadership shifted its attention to trying to restore credibility to its beleaguered regime. The fact that the government had launched a stern retrenchment program and that foreign investors had pulled back from China, causing the economy to sag, made their task all the more daunting. More than ever, it was essential that Deng and his allies erase the prevailing sense that their regime had lost its "mandate of heaven" and was on the downward slope of an unstoppable cycle of decline that would see the government and all its Marxist-Leninist-Maoist ideology swept away by a new dynasty. Having secured military control of the capital, the Party now needed to resecure its political legitimacy. Predictably, its leaders focused on Tiananmen Square, where the challenge was to make it appear as if this central political shrine had been restored to its rightful heir—the Chinese Communist Party. The fortieth anniversary of the PRC on October 1 provided them with an opportunity.

Under normal circumstances, the government would probably have commemorated the occasion with a public rally in the Square. But with martial law still in effect, it was still too dangerous to risk such a mass event, especially with a nationwide television audience looking on. After all, malcontents might try to embarrass the leadership by infiltrating the festivities and pulling off some highly visible guerrilla protest. On the other hand, not to hold a "celebration" would be interpreted as defaulting on their claim to the Square and an admission that the leaders feared "the people." Hopeful of finding a way to mark the occasion with an event that would bolster their damaged image without risking more humiliation, Party propagandists devised a *grand spectacle* that would give the appearance of a mass event without actually involving any uncontrollable "masses."

When October 1 finally rolled around, the Square remained hermetically sealed off from the public. Not wanting to take any chances, the Party put special security measures in place throughout the city. Those non-Beijingers who were staying in hotels were placed under curfew and residents were ordered not to leave their homes. All major intersections within a mile of the Square were put under patrol by riot police. To replace the missing "masses," the Party filled the bleachers flanking the Tiananmen Gate rostrum with 20,000 "celebrants" ordered to attend by their work units. These handpicked "invitees" were to function much like the studio audience of a taped TV sitcom, to provide on-cue applause and the semblance of participation. By carefully choreographing a lavish procession within the Square, it was hoped all the images of bullhorn-wielding students standing under caustic protest banners and of troops firing on unarmed civilians could be erased.

No effort or cost was spared on this coming-out party for China's new hard-line leadership. Two specially made red neon signs—"Invigorate China" and "Long Live the Motherland"—were installed on either side of the portals of Tiananmen. As the *People's Daily* later so aptly put it, "to love the motherland today means also to love socialism." The Square was festooned with rafts of potted flowers, and the surrounding trees on the Avenue of Eternal Peace were draped with Christmas-tree–like lights. To link the festivities to the neo-imperial aura of Mao Zedong, China's latest crop of Party grandees, led by Deng Xiaoping, watched this socialist halftime show unfold from the very spot atop Tiananmen Gate that Mao had immortalized with his own many theatrical appearances.

Unlike previous National Day events, which had usually been well attended by many high-ranking officials from foreign countries, the guest list this October was embarrassingly spare. Joining Chinese leaders on the rostrum were only a few lackluster representatives from "fraternal" socialist states, including a vice-president from the Democratic People's Republic of Korea, an unofficial emissary from the Soviet-Chinese Friendship Society, a member of the Czech Communist Party's Presidium, and Egon Krenz, a Politburo member from the

German Democratic Republic who would soon be toppled from power and defrocked. During the "celebration" the U.S. was unofficially represented by former Secretary of State Alexander Haig. Haig was greeted on the rostrum of Tiananmen Gate by Deng himself, who pointedly commended him for attending by saying, "You are a brave man."

So that "the broad masses" could glimpse this contrived event on TV, once again, the Square had been transformed into a giant video soundstage. But now instead of demonstrators acting out spontaneous roles in their unrehearsed protest movement, there was a one-thousand-man drill team from the Capital Iron and Steel Works whose placards produced a Chinese flag pattern on command; military bands oom-pah-pah-ing out such socialist favorites as "Our Workers Have Strength" and "The Red Sun Will Never Set"; and a chorus of uncertain origins chanting "Warmly Hail the Victory in Stopping Turmoil and in Quelling the Counterrevolutionary Rebellion!" Over in the northwest corner of the Square an army of university students decked out with patriotic banners did a listless loyalty dance. What TV viewers had no way of knowing was that this amateur ballet troupe included no students from either Beida or Beishida, or that the dancers had been induced to participate by threats of a month in military camp; organizers had even had them strip-searched before dragooning them into the Square to "perform."

It was fitting that one of the main contingents in this synthetic spectacle was the army, which dispatched units that an NCNA report identified as having taken part in "the cleaning-up" of the Square. According to the agency, some of these "valiant guards" of the Party were unable to "hold back their joyous tears when they looked up at the lofty and solemn Tiananmen rostrum and the beautiful night scene of trees decorated with colored lights." Indeed, Xu Qixuan, the director of the political department of one regiment that had taken part in the June 4 assault, was reported to have been so overcome by emotion upon returning to his beloved Square that he blurted out to a group of official reporters, "Please, look how happily these fighters are singing and dancing! Their singing and dancing contains their profound love for the Republic! I want to shout: We love you, People's Republic! We will always be your loyal defender!"

As a grand finale, the Party put on a display of fireworks that rivaled any in recent memory. But for some, the pyrotechnics were hauntingly reminiscent of that night in June when the skies over Tiananmen Square had last been artificially illuminated, only with tracer bullets and military flares rather than Roman candles and pinwheels.

Several weeks after this spectacle, I arrived back in China. I had left

Beijing just after martial law was declared and had not witnessed the events of June 3–4, but as my taxi made its way from the airport toward the center of the city, I saw not the slightest reminder of what had happened that bloody night. Street scenes were deceptively banal. Traffic flowed normally. The usual groups of old men sat on curbs under streetlamps playing Chinese checkers. Couples walked arm-in-arm down shadowy sidewalks.

Looking out at the stubbornly ordinary facade of urban life that was going by, I understood more clearly than ever the impulse that prompts human beings to erect monuments in commemoration of painful events—like the Monument to the Martyrs of the People in Tiananmen Square itself and the shrines and museums elsewhere in the world that have been made out of such somber places as death camps and prisons. Only by such ritual acts of remembering do we manage to keep alive the hope that we will not repeat our mistakes.

It was hard to imagine how Chinese who had witnessed the bloody events of June 4—much less lost friends or family members—would ever be able to come to terms with the tragedy without being allowed to participate in some public ceremony of grieving. After the Goddess of Democracy had been toppled, Cao Xingyuan had written, "I envision a day when a replica, as large as the original and more permanent, stands in Tiananmen Square, with the names of those who died there written in gold on its base." And then as an afterthought she added, "It may well stand there after Chairman Mao's mausoleum has, in its turn, been pulled down."

But such projects would have to wait until the twists and turns of Chinese politics someday led to a "reversal of the verdict" on *liusi*—literally "the fourth day of the six month" as June 4 had come to be known—and this "counterrevolutionary rebellion" became "reclassified" as a "patriotic democratic movement." This is what had happened to the Tiananmen Square Incident mourning Zhou Enlai's death in 1976 after Deng's final return to power. One thing was certain, however; *liusi* would most certainly not be "reclassified" until after Deng died.

Just as on that first morning in 1975, I again awoke at dawn possessed by a sense of urgency to visit the Square. Dressing quickly, I went down to the lobby, borrowed a bicycle from the hotel concierge, and set out through the labyrinthine network of *hutong* that still vein the old quarters of Beijing. As always, clouds of bituminous smoke billowed up from behind the gray walls of ancient courtyard houses as people lit their morning breakfast fires. The smell of frying *youtiao* (Chinese-style crullers) wafting out from the small private stalls filled the air with their enticing aroma. As people pedaled off to work, the *hutong* were filled with the familiar whirring sound of bicycle wheels, the soft jingle of bells, and, in the distance, the hooting of early-morning trains pulling in and out of the Beijing Railway Station.

Along the way I passed the houses of several friends I had often visited over the course of the preceding decade. In the tense political climate that prevailed, dropping in on them was now out of the question. For a Chinese to entertain a foreign journalist, even an old friend, was certain to attract unwanted attention from neighbors and the PSB.

As I pedaled by a low-lying apartment building where one old friend and his wife lived, I saw their family cat sitting outside their living-room window and I was gripped with a sense of loss for all the evenings we had shared, especially during the heady days of the previous spring when almost everyone had allowed themselves to become swept up in the excitement that emanated from the Square. Now it was difficult to feel anything but despair about the sense of lost hope and the fatalistic political silence that had settled over China. As painter Zhang Peili told writer Andrew Solomon: "Before the massacre, there was so much noise, a deafening political roar of protest. Then the tanks came and everyone immediately fell silent. For me, that silence was far more terrifying than the tanks."

Many of my friends were now either in prison, in exile, or lying low, making me feel almost as if I had returned in apparitional form—a perplexing reversal of what I had felt during the massacre itself. Then my physical absence from Beijing had only heightened the feeling of emotional connection to both the city and its people. But now that I was actually present at the scene of the tragedy, I paradoxically felt more isolated than when I had been away.

As I neared the Beijing Hotel, I began cycling right over the section of the Avenue of Eternal Peace where troops guarding the Square had fired point-blank into crowds of jeering people on the morning of June 4. But with throngs of bike riders now pedaling so determinedly off to work and crowded city buses lumbering down the avenue belching great clouds of blue exhaust as always, it was not easy to conjure up images of the carnage that had once littered this street.

As I approached the Square itself, however, my bike tires suddenly rippled over a stretch of pavement with the texture of a washboard. Looking down, I saw that I was passing over several corrugated, fan-shaped patterns etched into the asphalt like the angel-wings children leave when playing in the snow. It took a moment to realize that they had been made by the steel tracks of armored vehicles furiously spinning around as they carried out their deadly orders that night five months before. They made me recall something Chai Ling had said in a taped interview from underground several days later. "Our fellow students were crushed under tanks so that even their corpses could not be pieced backed together. They will never come back to life, but will remain forever on the Avenue of Eternal Peace."

Moments later I spotted pockmarks on the ancient masonry of the gate that arches over the entrance to Nanchizi Street, and just ahead on the vermilion stucco wall that surrounds the Imperial City was a stitching of holes where soldiers had squeezed off stray bursts of automatic-weapons fire.

As the rush-hour flood of bicycles thinned out, I entered the north end of the Square. Just as on that first morning so many years ago, it was empty except for the vehicular traffic that flowed around its still well-guarded perimeters. Otherwise, where once there had been massive crowds of chanting demonstrators and roiling banners stretching as far as the eye could see, now there were only concrete paving stones. As I approached Tiananmen Gate, however, I saw that there was, in fact, one object breaking the unrelieved emptiness of the Square, something that from far away resembled a sailing ship on an ocean horizon. As I drew nearer, this enigmatic object revealed itself to be a large white sculpture of a worker, a peasant, a soldier, and an intellectual standing together in a resolute pose of socialist solidarity. It had been erected by the Party exactly on the spot where the Goddess of Democracy had risen—presumably to help people forget what had previously stood there.

Otherwise, the Square looked as if it had been mothballed—like a historic battlefield long abandoned. Not only were there no demonstrators, but gone, too, were the usual droves of tourists from the provinces, the Popsicle vendors, the children flying kites, and the photographers under their colored umbrellas ready to snap pictures of visitors posing in front of Mao's famous portrait. As I passed the two marble *huabiao* and looked toward the Monument, there was not a single ordinary person anywhere. I felt as if I had strayed onto the back lot of a bankrupt film studio that had once been in the business of shooting big-budget biblical epics. All that remained were armed troops standing at rigid attention around the Square's periphery. From a distance the vast emptiness engulfed them, making them look oddly like toy soldiers. Only as I drew near enough to distinguish their camouflaged fatigues, steel battle helmets, and automatic rifles did they take on any air of menace. But as I pedaled past them, I was surprised to see that they were actually just young kids, beardless country boys whose cheeks were burned brown from hours of guard duty in the sun, whose unblinking gaze reflected more uncertainty and slow-eyed puzzlement than defiance or hatred. Even so, they were palpable reminders of the formidable power that China's 3-million-strong People's Liberation Army and the untold tens of thousands who made up the People's Armed Military Police could project when called on by their masters.

As if the Chairman himself rather than Deng Xiaoping were still their supreme commander, Mao's painted visage gazed imperiously down on these troops from its gold frame on Tiananmen Gate. No single image in China was more renowned or charged with symbolism than this portrait. Although most other Mao images had long since been removed, this mother-of-all-icons clung stubbornly to its niche because, even though the cult of Mao had been deemphasized, to remove this last image would have been tantamount to acknowledging that his revolution had ended and that the Party he had helped found no longer held "the mandate of heaven" or the right to rule unilaterally.

In fact, so exalted was this portrait that when on May 23 three youths from Hunan Province threw eggs filled with ink at it, the defacers were apprehended not by police but by students themselves. One might have imagined protesters would have opposed what Mao stood for. On the contrary, not only were they unsympathetic to this act of desecration, but they turned the three miscreants over to the PSB, which sent them promptly to prison with sentences from sixteen years to life. An unblemished duplicate almost immediately appeared in place of the old portrait, and has remained undefiled since.

Just past Tiananmen Gate, near the spot where Han Dongfang's workers' federation had its tent pitched on June 3, I stopped and got off my bike for a moment, pretending to tie my shoe, but actually to jot down a few quick thoughts in a notebook. As soon as my feet hit the ground, two of the soldiers I had just passed broke ranks.

"It's forbidden to stop!" screamed one.

"Get out of here!" yelled the other.

Before I could do anything, they had lowered their Kalashnikovs and begun running toward me. I leapt back on my bike and, with my heart pounding, pedaled away as fast as I could.

Turning off the Avenue of Eternal Peace, I approached the steps of the Great Hall of the People where the three students had prostrated themselves during Hu Yaobang's funeral. Now, instead of Wu'er Kaixi with his bullhorn chanting, "Dialogue! Dialogue! Dialogue!" an officer in camouflage fatigues was shouting commands to a column of troops in full combat gear practicing a goose-stepping drill. Chastened by my last encounter, I did not slow down until I reached the south end near the Front Gate. Here a convoy of buses was parked behind Mao's mausoleum, letting off hundreds of high-school children in the red scarves and white shirts of the Young Pioneers, the Communist Party's youth organization. Perplexed by what brought them here, I pedaled in a circle to watch. But almost immediately, I attracted the attention of soldiers standing guard in the area. Heading up the east side of the Square, I saw the students forming into tidy columns. Then like a sports team taking the field, they filed out into the middle of the empty Square behind a fluttering banner reading "Guardians of China"—the honorific title conferred by the government on those soldiers and policemen who died on June 4.

By the time the Young Pioneers had arranged themselves around the Monument, I was at the Museum of the Chinese Revolution. From there I watched as several students marched forward to the Monument and lay memorial wreaths at its base, just as demonstrators had done that April. As soon as the wreaths were in place, the students all snapped to attention, gave a perfectly synchronized salute, and then what sounded like an oath of allegiance drifted toward me over the same outdoor public address system that the government had used to warn the hunger strikers to abandon the Square.

After the oath, one young boy stiffly stepped forward to address his fellow classmates. I could catch only fragmented snatches in between bursts of static and feedback: "Love the socialist motherland . . . ," ". . . determination to learn from the guardians of the Republic . . . ," ". . . under the leadership of the Communist Party . . ." Then, like a shortwave broadcast that suddenly blasts out with ear-splitting volume before fading away entirely, I heard him proclaim, "Carry out the behest of the martyrs and be prepared at all times to struggle for the Communist cause!"

China's holiest enclave, Tiananmen Square, continued to be caught in a tug-of-war. Wrenched from the hands of the Party by infidel students, the Square had been retaken by well-armed crusaders from the PLA. Now, five months later, the Party was still trying to recon-secrate it to its own official purposes.

It was obvious from the bellicose looks being cast my way by ubiquitous sentries that if I lingered much longer they would be on me again. And so, filled with resignation, I headed back toward the Avenue of Eternal Peace and did not stop until I was once again part of a flow of traffic. As I passed by Nanchizi once more, I recalled that the home of a friend was close by. Because of its proximity to the northeast corner of the Square, the traditional courtyard-style house of Zhang Langlang's family had served as a makeshift headquarters for a number of student activists during the spring demonstrations. After the crackdown Langlang—who had been sentenced to death and then spent ten years in prison during the Cultural Revolution—was forced to flee to the United States. There he wrote an article for the Hong Kong magazine *The Nineties* that captured something of the same wistful sense of loss the Square now evoked for me.

"One day the streets will be repaired, the Square resurfaced, hosed down and cleaned up, but how can we go out for our morning exercise as though nothing ever happened?" Langlang wrote. "How can we take a stroll around the corner to the Square or go fly kites? . . . How can we ever be happy here again?"

22

Learning to Love
Socialism and
the Army

"The Party's salvation lies in renewed indoctrination and propaganda efforts," proclaimed a *People's Daily* editorial in January 1990. As far as hard-liners were concerned, the best hope for controlling the scourge of "bourgeois liberalization" (the corruption of Chinese socialism by bourgeois liberal ideology) and arresting the insidious process of "peaceful evolution" (whereby outside enemies of socialism were suspected of trying to change China's system not by war but by infusing the country with bourgeois influences) was a strong reassertion of Marxist-Leninist-Maoist thought. Such tonic doses of thought reform had traditionally been administered through a regimen of Party-organized *xuexi hui,* or political study sessions. Once an unavoidable part of Chinese life, such compulsory classes had largely disappeared during the late 1980s. By the beginning of 1990, however, the Central Committee had ordered Party branches throughout the country to undertake a new round of such "ideological work." While ostensibly the point of herding everyone back into such classes was to teach them how "to love socialism and love the army," the real intent was probably more to remind them of the Party's right to intervene in their lives on questions of ideology and to harass them if they did not at least appear to give up unorthodox views.

The drill that followed was in certain ways reminiscent of what Qin Shihuang, China's autocratic first emperor, had done two millennia before when he, too, had felt threatened by officials who insisted on thinking for themselves. Summoning his courtiers to the palace, he showed them a deer, but insisted that it was a horse. Those who corrected him were executed for their disloyalty, while those who agreed were rewarded with high office. Today Chinese still use the expression *zhilu weima*, "to point at a deer but call it a horse," to refer to such official manipulations of the truth. Now much of the country was being sent back to "school" to be taught that a deer was a horse. In fact, because the Party viewed China's most prestigious universities as the epicenters of the political unrest, the incoming 1989–90 freshman classes at both Beijing University and Fudan University in Shanghai were shipped off at great expense for a year of military training and ideological study to dissuade them from future acts of political insubordination. Beida students ended up at the Shijiazhuang Military Academy, where twenty of them became so psychologically disturbed that they had to be sent for treatment at a mental hospital.

Party elders still recalled with nostalgia the time when such strongarm tactics were successful in "correcting" people's thinking and inducing ideological "unity." But what they only dimly comprehended was that "bourgeois liberalism" was no longer a minor illness without a class base. It had become a chronic condition—a confirmed way of life and of viewing one's self in relation to the world. Whereas once the state had been able to control every aspect of life because of the way in which agriculture had been collectivized and industry nationalized, by 1989 the growth of the private economic sector had afforded Chinese new possibilities for escaping the suffocating grip of the state. Tens of millions of workers had been shed by state industries and, in effect, forced to become private entrepreneurs. At the same time, hundreds of millions more had been spun loose from rural communes to become day laborers, so that the Party now found it difficult to maintain its system of *dangan* (dossiers) which had once been the key mechanism for keeping track of everyone.

Before Deng's reforms, China had been so isolated from the outside world that virtually no foreign publications, films, radio shows, television programs, or cultural performances—much less foreign students, businessmen, and tourists—had been allowed in to challenge the Party's definition of how the world worked. But having created a nascent marketplace within China's once centralized economy, Party elders were now confronted with an equally competitive marketplace of ideology, just when they most needed to reregiment political thought. Their response was to order as many as possible of the Party's 44 million members into compulsory study sessions to read mind-

numbing Marxist texts about the superiority of socialism, watch
government-made videos about the "peaceful quelling" of the "counterrevolutionary rebellion," engage in "theoretical discussions," and
then cough up their newly corrected thought in long essays. Those
suspected of having sympathized with or participated in the protest
movement were also ordered to write detailed confessional logs describing their daily activities between April 15 and June 4. Known as
jiang qingchu (making things clear), this process involved recounting
one's whereabouts by the hour, and sometimes by the minute. Those
who were discovered to have actively participated in some aspect of
the protest—even to have gone to the Square simply to see what was
happening—were expected to *tanbai* (acknowledge) any incorrect sentiments they might still harbor and to earn absolution by *biaotai* (taking
a clear-cut stand) in favor of the current Party line.

In the Maoist era, when patriotism was synonymous with loving the
Party and when Chinese had no alternative but to submit to such
indignities, the accused were usually grateful to be offered any way at
all of absolving themselves, even if it involved complete self-
abnegation. The penal system's slogan, "Leniency for those who confess, severity for those who resist," applied to "thought reform" work
among ordinary Chinese just as much as to those in prison.

In the mid-1970s I had a chance to observe several political-study
sessions. Although it was difficult to know what combination of fear
and political interest motivated participants, people were usually serious about these activities and the cultivation of their political lives.
Most Chinese actually studied the materials given to them and participated in group discussions. By 1989, however, such rituals had come
to be looked upon with more contempt than fear. One survey conducted in 1990 by the Hangzhou Electronic Research Institute revealed
that only 2 to 3 percent of students queried "deeply believed" the
Party's version of events in 1989, while only 24 percent embraced the
Party's attempts at political reindoctrination. Most Chinese attended
political-study sessions only if they were absolutely unavoidable, and
then sat through them with the same kind of ennui as Americans forced
to attend traffic school. When compelled to write confessions or self-
criticisms, most just lied. Like officials agreeing with Qin Shihuang,
"students" told cadres whatever it was they wanted to hear just to get
the tedious business of having their thought "rectified" over with as
quickly as possible. The only thing that kept most from refusing to
participate in these rituals altogether was their awareness that the Party
still controlled so many practical aspects of everyday life, including
housing assignments, school entrance, career advancement, and per-

mission to travel abroad. But they approached their task with the kind of cynicism expressed in the following joke: Two police are on guard in Tiananmen Square when Policeman No. 1 asks Policeman No. 2 his views about June 4. "Oh, I'm not really sure about it. What do you think of it?" replies Policeman No. 2. "I'm also pretty unclear, but I probably feel about it the way you do," answers Policeman No. 1. "Well, if you feel about it the way I do, I'm sorry, but I'm going to have to arrest you," rejoins Policeman No. 2.

When these "study sessions" had been going on for some time, my wife and I visited a friend in Beijing whose "work unit" was in the throes of an intensive period of political indoctrination. Xiaohu is a bright, single woman in her mid-thirties who worked in a state-run municipal enterprise and lived in one of the hundreds of new but cheerless high-rise apartment buildings that rose like tombstones in the 1980s around the edges of what used to be old Beijing. As we sipped tea and chatted in her one-room flat, I noticed two pamphlets lying on a table. The thinnest one was entitled *An Outline of Certain Questions About Socialism.* What caught my eye was the line of red characters just below the title that warned: Internal Materials. Keep Confidential.

Aware that it was forbidden for Chinese to show such "internal materials" to foreigners, and not wanting to put Xiaohu in an awkward position, I didn't ask her about the pamphlets. But the next thing I knew, she was looking at me, smiling conspiratorially, and saying, "So, you're interested in those, are you?" I nodded. "They're my homework." She said the word "homework" puckering up her mouth as if she had just bitten into an unripe persimmon. "But, hey! Go ahead," she said with a laugh, waving dismissively at the pamphlets. "Look at them if you want. You're probably one of the few people on the face of the earth who would find them interesting!"

These pamphlets were part of a monthlong "socialist education" course being given to Xiaohu's work unit. Not only was she obliged to attend this course, but she was required to live in a dormitory at a suburban Party "school" and allowed to return home only on weekends. The *Outline* was divided into several sections, each a précis of longer arguments in the thicker volume that lay on the table. Realistic enough to recognize that few comrades would wade through endless pages of dogma, Party propagandists had packaged an abbreviated version. But the quickest glance left me wondering how many would even make it through the table of contents of the condensed version. The title of the first précis was "Scientific Socialism Reveals That the Main Historical Trend Is That Socialism Is Replacing Capitalism and That in the Last Twenty Years the Presence and Development of the

244 / MANDATE OF HEAVEN

Socialist System Has Made an Enormous Contribution Toward the Progress of Both Humanity and World Peace.'' The title of the second was ''The Replacement of Capitalism by Socialism Is a Long-term Historical Process and This New Social System Can Only Come of Age and Succeed After Going Through Numerous Complex Ups and Downs and by Continuing to Accumulate Experience.'' The third title was even more bloated: ''Although After World War II Imperialism Showed Relative Stability and Development, It Has Nonetheless Brought Many Large-Scale Disasters to Mankind and Has Never Rid Itself of Its Age-old Contradictions.'' And there were seven more such topics in all, each with a title longer than the last! It seemed as if Party propagandists had concluded that even their *Outline* was too dense and had thus performed the ultimate act of reductionism—shrinking hundreds of thousands of characters down to seven ponderous titles.

Reading the texts that followed was like listening to an insecure person who can't stop talking until he has exhausted every conceivable argument in his defense. No amount of self-justification seemed adequate. Moreover, in an effort to prove that the Party's various analyses and lines were, in fact, ''correct,'' the authors first raised every possible ''incorrect'' critique as a prelude to refutation. Alas, as presented, the ''incorrect'' critiques sounded more convincing by far.

As I browsed, it struck me as completely understandable that the Party would not want foreigners to see such ''internal materials.'' If the object in preparing these study materials was to convey a sense of confidence, conviction, and strength, in an all-too-embarrassing way these polemics accomplished the opposite effect by transparently revealing the Party's deepest fears and weaknesses. What radiated through their militant bluster was not the kind of self-assurance the Party was so eager to project, but an unmistakable air of self-doubt and failed nerve.

When I asked Xiaohu if her friends and colleagues found the ongoing political campaign forbidding, she replied, ''In the beginning no one was quite sure how far things would go, so naturally it was somewhat frightening. But now these stupid classes last a whole month!'' She rolled her eyes upward. ''All we do is sit and listen to dull lectures about political theory that nobody—not even the teachers—believes. We even have to take exams and write papers! My only fear is that I might die of boredom!''

At this point she started whispering in a conspiratorial manner. ''My boyfriend has already taken the same study course with his own work unit, so instead of wasting time writing a paper, I'm just going to hand in a copy of his.'' I clucked in mock horror at her disclosure. ''Oh, you shouldn't be surprised!'' she said sardonically, wagging an index finger at me. ''Perhaps you foreigners don't understand, but we know that they are lying to us, and they know that we are lying to them. In fact, everybody knows that everyone is lying to everyone else. So you might say that the system is working just as it's supposed to.''

It was hard not to be struck by the absurdity of the situation. To give state workers paid time off from their regular jobs to study political theory and to ruminate on the important issues confronting their country was certainly, in principle, a noble idea. And here was a government—perhaps the only one in the world—that not only gave its employees time to engage in such study, but also paid to house and feed them during the process. In the abstract, it seemed like a dream situation. The reality, of course, was rather different. By 1991 almost nobody in China was taking Marxism seriously. So instead of creating a greater receptivity to socialist theory, the Party's efforts only worsened an already advanced case of political alienation. The Party might force people like Xiaohu to attend a month of political study, but whether leaders knew it or not, long before she even arrived at her ''Party school'' dorm, she was already mentally beyond the reach of their turgid preachments.

However, since she was no political hero and had no urge to become a ''dissident,'' the Party did not really need to fear her either. Like those journalists who privately scorned the Party but went to work each day to put out its propaganda, her ambition was to elude the government's repressiveness by keeping her head down. Her greatest aspiration was to be left alone to lead her life.

This did not mean, however, that Xiaohu had been unsympathetic to the prodemocracy activists in 1989. In fact, she had been touched by their foolhardy bravery. Had they somehow managed to prevail, she might have welcomed a new government. But for now, like so many other educated Chinese, her strategy was to bide her time on the sidelines, suffer through her political-study sessions, and hope that things would ultimately change for the better.

23

The Spirit of
a Screw

Xiaohu's "internal materials" were only a small drop of the tidal wave of propaganda that crested over China after June 4, 1989. Just as most of the political ideas and jargon pressed into service in her pamphlets were reprised from earlier times in the Party's struggle against "incorrect thinking," many of the symbols were also lifted from previous political campaigns. Of all the resurrected symbols, none was wearier and more hackneyed than that of Lei Feng.

Lei had been a PLA soldier from a poor family in Hunan Province whom the Party had transformed into the paradigm of "service to the people" after he was ingloriously killed by a falling telephone pole in 1963. Immediately thereafter, Mao dubbed him a "revolutionary martyr" by uttering four simple words, "Learn from Lei Feng." Party hagiographers did the rest. They conveniently "discovered" a personal diary filled with testimonials to Lei's undying commitment to the Revolution, loyalty to the Party, love of Chairman Mao, and dedication to serving the masses. Because Mao himself had done the calligraphy for the title page, the diary was added to the canon of China's sacred socialist classics. It did not matter that it was almost certainly at least a partial forgery.

Lei Feng and his homilies soon became familiar to almost every Chinese. "Whatever Chairman Mao says, that I will do," was perhaps his best known line. "I have only one desire in my heart. I want to be wholeheartedly dedicated to the Party, socialism, and Communism,'' was a close runner-up.

Such expressions of slavish obedience to Mao and the Party made Lei Feng an enduring favorite of hard-liners nostalgic for the days before cynicism and dissent ran rampant. Since his canonization, Lei was frequently resurrected as an antidote to such ideologically poisonous phenomena as ''bourgeois liberalization,'' ''peaceful evolution,'' ''wholesale Westernization,'' and ''spiritual pollution.'' Each exhumation brought a new wave of Lei Feng study conferences, Lei Feng memorial meetings, Lei Feng books, Lei Feng photo albums, Lei Feng posters, Lei Feng stamps, Lei Feng calendars, and Lei Feng songs. Nothing captured ''the Lei Feng spirit'' and the numerous political campaigns in which he served as a posthumous veteran better than the song ''Emulate the Good Example of Lei Feng,'' written to ''commemorate'' his enshrinement in the pantheon of Maoist model proletarians. It went, in part:

> Emulate the fine example of Lei Feng,
> ever frugal and simple,
> ever willing to be a screw in the machine of revolution.
> All he ever wanted was for collectivism to shine!
> For collectivism to shine.
>
> Emulate the fine example of Lei Feng,
> who kept Chairman Mao's teachings ever in his heart
> and always served the people wholeheartedly.
> How exalted was his moral Communist character!

I first encountered this paragon of socialist virtue in 1975, sometime before Comrade Lei was completely drained of his credibility by overuse. Before being transformed after ''liberation'' into the prim Shanghai Youth Palace, the Great World was an amusement spot frequented by bon vivants and underworld figures that boasted six floors of gamblers, jugglers, masseurs, exotic sideshows, fortune-tellers, herbal practitioners offering remedies for everything, teahouses, dance halls, peep shows, and, of course, call girls. One night while being given a tour of the Great World in its latter-day incarnation of ''youth palace,'' I stumbled on an exhibit of Lei Feng memorabilia that included scores of black and white photographic blowups of Lei selflessly serving in the army, as well as a display of personal effects. Arranged and labeled in glass cases with all the care of a curated exhibit of Ming Dynasty porcelains was a dented face pan, a rusted tin cup, a fountain pen, a tattered pair of straw sandals, and an almost bristleless toothbrush that seemed to suggest that Lei brushed his teeth with no less ardor than he supported Chairman Mao and the Communist Revolution. Arrayed in little fanlike patterns under protective glass so that they looked almost as venerable as fragments of the Dead Sea Scrolls were a number of yellowing pages from Lei's hallowed handwritten diary.

As I came to the end of this reverential exhibit, I wondered who had had the foresight to save such mundane effluvia for the benefit of posterity, especially since Lei was not canonized by Mao until months after the telephone pole had done its dastardly work. When I asked an attendant how they had succeeded in assembling so many real artifacts from Lei's life, with all the surprise of an undertaker who has been asked if the Astroturf around a grave site needs watering, he replied, "Real? No! These things are all *fuzhipin!*" I still remember his reply, because not knowing the Chinese word for "facsimile," I had to ask its meaning before I could fully grasp what I had been told.

Since 1975 numerous other "emulate Lei Feng" campaigns had been launched, the last one after the student demonstrations in 1986. For the umpteenth time Party and army propagandists extravagantly extolled those willing to become Lei Feng–like "screws that will never rust" and will "glitter anywhere" they are placed in the machine of revolution. By then, however, most urban youth seemed to consider Lei a colossal joke, a kind of socialist Alfred E. Neuman, and they treated his reappearance in Party propaganda with sneering cynicism. Never imagining that he would survive the derision of another post-humous tour of duty, I wrote what I was certain would be a farewell epitaph to Lei in my 1988 book *Discos and Democracy*. But I had underestimated the tenacity and failing imagination of hard-line Party propagandists.

Soon after the Beijing massacre, Lei was quick-marched into the time warp once again. His reappearance was heralded in a front-page tribute that appeared in the December 15, 1989, issue of the *China Youth News* entitled "The Torch of Lei Feng's Spirit Will Never Go Out." On December 25 the New China News Agency began a six-part series glorifying the PLA and extolling Lei Feng's call for the masses to serve the army and the Party. That February the *People's Daily* was reporting that dozens of "living Lei Fengs"—a term that was strangely evocative of *huofu* (living Buddhas), whom Tibetans believe to be the reincarnations of enlightened lamas—had been identified around the country. On March 5, the anniversary of Mao's canonization of Lei, even the *Nanfang Ribao*, a daily newspaper published in Canton—a city filled with boutiques and fashion-conscious, narcissistic youth, where Lei's ethic of selfless service had been almost completely eclipsed by the Hong Kong ethic of making money—carried the headline "Gain a Profound Understanding of the Spirit of Lei Feng, and Carry Out Widespread Activities to Learn from Lei Feng." The accompanying article noted that Party General Secretary Jiang Zemin, Premier Li Peng, and President Yang Shangkun had all written inscriptions in their own calligraphy "calling on the whole Party, the whole army, and the people throughout the whole country to learn from the spirit of Lei Feng, to take the path of Lei Feng, and to set off a new surge of learning about Lei Feng." The Party also proceeded to release half a million freshly minted Lei Feng diaries and an equal number of tapes of old songs glorifying him. Included in the medley were such favorites as "Emulate Lei Feng," "Lei Feng, Our Comrade-in-Arms," and "I'm Willing to Be That Kind of Fool."

Curious to find out if Lei Feng mythology had been given any new twists since June 4, I made a pilgrimage in the fall of 1990 to the Military Museum in Beijing where yet another Lei Feng exhibit had recently opened.

The first thing that caught my eye inside the museum's rotunda was a heroic statue of Mao Zedong, one of the diminishing flock on public display in Beijing. It was flanked by busts of Marx, Engels, Lenin, and Stalin, reminders that before Deng's reforms these hirsute apostles of socialism were the only Westerners most ordinary Chinese had any familiarity with. Almost immediately, I made a wrong turn and unexpectedly found myself in a cavernous hall containing displays of rifles, bayonets, hand grenades, machine guns, mortars, and rocket launchers—a full arsenal of PLA weapons. Amid all this ordnance I felt as if I had strayed into a military compound. Even more disconcerting, I seemed to be the only foreigner there. Almost all the other visitors were young khaki-clad soldiers who locked onto me with radar-like stares, their faces displaying the same looks of suspicion I remembered from my bike tour of Tiananmen Square the year before. It occurred to me that it was at these young peasant soldiers—for whom the PLA had undoubtedly been an avenue out of poverty-stricken rural China—not alienated students or urban youth, that the new Lei Feng campaign was aimed.

Although during the eighties Deng initiated an ambitious program to transform the PLA from a guerrilla army stressing "redness," or revolutionary spirit and ideological purity, into a modern professional force emphasizing "expertise," or skill and new technology, the program was suspended in the wake of June 4, when once again political reliability rather than military professionalism was emphasized. As the secretary of the Military Affairs Commission's Discipline and Inspection Committee put it, "The armed forces' most important mission is to make sure that they are up to standards politically." The official military paper *Liberation Army Daily* was blunter. "Under any circumstances, we must firmly maintain the principle that the Party commands the gun. The army is a proletarian military force created and led by the Chinese Communist Party, and is an armed group for carrying out the Party's political tasks." In a China no longer threatened by foreign armies, there was, in fact, no other task besides the defense of the Party.

Taking yet another wrong turn, I next found myself in an open courtyard amid a display of camouflaged armored vehicles and tanks equipped with turret cannons and machine guns that looked almost as if they were being garaged here until the next insurrection. It was something of a relief when I finally found my way out of this intimidating armory into the Lei Feng exhibit itself where there were suddenly so many photos and portraits of the smiling soldier-hero gazing down at me that I felt as if I was in a house of mirrors. There were blowups of Lei beaming as he studied Chairman Mao's works in his pug-nosed PLA summer cap and as he repaired an army truck in his fur-lined ear-flapped winter hat; as he dutifully sewed his own clothes; as he stood in front of a bust of Mao; and smiling as he threw a hand grenade at some unidentified mock enemy. In every photo he grinned uncontrollably with nonstop socialist ecstasy.

Just past a brown bust of Lei that looked as if it had been sculpted out of baked meat loaf was a collection of memorabilia even more extensive than the one I had seen in 1975. It had the ambience of those American displays of mementos celebrating pop-music legends like Elvis Presley and Liberace. Nothing was too ordinary for veneration: Lei's driver's license, one of his mittens, a pair of old socks, a set of wrenches, a soldering iron, a pistol, a pair of boots, even some discolored underwear, and, of course, pages from his celebrated diary were all here. I almost expected to round a corner and find a vial of toenail clippings, like those relics of Catholic saints preserved in crypts beneath European cathedrals. But whereas the remains of saints are enshrined in such a way as to convey a sense of martyred greatness, this mass of Lei Feng flotsam and jetsam conveyed only a sense of the pedestrian—like a deceased relative's household effects that need to be dispatched to a Salvation Army thrift shop.

As I made my way through the displays, I of course wondered whether these so convincingly tattered, stained, discolored, and faded artifacts were not also *fuzhipin*. Pragmatist Deng Xiaoping's best-known motto may have been "Seek Truth from Facts," but when it came to propaganda, the authenticity of "facts" and "evidence" was not always of the greatest concern to the Party. If the appropriate facts, or even worn-out toothbrushes and yellowed underwear, did not exist, it was always justifiable to fabricate them. Was there not a factory somewhere—The East Is Red No. 3 Lei Feng Facsimile Products Works—dedicated exclusively to mass-producing Lei's specially antiqued memorabilia for exhibits around the country? I wondered.

It seemed extremely unlikely to me that the Party would be successful in influencing students or intellectuals with such simple-minded propaganda. In fact, one survey of universities in Jiangxi Province showed that as early as 1988 only 2 percent of the student body considered Lei a worthy model. Only at the end of the exhibit did the target of this most recent Lei Feng revival became clear to me. Opposite the last cases displaying Lei's personal effects stood a row of life-sized busts made out of the same meatloaf-like substance used to sculpt Lei himself. Each one bore the inscription "Guardian of China," and each had a red scarf tied around its mottled brown neck like those worn by the Young Pioneers I had seen in Tiananmen Square. Plaques affixed to their pedestals identified the busts as likenesses of those soldiers who had died on the night of June 4. While the difference between being beaned by a falling telephone pole and ripped apart in the streets of Beijing by "the people" was enormous, what Party propagandists wished to emphasize by putting Lei and these soldiers on pedestals was their unflinching willingness to take orders, whatever the consequences. In an age of galloping individualism and persistent challenges to authority, the army and the Party desperately needed more Lei Feng–like "screws" who could be inserted into the military machine and relied upon to be obedient—even to "serve" against "the people" if commanded to do so.

Soldiers had been bivouacked in this museum and the street in front had been one of the worst killing grounds during the early night hours of June 3–4. The next morning hysterical crowds had gathered around the steel fence circumscribing the museum. "There were two rows of soldiers standing very close to the fence holding guns across their chests," remembered one resident who lived nearby. "Outside there were people grabbing onto the fence, crowding up against it, crying, and cursing. There was one student who said he was from Qinghua University . . . who cried so hard that he was out of breath. He looked as if he wanted to die right there, and he told the surrounding people, 'My classmate died right in my arms with blood and brains spilling onto my hands!' Then he grabbed onto the iron fence, shouting at the army, 'You and I are both twenty-year-olds, so why are we killing each other to maintain the positions of those eighty-year olds?' ''

It was all well and good to make a camp joke out of Lei Feng, but he had, after all, been a PLA soldier, and if ordered to do so, there is no doubt that he would have been among the first to charge the barricades here at Muxidi with his AK-47 blazing away.

24

Interrogation and Surveillance

With newspapers and magazines back under Party control and the country awash with propaganda about the likes of Lei Feng, within China only the overseas press corps remained able to openly discuss sensitive political subjects. Needless to say, Party leaders struggling to control the flow of information were infuriated when foreign correspondents continued to file stories about the detentions, arrests, trials, sentences, and executions of those accused of participating in the "turmoil." Since these stories were negatively influencing international perceptions of China, and in some instances becoming serious impediments to normal diplomatic and trade relations, the Beijing-based foreign press corps were more than ever viewed by hard-liners as part of a conspiracy of "hostile foreign forces" and "domestic counterrevolutionaries" bent on undermining China's stability and sabotaging its socialist system.

In the spring of 1991, a succession of occurrences around the second anniversary of the Beijing massacre revealed just how deep the animosity toward the foreign press had become. On June 6, after getting hold of a newsletter that identified me as vice-chair of Asia Watch, the PSB unexpectedly banned a talk I was scheduled to give at the Sheraton Great Wall Hotel to the Beijing Foreign Correspondents' Club (BFCC). The talk, entitled "The Silence of Chinese Intellectuals," was scheduled to be given at a foreign joint-venture hotel to a foreign audience with no Chinese in attendance. It was the first time anyone could recall the government's intruding on an event organized by and for members of the foreign community.

At the same time, the PSB ordered managers at the Sheraton to cancel the BFCC's annual spring ball. In this case, some high-ranking Party official had been offended by the way organizers had facetiously called their get-together "The Peaceful Evolution Ball," and then billed it as an event where "bourgeois liberals could liberalize." Not surprisingly, the BFCC, whose president was the *Wall Street Journal*'s James McGregor, viewed the PSB order as an alarming intrusion into the club's own "internal affairs."

The third danger signal that spring was a rumor that the PSB had caught a foreign correspondent with a "top secret" government document in his possession and were weighing measures in retaliation. Although I had hoped few would notice, in this tense atmosphere word about the cancellation of my talk quickly appeared in newspapers around the world, from the *Washington Post* and the *International Herald Tribune* to the French paper *Le Monde* and Hong Kong's *South China Morning Post*. Even the *People's Daily* joined the chorus. "Some foreign enemies of socialist China and a very few of the elite leaders of the turmoil who escaped the country hate the stability, prosperity, and development of Beijing and the whole nation," said an editorial that left every foreign journalist feeling menaced by the possibility of an expulsion.

A few days later when I had lunch with an old friend, the son of a high-ranking Chinese leader, he told me that he had heard a good deal about the BFCC incident although he had not realized I was involved. When I asked if he knew who had ordered the cancellation, he paused for a long time and then silently pointed toward the ceiling.

"The order came from the top," he said in a whisper. "If you had gone to the luncheon, the consequences would have been dire. I think you would have been picked up."

After delivering this upsetting news, he allowed that he would never have come to lunch if had he known my speech was the casus belli. Then he asked me to stay seated while he left the restaurant alone so we would not be spotted departing together. The process of social isolation, long the fate of Chinese who fall under political suspicion, seemed to be setting in. As word of "my situation" got around, X and his wife, two very old Chinese friends who had only recently been enthusiastically urging me to come for dinner, suddenly became vague about getting together. Likewise, after repeated expressions of enthusiasm before my arrival about our seeing one another, Z and her husband suddenly became so "busy" that the date had to be postponed.

I arrived back at the hotel from lunch to find a cryptic message at the front desk: "Please contact reception regarding your message." A nervous-looking concierge gave me a handwritten note: "Contact Director Ma at the Beijing Public Security Bureau's Department of Foreign Affairs on Beichizi at 2:30."

Fearing the worst, my Chinese-born wife and I hastily gathered up our address books, computer discs, and notebooks and, for what it was worth, locked them up in a hotel strongbox. Should the PSB choose to search our things, the last thing we wanted was to give them access to a list of our friends and contacts, many of whom were dissident intellectuals who already had enough problems of their own. In a state of shock, we hailed a pedicab and set off. Not the least of my worries was the effect all this might have on my wife, who was six months pregnant and who, although she now carried an American passport, still had relatives in China.

Suddenly, we were standing in front of the PSB compound. We gave our name to the gatekeeper, and as we waited, I tried to slow my mind down, to decide how we should approach whatever might follow. I knew that the PSB rarely admitted to hauling people in for political reasons, and usually used technical violations as a cover to express other kinds of displeasure. But as far as I could tell, I'd done nothing illegal. My thoughts were suddenly interrupted by two police officers in front of us.

"You are to be questioned in different rooms," one of them announced in wooden English.

"I'm very sorry, but I will not be separated from my wife," I responded as calmly as I could.

"According to our internal regulations you will be—"

"Why have we been summoned here?" I demanded.

"You must go to separate rooms for questioning."

At this point Director Ma appeared.

"My wife is pregnant, and if you wish to charge us with some offense, I wish you would let us know what we have done wrong." There was a moment of silence, but from the opaque look on his face it was obvious that Director Ma did not understand English. "If we are going to engage in friendly exchange," I continued, using Chinese, "we must be in the same room."

"This is not a friendly conversation," Director Ma's adjutant shot back. "This is an investigation!"

A providential spring thundershower suddenly arrived, and as large raindrops began making dark gray splash marks on the policemen's khaki uniforms, they grudgingly escorted us together into a dingy room across the courtyard. Like most official meeting rooms in China, it was filled with elephantine stuffed chairs and sofas adorned with lace antimacassars. A stained rug covered the floor and a lone landscape painting hung curling with age on one discolored wall. As my wife and I took a seat on one of the couches and several other policemen materialized in the room, Director Ma took his place behind a table in front of us. A woman sat beside him with pen poised to take notes. Director Ma opened a file in front of him. Was this my *dangan* (dossier)? Had they been gathering information on me for years just as they did on their own citizens? Its heft was almost flattering.

"Show me your passports," demanded Director Ma.

I handed the documents to a sour-looking officer who arose from an adjacent couch, but as he began leafing through the pages, I immediately regretted having relinquished them.

"When did you enter China?" "What is your profession?" "Why are you here?" "Where did you get your visa?" The questions came like machine-gun fire. Their relentlessness was almost hypnotic, and my answers sounded like part of someone else's conversation. Meanwhile, the other policemen stared at us blankly and chain-smoked cigarettes, filling the room with suffocating clouds of smoke.

"What is your wife's full name?" "Where was she born?" "What is her profession?" "When did she arrive?" My wife sat glumly beside me on the verge of tears. "Where are you staying?" "What is your room number?" "How many other people are staying in your room?" "Did you register when you came in?" "When did you, in fact, register?"

As I replied, I recalled the strangely urgent 11 P.M. phone call I had received from the reception desk two nights previously. I had been almost asleep at the time, but the clerk had insisted that I go down to the lobby and fill in a registration form immediately. I had notified the front desk of my arrival so that I could receive phone calls, but since my wife had been in Beijing and registered for the room before I landed, it had not occurred to me to fill out a separate form of my own. It was beginning to dawn on me that this was my technical offense.

"So, you arrived on the fifth, but it was not until June eighth that you registered?" intoned Director Ma, plucking my hotel registration form out of the file and holding it up like a piece of evidence on display at a trial.

"Well, this was hardly an intentional act. It never really occurred to me that both members of a married couple had to—"

"Just answer the question, yes or no, because our computer link with the hotel will tell us the truth," said Director Ma, glancing down at the notes that a female officer beside him was scribbling.

"What I am saying is that my failure to fill in this form was not a purposeful act. At hotels abroad, it is quite adequate for one member of a couple to register." The police officers arrayed around the room glowered, making it obvious that such invidious comparisons with the West would only make matters worse.

"So, you admit your errors?"

"No, I—"

"Did you not violate the regulations of the People's Republic of China by entering the hotel without first registering or not?"

"I didn't even know that there were such regulations."

"It is the responsibility of all foreign guests to—"

"You're just searching for bones in an egg!" exploded my wife in Chinese, unable to contain her frustration and annoyance any longer. Ma gave her a wrathful glance. While I was an auslander and might be excused for certain errant tendencies, she was a native Chinese from Beijing for whom such insubordination was tantamount to treason.

"I am very sorry if I have done anything to inconvenience anyone," I said, trying to calm things down.

"So you admit that you were wrong," Ma proclaimed, a note of triumph in his voice.

My wife had begun to cry, and even though I hadn't the foggiest idea what the regulations were to which my accusers were referring, by then I was tempted to confess to whatever he wanted just to end the upsetting charade.

"I admit that I registered several days after arriving because I assumed—"

"You realize this is a very serious matter," interrupted Ma. "You have violated Chinese law. To require guests to register at a hotel is an internationally recognized sovereign right of any government." He held up a pamphlet entitled *The Laws of the People's Republic of China on Entry and Exit of Aliens,* opened it, and began reading like a preacher citing a scriptural lesson.

"I admit registering a few days after I arrived in Beijing, but that was two days ago," I interrupted. "What is the real reason you have summoned us here?"

"There is no other reason," said Ma preemptively. "Now that you understand our rules and regulations, perhaps you will not make such a mistake again." He seemed to be softening a bit. "Whether intentional or not, you broke the law. You have admitted your error, and now you will have to pay a fine.''

"Pay a fine?" I yelped in surprise. Then it occurred to me that this might simply be a very Chinese way of ending the affair without either side losing face, the equivalent of a nolo contendere plea. "Please tell me how much," I said, making a gesture to reach for my wallet.

"Ah no!" said Ma, raising a hand as if he were a street cop halting traffic. "We will investigate this matter and deliver a judgment later. For the next few days you must stay by your phone and remain in Beijing."

Just when I thought that at last we would be able to leave, another police officer changed places with Ma behind the inquisitor's table and the interrogation started all over again, this time with my wife in the docket.

Two and a half exhausting hours after we first sat down, the woman who had been scribbling notes rose from the table and presented us with what she called "a transcript," a jumble of bowdlerized snatches from the interrogations. "You must sign these in accordance with our regulations," she said icily.

At this point my wife leaned over and told me that her stomach had begun to hurt. I, too, felt exhausted. It was unsettling, although revealing, to see how quickly this experience had undermined both of our powers of resistance. I finally suggested that at the bottom of each of these two confessions-masquerading-as-transcripts, we write, "This is only a rough précis of our questioning on June 10," and then sign our names.

As we walked down Donghuamen toward the outdoor food stalls that were just beginning to open in the Night Market, something suddenly clicked in my mind. I recalled that toward the end of my interrogation, Director Ma had referred to a computer link between the big joint-venture hotels and the PSB. Could it have been that when the brouhaha over the cancellation of my BFCC talk erupted, the PSB had been embarrassingly unable to find me because my name did not appear in their computer? Had they only been able to locate my whereabouts by physically tracking me to the Palace Hotel, which was when I received the urgent 11 o'clock phone call demanding that I come down to the lobby and register? Whatever the genesis of my summons, as we left the PSB office, I naively hoped that my problems were now over.

I first became suspicious that I was being followed when I came out of a shop that evening and noticed a familiar-looking man wearing dark glasses and carrying a small black leatherette case the size of a collapsible umbrella standing at a bus stop. When I stared at him, he turned and began walking away. I recognized him as one of the men who often lounged on the lobby couches in our hotel, chain-smoking and staring off into a haze of cigarette smoke.

The next morning as I left the hotel, I saw him again. Once outside the front door, I ducked behind a tour bus in the parking area to see if he really was shadowing me. Moments later, almost at a run, he rounded the front of the bus and practically bumped into me. With a chagrined look on his face, he again beat a hasty retreat. When I hailed a cab in the street, I saw him standing just outside the hotel's main entrance watching. Then as my cab pulled away, he raised the small black case to his mouth.

That afternoon my wife and I took a walk. No sooner had we crossed the first intersection at Wangfujing than we spotted a second man in sunglasses standing in a doorway raise a black case to his mouth. On the next corner there was another of these sullen sentries with the same black case, standing against a store window.

At the third intersection there was yet another. With PSB clones skulking everywhere, our stroll felt more and more like a manhunt. Their ubiquity made us suspect that they had always been there and we had just innocently overlooked them. No longer really caring where we were going, we began dodging and weaving down the street, possessed by an irrepressible urge to free ourselves from the suffocating sense of entrapment that all this surveillance induced. Although I knew that almost every foreign journalist in Beijing had also been followed at one time or another, and that our U.S. passports would ultimately protect us from any serious harm, such knowledge did little to miligate against the unsettling, even alarming feeling of being stalked. The only constructive side of the experience, I tried to remind myself, was that it gave me a hint of how so many Chinese have felt over the past four decades as they have faced the inescapable and implacable power of the state.

When we were halfway down Nanchizi, heading toward the Square, I spotted an empty cab and impulsively flagged it down. Glancing back through the rear window and not seeing anyone following, for an instant I allowed myself to hope that we had shaken our pursuers. But suddenly a red motorcycle with two helmeted riders emerged from a side alley and proceeded to trail along about fifty yards behind us. Involuntarily, I thought about stopping the cab so that my wife and I could flee in different directions. But since we had no place to go except back to our hotel, where we would be more exposed than ever to our pursuers, the absurdity of this impulse became immediately obvious.

The motorcycle was still with us when we reached the Avenue of Eternal Peace. And as if towed by a cable attached to the bumper of our taxi it remained right behind us as we passed Chairman Mao's portrait and swung around the Great Hall of the People. When we pulled up at Liulichang, an alley lined with bookstores and art galleries, our shadow stopped, too. Walking down the alley, I noted with dismay that we were now being pursued by three new tails who were on foot: two shady-looking young guys in white drip-dry shirts, drab slacks, and regimental dark glasses, and the third, a corpulent character incongruously garbed in a tank top, shorts, and sockless high-heeled plastic sandals, a mutant form of male footwear then considered à la mode. It seemed that PSB operatives were capable of handing off their quarries from one team to another with astonishing precision.

When we stepped into a shop that sold books and stone rubbings, one of our new tails followed us inside, sat down on a chair next to the shelves on which history books were displayed, yawned, and lit up a cigarette. He was a squat young man with Brylcreemed hair and the suggestion of a mustache. Being able to scrutinize one of our pursuers in such mortal closeness was strangely calming. Instead of avoiding him, I found myself drawn to where he sat by the prospect of escaping the role of the passive, hunted prey and of somehow turning the tables on him.

"How are you?" I heard myself say in Chinese. He blinked up at me as if he had been awakened in the middle of a deep sleep by a bright light shining into his eyes. "So, are you interested in history?" I asked with a synthetic cheerfulness, glancing up at the books behind him. He looked up at the shelves with bewilderment, and then uncomfortably stammered, "Uh, well, yes."

"Ah, good! I love Chinese history, too! Tell me, what dynastic periods particularly interest you? Maybe we can become friends!" I exclaimed, parroting a line that Chinese themselves often use in approaching foreigners to learn English under the pretext of "building friendship."

"Oh, umm . . . well, actually I like literature," he demurred.

"Well, I'm also interested in literature," I replied agreeably. "What kind of literature do you like?"

"Oh, well . . . essays, and . . ." His eyes began to dart around.

"Oh really?" I crooned. "I also love essays. I am even a writer. In fact, sometimes I write essays on modern Chinese history, student demonstrations, security police, and even prisons—things like that. So, maybe we could get together sometime and talk.''

He stared up at me wide-eyed. My wife, who was leafing through a book of stone rubbings, also looked at me as if I had lost my senses. Then suddenly our tail stood up. ''I have to go now,'' he said, and like a kid who suddenly realizes he is late for dinner, streaked out the door.

I watched out the window as in the alleyway he conferred with his buddies, who began furtively glancing back at the shop just as earlier I had been looking over my own shoulder at them. I found my spirits somehow buoyed.

Liulichang alley, where this cat-and-mouse game was going on, is situated in a very old part of Beijing where twisting *hutong* crisscross the neighborhood like a complex web of tiny capillaries. As we approached one side *hutong*, and the line of sight between our tails and us was momentarily obscured by a tour group from Japan, I impulsively pulled my wife by the arm into this narrow alley and we began walking, almost running. Just before we slipped around a corner at the far end, I glanced back toward Liulichang. No one was following. Ten minutes later when we emerged on Xuanwumen Avenue, and I hailed another cab, there was still no evidence of our pursuers. As we sped away, I felt giddy with success!

But because in this People's Republic there has never been any final escape from government surveillance, our ''victory'' was short-lived. That night we were to attend the birthday party of a close Chinese friend. As we left the hotel, we were again followed. Because we feared the effect our presence would have on our friend, we almost turned back. But since we were also concerned that our host would feel slighted if we inexplicably failed to appear, we pressed on.

As we should have expected, the party was agony. Word of my canceled talk had reached many of the well-connected guests, and I could sense a distinct aloofness from some of them. Few people in China want to maintain contact with someone who is in political trouble. Though I understood the logic behind this standoffishness, the feeling of quarantine made the time before we felt able to say our goodbyes move with painful slowness. At that moment, had there been a way to expiate my ''sins''—whatever they were—and escape the uncomfortable feeling of being an outcast and so contaminating to everyone around us, I would have welcomed it.

In retrospect, we probably made the wrong decision in going to the party. At the time, I was still somewhat disbelieving that all this could be happening to me. Later on, after I had left the country, I learned that our friend had indeed been called in by superiors at her ''work unit'' for an explanation of my presence in her house and that she was upset with us for attending her party.

Although ultimately I was not required to pay a fine and was able to leave the country without incident, the whole experience highlighted for me the way that the state has succeeded in using fear and ostracism to isolate and control anyone it views as politically suspect. Once an individual is tainted by accusation, he becomes ensnared in a crippling psychological paradox. Not only is he made to feel sullied, but at the same time he also acquires the unshakable capacity to sully everyone he comes in contact with as well. Thus in one deft stroke, the Party is able to contrive a devastating condition of double jeopardy. First, it cripples those it condemns with accusations of political incorrectness, and then it delivers a *coup de grace* by transforming the accused from simple victims into potential destroyers of all their friends and relatives as well. A few exceptional people may remain loyal under such circumstances, but historically, many more Chinese have found it expedient to abandon friends and colleagues—sometimes even divorce spouses, and sever all connection with parents and children—to escape guilt by association.

At this birthday party, as in the interrogation room and when shadowed through the streets of Beijing, I had brushed up against an aspect of China's system of social and political control that eluded most foreigners. Instead of being just another "China watcher," for a brief moment I glimpsed an experience that has long been seminal in controlling educated Chinese. After groping for years to understand the paralysis that gripped Chinese intellectuals until this newest generation of students revived the May Fourth tradition in Tiananmen Square, I had now sensed within myself hints of the intimidated and fearful state of mind that had kept them silent for so long. Of course, compared to theirs, my own travails were inconsequential. But what had happened made me more curious than ever to probe the range of subtle yet powerful pressures that the Party has employed so successfully to suppress dissent, and to better understand the deep scars that this suppression has left on the psyches of China's intelligentsia.

If prisons are the ultimate way to silence political opposition, in China they have been a choice of last resort because the government has had a whole arsenal of other highly effective intermediate measures at its disposal to assure ideological uniformity and political obedience. When propaganda, ideological study sessions, political campaigns, and societal pressure failed to bring a comrade into line, the threat of having one's thought or activity publicly labeled politically "incorrect" and one's reputation ruined has usually been more than enough inducement to deter critics from further resistance. It would not be too extreme to say that the Party's power to accuse has been its most effective weapon in creating ideological uniformity. Whether made against whole classes of people as during the Antirightist Campaign in the late 1950s or during the early stages of the Cultural Revolution during the mid 1960s, accusations of incorrect thinking left individual victims feeling so isolated and paralyzed with self-doubt and guilt that there was usually no need to actually imprison them.

In describing his experience of being labeled a "rightist" in the late fifties, former *People's Daily* reporter Liu Binyan has spoken of how the constant drone of accusation made him "lose confidence" in his own sense of innocence. "Was I without fault?" he wrote in his autobiography, *A Higher Kind of Loyalty*. "Of course not. . . . Could I honestly say that I had joined the Party solely for the liberation of the Chinese people with no ulterior motives? Of course not. There was at least some element of self-fulfillment. And then there was my writing. Could I honestly say that I never had an eye on publicity and profit? Of course not."

The way in which official accusation exaggerated Liu's self-doubt and generated the urge toward guilty self-flagellation was characteristic of what happened to almost every intellectual who came under political attack. No matter how ardently Liu or other "rightists" criticized themselves, or each other, the authorities continued to accuse them of "insufficient awareness" of their guilt and "insufficient resolution to undergo thorough and complete reform of the self." Since in the eyes of the Party no amount of intellectual self-immolation was ever sufficient penance, it was impossible to ever win complete absolution from the crushing burden of guilt.

Looking back upon the twenty-two years of political persecution he endured, Liu recalled elsewhere how he became filled "with a sense of humiliation" that silently reminded him that he "was the lowest of the low, that I had injured my wife and children, [and] that I had no hope of exoneration in this life." The "endless charges" that were leveled against him were "very effective," says Liu, not only in adding to his "load of guilt," but in reducing him to a state of penitent acquiescence. What he craved was not the catharsis of revolt but the "sigh of relief" promised by self-confession. As the Russian poet and Nobel laureate Joseph Brodsky noted about his own experience under Communism in an exchange with Czech President Vaclav Havel, "One may be perfectly convinced that the state is wrong, but one is seldom confident of one's own virtue."

It was, no doubt, such a political climate of guilt that Party hard-liners dreamed of reestablishing after June 4. They seemed to have recognized that it was precisely the breakdown of this complicated system of guilt-induced self-censorship and self-control that had allowed so many people to break free from the Party's gravitational field and fearlessly fill Tiananmen Square with protest. And it was an awareness of their inability to replicate this fearful state of guilt-induced submission among the newest generation of intellectuals that helped create such a feeling of paranoia among hard-line leaders.

Shortly after my own interrogation, the Chinese government, as many had expected, expelled a foreign journalist. Andrew Higgins, bureau chief for the British paper the *Independent* and coauthor of the book *Tiananmen: The Rape of Peking,* was kicked out for possession of classified Chinese documents. It was interesting to watch the effect of Higgins's expulsion. Many other foreign reporters, worried about having their own careers interrupted, shied away for the moment from the kind of hard-hitting investigative stories about dissidents, prisons, or Party leaders that might incur official wrath.

Even after a decade of reform and ''opening up to the outside world,'' the Chinese state could still be an awesomely intimidating force. While it could no longer watch everyone, when it chose to target a lone individual for harassment, it could still be effective in stilling dissent. Nonetheless, things were changing in fundamental ways. A new generation of Chinese whose primal experience was not Mao's revolution but the protest movements and the entrepreneurial frenzy of the 1980s was coming of age. Even as the government attempted to initiate new campaigns of propaganda and political harassment in hopes of exploiting the kinds of insecurities that make all human beings vulnerable to self-blame and self-censorship, it found itself confronting a younger generation far less willing to surrender its urge for some kind of independence. And as more time elapsed after the trauma of June 4, it became clear that while hard-liners might temporarily succeed in bullying the Chinese into an appearance of political submission, they were not going to be successful in returning the country to a neo-Maoist era.

25

Miniature Rebellions

To mark National Day on October 1, 1991, Party leaders turned once again to Tiananmen Square. Instead of holding a parade, this time, they filled the Square with a floral spectacular composed of more than 160,000 pots of chrysanthemums arrayed around a series of portable fountains. The *pièce de résistance* was a giant crimson star composed of red flowers with sunbursts of golden blossoms emanating outward from the center like the rays of a halo. And then opposite Mao's portrait, organizers contrived another arrangement of potted flowers spelling out "Socialism Is Good!" Short of "Jesus Wept," it was hard to think of a more blunt utterance.

For the first time since the spring of 1989, tens of thousands of ordinary people were allowed into the Square at one time. It was a sign that the government was feeling more secure, and the sight of the crowds milling about this most symbolic of all Chinese public places once more did make it seem, as surely it was meant, that 1989 had been a bad dream. In fact, like a hurricane advisory that is downgraded as a storm blows out to sea, Party propagandists were no longer referring to what had happened as a "counterrevolutionary rebellion," but simply as "the turmoil." The impression they wished to convey was of a country that was now as unperturbed by dissension as the gargantuan flower arrangement filling the Square. As Jiang Zemin had wishfully just told Barbara Walters when she asked him how he looked back on the events of 1989, "It's like much ado about nothing."

This carefully curried semblance of order was deceptive. Not only were there hundreds of plainclothes police agents drifting unobtrusively through the crowd lest unscheduled acts of protest erupt, but the cheerful mien of the flower-bedecked Square hardly represented how most ordinary people actually felt. Like an uninterred body, June 4 continued to cry out for an appropriate and respectable burial. The yearning that many continued to feel for some sort of commemoration could never be fulfilled by parades or crimson stars fashioned out of potted flowers. But since the government stubbornly refused to acknowledge the tragic significance of what had happened, much less allow for a ceremony at which those who had died could be properly remembered, the Square remained charged with unresolved energy and, like a lodestone, kept drawing defiant demonstrators back into its embrace to engage in solitary acts of guerrilla mourning.

Such observances were, of course, politically suicidal. As soon as anyone began such a ritual protest, plainclothes policemen materialized as if out of nowhere. Within moments the offenders were surrounded, seized, and dragged away. Only on those rare occasions when foreign journalists had been alerted in advance or happened to be at the Square for other reasons were such fleeting moments of defiance recorded. But then, like shooting stars in the night sky, these usually nameless protesters would disappear.

On the first anniversary of June 4, a lone figure had walked up to the Monument and nervously fumbled to display a handmade banner; moments later he was seized and taken away. That night at Beida, a young economics student named Li Minqi, who had been active in the outlawed BASF, tried to mark the anniversary by addressing a spontaneous midnight rally on campus where he indignantly referred to China's current leaders as "wild and savage autocrats" and called for an elective government that could supervise the Communist Party. Li was not only promptly expelled from Beida, but arrested, labeled a "chief instigator of an anti-Party conspiracy," accused of "counterrevolutionary propaganda and incitement," and sentenced to two years in prison.

On the second anniversary of the massacre, a young woman dressed in funeral white appeared in front of the Monument to observe a moment of silence. "I came to remember," she told a *South China Morning Post* correspondent before drifting away just as suspicious undercover agents began to close in.

Then in 1992, on the third anniversary of the massacre, a young worker named Wang Wanxing appeared not far from where a new sign warned visitors that it was illegal to lay memorial wreaths in front of the Monument without prior approval. After unfurling a banner calling on Deng to apologize for the crackdown that followed the protest, he was seized, dragged away, and committed to a mental hospital. In a letter to U.N. Secretary-General Boutros Boutros-Ghali smuggled out of China a month later, Wang asserted that not only was he being held against his will in Shanghai's Ankang Psychiatric Hospital for the criminally insane, but he was being forced to take psychotropic drugs.

Not everyone who felt the urge to remember could afford to be so open. Many Chinese settled for more oblique forms of protest, furtive and indirect miniature rebellions that could be carried out without getting the perpetrators caught. In the spring of 1991, during the period leading up to the second anniversary of June 4, a whole host of such protests erupted. One that attracted much international attention involved a pseudonymous poem entitled "Yuanxiao" (Lantern Festival), which slipped past *People's Daily* editors and into the paper's March 19 Overseas Edition. At first glance, the poem appeared to be nothing more than an innocuous ode to spring written in a traditional style. When discerning readers studied the text carefully, however, they discovered that it included an acrostic. If read diagonally from the top right-hand corner to the bottom left-hand corner, the poem contained a line of characters reading, *"Li Peng xiatai ping minhen"* ("Li Peng must step down to appease the anger of the people").

When a reporter managed to query Li Peng about the offending verse at a press conference a month later, Li downplayed the whole affair. "This is a small incident, and not worth mentioning," he replied coolly. "China is a vast country with a huge population, and in my opinion it is not surprising that there are some individuals who oppose the current policy of the Party and government. . . . I do not think the author of this poem represents the will of the people."

On the morning of May 1, a day that is celebrated in China as International Labor Day, citizens in the Tiantan Park area of Beijing awoke to find a battery of kites flying over Longtan Lake inscribed with "Bury the Li Peng and Yang Shangkun Regime and Joyously Celebrate May Day."

Three days later, dissident employees at the People's Broadcasting Station in Beijing were reported in the Hong Kong press to have almost succeeded in pulling off their own covert media coup. Two defamatory slogans—"Deng-Li-Yang Are Murderers!" and "Abolish One-Party

Dictatorship!''—were dubbed onto a tape scheduled for airing during an evening newscast, and were discovered only minutes before broadcast time by a wary news director.

Computer hackers were also busy that spring waging electronic warfare by introducing rogue viruses into software programs used on government computers. One such virus caused the words "Remember June 4" to appear on display terminals, while another flashed the slogan "Bloody June 4" as soon as computers at certain state enterprises were booted up. A more elaborate virus required operators to respond with a "Yes" or "No" to the statement "Down with Li Peng." If an operator answered "Yes," the program allowed the user to proceed. If the user answered "No," the machine automatically turned off or erased all stored files.

Despite increased campus surveillance, on May 28, 1991, Beida students managed to hang cloth streamers out of two dorm windows declaring, "We Will Never Forget June 4!" Leaflets recalling the events of 1989 also appeared in the student canteen. "Those were days that woke the heart and moved the spirit! Then the hue and cry became the sound of suffocation in a pool of blood . . . and for the last two years the earth has been sunk in an abyss." And a few days later as the June 4 anniversary approached, students began throwing bottles from their dorm windows to smash them on the pavement below. It was a telling if comical indication of how sensitive the leadership was to such forms of Deng mockery that in the preceding weeks university authorities had sent recycling teams to dormitories offering Beida students four cents each for empties in order to deplete stocks of this highly symbolic ammunition.

Occasionally, older, more established Chinese intellectuals also found ways to make covert protests. In Shanghai, for instance, authorities were infuriated when a spate of unflattering articles from the Hong Kong press mysteriously began to surface around town. This network of "anti-Party" literature turned out to be the handiwork of a group associated with essayist Wang Ruowang. Despite being seventy-two years old and having just been released from over a year in jail, Wang had not only helped organize an underground journal called *Democracy Forum*, but had taken to circulating forbidden articles reproduced on copy machines around Shanghai. When in April 1991 the PSB uncovered the source of these articles, authorities detained and interrogated Wang for thirty hours, confiscated all of *Democracy Forum*'s office equipment, and then held two younger members of the group for several months.

In January 1992 another underground workers' group, the Preparatory Committee of the Free Labor Union of China, printed up and mailed a bold manifesto to some two thousand government work units. "The right of workers to organize free trade unions is an internationally recognized right," it declared. "Didn't Poland's Solidarity get banned and suppressed ten years ago? And what were the results? Solidarity won and its oppressor fell."

This union was just one of a whole list of nascent underground groups that had started to spring up. Just the month before, Qiao Shi, the Politburo member in charge of security, had told a conference attended by representatives of state judicial and security organs that although nearly six hundred dissident organizations had been uncovered since the spring of 1989, many others continued to elude the government. His prescription was to "smash" them "mercilessly."

Another protest tactic involved filing lawsuits. Using the legal codes that had recently been passed to give China a gloss of conformity to international standards, disaffected Chinese sought to beat the government with its own stick. Since the leadership insisted that all judicial matters, especially political cases, were being handled "according to law," such renegade legal actions forced officials to perform bizarre judicial charades, and gave human rights advocates and the foreign press a chance to point out the inconsistencies in China's legal system.

One of the best-publicized of these cases was initiated in October 1991 by the writer and former Minister of Culture Wang Meng, who used a recently enacted libel law to file suit against a Party-controlled journal. Wang, who was one of China's best-known writers of fiction, had been accused of bourgeois thinking during the Antirightist Campaign in 1957 and sent into twenty years of internal exile at a Xinjiang Province reform-through-labor camp. He did not write again until after he was "rehabilitated" in 1978. Then in 1986, during a politically very liberal period, Wang found himself elevated to the position of minister of culture.

Wang's time in official favor was short-lived, however. After June 4 he was labeled an exponent of "bourgeois liberalization," accused of having "doubted Marxism" and of supporting "the pluralistic nature of literature," and forced to resign. The ostensible motive for Wang's libel suit was not, however, his removal from office, but a letter to the editor of the state-owned journal *Literature and Art Gazette* attacking a story, "Thin Porridge," that Wang had published in the February 1989 issue of the magazine *Chinese Writer*. The letter had alleged that the story "tacitly satirized and criticized the Chinese Communist system under Deng Xiaoping's leadership" and hinted that Deng should retire. It was signed with a pen name widely assumed to be that of the *Literature and Art Gazette*'s own hard-line editor in chief, Zheng Bonong.

Wang's civil suit accused both the journal and its editor of having violated Article 120 of the 1986 General Principles of Civil Law establishing a citizen's right to protect his "name, likeness, reputation, or honor." Wang demanded both a public apology and 2,000 yuan in damages for the harm done to his reputation. Not surprisingly, the various ascending levels of courts to which Wang appealed rejected his arguments. However, at a time when most other intellectuals were still lying low, Wang's feisty action against the government attracted a good deal of notice. Even after the Central Committee's Propaganda Department issued an order forbidding the media from reporting on the progress of Wang's suit, several publications went ahead and ran articles in which Wang was allowed to defend his position. Such insubordination was a hint of how, despite the efforts of hard-liners, government controls, particularly in culture, were beginning to weaken.

If Wang's suit represented a startling departure from the kind of passivity that had been the hallmark of politically harassed intellectuals in the past, it was not, however, quite the unalloyed defense of free expression that some at first assumed it to be. What Wang argued in his suit was not that his right to free speech had been abrogated, but that he had been libelously accused of "mocking" Deng's reforms when, in fact, he actually supported them.

Like Wang, Nanjing University philosophy professor Guo Luoji had also been labeled a "rightist" and sent to a labor camp in the late 1950s. His crime was giving Mao's daughter a barely passing grade in a Beida course on Marxist theory. After a belated rehabilitation, Guo ran afoul of the Party leadership again in 1979 when he wrote an article for the *People's Daily* raising sensitive questions about the rights of Chinese to freedom of speech during the trial of Democracy Wall activist Wei Jingsheng. This time Guo's outspokenness evoked the ire of Deng himself, who saw to it that he was banished from Beijing to Nanjing. But Guo kept speaking out. In June 1989 he protested against the crackdown, provoking Nanjing University's Party organization to charge him with being *zhengzi shang bu hege* (politically unqualified) to hold his academic position. As a result, he was deprived of his academic title, expelled from the Party, stripped of the right to teach, denied permission to go abroad, and had his salary reduced. But Guo, whose slight build and scholarly demeanor belie his tenacity, fought back, using what he called "democratic means to confront our undemocratic system."

Just before the student demonstrations began, the National People's Congress had passed a new Administrative Procedure Law. By creating a codified procedure for filing suits against government officials and state organizations when plaintiffs believed their rights had been infringed upon, the Congress took an important step toward establishing the principle of judicial review. It was this law that Guo used to sue the State Education Commission for unlawfully depriving him of his income. In a separate suit he went after his university's Party Committee for violating Article 5 of the Constitution by depriving him of his job, damaging both his reputation and financial condition. As Guo later told me, he had taken this legal action to help "teach people how to overcome their fear of officialdom" by challenging the government in court. Insisting that what China needed was "a people's law movement," Guo maintained that even though "a constitution is there, it cannot really be said to exist if people do not put it to use."

As in Wang Meng's libel case, the courts refused to hear Guo's briefs, claiming that Communist Party organs could not be sued under the Administrative Procedure Law. Higher-level courts also threw out Guo's appeals. However, by simply engaging the process, he achieved his goal. The cases allowed Guo to write a number of long and reflective legal briefs discussing both the technicalities and the theory of the laws he was using to challenge the government. When supporters got hold of these briefs, they began making copies and disseminating them around the country. "Many people said my briefs were more like essays than legal documents," Guo told me with a satisfied chuckle. "They seemed to like what I was saying, that law must rule politics, and soon my case began to be widely known."

After Guo's appeals were rejected, he stepped up the level of his protest by taking the unprecedented step of publicly joining the New York–based group Human Rights in China, becoming its first board member inside mainland China. When his move was announced over the VOA and the BBC, Guo's Nanjing apartment was flooded with letters from admirers all across China. By the fall of 1992, officials seemed to have so wearied of his relentless pecking at them and the bad international publicity it involved that they finally granted him a passport and allowed him to go abroad.

By then so many aggrieved Chinese were filing suits against organs of the government that lawyers spoke of the country as being in the grip of *susong re* (litigation fever). The Supreme People's Court reported that in 1991 alone the number of administrative law cases against the government—most of which were economic in nature—rose to 25,667, twice the number of the previous year. The list of litigants soon included such political dissidents as investigative journalist Dai Qing, who had spent fifteen months in jail after June 4; journalist Zhang Weiguo, who had spent twenty months in jail in Shanghai for his prodemocracy political activities; Wang Juntao, the former head of the Social and Economic Sciences Research Institute (who was given a thirteen-year sentence for "counterrevolutionary incitement and instigation" for his role in the 1989 movement but was released in April 1994); and Wang Xizhe, who was released in 1993 after twelve years in prison. The administrative and constitutional violations they alleged ranged from defamation of character and physical mistreatment to illegal seizure of property and arbitrary imprisonment. The urge to sue the government was becoming so commonplace that in late 1992 a man even pressed charges against the Shenyang Canine Control Office for beating his family dog to death as part of a crackdown against such pets, which were technically still illegal in Chinese cities.

The fact that politically sensitive suits were regularly thrown out served as a reminder that when it came to politics, the government and the Party were still not prepared to make themselves subject to the rule of law. They did, however, publicize the fact that ordinary people now had the theoretical right to sue the government. As John Sullivan, one of the first Americans to work for a Chinese law firm, the Junhe Law Office in Beijing, later observed, "Chinese are becoming more aware of their legal system through these suits. They now realize they can go to the courts for some kind of remedy."

Most ordinary people were neither filing suits against the government, demonstrating in the Square, nor covertly distributing prodemocracy articles. But many did engage in less confrontational ways of expressing disaffection. A favorite tactic among students was to sing "revolutionary songs" at inappropriate moments or at half-speed. For instance, to mark the hundred-day anniversary of the Beijing massacre, Beida students trooped around their campus in a dirge-like conga line singing "Without the Communist Party There Would Be No New China."

Another favorite way for ordinary people to express discontent was by distorting political slogans, spoofing jargon-filled texts, perverting the well-known quotations of important leaders, tampering with the words of Party songs, or making up jingles and doggerel. One piece of doggerel popular in the early nineties satirized the Party's everchanging "correct lines."

In the 1950s we helped one another,
In the 1960s we denounced one another,
In the 1970s we doubted each other,
In the 1980s we swindled each other.

Another made fun of the so-called *San Da Zuofeng* (Three Important Styles of Work), an effort by the Party to codify three principles that were supposed to ideologically guide the work habits of good Party members. Accordingly, everyone was supposed to

Closely unite theory with practice,
Closely unite with the masses,
Closely unite criticism and self-criticism.

Worked over by cynics, it came out:

Closely unite theory with material benefits,
Closely unite pandering with influential leaders,
Closely unite flattery of others with praise of oneself.

People also manifested their disrespect for leaders, especially Premier Li Peng, by lampooning them in jokes. "Two prodemocracy demonstrators are about to be sentenced for their protest activities," began a typical one. "The first receives a five-year prison term for carrying a poster reading 'Overthrow Li Peng!' The second receives fifteen years for carrying a banner that says, 'Li Peng Is a Fool!' Outraged by the discrepancy between the two sentences, the second demonstrator approaches the bench to demand why his sentence is so much more severe. 'While it is true that you are both guilty of counterrevolutionary incitement and propaganda,' replies the judge, 'you are also guilty of having revealed a state secret.' "

Another form of oblique protest was *wenhua shan* (culture T-shirts, or dissatisfaction T-shirts) that came into vogue among Chinese youths during the spring of 1991. Influenced by Western garments with ads and logos on them, enterprising but alienated young artists took to decorating T-shirts with a host of cryptic, often cynical legends taken from Party propaganda, Big Leader preachments, Beijing slang, pop music, and even Daoist texts. The prime mover behind culture T-shirts was former Beijing Municipal School of Art and Design student turned entrepreneur Kong Yongqian, who designed and marketed more than fifty different shirts, almost single-handedly creating a whole fashion craze.

One shirt featured a picture of a weeping cat over characters that read, "Black Cat, White Cat; It Doesn't Matter as Long as It Catches Mice." This was Deng's well-known slogan extolling economic pragmatism, but worn on the chest of a surly, deviant youth in post–June 4 China, it conveyed a sense of skeptical disparagement.

Other shirts borrowed Mao images and quotations, like the famous final line from a poem Mao had written in 1963 while contemplating the need for a "cultural revolution" to sweep away all "rightists" and "capitalist roaders," and which ended, "Sweep away all pests." Another best-seller featured a crimson silk-screened image of Mao with the caption "A Single Spark Can Light a Prairie Fire," a quotation lifted from Mao's well-known 1930 essay describing China as a country "littered with dry wood that will soon be aflame." All that was needed, predicted Mao, was a "single spark" to ignite it. The inference that China could now do with another "prairie fire" was unmistakable. A third was inscribed simply with the five familiar characters for "Serve the People." This renowned exhortation of Mao's had once been emblazoned on everything from walls and smokestacks to notebooks and thermos bottles as a reminder for everyone to put the interests of the commonweal first. However, during the "To Get Rich Is Glorious" Deng era after private greed had long since eclipsed such ideals of public service, a shirt sporting this old adage had the effect of making people snigger.

Another line of T-shirts expressed frustration with the dead-end quality of life for young people. "I'm Pissed Off! Get Out of My Face!" one of the most popular of this genre asserted. "There Is No Way Out!" another declared in a tone of existential weariness. "I'm Just Sick of Everything!" proclaimed a third, expressing the malaise that had become so characteristic of urban youth.

While China continued to be politically stifled, the market nonetheless continued to breathe. In fact, culture T-shirts became such a popular means of expressing the prevalent mood of ennui, dissatisfaction, and alienation, that private entrepreneurs like Kong were able to do very well commercially. Designed by iconoclastic art students, manufactured and distributed by entrepreneurs with an eye for the latest trends in the youth-culture market, hawked by *geti hu* (private entrepreneurs) shop owners, and street-stall vendors, and worn by everyone from members of the student literary avant-garde and the countercultural rock scene to taxi drivers and street hustlers, culture T-shirts were the perfect emblem of that expanding element in urban Chinese society that in spite of the crackdown continued to develop its own irreverent and independent lifestyle. As one official critic put it, "They carry gloomy, negative and cynical messages which do one thing and one thing only; encourage a sense of decadence."

As Australian Sinologist Geremie Barmé has commented, the culture T-shirt phenomenon provided people with an opportunity "to release pent-up emotions and frustrations, whether personal, social or political'' by creating ''a popular, unspoken conspiracy of self-expression writ large in satirical and ironical terms.''

Recognizing these curious garments as obvious expressions of a larger and more dangerous trend of cultural estrangement, Party watchdogs moved to deal with them the same way they had dealt with most other kinds of iconoclasm—with a ban. In late June 1991, Kong, who had been so instrumental in starting the fad, was detained by the police, interrogated for three days, and fined 30,000 yuan ($6,000) for ''disrupting the planned socialist economy.'' First the Beijing Municipal Industrial and Commercial Administration Bureau banned production, sale, and display of all ''products carrying unhealthy designs and wording.'' Then the PSB began confiscating shirts from street stalls.

Though a period of ''dead time'' was to continue in the political sphere with few signs of overt protest, such phenomena as culture T-shirts were an indication that the free-spirited economic and cultural energy that had developed in the late 1980s had not entirely vanished. Instead of manifesting itself through direct political action as protesters had in the Square, it was now expressing itself through various forms of underground culture and the marketplace.

''I do not believe that the Chinese will forever refuse to think for themselves,'' wrote the journalist Dai Qing, who had spent ten months in prison after 1989. ''I do not believe that the Chinese will never speak out through their writings; I do not believe that morality and justice will vanish in the face of repression; I do not believe, in this age in which we are in communication with the world, that freedom of speech will remain an empty phrase.''

Whether such optimism was called for was still difficult to discern in 1991. Chinese society had turned into a curious hybrid in which market forces, an entrepreneurial class, and an alienated counterculture coexisted with a one-party state, a repressive police apparatus, and an extensive system of prison labor camps. How these opposing forces would realign themselves in the months and years to come would determine the fate of China.

Part IV

The Second Channel

26

Chairman Mao as Pop Art

While Mao lived, his visage gazed down from the walls of public rooms, white ceramic busts were on display in schools, towering concrete statues loomed at the front of important buildings, and almost every Chinese household boasted Little Red Books, collections of posters, buttons, and other Mao icons. When, after Mao's death, it was no longer fashionable to collect such things Chinese were confronted with a tricky problem: how to dispose of their accumulated caches of Mao trinkets. Still fearful of being accused of lèse majesté if they got rid of them by ordinary means, people devised elaborate strategies for disposal, such as burying them at night in public parks, smelting them down in boiler-room furnaces, or deep-sixing them in canals and lakes.

When Deng Xiaoping took power, he had his own disposal problem. To repudiate the Great Helmsman's legacy, as Khrushchev had "de-Stalinized" the Soviet Union, would not only have kicked loose the keystone of the ideological arch that supported the Party's "democratic dictatorship," it would have sparked opposition from powerful Party leaders who continued to venerate Mao's teachings.

Yet to perpetuate Mao's ideology in toto would preclude the market-oriented reforms Deng deemed essential to China's development and the Party's survival. Characteristically, Deng dealt pragmatically with the problem by giving something to each side. "On no account can we discard the banner of Mao Zedong thought," because to do so would be to "negate the glorious history of our Party," he declared. On the other hand, he repudiated the notion of Mao's complete infallibility, judging that "the Chairman," as many people referred to him, had been only 70 percent correct in his policies and 30 percent in error. It was the same success-failure ratio that Mao himself had once used in evaluating the legacy of Stalin.

Although Party leaders still paid technical fealty to Mao as grand revolutionary progenitor, during the eighties there was a noticeable diminution in his hagiography. Just as Confucius said of the spirits, "They must be respected but kept at a distance," Deng tried quietly to distance himself from Maoism without rejecting it altogether. Mao's remains were left on display in his memorial mausoleum, but even there Deng contrived to water down their symbolic import by adding three new memorial rooms commemorating Zhou Enlai, Liu Shaoqi, and Zhu De. Mere sideshows compared to the main hall where the Chairman lay in state, they nonetheless served as reminders that while Mao had reigned supreme in life, he was now reduced to being first among equals in death.

Most ordinary Chinese were relieved to rid themselves of all the Maoist effluvia that had inundated their lives for so long. By the mid-1980s Mao's image had become sufficiently denatured that the government felt able to order urban trash recycling centers to "receive" unwanted Mao buttons for certain kinds of dignified disposal. Since most of them were made out of aluminum, many were melted down and then recycled in what amounted to a quasi-cremation. Mao portraits were quietly removed from public spaces, and concrete statues in front of official buildings were dynamited under the cover of darkness. Among the few prominently placed images of Mao to survive was the portrait hanging on Tiananmen Gate.

By the late eighties, Mao images were found almost nowhere except in curio shops among mass-produced laughing Buddhas, cloisonné bracelets, and cheap lacquerware trays covered with frolicking pandas. Perplexed clerks looked on as Westerners with a fascination for socialist kitsch snapped up Mao memorabilia as if they were Tang Dynasty ceramics or Qing Dynasty landscape paintings. Although by the beginning of 1989 many ideologically minded older Party leaders still held *ta laorenjia* (the old guy), as Mao was also known in the vernacular, dear to their hearts, most people were pleased to see his patrimony passing into oblivion. But just as the student protests in 1986 had prompted hardliners to a new burst of Maoist pronunciamentos, the 1989 demonstrations presaged another Party effort to revive Mao as a political cult figure. Curiously, certain aspects of this new revival found unexpected resonance among ordinary people. In fact, a Mao craze of sorts began. Although it lacked anything like the frenzy of the Cultural Revolution, the way this new infatuation spread across the country took most observers by surprise. It was not only difficult to know who, if anyone, was behind it, but also to ascertain whether those embracing this neo-Mao *Kultur* were expressing nostalgic support for the Chairman's political ideals or indulging in underhanded satire.

The first signs of what came to be called "the Mao phenomenon" revealed themselves during 1991 in South China where Mao images began popping up in unexpected places. By far the most ubiquitous manifestations were playing card–sized photos of Mao laminated in plastic like I.D. cards that appeared hanging from vehicle rearview mirrors like amulets. One side featured a colorized photo of a flinty-eyed, youthful Mao in a Red Army cap taken by American journalist Edgar Snow after the Long March, the other a mature, corpulent Mao best known from his Tiananmen Gate portrait.

By the next year other kinds of images also began appearing. In Nanjing I came across street peddlers hawking key-chain pendants adorned with Mao's photograph. In Wuxi, a city known for its traditional *niren* clay images, shops had expanded inventories to include not only Mickey Mouse figurines and statues of Beethoven, but a freshly minted line of Mao busts updated with gold glaze. Standing alongside their "traditional" white ceramic counterparts on store shelves, they looked like so many gold-capped front teeth set in a mouthful of ordinary dentures. A souvenir shop at the Jingguang Business Center in Beijing had 3-D renditions of the statue that stands inside the entrance to Mao's mausoleum stacked up for sale like pope plates at souvenir stands outside the Vatican. Street markets were running over with tubs of old Mao badges, tattered Mao posters, Mao cups, Mao embroideries, Mao busts (including glow-in-the-dark versions that looked as if they might be radioactive!), and alarm clocks decorated with Red Guards whose mechanical arms waved Little Red Books with each tick. People with dreams of fat profits from foreigners began scouring their closets for more such memorabilia.

Soon a new generation of Chinese began collecting as well. One aficionado in Sichuan Province was reported to have gathered 18,000 different pieces of Mao paraphernalia. An NCNA report claimed that an employee of the Zhuhai Department of Civil Affairs in Guangdong Province had assembled a collection of Mao buttons so large—this treasure trove contained a total of 101,688 badges of more than 4,000 different types, weighing a total of 493 kilograms, with the largest being 33 centimeters in diameter—that it covered every square inch of wall space in his three-room apartment. And a technical-school teacher in Guizhou Province was reported not only to have assembled a collection of 34,000 badges (including 19,000 varieties!) but to have written a 250,000-character treatise on the evolution of this unique art form. Another collector assembled so many badges in his twenty-square-meter home that he won mention in *The Guinness Book of World Records*. As interest in Mao buttons increased, collectors got together like philatelists to set up a Mao Zedong Badge Collection and Research Society, organize exhibits, and put out newsletters and publications.

Hard-liners were initially thrilled about the Chairman's second coming. Some observers even surmised that hard-liners had initiated the fad. Commenting on the avalanche of Mao knickknacks that suddenly reappeared in western Hunan Province's Huaihua County, the *People's Daily* noted proudly that "in analyzing the phenomenon, we can see that the inhabitants of Huaihua have a deep admiration for the leaders of the Chinese Revolution, and especially for Chairman Mao as well as for Communist and socialist values." In a November 1991 article appearing in the *Guangming Daily*, hard-line ideologue Deng Liqun went so far as to claim that "the Mao craze" was a "miracle in the history of socialist China, in fact, in the history of the Communist movement as a whole."

But the truth was that Mao was being reborn not because "the masses" wanted another episode of "permanent revolution," but because they were beginning to treat Mao as part of a pop-culture fad with little more ideological seriousness than crazes for hula hoops, Silly Putty, or bubble-gum cards. Chinese collected Mao memorabilia because it was there, an inescapable part of their recent history. Elsewhere they might have collected old hubcaps, comic books, or beer cans instead. And, of course, it didn't hurt that all this Mao detritus now had real market value.

As entrepreneurs in the south discovered that Mao amulets sold like hotcakes, the fad spread. Within months every other taxi, bus, and truck driver seemed to have one dangling from his rearview mirror. Soon manufacturers were making more sophisticated versions that came with ceremonial red tassels, brass bells, and other glitzy gee-gaws. Merchants started hanging them inside their shops as good-luck charms and homemakers affixed them to the entrances of their homes as protective door gods. Incredible as it seemed, Mao Zedong, the enemy of feudal tradition, was being enthroned in the pantheon of traditional folk gods to whom superstitious Chinese were once again appealing in times of need.

Factories—perhaps the same ones that had been minting facsimile Lei Feng underwear and toothbrushes—began churning out replica buttons, busts, and posters, as well as tacky Mao ballpoint pens, Mao tie clips, Mao umbrellas, and Mao calendars. A distillery began marketing an "East Is Red" wine, which it sold in a fancy box complete with a Mao badge on a yellow silk ribbon tied around it. The Shanghai Watch Factory introduced a new line of wristwatches featuring three different Maos on their dials: Mao as slender young guerrilla commander, as middle-aged army leader, and as aging Chairman. As the hundredth anniversary of Mao's birth approached on December 26, 1993, a plethora of Mao watches began appearing around the country. The souvenir counter on the top of Tiananmen Gate even sold a pocket watch with a hologram of Mao's face on the crystal. One factory started marketing an upscale limited-edition Mao watch complete with diamond- and sapphire-studded gold casing that cost $1,500. So many buyers mobbed the distributor when it went on sale that police had to be called in to keep order. (Alas, a short time later, the "diamonds" were reported to be fakes.) My favorite new line of Mao gimmicks were cigarette lighters with gaudy vinyl renderings of the Chairman in their sides which, when flicked open, beeped out an electronic version of the "The East Is Red" like a car-door alarm gone berserk.

One of the most prolific fountainheads of such products was Mao's Shaoshan birthplace in Hunan Province. When peasant Tian Yongjun realized that all the Mao busts being sold to tourists in Shaoshan were made elsewhere, he abandoned farming and opened up the Shaoshan Statue Company, and by the end of 1992 was annually producing tens of thousands of busts. By the end of 1993, some 2,000 other Shaoshan peasants were also cranking out Mao tchotchkes.

Even the lumbering Xinhua Bookstore monopoly jumped on the Mao bandwagon by issuing 10 million copies of a new four-volume edition of Mao's collected works. China's infant laser-disc industry began selling editions of Mao speeches entitled "Voice of the Giant." Film studios began cranking out Mao docudramas. The 1991 *Mao Zedong and His Son* emphasized Mao's human side by highlighting the emotional torment he endured after learning that his son, Mao Anying, had been killed in the Korean War by American fighter bombers. *The Mao Zedong Story* was released in 1992, and the NCNA claimed that the film would "touch" viewers with "Mao's wisdom and humor; his simple, kind, and considerate nature; his relations with bodyguards, his personal doctors, and female servants on his special train.'' No mention was made of Mao's legendary sexual appetite for these same young ''female servants.''

Beijing Television weighed in with an American-style quiz show called ''The Sun and Truth.'' Taped before a live audience and presided over by a dapperly dressed TV personality named Chao Shan, the program pitted teams from different state enterprises against one another in competition to recite well-known Mao quotations on command and to identify the dates, places, and contexts of others.

Mao, who had once crusaded zealously against superstition and capitalism, now seemed to have been reborn as an agent of both. His perplexing reincarnation raised a troubling question: If the Party's foremost revolutionary hero could be hijacked by the market, what part of revolutionary China was safe from being commercially consumed by Deng's new brand of ''market socialism''?

Whenever I asked what they thought was behind Mao's reprise, people usually just shook their heads and laughed. ''For us little people this Mao thing means nothing except that 'the old guy' just makes us feel good,'' a Beijing cabdriver told me, snapping his tasseled Mao amulet irreverently with an index finger so that it danced alongside the air-freshener dispenser with which it hung from the rearview mirror. ''For us the old guy is like . . . well, like the Great Wall.''

''People say Mao has become divine like a God and can bring good luck,'' giggled an embarrassed shopkeeper in Wuxi as she wrapped up some Mao pendants for me. ''Some people say he can even protect you from bad fortune!''

A bus driver in Nanjing snorted with laughter when I asked him why he had hung a Mao pendant from his sunshade like a St. Christopher medal. ''Hey! Why take chances?'' he replied. ''Who can say if he can do anything for you or not?''

Everywhere one heard tales about people who had been ''saved'' by Mao. There were automobile drivers who walked away uninjured from hideous crashes; street vendors who escaped from robberies; and even survivors of murder attempts who claimed they had been shielded by their Mao pendants. During the summer of 1991 thousands of destitute peasants in southern China were reported to have purchased Mao talismans after the region was inundated by catastrophic floods.

Hao Zhiqiang, a young documentary filmmaker from CCTV, became so intrigued by the Mao craze that he and several former classmates from the Beijing Film Academy set off on a cross-country trip in early 1992 to plumb its significance by shooting cinema verité–style interviews in the streets of Shanghai, Canton, and Shaoshan. Keeping an unobtrusive Minicam rolling, they queried pedestrians about why people were once again so enamored of Mao, and how they imagined "the old guy" would react if he returned and saw what was happening. While none of the subjects expressed a desire to return to the Maoist era itself, many seemed drawn in an almost primal way toward Mao's mystique. Most of the interviewees were well aware of Mao's excesses, but in their view, to attack him seemed almost tantamount to attacking China itself. "Mao did make mistakes in his late years, but he is still a superman in modern Chinese history," declared a telling article in the *Beijing Review*. "In a nutshell, the position Mao Zedong holds in the minds of the Chinese is so paramount that he is seen as having become synonymous with the Chinese nation."

Just as earlier generations of Chinese often looked backward during times of cultural ambiguity and social chaos to the mythical Yellow Emperor and the prehistorical sage-kings Yao and Shun, the uncertainty of the present period now seemed to make many Chinese yearn for a more recent golden age. For them, "the good old days" were the early fifties when, as one *China Daily* article put it, "prices were stable, personal relations warmer, and people put the interests of the country before their own."

"In many ways I think Mao appeals to people on a very subconscious level," Hao told me when we met to watch some of the raw footage he had shot. "What draws people toward Mao more than anything else is his familiarity. So many leaders have come and gone and things have been changing with such confusing speed that people find Mao's unchanging face comforting." Then, in a way that seemed to suggest that even he was not immune to such yearnings, he added, "I think what people are searching for is some connection to the past—something constant."

Rediscovering Mao was also a way of making money, and with the hundredth anniversary of his birth approaching, everyone was looking for some way to get in on the spoils. The *Farmer's Daily* reported that officials on Hainan Island had found a mountain that was "a perfect likeness" of Mao's profile and had persuaded his daughter, Li Na, to endorse opening it to the public as a tourist attraction. In Nanjing, a private restaurateur not only named his eatery after Mao (calling it the Runzhi restaurant using the name Mao had been given at birth before he changed it as a guerrilla), but decked it out with Mao statues and waitresses done up in period-piece Mao suits complete with Mao badges. Back in Beijing, a spate of restaurants decorated with Cultural Revolution posters, Mao buttons, huge photos of Red Guards, and even Lei Feng statues cropped up and quickly became the rage among middle-aged Chinese who had come of age during the 1960s.

Some were not thrilled by the commercial way the Mao craze was developing. "Drinking and playing drinking games under Mao portraits while listening to Mao-extolling music is almost blasphemous," complained the *Wenhui Daily*. "If other people follow suit, then dance halls, cafeterias, and public bathrooms could all use the Great Leader's name on their billboards."

Mao's pop resurrection may have been started by Maoist hardliners, but it was soon hard to tell whether their patron saint was being adored or defamed. In the politically repressive climate of 1991, feelings of discontent had a way of leaking out in convoluted and roundabout ways. In this case, the very tawdriness of dangling Mao's image on cheap key rings or from rearview mirrors seemed to suggest that the revival might be as much a backhanded way to declaim his legacy as proclaim it. Nowhere did this ambiguity seem more implicit than in the unexpected revival of "revolutionary songs" from the 1950s and 1960s that suddenly swept China.

In 1991, state-owned recording companies began to jazz up Party anthems with disco, country-and-western, and rock-and-roll arrangements, and to sell them as tape-cassette albums. To hear lyrics once sung by militant Red Guards and Red Army choruses exhorting the masses to struggle against imperialism and class enemies warbled by pop singers to the accompaniment of drum machines, electronic synthesizers, and electric guitars was mind-bending.

Among the first to be resurrected from the deep freeze of the Maoist era was the mother of all anthems, "The East Is Red." One might have thought that its polemical lyrics and strident music would have forever disqualified it from ever achieving chart-busting success on the Chinese pop hit parade. Moreover, for anyone who had known China during the heyday of the Cultural Revolution when tampering with the words of such a sacred Party hymn ("The red in the East raises the sun, / China gives forth a Mao Zedong, / He works for the happiness of the people, / He shall be China's saving star. / The East is Red!") would have been unthinkable, and the idea of retrofitting it with a boogie beat and wah-wah electric guitar licks, beyond the pale. Nonetheless, this is what happened, and the result was a smash hit.

Westernized disco music was, of course, nothing new in the People's Republic. As Deng's "open door" exposed the country to more and more outside influences in the mid-eighties, pop culture established its first beachhead. For Chinese youths, such music provided a welcome escape from the dreariness of their lives and a way to vicariously brush against a Western cultural world that represented freedom, wealth, style, sex, fun, and glamour. This tendency to believe that "the moon was rounder abroad than in China" infuriated many old revolutionaries. So when pop music made an unexpected U-turn and began embracing old revolutionary standards, many of them were at first relieved and gratified. The problem was that, after being revamped, the revolutionary essence of these songs was completely lost. What was a veteran revolutionary to make of a get-down version of "Ah, Chairman Mao, How the People from the Grasslands Long to Behold You!"?

This new craze really took off in December 1991 when the Shanghai branch of the China Record Company released two new albums, "The East Is Red" and "The Red Sun—An Anthology of Odes to Mao Zedong Newly Sung." They included such classic favorites as "The Sun Is Most Red And Chairman Mao Is Most Dear" and "Our Leader, Chairman Mao." By 1993 "Red Sun" alone had sold over 14 million copies.

What worried reform-minded Party leaders about the new Mao fad was not only the way it seemed to deify the Chairman, but the possibility that despite their lighthearted veneer, these old songs might somehow allow hard-liners to foment a resurgence of dogmatic "leftism." Li Ruihuan, a reform-minded vice-premier with responsibility for overseeing culture, was reported to have circulated a document in the name of the Central Committee's Secretariat arguing that the broadcast of these reconstituted songs from the Cultural Revolution should be suspended. In February the Shanghai newspaper *Wenhui Daily* convened a scholarly gathering to discuss the significance of the Mao phenomenon, and one of the conclusions of conferees was that the Mao craze showed that efforts "to negate" the Cultural Revolution had been "insufficient," and that the Party had "failed to approach its harmfulness to the entire nation from the high plane of reason."

It was not long before even Deng himself weighed in. "In my view the campaign is abnormal," he said of the Mao craze. "Young people today who do not understand the last forty years of our country's history may be given the wrong impression."

Such admonitions did nothing, however, to stem the flood of crypto-revolutionary cassettes emblazoned with Mao photos that were flooding the market. The Anhui Recording Studio's *Our Star of Salvation* featured a jacket with a portrait of the Chairman set in the middle of a crimson globe that hovered around his head like a halo. Graphics for the Jiangsu Recording Studio's double cassette album *May the Red Sun Shine for a Thousand Years* showed an oversized Mao looming over Tiananmen Square like the Incredible Hulk.

The fact that most Chinese had learned the words to these proletarian golden-oldies as students, in the army, at cadre training schools, or in reform-through-labor camps, was certainly an important factor in their appeal. They were to Chinese what "Home on the Range" and "This Land Is Your Land" are to Americans, and it was not long before they were outselling even the once-dominant "Canto-pop" music from Hong Kong. Some stores had a hard time even keeping them in stock. At one point the Ganjiakou Electric Appliance Sales and Service Department in Beijing reported that it was selling almost a cassette a minute, forcing its distributor to take the extreme measure of airlifting a fresh shipment in from Shanghai to meet demand.

Deng, like Mao, had always urged his people to "take the best from East and West." But this combination of socialist lyrics and capitalist Muzak seemed to combine the very worst of East and West—a weird juxtaposition whose end products rivaled even numbers from Mel Brooks's Broadway musical satire *Springtime for Hitler* for sheer bizarreness. It was difficult to keep a straight face through a country-and-western rendition of "Mao and the People Together" accompanied by between-verse cadenzas played on a pedal steel guitar, or an "easy listening" version of "The Sun Is Most Red and Chairman Mao Our Most Beloved" sung in close harmony.

Early in 1992 the Mao pop-song craze took another giant evolutionary step when a spate of "revolutionary karaoke" videocassettes began appearing. Karaoke—which allows amateurs to sing along to taped musical accompaniment and subtitled lyrics—had been Japan's main cultural contribution to China's pop revolution. Since the mid-1980s when karaoke started taking the country by storm, Chinese cities had become full of bars with huge overhead projection screens on which documentary footage of Mao during his early years as a revolutionary were accompanied by lyrics crawling across the bottom of the video screen like stock reports on a cable channel, as musical accompaniment boomed out of speakers. Soon, even the Central Propaganda Department decided to grab a share of the fun and profit by issuing the *Everyone Sing Along Chinese Karaoke Treasury of Songs,* a video extravaganza including hundreds of reprised Mao-era favorites in karaoke form. Soon there were even laser disc collections of karaoke-ized Mao-era songs, complete with footage of Tibetans doing loyalty dances to the PLA and "the Chairman" swimming the Yangtze River.

Almost everywhere one went in urban China during 1992, the sound of these transvestite-like songs blared out of music shops, hair salons, department stores, hotel lobbies, airport waiting rooms, restaurants, dance halls, bars, and even train-car speakers. Twenty years earlier, citizens had been involuntarily roused from their slumber by the same tunes blasted at them each morning over tinny outdoor loudspeakers. Deng's decade of reform had held out the promise that such unsolicited acoustic pollution was finished. Now, however, it was back—only this time voluntarily self-inflicted. While it is improbable that most of those involved in marketing or buying this music were consciously trying to trivialize either China's revolutionary mythology or Mao, in myriad subtle ways this was precisely the effect. Mao and Party culture were being cannibalized by market forces and turned into marketable pop culture. It was hard to know where the process would end, especially when Pierre Cardin's bistro-cum-disco, Maxim's, hosted a 1993 high-camp yuletide disco event that featured Beijing's avant-garde dressed as political persecutees and Red Guards dancing around a Christmas tree decorated with Mao ornaments.

If the reappearance of Mao memorabilia and revolutionary pop songs was having an unpremediated subversive effect on official culture, the impact of avant-garde art was decidedly more calculated. During the late 1980s as more and more artists began experimenting with new styles, the visual arts broke loose from their socialist-realist moorings. After the 1989 crackdown, nothing proved more tantalizing for artistic pioneers than repossessing revolutionary imagery and exploiting it for artistic purposes. In 1990, Wang Guangyi, a graduate of the Zhejiang Art Academy, who had already won notoriety both at home and abroad for superimposing suggestive barlike grids over a series of postmodernist portraits of Mao, began what he called his "Great Criticism" series. It consisted of art-for-the-masses images from Cultural Revolution propaganda posters counterposed against commercial advertisements for Western products like Maxwell House coffee, Kodak film, Tang breakfast drink, Marlboro cigarettes, Nestlé instant coffee, and Coca-Cola. "Workers, Peasants, Soldiers, and Coca Cola," for instance, featured a Holy Trinity of defiant model proletarians thrusting the crimson banner of socialism out over a Coke logo. Such juxtapositions made one wonder how long it would be before some upstart advertising account executive—and there were more and more of them in China every day—would slap Mao's mug on a soft-drink bottle or a detergent box. After all, at a 1992 exhibit in Wuhan, two panels counterpoised the Chairman and Marilyn Monroe à la Andy Warhol, and the Shanghai-based artist Yu Youhan had produced a series of playful portraits, including one entitled *Mao: With Love, Whitney* that showed the Great Helmsman sitting before a bank of microphones next to a portrait of the American pop singer Whitney Houston. Yu's *Mao Zedong Age Series* centered around silhouettes of

Mao outlandishly filled in with chintz and paisley-like patterns as if Laura Ashley had designed a special line of Mao suits.

And then there was the Qingdao painter Liu Dahong, who made traditional protective door-gods out of images of Marx, Lenin, Engels, and Stalin. He also did an oil entitled *The Honeymoon* that showed a beaming Mao presiding over a wedding populated by a host of famous "model" workers, peasants, and soldiers, including a doltish Lei Feng riding around on a tricycle while reading his own diary.

Not surprisingly, the most explicit of these "deconstructionist" Mao image manipulations (dubbed the Cynical Realism, or Political Pop, School of painting) were done in exile, where artists did not need to fear reprisal. Some of the most arresting were those of Zhang Hongtu, a painter who had attended the Central Academy of Fine Arts in Beijing before leaving to study in the United States. After 1989, Zhang produced a series of distorted Mao likenesses that he called the "Chairmen Mao Series." Included were works depicting the Chairman wearing a headband inscribed with the motto "Serve the People" standing in front of banner-waving student demonstrators in the Square; Mao with his head dissolving into a blur like a television image distorted by bad reception and the caption "Either the east wind prevails over the west wind, or the west wind prevails over the east wind"; a randy-looking Mao ogling the Goddess of Democracy while exclaiming in an overhead speech bubble, "Women!"; and an empty silhouette of Mao's head with the likeness of Wu'er Kaixi with bullhorn interposed on it. Zhang's *The Last Banquet* is a hilarious rendition of the Central Committee done in the manner of Leonardo da Vinci's *Last Supper*. The apostles, all outfitted in Mao suits, Mao caps, and even Mao faces, sit at a long table arranged with chopsticks, spittoons, ashtrays, and microphones. In 1993, Zhang was just completing another series, a collection of sculptures fabricated out of everything from wire, steel, brick, and concrete, to rice, grass, burlap, and fur to create a sequence of Mao depictions that he called *Material Mao*.

"Before 1989 I had imagined that I could escape China and politics into my own artistic creations," Zhang, a gray-haired but energetic forty-seven-year-old, told me when I visited his Brooklyn studio. "As I watched those demonstrations on television, however, I found myself feeling Chinese again. My whole attitude began to change, and I no longer felt that I wanted to isolate myself." Zhang explained that his fascination with Mao's image grew out of the power the leader had exerted over him as a boy. "When I was growing up Mao was everywhere. He was like a god. After 1989 I found myself wanting to play with that sacred image, to transform it from a god's face into that of a moved person.''

Zhang readily acknowledges the tremendous power that Mao's image still retains for him, even in America. "When I first cut up a photo of Mao's face to make a collage, I felt as if I were sinning. Such feelings have made me realize how my work is really an effort to break the psychological authority that Mao as an image continues to hold over all Chinese. For me, working on Mao became a form of exorcism.''

It was a paradox that just as ordinary Chinese were turning Mao into a tutelary demigod, artists were trying to demystify him by turning him into pop art. The effect of these unauthorized artistic expropriations of Mao images was the reverse of what Andy Warhol did when he took mundane commercial images and elevated them to the level of art. By doing so, he transformed the profane into the sacred. By taking politically sacrosanct Mao images and converting them into commercialized pop-culture commodities, contemporary Chinese artists were transforming the sacred into the profane.

Although such artworks were too avant-garde for local buyers, collectors from Hong Kong and Taiwan quickly snapped them up. By 1993, Hong Kong was even having art shows such as "China's New Art, Post-1989" complete with an expensive color catalogue divided into such categories as "political pop art," "cynical realism," "wounded romanticism," "fetishism," and "sadomasochism." Almost any indignity, it seemed, could now be inflicted on Mao for the sake of commerce as long as it was not overtly political in nature.

The irony here was that the debasement of Mao's image was not happening because Chinese dissidents had decided that the Great Helmsman's political vision was too brutalizing, but because Deng's "market socialism" needed fuel, even if that fuel ended up being China's revolutionary escutcheon. The Party's perverse quest to sustain itself by unleashing the productive forces of entrepreneurial capitalism were making whole chunks of Mao's revolution expendable— everything, that is, except the Party's right to rule unilaterally. Like a banked blast furnace that demands an ever larger supply of combustible material as it is refired, by the end of 1991 Deng's revived private sector had grown to the point that it had begun to consume even Mao. By 1994 this trend had advanced to such a stage that people hardly blinked when, in April, a Beijing Hard Rock Café opened, featuring a portrait of Chairman Mao alongside such Western pop idols as the Beatles, Elvis, and Chuck Berry. As Liu Xiaobo sardonically put it,

"What intellectuals could not do by way of dethroning Mao during the protest movement is now being done by the market. Mao has been transformed from 'the Chairman' into an entertainment star who can make people rich."

Behind the often deceptive facade of the official media, there were myriad other telltale indications that despite the crackdown, elements of Chinese society were detaching themselves from the Party and its tedious regimen of sloganeering and revolutionary posturing. The Mao craze was only one of numerous manifestations of a larger change in zeitgeist that began to reveal themselves as it became clear that Deng was not going to allow hard-liners either to abandon his program of market reforms or to reimpose the kinds of rigid cultural controls of which many of them doubtless still dreamed.

27

The Second Channel

When I was introduced to Jia Lusheng during the spring of 1989, there was little about him to suggest that he was one of the pioneers of a new style of reporting called *baogao wenxue* (literary reportage), a popular genre of investigative journalism that encouraged writers to *ganyu,* or delve into their subject matter in order to portray real-life situations with down-to-earth dialogue and descriptions. "Literary reportage," which shared certain similarities with American "new journalism," had gained great popularity over the preceding decade, even spawning a journal by the same name. Contributors prided themselves in covering topics from underground political movements and prison conditions to official malfeasance and China's growing underclass. The revelations by this new generation of investigative reporting played an important role in articulating the dissatisfaction that erupted in the Square.

Focusing on the seamy side of contemporary life, Jia became one of the better-known writers of literary reportage. Born in 1950 in Qufu, the birthplace of Confucius, Jia began his writing career while serving as a soldier in the information office of the PLA, and soon became a Party member. However, once out of the army, he began blazing a trail all his own. In fact, few other Chinese writers were more dedicated to escaping from the stultifying embrace of Party-sponsored literary circles. Submerging himself for months at a time along what he called the *heidao* (black route) among down-and-out beggars, petty criminals, street urchins, mentally ill homeless drifters, entrepreneurial hustlers, prostitutes, political outcasts, and prisoners, Jia probed special pockets that more "respectable" writers refused to heed. The result was a collection of personal explorations that tore the shroud off a whole level of Chinese society that the Party did not wish to see described in print.

To research his 1986 exposé *China's Vast Western Desert Gulag*, Jia had infiltrated a network of reeducation and reform-through-labor camps in Xinjiang Province where victims of the 1984 anticrime and "anti–spiritual pollution" campaign had been dumped on the desert behind barbed wire and forgotten. Shortly after it appeared, the book was banned by the government. To write his 1987 account *Drifting with Beggar Gangs*, Jia spent weeks hanging out with a "brotherhood" of Chinese hoboes, part of China's roughly 80 million homeless and unemployed *liudong renkou* (floating population). In 1989 he did a study of street vernacular that he published as *The Lingo of Thieves*. And using confidential files to which he had gained access, Jia documented cases of all the antisocial acts committed in and around Tiananmen Square over the period of a single year. Many of the perpetrators were politically persecuted Chinese who had come to the capital desperately seeking to win a "reversal of their verdicts," handed down during earlier political campaigns. It was yet another measure of the Square's drawing power as a place of remonstration that when they got no satisfaction from officialdom, these unfortunates ended up committing often bizarre acts of protest in the Square. A man who had had his legs broken and was then forced to kneel in front of a portrait of Mao during the Cultural Revolution hurled a car axle at Mao's crystal sarcophagus. Someone else had tried to plant explosives near the Great Hall. Others attempted suicide by jumping off Tiananmen Gate. Even the muckraking *Baogao Wenxue* (Literary Reportage) would not risk publishing Jia's daring piece.

"Our society is filled with such a division of lightness and darkness," Jia told me over lunch in 1989. "We writers live in a rarefied place of lightness, and only when we go into the blackness at the bottom do we discover how dark our society actually is and how few from the top have ever been down there to see what it's like."

Jia's exposés quickly earned him a reputation as a literary maverick. They also caused him to be accused of "yellow journalism," and in 1988 to be expelled from his official "work unit," the Shandong Provincial Writers' Association. By his own description he was a monk with a *waizui* (mouth that's off-center). One did not have to listen long to pick up his distaste for Party-sponsored intellectuals. A biographical account by Suzhou University professor Zhu Zhinan quotes Jia as saying, "Chinese writers are too lacking in the spirit of risk taking. . . . I wish they had more of the consciousness of ordinary people."

It was typical that Jia preferred living in the provinces with ordinary people rather than the official life of Beijing. Among those things that seemed to fascinate him most was the urban street life to which Deng's economic reforms had given rise. His conviction that writing was really just a commodity that ought to compete on the open market with everything else was not one shared openly by most other intellectuals of the time. His respect for the marketplace gave him a natural affinity for those private entrepreneurs who were filling China's cities with a rough-and-tumble commercial energy. He is even reputed to have once said that "a single private entrepreneur is worth a hundred Liu Bin-yans." Liu represented an older, more conventional and cautious style of investigative reportage.

"Everyone has been so afraid, and this fearful state of mind has led to such an obsession that we Chinese writers have turned into our own censors," he told me. "Our problem is that as soon as we pick up our pens, rather than concentrating on producing a good article or book, we first have to think about whether or not we can get the piece published. Only over the last few years have things started to change, and this has been because a new world of underground publishing has sprung up out of the marketplace and started to challenge the state monopoly."

Jia's interest in this "new world" of market-oriented publishing grew not only out of his fascination with everything "underground," but out of necessity. Having been expelled from the official writers' association, and no longer able to rely on the state for support, he himself became an outcast of sorts. "Since I no longer have an 'iron rice bowl' and very few people want to have much to do with a writer who has no 'unit,' the only way I can survive now is to give my stuff to the second channel," he said. The nebulous galaxy of underground publishers and distributors called the "second channel" that had begun to challenge the state's control over the printed word held such special meaning for Jia that in 1988 he published a pathbreaking article in *Literary Reportage* describing how it worked.

Before the privatization of China's economy had gathered real momentum from Deng's reforms, the publication and distribution of books were part of a huge state-run monopoly operated under the scrutiny of the State General Publishing Administration (SGPA), an organization that technically answered to the government's State Council but was actually under the thumb of the Party Central Committee's Propaganda Department. Professional writers were all employees of this monopoly. Only after being carefully screened was a candidate admitted to one of the branches of the official Chinese Writers' Association, which paid their salaries and provided such crucial necessities as housing, health care, and travel privileges. It was virtually impossible for a writer to survive, or even to get published, outside this system. Only after a manuscript passed muster at an official publishing house was it given a *shuhao* (book registration number), the Chinese equivalent of an ISBN number. Without a *shuhao*, no volume could be legally published or distributed through the state-owned Xinhua Book Distribution Company monopoly. *Shuhao* were controlled by the SGPA which, in an attempt to tighten its grip over what was published after the student demonstrations in 1986, was rechristened the State General Press and Publication Administration (SGPPA) and given responsibility for overseeing the publication of magazines, newspapers, and periodicals as well as books.

Despite this megalithic system, what appeared in print was not controlled by a Soviet-style, centralized watchdog bureaucracy of censors scrutinizing every word before presses were allowed to roll. Instead, China relied on a system that Liu Binyan described as "postpublication censorship" in which guidelines for what was acceptable were delineated ex post facto after books appeared and were banned and writers and editors blacklisted. By far the most effective censoring mechanism was the ethos that grew out of the Party's numerous ideological campaigns, which at any given moment gave writers and editors an instinctive sense of what was permissible and what was not. To be a "literary worker," as writers, editors, and publishers were dubbed by the Party, demanded an alert and keen sense of shifting ideological boundaries. Because everyone knew that transgressions led to censure, demotion, dismissal, and even worse, most literary workers were careful to sanitize their own work, or any work that crossed their desk, so that there was little need for a censorate to make actual changes for them. "It's not so much a question of institutional censorship per se," explained Zhang Weiguo, the former Beijing correspondent for the *World Economic Herald,* which was closed down in 1989. "However, since it is always clear that punishment will be meted out after unorthodox articles appear, this creates obvious pressure for self-censorship."

Despite periodic crackdowns on deviant culture, this system of self-censorship had been eroding during the 1980s as writers and editors became increasingly resistant to such ideological pressure. Although the Party still controlled major publishing houses and newspapers, privatization had prompted the appearance of new kinds of publishing enterprises whose aim was to make money rather than to spread the Party's political gospel. Trashy tabloid magazines such as *Police Digest, Motorcycle,* and *Bodybuilding,* and works of pulp fiction that focused on romance, sex, martial arts, crime, and the supernatural began proliferating. This new laxness also allowed for a range of more serious writing by muckrakers such as Liu Binyan, Dai Qing, Su Xiaokang, and Jia Lusheng that explored previously taboo subjects. Even some publications directly under state control, like *China Youth News*, the *Farmer's Daily*, and the *World Economic Herald*, found ways to run articles that were surprisingly straightforward about the "dark side" of China's economic and political system. Translations of foreign works also abounded, further challenging the boundaries of official tolerance. To browse privately run outdoor bookstalls during this period was to enter a new world where the writings of Sigmund Freud, Carl Jung, John Locke, Friedrich Nietzsche, and Thomas Jefferson competed for space alongside kung fu novels, autobiographies by Richard Nixon and Lee Iacocca, and the first marriage and sex manuals ever published in the People's Republic.

When I spoke with Jia in 1989, the government's publishing and distribution monopoly was being challenged in ways that would have been unimaginable only a few years before. He laughed when I asked him to describe how the second channel had changed things and said that the situation was not easy to understand. Then he launched into an explanation of how publishing was being divided into three different color-coded "channels." The "red channel" was composed of the state-run publishing houses, the Xinhua Book Distribution Company system, and its thousands of Xinhua bookstores located throughout China. The "white channel" was made up of a new network of nongovernmental distributors run by so-called "book kings" who were wealthy private entrepreneurs. Although technically they were only allowed to distribute a restricted variety of publications within local areas, many of them had begun to branch out, not only setting up alternative, sub rosa distribution systems, but commissioning and publishing manuscripts as well. The "black channel" was made up of unlicensed and illegal fly-by-night publishers, printers, and distributors operating without any government sanction whatsoever. Although they tended to be heavily involved in the production of pornography, they were willing to publish and distribute almost anything that made money.

According to Jia, the basic building blocks of the second channel, which was a combination of the white and black channels, were the book kings. Since by 1989 they were offering advances that were far higher than those from state publishing houses, and since their books could be produced rapidly and were thus able to capitalize on market trends, authors found deals with book kings irresistibly lucrative.

If a second-channel manuscript was too controversial, once it was written and edited—a very cursory process in this "quickie" world of subterranean publishing—book kings could arrange for it to be printed illegally by a small underground press and distributed via the black channel. If the topic was relatively safe, a book king might negotiate with a state-run house to buy the use of its name and one of its *shuhao*, which created the appearance that the book had been contracted for and edited and published by the state-owned house itself.

For example, when in response to the Mao craze Jia Lusheng rushed out an analysis of the phenomenon, *The Sun That Never Sets,* although the title page listed it as being put out by the Central Plains Peasant Publishing Company in Henan Province and printed by the Loyang Yuxi Printing Company, and although it bore the imprimatur of the Henan branch of the Xinhua Book Distribution Company, it was impossible to know its actual lineage. Although selling *shuhao* was illegal, the bribes that book kings were willing to pay (usually in cash) to state-owned publishing houses were usually sufficient to turn managers into accomplices. Besides, if anyone did threaten to blow the whistle on them, it was always possible to pay another bribe in the form of a special "tax" to local officials in order to derail further investigation. The reason the whole system worked was that everyone got a cut. "The second channel consisted of people with money, or to be more precise, of people with money over which they have control, and they could afford to buy novels at higher prices than government publishing houses, and to spend money on gifts," Jia wrote in *Literary Reportage.* "During the era when we refused to accept the laws of commercial economic activity, hardly any consideration was given to making money in publishing. The only criteria were political. But now things have changed, and the laws of commerce have become the determining factor in publishing, and the books that get put out are those that make money."

Three of the most lucrative second-channel topics were sex, politics, and the occult. However, since white-channel publishers were fearful of books that might provoke the SGPPA to crack down on their whole operation, such topics often fell to black-channel operators. By the late eighties, China was awash in black-channel pornography, much of it imported from abroad and then reprinted. Another black-channel specialty was reprints of materials originally published by the Party in *neibu* (for internal circulation only) editions which often included critical foreign views of China, critiques of past Party policies, and unflattering accounts of deposed leaders.

As Jia discovered, there were whole townships that specialized in such underground publishing. After being blindfolded and taken to one such place in his native province, Jia not only found printing presses hidden in cellars, but he discovered that the whole town was involved in laying out, printing, and binding illicit publications.

By 1989 the second channel had also developed its own distribution network. Jia described it as being like a giant underground "irrigation system" veining the country with a complex web of interconnected entrepreneurial enterprises that were able to deliver products into the hands of thousands of outdoor *shutan* (private street stalls) with amazing speed. These men, wrote Jia, "represent the promise that money has made to literature." Organized almost like the Mafia on the basis of personal ties, networks of book kings got around regulations restricting their distribution by making informal intercity alliances with one another. On paper, companies looked local, but in reality they embraced whole regions, and in some cases much of the country. Some book kings even poached directly on red-channel territory by competing with Xinhua in the distribution of books with good market prospects put out by state-owned publishers themselves. By paying off state printers to do extra runs of popular volumes and then buying them through the "back door," book kings were even able to beat the sluggish Xinhua distributors to market with their own goods. As Jia told Cornell University China scholar Thomas Moran, "*Geti hu* with a small operation can run circles around the managers of a state enterprise until the latter don't know whether to laugh or cry."

Needless to say, their competition made Xinhua managers very uneasy. "All they do is sell martial-arts stuff, romance stories, murder mysteries, and porno, and they're just messing up the book and periodical market," the manager of one county-level Xinhua bookstore carped to Jia. "What's more, by feeding readers all kinds of unhealthy psychological stuff, they are damaging the building of socialist spiritual civilization, which is really criminal."

So well organized and so successful did second-channel distributors become that they began holding their own trade conventions. The First Non-governmental Book Distribution Work Conference was held in 1987 in Leshan, Sichuan Province. Neo-Maoists in Beijing were far from pleased to see their once absolute control over the printed word challenged by so many dynamic competitors, but they knew that closing down the second channel would not only be difficult, but would have a potentially ruinous effect on many state-owned publishers. With state subsidies being slashed, and state-owned houses increasingly reliant on their actual earnings, a growing portion of their income came from "fees" for *shuhao*. What is more, a crackdown could boomerang on the Party by driving white-channel publishers into the black channel, where they would be even more unmanageable. Given these constraints, the best officials could do was to harass certain book kings with threats, periodic fines, and from time to time close some of them down as demonstrations of who retained ultimate authority.

One such closure involved the Expectations Book and Periodical Distribution Service Agency, run by a semiliterate entrepreneur in his mid-twenties. Chen Dadong got his start setting up a string of independent book retail outlets in southwestern Shandong Province, a backward region that Xinhua had refused to service. As he became more successful, Chen's dreams of entrepreneurial grandeur grew. He built a ten-story flagship headquarters in the capital city of Jinan, established a national prize for literature, and moved to set up China's first truly independent publishing house. Chen's successes made authorities wary, and eager to find some pretext to cut him down to size. After an anonymous letter accusing him of selling pornographic literature surfaced in September 1987, the local Industrial and Commercial Management Bureau canceled his business license, fined him 110,000 yuan ($20,000), confiscated some 115,000 yuan ($21,000) in company funds, and closed his operation. "In effect, whatever the government does becomes legal, while whatever private individuals do puts them in violation of the law," commented Jia.

When Jia and I first spoke, there were hundreds of thousands of protesters in the Square, and the freedom writers were enjoying made it possible to imagine that publishing was poised to take another giant leap toward openness. Less than a month later, however, the crackdown was in high gear and Jia had disappeared underground. But if there was one writer in China with enough practice living by his wits to survive, it was Jia. However, as the repression deepened, it appeared uncertain that the second channel would survive. Many of China's most talented writers had been detained or driven into exile, and among those who remained in China, despair and frustration prompted many to give up writing. In fact, so many works-in-progress were abandoned that the term *chouti wenxue* (drawer literature) came into common parlance to describe all the manuscripts left in drawers unsubmitted to publishers.

With hard-liners back in control, SGPPA officials began issuing plump new compendiums of banned-book titles. For example, as China specialist Sophia Woodman discovered, in 1990 Yunnan Province issued a "for internal circulation only" handbook listing 41 closed state publishing houses and 1,300 banned books. The blacklist included erotic titles such as *The Abyss of Love* and *Perfume Stolen at Daylight*, but also politically unacceptable titles such as *Lessons for Chinese Youths: Rethinking the Pursuit of Democracy* (said to contain "political errors"), *On Human Rights* (described as having "serious problems in content"), and all the works of investigative writer Dai Qing.

It soon became clear, however, that while political debate had been silenced, suppression of indirectly errant forms of culture, particularly those tied to the market, would be nowhere near as thorough. In fact, after a tense post–June 4 hiatus of watching and waiting, book kings began picking up where they had left off and, by sticking with works that were largely nonpolitical, were soon expanding their operations again. With everyone trying to recover from the shock of what had happened, there was more money than ever to be made in escapist paperbacks and magazines on fashion, pop-music, and disco trends; in how-to books on improving one's sex life, investing in stocks, and redecorating the family bathroom; in tabloid magazines such as *Gun Culture, Tales of the Occult,* and *Secret Pleasures of Couples* featuring articles on executions, fortune-telling, and orgasm; and in soft-core porn, called *renti yishu* (body art), and sexually titillating fiction (which included everything from Chinese classics like the sixteenth-century *Golden Lotus* and *The Mat of Flesh* to translations of William Burroughs's *Naked Lunch* and the oeuvre of novelist Jackie Collins). One pulp tabloid called *Peach Flower Cave* even ran an article entitled "Teach Me How to Rape You." But almost any tabloid with a décolleté young woman on the cover, teasing headlines about movie stars, or articles about China's burgeoning class of "millionaires" sold out almost instantly.

Under such market pressure, the circulation of official Party publications plunged. To stem this hemorrhage of red ink, even such ideologically stodgy papers as the *People's Daily* and the *Liberation Army Daily* began putting out racier weekend magazines, featuring more marketable kinds of entertainment, to make money. It didn't take long for hard-liners to realize that it was time to triage the situation—to reserve the Party's suppressive firepower for manifestations of more overt political opposition and lob only occasional warning shots across the bow of upstart publishers. It was an astute strategy—at least in the short run. Even though the second channel undermined government control, it also helped neutralize vocal writers, editors, and publishers by giving them a shot at new wealth.

When in 1992 I asked what had become of Jia, a mutual friend in Beijing who had worked with him at *Literary Reportage* laughed and said, "Oh, Jia! He's out making money." Jia had been working out of Zhengzhou, the capital of Henan Province. He had not only survived 1989 but had successfully transformed himself from a déclassé investigative journalist with a smashed iron rice bowl into a book king who moved in a world where successful entrepreneurs enjoyed expensive banquets, drove Mercedes-Benzes, and clinched deals over car phones. In fact, by then many other intellectuals had also begun drifting away from their old state-run "work units" to the marketplace. As Zhang Weiguo said, "Before 1989 the most talented people in China were all trying to reform the system from within by working at Party-controlled publications or reform-minded think tanks. But when the Beijing massacre destroyed hopes for such political reform, most of them just dropped out of politics and went into business."

From the Party's perspective, making money was the perfect palliative for political malaise. In fact, officials even averted their gaze when blacklisted writers—whom not even the second channel would publish—submitted articles and books to Chinese-language publications in Taiwan, Singapore, Hong Kong, and the United States. After her release from prison in May 1990, Dai Qing managed to get her Qincheng Prison diary serialized in Hong Kong's daily, *Mingbao*. After his release that November, writer Wang Ruowang also got parts of his autobiographical prison novel, *Hunger Trilogy,* published by *Mingbao*. And when Zhang Weiguo was released from detention in February 1991, he was able to support himself by doing pieces for *Mingbao* and the *United Daily News* in Taiwan. The Party seemed to view writing for publications outside of China something like the export of toxic industrial waste—better to dump it abroad than keep it stored inside China.

By 1992 new market-driven publishing companies were springing up all over. Of course, each of them had to be affiliated with some official organization in order to get approval from the SGPPA, but these marriages of convenience were easily arranged—for a price. Everyone, it seemed, was now interested in making money. Even printing houses that had turned out nothing but Party documents and propaganda tracts and university presses specializing in scholarly works and textbooks joined the crush to publish children's books, girlie calendars, romance novels, and ten-step programs on how to get rich. The Expectations Book and Periodical Distribution Service

Agency, which Jia had told me about back in 1989, had even managed to reemerge. When Sophia Woodman visited Chengdu in 1992, she found that despite the challenge to Xinhua's book-distribution monopoly, Xinhua had rented office space to the upstart company! One of Xinhua's most pressing problems was that many of its most able employees had started to defect to the private sector. If it could not win in the increasingly competitive book-distribution business, it might at least make money as a landlord by renting out its not inconsiderable facilities, its managers seemed to reason. Under the circumstances, it was not surprising to find the second channel publishing a number of popular books on real estate.

The presence of the Expectations company in Xinhua's Chengdu building was the result of a new plan to "revitalize" the state-run book monopoly in innovative ways. In July 1992, Wang Yiquan, general manager of the head office of Xinhua's bookstore network, announced that they were setting up a national network of "book-marketing centers" in which the state would lease space to private book dealers. Indeed, in March 1993 the Chaoyang District People's Government and the Beijing Press and Publication Bureau got together with the Chaoyang City Construction Company to open the Beijing Magazine and Booksale Trade Mart on a dead-end street in the eastern part of the capital. In spite of the fact that monthly rent on booths was a stiff 1150 yuan ($230) and that the presence of wholesale dealers at the Mart made them easy prey for tax collectors and Commercial Bureau inspectors collecting license fees, by the time I visited the Mart in 1994, it had become a beehive of activity. With 120 booths and over 220 different publishers represented, buyers from private retail bookstalls welcomed its one-stop convenience. The second channel would be tolerated, even embraced, it seemed, as long as it did not publish material that offended Party leaders. But when such material did appear, officials were still obliged to act.

Who Will Take Charge?, which focused on China's then beleaguered economy, was Jia Lusheng's first post–June 4 work and was coauthored with Su Ya and put out by the Huacheng Publishing Company in Canton. The cover featured a large question mark superimposed over a map of China. Since China's stability, economic and otherwise, was an extremely sensitive issue at the time, the book was banned by the SGPPA, although not before it had become a best-seller. However, as soon as Huacheng stopped its presses, the book resurfaced in black-channel editions so that by the end of 1991 it was estimated to have sold almost a million copies.

As market demand for popular books grew in the post-1989 era, book kings, who had begun to refer to themselves by the slightly more dignified sobriquet of *shushang* (book traders), soon found themselves in competition with new kinds of upstart guerrilla publishers. *Feixing daxia* (flying knights) were one such new species. Some were ex-cons, but most were poorly educated young men who got started operating street stalls, where they gained a sense of how rapidly changing trends influenced what sells. They kept no offices and had no permanent phone numbers. Operating out of hotel rooms under assumed names, they simply appeared with satchels of money to pay off writers for manuscripts on hot subjects, usually potboilers containing lots of steamy sex and violence. Even well-known authors succumbed to their large cash advances, although they often wrote under pseudonyms.

Once a *feixing daxia* had a manuscript in hand, he would jump on a train or plane and, ignoring the niceties of book registration numbers, rendezvous directly with an underground printer who was willing to start his presses without a deposit. To raise capital the *feixing daxia* would then solicit prepaid orders from second-channel distributors so that when the book was printed and bound, his pyramid scheme would have produced enough not only to pay off the printer, but to provide a fat premium for himself as well.

The second channel worked so fast that such books usually got printed and distributed before anyone in authority got wind of them, much less got around to ordering a ban. And since the palms of local officials were easily greased, even when higher-ups were offended, officials would frequently do little more than go through the motions of "investigating." But even if they were serious about halting distribution of a given book, there was actually very little officials could do to control black-channel editions that invariably cropped up right after any banning.

For example, *The Tide of History* was a collection of articles written by seventeen intellectuals, many of whom had previously run afoul of Party hard-liners. It was edited by Beijing University law professor Yuan Hongbing, who had lost his job during the 1989 crackdown, and was published in the spring of 1992 by the People's University Press. While its essays extolled Deng's economic-reform policies, they also criticized the Party's history of leftist excesses under Mao and those hard-liners who had been appointed after 1989 to oversee media and culture. Almost as soon as the *The Tide of History* appeared, the SGPPA criticized it for having "serious political problems," banned it, and ordered the remaining 20,000 warehoused copies seized and destroyed. In the old days this might have been the end of the book. But as far as the market was concerned, there was no better testimonial to a work's perspicacity than Party censure. Like a rave review on the front page of the *New York Times Book Review,* Party censure made almost any book an instant best-seller. In no time at all second-channel entrepreneurs of the "black" variety were reproducing pirated editions of *The Tide of History,* and bookstall vendors were selling them for five to ten times the price of the original volume.

In 1993 a steamy sex-fest of a novel entitled *Feidu* (Defunct Capital) came out after its author, Jia Pinggao, had received a lump-sum advance from a second-channel operator. Shortly thereafter, it, too, was banned. But in a matter of weeks some 2 million black-channel volumes were flooding the market. "These days writers are never quite sure what happens once their books are published," Shanghai writer Sun Ganlu told me. "You never know how many copies are out there, because you don't know if they've been pirated and reprinted or what."

By February 1992, Party propaganda chief Wang Renzhi had become so concerned about what was happening, that he accused book kings for "getting up to their old tricks" and reproached them for failing to resist the seductions of the "fast track to fame, promotion, and wealth." He warned officials that "the moment they stick out their heads, we must beat the war drums and attack. Our newspapers, magazines, publishing houses, radio and television stations must never again provide a forum for such bourgeois liberalization."

With the hundredth anniversary of Mao's birth approaching and with the craze for Mao memorabilia and lore sweeping the country, the SGPPA was presented with yet another problem—how to protect the Chairman's reputation from all the *mishi* (secret histories) about his private life being published, via the second channel, that revealed his lechery toward women and his perfidy toward old comrades-in-arms. Popular favorites recounted Mao's affairs with his "nurse" Zhang Yufeng and film star Liu Xiaoqing. So in March of 1993 the SGPPA launched a "rectification" drive to control "irresponsible" and "vulgar" accounts that threatened to mar the work of Party hagiographers. Several magazines, including a spring issue of *Bridge,* in which excerpts were run of a book by Mao's former secretary, Li Rui, chronicling the Chairman's last years in office, were shut down, more than a dozen dailies were reprimanded, and regulations were issued requiring that all book-length biographies about Mao (and other high-ranking leaders) be approved by the Propaganda Department before publication. It further decreed that only six centrally controlled houses were authorized to publish such sensitive materials.

To remind everyone that it was not yet willing to relinquish control over the printed word and that it could still act with resolve when it chose to, the Party felt called on to make occasional dramatic gestures. In April 1993, for instance, the Beijing Intermediate Court made an example of book king Wang Shuxiang. He was sentenced to death for trafficking in *shuhao* and publishing almost a million copies of such "pornographic" books as *An Elementary Course for Marriage* and *Sexual Desire*. Although Wang's death sentence was suspended for two years to give him a chance to repent, all his assets—estimated to be worth more than half a million U.S. dollars—were confiscated and Wang was thrown in prison. That October the SGPPA and the Party's Propaganda Department issued a stern seven-point reminder: "Any unit or individual is strictly prohibited from purchasing *shuhao* in any form. Any publication put out under the imprint of a purchased number will be classified as illegal and will be banned . . . Ring-leaders will be sought out, and those responsible will be held culpable . . . [for] publishing books that contain grave political errors, leak state secrets, undermine national unity, contradict foreign policy, promote feudal-istic and superstitious practices, and feature pornographic and obscene material."

As China moved into the mid-1990s, forces similar to those trans-forming publishing were also beginning to influence state-owned elec-tronic media as well. Pirate record producers also began assuming entrepreneurial roles. "It used to be that we all had to 'link up' with the Party," one independent Shanghai record producer told me. "Now, we link up with the market." In broadcasting, similar phenomena were arising. For decades the central government had not permitted Chinese cities to have more than one local radio and television station. Of course, when the VOA and the BBC were not jammed, tens of millions of Chinese were able to tune in their Chinese-language radio broad-casts. And by setting up special "fishbone antennas," Chinese in Guangdong Province had long been able to watch Hong Kong televi-sion, while people living in coastal Fujian Province were able to tune in Taiwan channels.

But in 1992, under the sponsorship of Shanghai's entrepreneurial vice-mayor Gong Xueping, a new precedent was set in China when the city was allowed to set up a new kind of radio station and TV channel. Although Eastern Radio and Oriental Television were to be operated under the aegis of the Shanghai Bureau of Radio, Film, and Televi-sion, instead of relying on government funding they were designed to be commercially self-supporting. Moreover, they were dedicated to a whole new kind of programming that emphasized live broadcasts, Western pop music, and telephone call-in shows that sometimes even included local government officials as guests. The *China Daily* went so far as to describe this new program mix as "revolutionizing China's conservative broadcast format." With a potential listening audience around Shanghai of almost 120 million people, Eastern Radio quickly gained a massive following. During call-in shows, thousands sometimes jammed the switchboard.

"General political problems are out, but cultural, family, and city problems are in," Oriental Television news editor Wu Chaoyang told me of his new channel's programming. "In" subjects dealt with such titillating topics as crime. "Dongfang 110," for instance, was a program featuring stories about actual criminal cases, that was not only coproduced with the Shanghai police but featured a uniformed cop as an anchorman. Eastern Radio featured such programs as "Emergency Room Hot Line," which broadcast a mélange of Western pop tunes and phoned-in consumer queries and complaints. As politically bland as these programs often were, they did allow Chinese an opportunity to publicly air their thoughts. Moreover, by mid-1993 there were more than fifty such new commercial stations operating in China, and it was not difficult to imagine the role they might play as a vector for public discussion if a new wave of political disturbances ever hit the country in the future.

Since virtually every urban household owned a TV set (80 percent had color sets by 1993), television had become the most influential medium of public communication. While there were still no truly independent TV channels, the ubiquity of VCRs meant there was no limit to what people could watch—from hard-core pornography and American cop shows to MTV rock-music videos and Hong Kong kung fu movies—in their own homes. In addition, thousands of satellite dishes had begun sprouting from Chinese rooftops, enabling viewers to tune into networks such as CNN and Star-TV. Rupert Murdoch had just bought a 63 percent interest in Star-TV for $525 million, and it was broadcasting everything from "The Simpsons" and "Oprah Winfrey" to the BBC World Service News (which Murdoch took off the air in 1994 after the Beijing government claimed its reports "hurt the feelings of the Chinese people") and international sports events to some 30 million households in China. NBC was also about to join the China video sweepstakes via the Apstar 2 satellite launched by a Chinese-made Long March rocket in 1994. Although a 1990 Chinese regulation made it illegal to use dishes for the purpose of tuning in such overseas broadcasts, authorities neither banned the sale nor the purchase of the dishes themselves. This ambiguity left loopholes for local manufacturers and salesmen to sell dishes (which cost from $300 to $600) and for purchasers to claim that they needed the satellite in order to get good reception of state-run Central Chinese Television (CCTV) broadcasts which, as it happened, were broadcast via the same satellite, AsiaSat 1, as Star-TV. Thus any dish aimed in the direction of AsiaSat 1 was conveniently able to receive both signals.

The animating force behind this subterfuge was, of course, money, and the list of those profiting from the sale of these space-age consumer items ironically included many state-owned enterprises. Like those publishers whose bottom lines had come to rely on the sale of *shuhao*, enterprises attached to such government organs as the Army General Staff Department and the Ministry of Radio, Film, and Television also had a vested interest in satellite dishes because they had begun to manufacture them. According to Zhang Weiguo, in 1992 Shanghai alone had at least seventeen different assembling factories using parts imported mostly from Taiwan, Japan, and the United States. The finished products were not only sold by department stores and electronics shops, but hawked in the streets by peddlers who were very difficult to control.

Certain state enterprises and Party-sponsored neighborhood committees had another kind of economic interest in satellite dishes. Beginning in the early nineties, people with an entrepreneurial instinct had begun setting up thousands of miniature cable-television systems that depended for programming on pirated videos of foreign films and satellite feeds from Star-TV. By buying a single dish and then selling hookups to subscribers in an apartment building, residential compound, or neighborhood, these nascent media moguls (by 1993, estimates placed their number at over 10,000 nationwide) were able to make handsome returns on relatively small investments.

In 1992 officials did try to reassert some measure of control over these networks. For example, one factory-based cable system in Manchuria that showed overseas videos was admonished by local authorities for being "in violation of state regulations" and for failing to be a "mouthpiece of the Party and people and an important front of socialist ideology." In late 1992 the Shanghai PSB confiscated a demonstration dish from a retail showroom and fined the store 50,000 yuan ($10,000). In response, the manager filed suit against the government, claiming that it was unfair to penalize a store where the dish was not even in use. Various newspapers quickly took up the store's cause, claiming that such harassment was bad for business, at which point the government just seemed to give up, and soon trade in dishes and activity at local cable operations were back to normal.

All this activity made it tempting to believe that the market had triumphed over politics. However, in October 1993, Premier Li Peng, who had been sidelined for months by a heart condition reemerged in public view and signed State Council Proclamation No. 129, making it illegal for individuals to sell, buy, install, or use satellite dishes without first obtaining a permit. According to the *People's Daily*, the object of the ban was to protect "social stability" and "socialist spiritual civilization," or what was left of it. The proclamation may also have been designed to protect China's grip on this very lucrative field of business. Violators who failed to make the application were threatened with not only having their dishes confiscated, but being fined up to 15,000 yuan ($3,000). Only those private citizens unable to receive a clear CCTV signal would be granted permits.

It was not long, however, before it became evident that Li's ban was going to be ineffective. By the time of his decree there were already so many dishes in use that, short of checking every rooftop, it was hard to imagine how the government might force compliance. As far as anyone had heard, by the middle of 1994 no one already hooked up to a dish had yet been challenged by authorities. Although demonstration models had disappeared from most store showrooms and sales of dishes had dropped to one-tenth their previous number, it was still possible to buy the devices and have them installed. Some observers began to wonder if, rather than intending an immediate crackdown, the government was not just laying groundwork with Proclamation No. 129 so that if there were political disturbances in the future it would have ready legal justification for clamping down. Meanwhile, if officials chose to, they could harass certain individuals and reap a bountiful harvest of fines.

Actually, the government had developed a far more effective strategy for controlling what people saw than simply cracking down on foreign broadcasts. Their answer was to deluge the country with an ever greater variety of local programming that they themselves could regulate. Toward this end, officials began approving more than fifty new cable channels as well as a new network of "educational" channels. Although these were licensed and controlled by local government jurisdictions, their reliance on commercial sponsors made them both more financially independent and more eager to pioneer new kinds of programming.

"I don't know if the government did it consciously or not," Wu Chaoyang told me, "but approving all these new sources of entertainment has had the undeniable effect of providing more competition for Star-TV."

By 1994 more than 600 urban cable services had been approved, creating so much media interest that in Beijing a magazine, *World*

Cable TV, even began to be published. Shanghai Cable, for instance, was a $115 million venture set up to offer twelve new channels of entertainment for a $25 hookup fee and a monthly charge thereafter of less than $1. Although the programming of these new channels was often quite poor, their sheer numbers and diversity were impressive. While for the moment they were not asserting much political independence, many stations managers were busy bending rules and making their own deals for foreign programming with overseas suppliers who were all too willing to barter an hour of some old American soap opera for a minute of commercial time. Just as in the second channel, it was not hard to see how this new welter of media outlets might someday provide a real challenge to government control over news and information.

"What's changed in China is the market, and what's driving things is money, not politics," explained Zhang Weiguo. "There are such enormous fortunes being made in underground newspapers, magazines and books, and now in radio and television as well, that the government has been left running around like a fire brigade putting out blazes that keep popping up everywhere. It's a rapidly changing and confusing situation, but whatever happens, I don't think it's realistic any longer for the government to think in terms of completely stopping the second channel."

"Oh sure, officials come in here and confiscate stuff from time to time," a clerk at a shop run by several university presses at the Beijing Magazine and Booksale Trade Mart told me as I was browsing one day. "The most they can hope to accomplish is to scare people who mess with politically sensitive subjects. But there's no longer any way they can actually control what's going on."

28

"Nothing to My Name"

Even though it was raining, a huge crowd made its way through the streets of Nanjing to the Wutaishan Sports Arena. Outside the gates, hopeful fans gathered to negotiate with scalpers for last-minute tickets to the sold-out May 1992 concert that were going for as much as $20—five times the original price and more than half the monthly salary of an average worker. Inside, the supercharged atmosphere was lent an added edge of excitement by the presence of hundreds of uniformed police. Even though the makeshift stage was still empty, the din was deafening as people cheered wildly and waved hand-lettered banners. One claque from a city almost a thousand miles away held up a banner that read, "Cui Jian: Your Buddies from Lanzhou Are Here!" A group of local fans had arranged itself in seats so that when each raised a placard the message read: "From Your Fans in Nanjing!"

Only when the houselights finally dimmed did the crowd hush. But as soon as the slender, pale, almost expressionless Cui Jian appeared in a pair of blue jeans and a tank top amid a billowing cloud of theatrical smoke and a blaze of flashing colored lights, the audience rose as one and roared. Cui surveyed his ecstatic fans for a few moments, and then with evident satisfaction proclaimed, "So, I see Nanjing is another of my liberated areas!" In response to this mocking allusion to the areas Chinese Communist guerrilla forces "liberated" from the Nationalists during the 1920s and 1930s, the crowd sent up another collective roar the likes of which I had not heard since I stood in the middle of the Square in 1989. When Cui released the first ear-splitting chord of "The New Long March of Rock-and-Roll" on his electric guitar, young fans jumped up and began dancing in front of their seats as if they had been waiting since that terrible June day for this single moment of cathartic release. "I love it here so much because I don't have to behave!" a young man sitting near me cried out.

"I feel something like I imagine the old guard of revolutionaries must have felt on the Long March," Cui would later tell a journalist from the Hong Kong–based *China Times Weekly* when asked why he had decided to name his concert tour after his song "The New Long March of Rock-and-Roll." Cui insisted that just like old-guard veterans, who after being "chased and embattled" had finally realized their dreams of revolution, he, too, hoped to "succeed in creating something unusual" in his life. He didn't indicate whether he meant a new zone of cultural autonomy or simply a chance to sing his own music, but whatever, old Long Marchers would probably not have had an easy time drawing parallels between their political odyssey and his. In fact, a block of people sitting to one side of the stage remained so noticeably motionlessness compared to the rest of the whooping, clapping, gyrating audience, that it seemed as if within this single zone everyone had been anesthetized by some mysterious and highly selective chemical agent. These were the seats that had been set aside for Party and government dignitaries attending this benefit in their official supervisory capacities. Cui had been allowed to play as part of a concert for Project Hope, an effort by a new Chinese foundation and the Communist Party Youth League to raise money for children whose rural parents were too poor to send them to school. These officials looked hopelessly trapped in this scene, which for many appeared to be a manifestation of their worst nightmares about the insidious effects of "bourgeois liberalization."

Only the rows of uniformed police officers who kept a nervous watch over the undulating crowd appeared more self-conscious and out of place than these officials. The more excited the crowd became, the more jittery the police grew. Initially, they tried to restrain a few of the more rambunctious youths as they jumped up to dance in the aisles, but it was a hopeless task, and they soon gave up. For the rest of the concert they remained awkwardly at attention, murmuring occasionally into their walkie-talkies.

As Cui sang, the sports arena became the same kind of self-contained oasis that the Square had been three years before. "I've given you my dreams, and given you my freedom / But you always just laugh at me for having nothing!" When he broke into "Nothing to My Name," a song that had been one of the anthems of the 1989 hunger strikers, the rigid dignitaries stared at the stage blankly. It was probably one of the few times since the televised contretemps between Premier Li Peng and the student leaders three years before that government representatives had been forced to listen to the real voice of the country's youth. How much of the message they understood was another matter, but they could not have failed to grasp the fact that these kids were cheering a performer who was spreading a gospel that obliquely repudiated almost everything the Party stood for. When Cui's band performed "Like a Knife" ("The guitar in my hands is like a knife, / I want to cut your face till all that's left is your mouth . . . / I don't care if you're an old man or a girl, / I want to cut your hypocrisy until I get some truth./ Now my heart is like a knife, that wants to pierce through your mouth; to kiss your lungs!"), the dignitaries hardly batted an eye. Only when Cui began playing a song called "The Last Shot" was there a flicker of recognition on their otherwise wooden faces.

Cui insisted that the "The Last Shot" had been written about the 1979 Sino-Vietnamese war, but the song was so poignantly evocative of 1989 that when his album *Nothing to My Name* was released that year, the lyric sheet left only a blank space where the words should have been. The missing words consisted of only two lines—"A wild shot hit my chest / And at that moment everything from my life surged through my heart"—followed by the song's title chanted over and over as bursts of machine-gun–like fire rolled from the drummer's snare. At this point, Nanjing fans, who seemed to have been waiting for this moment, lit candles and began to sway back and forth as he played. The flickering lights merged with the final spine-tingling, tapslike solo Cui played on the trumpet to create an almost funereal atmosphere.

Born in 1961, Cui Jian was taught music by his father who played with an air force band. After graduating in 1981 from a high school attached to the Beijing Industrial Institute, Cui won a position as a classical trumpeter with the prestigious Beijing Philharmonic Orchestra. But after listening to the music of John Denver, Andy Williams, and Simon and Garfunkel, whose recordings were among the first nonclassical Western works to enter China during the early 1980s, Cui started playing hooky from the orchestra to try his own hand at popular music. With six other classical musicians, he formed the Building Blocks, one of the first independent music groups of its kind in the People's Republic. "I worked hard, said farewell to my old life, and started life from zero," said Cui of his plunge.

Cui's decision to relinquish his "iron rice bowl" and live on the fringes of official society was an act of considerable boldness in the mid-eighties, especially for an aspiring rock musician. Like Jia Lusheng after his expulsion from the Writers' Association, Cui found himself without a monthly salary, housing, or medical care. Even if the Party had not been opposed to "spiritual pollution" from the West, living in a poor country where decent instruments, amplifiers, practice space, recording facilities, and performance halls were extremely difficult to find made surviving a daunting proposition. On the other hand, Cui had gained an unprecedented degree of freedom to develop both his music and an unorthodox lifestyle. "Of course, when you are the first, there are a lot of problems," he told an interviewer in 1992. "But I also think one is lucky because no one will control you. You can do anything you want."

By 1986, Cui was listening to recordings of the Beatles, the Rolling Stones, Talking Heads, and Sting, and his own songwriting had begun to show signs of increasing sophistication. In May of that year, he got an unexpected break when he was invited to sing at Beijing's Workers' Stadium on a nationally televised music competition called "One Hundred Pop Stars." Chinese popular music then consisted largely of saccharine love ballads and derivative Western-style disco tunes, and nobody was prepared for what followed. When Cui walked on stage wearing a pair of tattered army fatigues and began gyrating his hips and singing in his gravelly voice, the audience lapsed into a dumbfounded silence. But by the time Cui finished his set, which included "Nothing to My Name," the crowd was cheering wildly and dancing in the aisles. Word of Cui's pathbreaking appearance spread quickly among trend-conscious youths, and it was not long before he was besieged with fan mail and bootlegged tapes of his performance were being sold in private music shops.

Taking up with several other independent-minded musicians—including two guitarists from Madagascar and Hungary, and several Chinese—Cui formed a group called ADO that combined electric guitars, synthesizers, woodwinds, and brass with an assortment of traditional Chinese instruments such as the oboe-like *suona,* the zither-like *guzheng,* and the reed-piped *sheng.* ADO developed an eclectic sound that mixed jazz, Afro-pop, reggae, and Western rock with Oriental flourishes. Cui lived a hand-to-mouth existence by playing gigs on Beijing college campuses, in dance halls, at private parties given by foreigners, and at the chic new after-hours discotheque opened at Pierre Cardin's Maxim's restaurant, where even the PSB was reluctant to intrude.

Because hard-line leaders viewed rock music as "spiritual pollution" and as a transmitter of antiauthoritarian attitudes and pernicious bourgeois influences, they made periodic attempts during these early years to stamp it out. But Deng had concluded that opening up the economic door inevitably meant tolerating certain undesirable outside influences. "When one opens the window, it is natural that some flies will come inside," he said, so such drives were ultimately short-lived, and pop music not only survived, but spread like wildfire. In fact, by 1987, the mantle of heroism for many of the country's urban youth had passed irrevocably from the likes of Lei Feng to pop-culture icons like Cui Jian and his ragtag band of nonconformist rockers. Party realists seem to have decided that pop music was both ineradicable and an important pressure-release valve for youthful energy that might otherwise seek political expression. Sometimes they even used it to sugarcoat their own Marxist messages with a veneer of contemporary trendiness. Not surprisingly, these efforts to wrap the Marxist wolf in a pop-culture sheepskin created some bizarre cultural collisions, such as electric-guitar–toting female PLA soldiers in high heels performing on TV and Party-sponsored disco dances at universities.

Understandably, the Party's cultural grand viziers far preferred *tongsu yinyue* (middle-of-the-road pop music) to the more hard-edged sound of *yaogun yinyue* (rock, or literally shaking and rolling music). There were, in fact, completely different sociologies behind these two musical forms. Whereas the *tongsu*/pop-music industry was vertically controlled by the government, which operated everything from state-run arts troupes where the songs were written to the TV shows where they were performed and the recording studios where albums were produced, *yaogun*/rock was controlled by the singers themselves, many of whom, like Cui, had dropped out of the official system. In short, *yaogun* was as much an attitude as a musical style.

The Party was well aware of rock's subversive nature, and sometimes sought to eradicate it. But efforts to limit the effect of rock by denying bands access to concert halls and excluding them from appearances on state radio and television only forced rockers to root themselves deeper in their own free-market underworld. It was in the privately run bars, restaurants, and dance halls that proliferated during the late 1980s that rock survived and acquired an outlaw cachet that enhanced its appeal among young people searching for alternatives to the mind-numbing monotony of official culture.

Although Cui's young fans clearly appreciated the way in which his songs often toyed with the Party's most cherished symbols and themes, his growing popularity stemmed primarily from his ability to articulate feelings of political frustration, sexual confusion, and social alienation without lapsing into overbearing didacticism. But in spite of his indirection, it was almost inevitable that sooner or later Cui would raise the Party's political hackles. One of his first scrapes occurred in 1987 after he revived the old Yan'an-era revolutionary ballad "Nanniwan" (South Muddy Bay) as a rock song. This trailblazing effort to recycle Party culture by adding a boogie beat to a familiar revolutionary tune paved the way for the updated Mao-era songs that were later to flood the market. But in 1987, Cui's new rendition of "Nanniwan" was considered almost as much of an abomination as making a jingle out of Deng's Four Basic Principles. Moreover, its debut happened to coincide with an earlier movement to halt the spread of "bourgeois liberalization," causing Cui's formal dismissal from the Beijing Philharmonic.

For Cui, the late 1980s were a high-wire survival act that mixed subtle defiance with calculated efforts at compromise. Fortunately, China's economy was being privatized and areas at the margins of official society where artists, entrepreneurs, nonconformists, dropouts, and even criminals could find refuge from government control were opening up. For a society that for over three decades had had no such sanctuaries, the reemergence of these littoral zones represented an important change, one which some hopefully viewed as the beginnings of civil society in the People's Republic.

Starting from these margins, Cui's musical reputation slowly grew. In March 1989, during the relative permissiveness of the period that preceded Hu Yaobang's death, Cui was even allowed to give a concert before thousands of fans at the Beijing Exhibition Hall. Once out on stage, he pulled out a bloodred scarf, blindfolded himself with it, and then lit into his song "A Piece of Red Cloth," an abstruse exploration of the complicated master-slave relationship that exists between oppressors and oppressed. Even for those who found the words enigmatic, there was nothing subtle about the blindfold, which had the haunting effect of making Cui look as if he was about to be executed. For those searching out even more symbolism, it was not difficult to interpret the blindfold as an emblem of the way in which revolutionary politics had blinded Chinese into self-subjugation.

Such oblique symbols were Cui's specialty. Continuing the tradition of culture T-shirts, he silk-screened a shirt emblazoned with two high brick walls linked by a strand of barbed wire. Confined in between the walls was a small green plant in the shape of the character *ren* (man). Taken together, the entire image formed the character *qiu* (to imprison). Yet, when asked about his political views, Cui always demurred. Even in the relative openness of the period, he seemed to have decided that it was not safe to be too explicit. On the eve of the Tiananmen Square demonstrations, an interviewer asked him if he saw himself as a political rebel. "We do not rebel," he replied obliquely. "We fight for personal liberation."

That April, Cui was signed to a record contract by EMI Music in Hong Kong and went to England to participate in the First Asian Popular Music Awards at London's Royal Albert Hall. By the time he returned to Beijing, demonstrations had already begun and his song "Nothing to My Name" had been appropriated as one of the protesters' favorite anthems. "We loved the kind of strong individual will that was expressed in 'Nothing To My Name,' " remembered Wu'er Kaixi. "I felt as if the song's title summed up our lives and our sentiments. Just think about our generation. Did we have anything? We did not have the goals for which our parents once strived, nor did we have the kinds of fanatic ideals our older brothers and sisters once had. . . . Apart from our strength, we had nothing to our name."

Finally, even Cui could not resist the temptation to get involved. On May 19, just before martial law was declared, he made a pilgrimage to the Square and sang "Opportunists," a song he had written for the hunger strikers. When it was reported that a wire-service photo showed him performing, Cui became inextricably identified with the protest movement.

Like so many others, Cui dropped from sight immediately after June 4. But after lying low for several months, he reemerged unscathed. As repressive as the crackdown was, pop music was one outlet for creative expression that remained relatively unperturbed. Only a few months after the crackdown began, Australian diplomat and novelist Nicholas Jose visited a Beijing dance hall near Liubukou, where the slaughter had been horrendous, and found a band calling itself 1989 I Love You belting out choruses of "Get Back" and "Let It Bleed" as a capacity crowd of young people danced in a frenzy. Before the band signed off that night, it played a deeply ironic version of the revolutionary standard "Without the Communist Party There Would Be No New China" that was reminiscent of Jimi Hendrix's Woodstock "Star-Spangled Banner." The improvisation was "a musical re-enactment of events still imprinted on everyone's mind," said Jose. "Nothing was said, and nothing needed to be said."

Some conjectured that the Party had decided to allow rebellious youth certain cultural diversions in hopes of keeping them out of political trouble, or that they had decided to relent on some cultural matters in order to concentrate their control mechanisms on activities that were more directly political in nature. Whatever the reason, rock bands continued to eke out marginal existences and, in the absence of other forms of public protest, to serve as a vicarious form of dissent.

Just as Deng's decision not to cancel economic reforms had allowed the second channel to maintain a niche outside of the state publishing and distribution system, so the market now afforded rock musicians like Cui a way to make a living. As the government sought to wean state-run companies off subsidies, recording studios were eager to find lucrative projects to shore up their bottom lines. As a substantial new market grew for rock music, studios started producing recordings of independent bands like Cui's. ADO's first major album was put out by none other than the state-run China Tourism Audiovisual Publishers.

The debacle of 1989 left China's leaders desperate to find ways to regain the respect of the world. The 1990 Asian Games, scheduled to take place in Beijing, were viewed in official circles as an opportunity to showcase the extent to which life in Beijing had returned to "normal." Casting about for ways to perform before larger audiences, Cui agreed to do a series of benefit concerts to help offset the Games' looming budget shortfall. His decision sparked some critics to charge that he had "sold out." But Cui insisted that he was neither a dissident nor a Party follower, just an artist. Besides, Cui the pragmatist knew that if he was going to sell albums, he needed to cultivate a following through public concerts, even if getting permission to perform entailed making certain accommodations. Behind Cui's decision beat the pulse of the market.

At each of his Asian Games benefit concerts, Cui was greeted by screaming fans waving posters, raising their fists in solidarity, and flashing the V-for-victory sign just like protesters in the Square. And when he performed "A Piece of Red Cloth" and provocatively wore his signature blindfold, crowds went crazy. With the memory of June 4 not yet a year old, the government was understandably concerned that this effusive outpouring of support for the upstart rocker might serve as a catalyst for some kind of new political upheaval. Halfway through Cui's eight-city tour, officials abruptly canceled the remaining concerts.

In the spring of 1992 the Party decided to give Cui another chance by recruiting him to play at the series of benefit concerts in Nanjing, where I saw the power that his music still had over China's youth. Despite Cui's claim that "politics is not my work," it was obvious from the concert that he did tap into a deep vein of suppressed rebelliousness. It was no accident that each June the Party banned all rock concerts. "Cui Jian's popularity is not just due to the skill of his music or his band, but because he expresses inner feelings that are rarely expressed in China,'' rock singer Zhao Li explained to Andrew Jones, whose book *Like a Knife* chronicles the Chinese rock scene in the early nineties. ''Rock is definitely about oppression, about rebellion. It's very provocative. It wants to stir people up. . . . Why is it today that the only music we can respect is Cui Jian's? It's because it is truthful. There are hardly any *tongsu* songs that are truthful.''

By the summer of 1992, the Chinese rock scene had developed a subculture all its own, with its own dress code, language, sexual mores, lifestyle, and even penchant for drugs, mostly hash and opium scored in Ganjiakou's Xinjiang Village, where many Muslim-style restaurants are situated in Beijing.

Another milestone in the history of Beijing rock-and-roll was reached in 1992 when Cui and a group of his musical cronies converted an old abandoned movie theater in the Xuanwu District into an after-hours club, giving the rock scene an actual locus. The Taijin, or Titanium Club as it was dubbed, became a hub not only for rock bands, but fans, groupies, fascinated foreign students, *geti hu* entrepreneurs, and assorted riffraff looking for ''a scene.'' An unprepossessing, win-dowless hall located on the second floor of a drab building, the Tita-nium featured a bar that served beer, a performance stage where bands could play, and a dance floor where the theater's seats had once been. On the walls was a collection of rock-star photographs and Mao-era records tacked up like so many 45's from the fifties. Night after night, bands jammed away in suffocating clouds of cigarette smoke and ear-splitting noise until the wee hours. Performing were such groups as the heavy-metal band Black Panther, punk rocker He Yong, and the all-female Women's Band, which included Wei Hua, the former CCTV English-language news anchor who had been sacked after giving an interview to ABC-TV's ''Nightline'' in 1989.

Although Cui was the most prominent figure in Beijing's rock demi-monde, by 1992 the iconoclasm of many younger singers and bands was beginning to make him seem almost tame. For instance, He Yong, whose former band, Mayday, had been renowned for the hard-core nihilism of such signature songs as ''Beijing Punk'' and ''Garbage Dump,'' a bleak, existential howl of a song whose lyrics are half-growled and half-shrieked over a cacophonous guitar line and an ec-centric alternating rhythm. (''Where we live is like a garbage dump./ People are like insects with everyone struggling and stealing./ First we eat our consciences, and then we shit ideology!'') At the end of the song, He screams, ''Is this a joke? No! Tear it down!''

''Saying the things you most desperately need to say [in China] is like trying to scream with your lips Krazy Glued together,'' He told Jones. ''When you finally get it out, there's blood dribbling down your chin.'' Despite the fact that it was still impossible to speak openly on political subjects, as China approached the third anniversary of June 4, there were so many heterodox ideas, weird fads, errant cultural tendencies, and unorthodox economic hustles going on that it was difficult to imagine how the Party would again rein these forces back in should it ever feel the need to do so. Since habitués of Beijing's rock subculture seemed to be doing nothing more than singing bizarre music and leading bohemian lifestyles, it was hard for Party elders to know how to deal with them. Perhaps they reasoned that under the circumstances, allowing stars like Cui—who unlike punker He Yong seemed to recognize certain limits of propriety—to reign as king was perhaps the most effective way of managing the unpredictable rock-music phenomenon.

Rock music was only one more of the host of indications that, despite the crackdown, certain social groupings were nonetheless finding ways to detach themselves from the grip of the Party. Their survival seemed to confirm that Deng was neither going to abandon his program of market reforms nor reimpose the kinds of harsh cultural controls that many hard-liners still favored. The resulting trends collectively comprised what China scholar Geremie Barmé began referring to as the "graying of Chinese culture." The term was borrowed from Eastern Europe, where people like Vaclav Havel had used the notion of a "gray zone" to describe the space occupied by those people who opposed the Communist system in passive rather than active ways. It was a vague term, but apt in the sense that it pointed out the way once hard-and-fast political distinctions were beginning to blur as more and more maverick Chinese animated by a pioneering sense of experimentation and adventure left the state sector to live in those marginal gray areas of life over which the Party no longer exercised complete control. What was significant about "gray culture" was that, despite its seeming lack of intention, it was almost as subversive to the established order as protesting students. By appealing indirectly to people's emotions rather than directly to their intellects or political sense and by being an exemplar of survival on that expanding edge of the economy that existed outside the state sector, Cui Jian was a perfect emblem of the kind of subtle rebellion that lay at the heart of gray culture.

29

The Graying of Chinese Culture

T he word "gray" describes both the process by which Chinese culture was being bleached of its Communist redness in the early 1990s and the appearance of those new "gray zones" of commercial and cultural activity that were arising outside of Party-state structures. As manifested in such areas as the Mao craze, second-channel publishing, commercial broadcasting, and rock music, gray culture was not so much a coherent movement as a state of mind—the zeitgeist of a new generation that had lost the grand hopes of radically reforming, much less unseating, China's Party-controlled political establishment. Gray culture was exemplified, wrote Geremie Barmé, by "hopelessness, uncertainty, and ennui" mixed with "irony, sarcasm, and a large dose of fatalism." Most young Chinese revealed their deepening sense of alienation by pursuing alternative lifestyles; innovative forms of artistic expression; rowdy, antisocial behavior; and most of all by making money. The challenge to members of this gray culture was not so much to confront the Party and official culture head-on with idealism but to make an existential statement out of one's lifestyle simply by living in a way that eschewed official values; to beard the Party dragon subtly without being caught. "Today, surrounded by the ruins of bankrupt idealism, people have finally come to an unavoidable conclusion: extreme resistance proves only just how powerful one's opponent is and how easily one can be hurt,'' wrote the critic Liao Wen. ''Humor and irony, on the other hand, may be a more corrosive agent.''

In 1989 the prime source of dissident energy had been students, but as privatization of the economy progressed, more and more new classes and groups began delaminating from established society. One of these was the *liumang,* young unemployed youths with little education and no stable families or permanent residences, who kept themselves in pocket money by one kind of illicit hustle or another. *Liumang* drifted around Chinese cities wearing looks of vapid boredom as they played snooker in tawdry pool halls, hung out with their buddies in karaoke bars and dance halls, and prowled the streets. It was a paradox of China's post-1989 situation that these *liumang* were far more estranged than the student activists of 1989. Despite the bitter disillusionment of students, they were still irrevocably a part of China's educated elite, and regardless of whether they were underground, in prison, or in exile, ultimately most of them would become part of the country's ruling class. But having never had faith in anything beyond their own survival, *liumang* did not even have the benefit of disillusioned idealism to give direction to their lives. As Wang Shou, a writer and creator of several wildly popular TV programs that were admired by disaffected youth, put it, ''I can't stand people with a sense of mission.'' If China was in danger of spiraling toward chaos anytime soon, the impetus was as likely to come from gangs of alienated *liumang* and unemployed workers as from banner-waving university students. Having cleared the political stage of critics who had been eager to reform the system from within, hard-line Party leaders now found themselves facing a far more inchoate and potentially destabilizing urban opposition—what some China scholars had begun to describe as ''uncivil society'' (in contradistinction to the newly independent ''civil society'') that was also appearing alongside official social structures.

The once discrete universes of these lumpen *liumang* and educated young Chinese had intersected briefly in the Square during 1989. Now as the political crackdown continued, they merged again in an unexpected way through the gray culture's burgeoning underground. Here the term *liumang,* once looked upon as purely pejorative, implying indolence, dishonesty, and criminality, was being appropriated by educated urban youths as a shorthand way to differentiate their new subculture of rebellion from *guanfang wenhua* (official culture). Particularly among rock musicians, the word *liumang* acquired positive new connotations centering around notions of individualism, defiance of authority, and the spirit of independence. Within the context of ''gray'' rock subculture, being known as a *liumang* conferred the luster of nonconformism, the equivalent to being called "bad" in American black culture. Among self-styled outcasts, the notion of a *liumang* also echoed with romantic associations of *jianghu haojie* (Robin Hood–like knights-errant) from classical Chinese literature whose righteous rebellions against unjust officialdom were for hundreds of years central to the Chinese version of the "outlaw ideal" or "honor among thieves" that Jia Lusheng had extolled in his writings about social rebels.

While visiting Beijing in 1992, I stumbled upon one pocket of gray culture where the glorification of *liumang*-ism by rock-and-rollers expressed itself in a most graphic way. The occasion was a shoot for a film called *Beijing Bastards* (*Beijing Zazhong*) that depicted the free-wheeling existence of a group of young rock musicians, songwriters, and painters surviving by their wits in Beijing as they did their art, hung out in restaurants, and brawled their way through bars and dives. The film was being directed by Zhang Yuan, whose credits included several experimental films and music videos for Cui Jian. What was more telling about *Beijing Bastards,* though, was that it was being independently produced outside the state film apparatus with money that Cui had earned from his albums and that Zhang had won at a French film festival, which made it the first second-channel–style film production in China.

The story's plot centered around a rock singer who, having been banned from giving public concerts by police, drifts aimlessly among Beijing's demimonde, smoking, drinking, carousing, doing drugs, and searching for his pregnant girlfriend. Instead of hiring professional actors and actresses, Zhang Yuan chose to create documentary authenticity by using actual rock musicians and artists for all the roles. The star of the film was none other than Cui Jian. And to capture the real ambience of the underground "scene," Zhang had been shooting at the Titanium with live crowds. The night that I caught up with him, he was doing a shoot outside of Beijing. According to rumors, it was going to be an all-night outdoor rock party, a real cinema verité bacchanal complete with bonfires, roast meat, beer, live music, dancing, and even young women who would purportedly strip before the cameras and dance in reckless abandon. The idea that such a scene might be shot in a country still fixated on the perils of "bourgeois liberalization" was just another example of the kind of cognitive dissonance that distinguished this "gray" period.

After our rented bus crammed full of musicians and hangers-on rattled to a stop in front of a large walled enclosure, I learned that we had arrived at a horse track in which a singer with the rock band Black

Panther was said to have a financial interest. Like so many others who had *xiahai* ("jumped into the ocean" of commerce), this new private enterprise had been importing burned-out racehorses from Hong Kong for the riding pleasure of Beijing's nouvelle equestrian set. Although the film had nothing to do with riding, the walled track provided a perfect setting for all the "Beijing bastards" who had gathered from far and near that night to eat, drink, play music, and be extras.

By dark, two huge bonfires had been lit in the middle of the track. Several freshly slaughtered goats hung undecorously from a hitching post by the entrance, and knots of young men dressed in high black boots, tight trousers, black T-shirts, and leather jackets milled around in the flickering firelight, chatting, laughing, smoking, drinking beer, and mingling with a contingent of unusually attractive and modishly attired young women. Not only were these people unlike the poster figures of ruddy-cheeked model workers, peasants, and soldiers that the Party had once put out, but they were also starkly different from the earnest, righteous, and politically didactic young students who had filled Tiananmen Square. Wondering what the line of succession was between those demonstrators and these rockers, I asked one young man in an army jacket if he had been in the Square in 1989. He said that he had, smiled, and then changed the subject as if I had asked him about some relative who had passed away under dubious circumstances. In fact, no one I talked to that night seemed to have any interest in the kind of political protest that had swept the city into such a furor only three years before.

Around midnight, Cui sat down on the ground next to one of the bonfires amid a throng of revelers and began vamping on an acoustic guitar. The fact that no one seemed to be in charge only enhanced the feeling of reality that this scene of feasting and merrymaking was supposed to depict. It was not until after one of the goats had been unceremoniously hacked into pieces by two shirtless young men and thrown into a cauldron on the coals of one of the fires that someone finally appeared with a clapstick. By then, however, the party had taken on a life of its own, and in the atmosphere of tipsy camaraderie, the presence of the rolling camera seemed almost irrelevant.

Sometime later I asked Zhang Yuan how the film's producers had been able to secure approval from the Chinese government. "Well, let's put it this way, we sort of got approval," he replied with a conspiratorial wink.

"The whole point of the film is to portray the kind of hand-to-mouth lives these guys live where people don't get permission," a young woman who had been talking with Zhang piped up. Gesturing toward the crowd cooking goat meat over the fires, she grinned and said, "The government claims that it wants to encourage private entrepreneurs as part of economic reform, so we're just taking the government at its word and extending the notion of private enterprise to include rock-and-roll and filmmaking." She gave a little chirrup of laughter, obviously enjoying the idea of besting the Party with its own "correct line."

However this production company had come into being, it was hard to imagine the Central Film Bureau—whose job was to keep account of all movies produced in China—ever approving the script for *Beijing Bastards,* if indeed there was a formal script. Films about Mao Zedong and Lei Feng were one thing, but films glorifying the lifestyle of this new class of cultural renegades was quite another.

It was well past midnight before Cui's band finally began to play. As bats flew through the showers of sparks rising from the bonfires and huge moths made kamikaze dives into the klieg lights, the band's electronically amplified sound boomed out over the dark fields surrounding the track at a volume loud enough to wake even the deafest peasant. Soon couples were dancing, but instead of moving with the self-conscious awkwardness that had characterized them when the Western pop-music and disco craze first hit China, these youths, many of whom had drunk a good deal of beer, moved with a new laid-back languor. And while they seemed oblivious to the incongruity of this heavy-metal hoedown in the middle of the Chinese countryside, I couldn't help wondering whether all the commotion wouldn't lead to official inquiries. Wouldn't the PSB bust up the party and haul everyone off for interrogation? After all, few things escape their notice, and what was going on here was not exactly subtle, which was exactly its point. Whereas in the past the Chinese had always been anxious about Big Brother's surveillance, now they seemed almost to feel validated by it. In a way that caught me quite by surprise, it was I, rather than they, who was now infected by such anxieties.

Then out of the corner of one eye I detected movement in the shadows near the entrance gate. To my alarm, I saw that two uniformed policemen had materialized. In their presence the bonfire-lit scene of dancing rockers seemed awfully fragile. Indeed, the whole gray zone in which this fledgling subculture existed seemed suddenly precarious. I braced for a confrontation, but none of the merrymakers showed the slightest alarm, and the policemen just stood there, hands clasped behind their backs, observing the festivities as if watching an innocuous sports event.

Finally, two young men who were evidently part of the production team sauntered over and began talking to them. A few minutes later the policemen left. Puzzled, I asked a long-haired young man what had happened. "Aw, they're just locals, and I guess they've been taken care of. Unless there's some order from above"—he pointed skyward with an index finger—"they won't bother us." He took a swig from a can of Qingdao and stared out at the dancers gyrating in front of Cui's band. Then as if he had read my thoughts, he added. "Hey, don't worry, it's no big deal! We're just a bunch of *liumang*. We do what we want, like the outlaws from *Shuihu*."

Shuihu Zhuan, variously translated as *All Men Are Brothers, The Water Margin,* or *Outlaws of the Marsh,* is a classic work of popular historical fiction set in the 12th century during the latter years of the Song Dynasty that recounts the exploits of a band of rebels dedicated to fighting official injustice. Led by superhero Song Jiang, these outlaws had their own unwritten code of rebel honor that emphasized personal camaraderie and brotherhood over allegiance to official institutions. The *Shuihu Zhuan* recounts stories of the band's bloody and heroic battles whose retelling has enthralled Chinese ever since the Ming Dynasty. Whereas in premodern times it was viewed as a handbook of sedition and banditry, the young Mao had regarded Song as a champion of peasant rebellion, even immodestly coming to view his own leadership of the Communist revolution as part of the grand tradition of Song's rebel populism.

Casting about in history for their own models of rebellion, Mao's successor generation was now adopting Song as a proto-*liumang* rebel without a political cause, which was probably far closer to the historical reality than Mao's rose-tinted version. While Mao saw Song's band as an idealized form of peasant rebellion against unjust authority, these contemporary "Beijing bastards" seemed to view him as a model of rebellion for rebellion's sake. It said something about the aspirations of gray-culture youth. They were seeking historical validation not for political reform or revolution, but for doing their own self-absorbed and often antisocial thing. It also said something about the Party's success in using repression to eliminate the ability of young Chinese to imagine political forms of rebellion.

But while it was true that this generation was not leading the sort of underground political revolution the Communist Party had once led, it was leading a cultural revolution. And if the past was any guide, it was just such cultural revolutions, however inchoate at first, that usually paved the way for political change.

Protesters of the 1980s had taken to the streets to establish the principle that all Chinese were entitled to certain fundamental rights.

Gray culturalists were manifesting their iconoclasm in a way that seemed almost Daoist in comparison. Artists manipulating Mao images, book kings surreptitiously competing with state publishing monopolies, rock singers becoming commercial pop heroes, and filmmakers chronicling China's new bohemian life were all part of this semi-autonomous new culture. Just like China's economy, which remained suspended somewhere between the centralized control of the state and the "invisible hand" of the free market, the world of culture was becoming ambiguous as gray culture quietly ate away at red culture.

Addressing the Second Plenum of the Seventh Party Central Committee in 1949, Mao Zedong had declared, "It has been proved that we cannot be conquered by force of arms. However, the flattery of the bourgeoisie may conquer the weak-willed in our ranks. There may be some Communists who were not conquered by enemies with guns, and were worthy of the name of heroes for standing up to these enemies, but who cannot withstand sugar-coated bullets."

The Party may not have wanted to acknowledge it, but purveyors of gray culture were, in fact, just such "sugar-coated bullets." Whether the sting of gray culture would ultimately prove fatal to the Party, or whether the Party would succeed in co-opting it, was in 1992 still not clear. However, if they continued to allow more and more entrepreneurial activity and permitted ever more Chinese to taste the sweetness of consumerism, and if they continued to "open up" to the outside world so ever more Chinese could glimpse something of values and life abroad, Party leaders would not only create a more prosperous society, they would also continue to weaken their own once absolute power over culture. Much of the ongoing factional struggle within the Central Committee revolved around a debate over the proper mix of *song* (relaxation) and *jin* (restrictiveness) in the control of culture, politics, and economics. It was a long-standing, unresolved contradiction that was soon to come to a head in an unexpected way.

Part V

The Boom

30

"Greater China"

In 1978, Shenzhen, a lazy fishing and farming community with a population of 70,000, was little more than a border stop on the railroad line between Hong Kong and Canton where passengers had to disembark and lug their baggage across the Lowu Bridge in order to reboard a Chinese train on the other side. In those days China was a defiant autarky that took pride in itself on its "self-reliance" and isolation from the contaminating capitalist world. However, when Deng initiated his new reform policies in the late 1970s, things suddenly began to change at this border. Because of its proximity to Hong Kong, in 1980 Shenzhen was designated one of four new experimental special economic zones (SEZs). These commercial enclaves were to have a dual purpose: to serve both as forward outposts of contact with the capitalist world and as buffer zones shielding the rest of the country from invading foreign influences. As the State Council Economic Research Center's Ji Chongwei wrote in 1984, by "taking in positive things and sifting out the negative aspects of Western culture," the SEZs would act as a filter to allow "market mechanisms and the law of value to operate under the guidance of the socialist planned economy."

By the end of the decade Shenzhen had been transformed into a commercial boomtown with a population of 2 million, broad boulevards lined with high-rise apartment blocks, office buildings, and luxury Western-style joint-venture hotels. During the 1989 crackdown, hard-liners, who had never been pleased by these capitalist cavities in the flank of Chinese socialism, tried to deemphasize the economic policies they represented. But since the SEZs were Deng's personal projects, they not only survived, but continued to flourish. In 1991, Shenzhen's gross domestic product (GDP) hit $3.16 billion, reflecting an average annual growth rate of 50 percent since 1980, and its exports reached $3.4 billion, having grown an average of 75 percent annually over the same period.

In this country where appearances so often triumphed over reality, massive show projects had a way of coming into being by fiat. This was how Tiananmen Square had been built, how agriculture had been communized, and how enormous public-works projects were constructed in the past. But like Plato's cave dwellers who knew no more of the outside world than what they saw reflected in shadow on their back walls, when elderly leaders tried to reproduce aspects of what they thought the outside foreign world was like, the results were often strange. After more and more of these leaders began going abroad in the 1980s, many of them were so chagrined by the disparity between what they saw and their own country's situation that they felt an urgent need to cosmeticize China with a few prominent landmarks that would give a semblance, at least, of modernity. During the 1980s one of the most popular symbols of such modernity was high-rise buildings topped with hat-like contrivances that mimicked the revolving restaurants crowning certain Western hotels. Not surprisingly, Shenzhen ended up with its share of these constructions, and from a distance they did, indeed, look impressive. But like screen sets, as one drew closer, such buildings became increasingly less convincing. They had a way of falling into such high-speed deterioration so that even before they became operational, many were ready for the wrecking ball.

I remember visiting one such building in the early eighties that had opened so recently that red bunting and wreaths still adorned the front portico. But once inside, I discovered that not only had the elevator already broken down, but crews of workers were busy bashing gaping holes in the concrete walls of the stairwells with sledgehammers, leaving the stairs almost impassable with rubble and covering the rest of the building with fine white dust. God knows what they were doing, but it looked as if in their haste to complete construction, they had forgotten to install electrical conduit or water pipes.

Although by 1991 building standards had risen considerably and the construction of the city proper was largely completed, walking the streets of Shenzhen was still strangely disorienting. For anyone accustomed to cities that have evolved over centuries, the SEZ was a charmless upstart. Having had no real history, it had no "old section," much less a heart, like Tiananmen Square, that focused everything toward a single central point. Its identity was equally as elusive. It was a bastard—a no-man's land that was in its weird way a perfect expression of its ambidextrous role as interface between a People's Republic and a British crown colony. Its new, gleaming, glass high-rise buildings were evocative of Hong Kong, while its cheerless apartment blocks and klunky office buildings were reminiscent of the bleak designlessness of China's provincial cities. And while there were jungles of blinking neon announcing bars, discos, karaoke clubs, restaurants, and fast-food joints, and endless rows of billboards with flashy capitalist iconography, its streets were also lined with the countervailing signboards from such stern, socialist mega-enterprises as the China National Cereals, Oils, and Foodstuffs Corporation and the China No. 2 Automobile Plant United.

By the time I arrived back in Shenzhen in 1991, it was sizzling with commercial energy. For businessmen, it was a new Mecca, a place where nothing but money mattered. Not only had it become the exit point for billions of dollars worth of goods draining out of all of South China into world markets, but it was the point of entry for fortunes in new investment capital from Taiwan, Hong Kong, and Singapore, which were converging with the Mainland to form what people were staring to refer to as "Greater China." These outlying Chinese territories provided a combination of capital, technical expertise, management, finance, transportation, and marketing, while China offered inexpensive labor, low-rent facilities, natural resources, and weak environmental controls. It was such a powerful combination that the World Bank estimated that by the year 2002 "Greater China's" collective domestic product would surpass that of the United States.

No matter where one looked in the new triangle of free enterprise, which stretched from Shenzhen up the Pearl River Delta to Canton and then back to the Zhuhai SEZ across the border from Macao, one saw signs of development and affluence. By the end of 1991 some 300,000 people in southern Guangdong alone were reported to have acquired electronic pagers, dubbed *bibiji* in Chinese because of their characteristic beeping noises, while another 30,000 had graduated to *dageda* (cellular phones). Less than a decade earlier, China had been a country where even in major cities phones were few enough to make telephoning a real travail; now demand for Shenzhen's regular phone service was growing so rapidly that the local telecommunications company was forced to add two new digits to all phone numbers in order to expand its circuit capacity to include the 5 million new lines it anticipated hooking up in the near future.

In almost every way, Shenzhen was a pacesetter. One of China's first eighteen-hole golf courses was the Shenzhen Golf Club Company, built in 1985, a facility complete with a clubhouse, a luxury hotel, tennis courts, a swimming pool, a bowling alley, and Japanese-style baths. In 1986, Shenzhen hosted the National Hercules Cup International Bodybuilding Tournament, China's first public bodybuilding competition to include bikini-clad female Chinese contestants. The country's first 7-Eleven store and first DKNY (Donna Karan) Boutique opened in Shenzhen. The city even boasted a branch of the notorious Bank of Credit and Commerce International. In 1979, there had been only three small hotels, whereas by 1992 there were over 300, of which 67 had won star-class ratings. "Now when you drop into Shenzhen you don't have to drop your standards," bragged the luxurious five-star Century Plaza Hotel in an ad aimed at all the international businessmen arriving in the city. "Every aspect of service and professionalism you are used to in Hong Kong is here at this magnificent hotel."

When the "open door" policy went into effect in the early eighties, Deng urged his people to "keep a clear head, firmly resist corruption by decadent ideas from abroad," and never to permit "bourgeois ways of life to spread" and "undermine socialism." But Shenzhen quickly became a petri dish of just such phenomena—of dance halls, gambling joints, smuggling rings, opium dens, massage parlors, and brothels. For instance, by the early 1990s it had become all the rage for wealthy Hong Kong and Taiwanese businessmen to keep Shenzhen mistresses for off-hours divertissement. The city was soon filled with thousands of young women from poor rural areas trying to get in on the lucrative hard-currency flesh trade. "Entertaining just one customer brings more than half a year's salary," was a common expression among such women. By July 1992 the situation had gotten so out of control that the Guangdong Provincial PSB launched what the *China Daily* indelicately called a "whore war"—a crackdown in which more than 5,000 people connected with organized prostitution were detained.

It didn't take long after my arrival on that hot August day in 1991 before I was looking forward to leaving Shenzhen's noise and smog for the Pearl River Delta, a stretch of countryside that I remembered from earlier trips as being quiet and green. When I had last made the journey to Canton, the narrow road had been traveled mainly by local farmers and occasional trucks. Now, even after my taxi passed through the internal checkpoint in the eighty-six-kilometer-long backup fence that was supposed to keep ordinary Chinese from entering the Shenzhen SEZ, development and traffic stretched on. The potholed, trash-strewn road was lined with an endless clutter of gas stations, snack stands, tire-repair shops, small stores, flophouses, restaurants, factories, and buildings under construction. And everywhere there were huge gashes in the red earth where hills were being leveled, valleys filled, and lots cleared for even more new construction.

As we pounded along, the radio blared a mixture of Canto-pop and Cantonese commercials quacked out by announcers who sounded like so many enraged ducks fighting. When I asked the driver if he was listening to a Chinese or a Hong Kong station, he said laconically, "No difference now." As the high-speed quacking continued, an endless procession of Mercedes went by in the other direction with their businessman occupants sitting behind tinted windows in air-conditioned comfort making deals on their *dageda* as their drivers did slaloms around the stop-and-go convoys of stalled trucks loaded with fabric, garments, shoes, toys, electronic components, and hundreds of other Guangdong-made products on their way to world markets.

In a few years a new road would open, financed by Hong Kong businessman Gordon Wu, whose Hopewell Holdings Ltd. had already sunk $1.5 billion into China. In 1994, Wu was slated to open the first 76-mile stretch of his 250-mile-long pride and joy—a six-lane "superhighway"—that would ultimately not only replace this crowded road between Shenzhen and Canton, but would also connect Canton to Zhuhai. Soon thereafter, another expressway would connect Shenzhen with Shantou, Guangdong's third SEZ, to the north.

I had interviewed Gordon Wu in his Hong Kong skyscraper in 1982 when Shenzhen was still of little consequence. When he told me he intended to build this privately financed highway, the idea that a capitalist mogul would construct a toll-road in a country with almost no private cars seemed almost laughable. But by 1991, Wu's fantastical project had not only been approved by the Chinese government and was under construction, but was becoming an acclaimed official model for the Ministry of Communications, which was in the process of adopting a whole new road-building policy of "Those who invest, benefit." According to this most un-Communist notion, whole segments of China's ambitious new road-building plan would be financed by foreign and private capital, whether from Chinese-owned cooperative ventures, Sino-foreign joint ventures, or even wholly foreign-owned ventures. For ten years after his $1.4 billion highway opened, Gordon Wu would get 40 percent of the $13 toll that each car would be charged to travel from Hong Kong to Canton, and he was estimating that by 1995 some 100,000 vehicles a day would be making the trip.

Given such economics, few were surprised that from 1988 to 1992, China saw a 3.4-fold increase in the number of miles of high-speed expressway built. Around the Pearl River Delta, road maps had a way of becoming outdated almost as soon as they were published. In fact, by 1993, Wu had a map on his office wall showing another "dream highway" stretching 700 miles from Hong Kong all the way to Chongqing on the upper reaches of the Yangtze River. Stuck in traffic on this narrow road outside of Shenzhen in suffocating tropical heat and dust as caravans of trucks belching black clouds of foul diesel exhaust inched their way toward Hong Kong, it was not hard to imagine how even stalwart Marxists might capitulate to capitalists like Gordon Wu just to get traffic moving.

If there is one thing overseas investors and manufacturers love, it is new pools of inexpensive labor, cheap land, and abundant natural resources. Although costs had been rising, in 1991 leases on land in southern Guangdong were still only 2 to 3 percent of what they were in Hong Kong and Taiwan, and labor costs were 10 to 20 percent. Since Guangdong's population of 80 million was being bolstered by millions of new refugees from poorer parts of China, including many children, overseas businessmen knew that for years their factories could rely on a virtually inexhaustible supply of cheap labor.

Of course, so many instant new industries and such large migrations of people created numerous problems. Work conditions were frequently unhealthy and dangerous as well as being environmentally destructive. Almost every week brought news of a factory that collapsed, burned, or exploded, killing and maiming scores. In May 1991 seventy-two workers locked in a squalid dorm at a privately run sleeping-bag factory in Dongguan burned to death. In August 1993 eight chemical warehouses in Shenzhen exploded, killing an estimated seventy people. That November eighty-one more workers died of smoke inhalation when trapped inside a burning toy factory in Kuiyong that had no emergency exits. Needless to say, such workers did not have any provisions for health care or disability pay, much less other kinds of welfare rights such as old age pensions or unemployment compensation that were still afforded to most workers in state enterprises. However, because virtually nobody wanted to slow down the RPMs of this production turbine, few concerned themselves with such problems. The truth was that even most children and young women laborers working under the worst conditions considered themselves lucky rather than victims. Piece-work salaries of 200 yuan ($40) a month may have put them at the bottom of the Pearl River Delta's earning curve, but they were still making far more than they could make farming back home. So what often seemed like glaring exploitation to an outsider was for poor Chinese migrants a welcome opportunity to escape rural poverty. For the moment a symbiosis of interest between "exploiter" and "exploited" seemed to exist in these boom-towns. How long it would last was another question.

The township of Houjie, for example, had an official population of 75,000, but was also home to another 100,000 migrant workers who kept its 900 factories producing. Because of this new supply of inexpensive labor, most Houjie natives had given up farming to become managers and entrepreneurs with a lifestyle and level of material consumption unimaginable under Mao. As Nicholas Kristof discovered when he visited the township shortly after my own trip, the local Party chief had long since abandoned ideology in favor of the affectations of a tycoon. Rather than making his appointed rounds in a Chinese-made Liberation-brand truck, he was ensconced in a chauffeur-driven air-conditioned Mercedes-Benz 300SEL complete with a *bibiji* and *dageda*. Towns like Houjie were commercial free-fire zones that moguls from postindustrial countries could only dream about. Passing through them made Ji Chongwei's hopes that Shenzhen might serve as a filter seem excessively naive. If Shenzhen was anything, it was more like an enormous intake valve sucking up all kinds of untreated heterodox influences and indiscriminately pumping them not only just across the border from Hong Kong into the SEZ, but up the hundred miracle miles of hyper-development to Canton, where almost overnight obscure villages were being transformed into full-blown cities and empty fields into thriving industrial centers as millions of migrant laborers flooded into Guangdong looking for work. Officials were only too willing to countenance this mass migration, often making fortunes themselves by selling illegal household registrations to these refugees.

With some of the highest growth rates in the world, the five counties between Shenzhen and Canton—Zhongshan, Dongguan, Shunde, Nanhai, and Bao'an—were being called the Five Small Dragons of South Guangdong, borrowed from the so-called Four Dragons of Asia—South Korea, Taiwan, Hong Kong, and Singapore—known for their legendary economic development. Amazingly, the growth rates in these five counties actually surpassed those of the Four Dragons during their own boom years. Between 1978 and 1990, the annual growth rates of these counties averaged more than 20 percent and had become the motor force pushing Guangdong's provincial GDP growth rate to almost 14 percent and its industrial output growth rate to over 27 percent. By 1991, the Hong Kong-Shenzhen-Canton axis was becoming a veritable Ripley's Believe It or Not of growth statistics.

Although Guangdong was only one of China's twenty-two provinces and five autonomous regions, by 1991 it contributed almost 20 percent of the nation's total GNP. The main stimulant of its fantastic growth was trade and investment from Hong Kong. Approximately 60 percent of China's direct external investment was coming through the colony, giving it the largest outside stake in China's economy. And every day more manufacturers were moving across the border. In 1982, Hong Kong boasted 3,200 toy factories, but by 1992, 97 percent of them had moved to Guangdong, and the total trade between Hong Kong and the Mainland had risen from $21 billion in 1978 to $136 billion. One more sign of how tightly fused Shenzhen was becoming with Hong Kong was the fact that by 1992 an estimated 20 percent of the colony's money supply had also jumped the border to circulate as the SEZ's main currency.

China had become almost as reliant on trade and investment from the Republic of China, aka Taiwan, the Mainland's nemesis ever since the end of the Civil War in 1949 when Chiang Kai-shek had been driven from the Mainland. It was a wry paradox that when Western tourism, trade, and investment suddenly dried up after June 4, China was rescued by a providential influx of "compatriots" from Taiwan. For almost thirty years Taiwan Chinese had been forbidden to travel to the Mainland, because the Taipei government viewed Mao's regime as "Communist bandit" usurpers. In 1987, however, Taipei began changing its policy, and by 1990 more than 3 million had crossed the Taiwan Strait, filling the newly built joint-venture hotels that had been left vacant by vanished Europeans and Americans. When Taipei announced in 1991 that the "period of Communist rebellion" was over, another million and a half Taiwanese "compatriots"—7 percent of the island's entire population—promptly visited the "motherland." Even though Taipei did not allow "direct" commerce, figures on "indirect" trade through Hong Kong skyrocketed from $4 billion in 1990 to $5.8 billion in 1991. And many analysts thought that when all the unrecorded transactions done under the table were accounted for, the tally could be twice as high. With a Taipei government survey estimating that Taiwanese businessmen were able to double their profits by moving manufacturing to mainland factories, it was not surprising that by 1993 cumulative Taiwanese investment in China was estimated to have reached $10 billion.

As Taiwan businessmen became more deeply involved in the economic future of China, the Nationalist government was forced to further temper its once-uncompromising anticommunism. Some Nationalist officials even anomalously began expressing reservations about weakening the Communist Party rule lest instability set in and create an unfavorable business climate. "A collapse would be a disaster for the Chinese people and China's peripheral areas," warned Ma Ying-jeou, vice-chairman of Taiwan's Mainland Affairs Council, a group set up to formulate policy toward Beijing. In 1992, P. K. Chiang, Taiwan's vice-minister for economic affairs, was quoted as saying, "The time has come to review our policies. We can't stop trade and the operations of a free market."

As my taxi approached Canton, I felt as if I were arriving at a completely new city. Whereas in the early eighties the outskirts of Canton had been a weave of flat green rice paddies and vegetable fields, now the land was so honeycombed with construction projects that the few fields remaining looked like part of a wool garment that was in the terminal stages of being devoured by moths. Whereas the city itself had previously boasted only a few tall buildings, before me was an imposing skyline of high-rises stabbing up into a penumbra of smog. Canton's downtown area was now filled with shops, offices, boutiques, restaurants, and department stores buzzing with high-speed activity. The Liuhua Hotel near the train station—where I stopped to eat—was overflowing with youths lounging, drinking beer, sipping instant coffee (the latest Western youth craze), and chain-smoking while a sound system blasted Cui Jian's "It's Not That I Don't Understand." Young women were dressed to the nines, their bright red lips and gaudy clothes the only relief from the surrounding smoky drabness. Just two years earlier Chinese youth had been so possessed with the urgency of political reform that almost everything else had seemed irrelevant. Now they appeared just as intent on making money, shopping, hanging out, and enjoying the good life. Each of these imperatives had its own different rhetoric, measurements, rationales, and superstars. What they shared was their totalism and willingness to forget their own history. China's capacity to cancel the past and reinvent a new future never ceased to amaze me.

If there was a disjuncture between the mercenary fever of southern Guangdong and the idealistic students of Tiananmen Square, there was also a jarring contradiction between the commercial boomtown ethic in the south and the militant Party propaganda emanating from Beijing that insisted Chairman Mao was still a "great leader" and that China was still "building socialism with Chinese characteristics." The fact that the Pearl River Delta was being saved from backwardness not by communism and Beijing, but by capitalism and Hong Kong, and was thereby turning China's old revolutionary ideology on its head did not, of course, sit well with many hard-liners. The *People's Daily* ran an article describing how one veteran Communist had wept upon arriving in Shenzhen. Pausing before a fluttering Chinese flag, he wept with "hot tears rolling down his cheeks" because "except for this red flag," there was "no more socialism left in Shenzhen." The paper admitted that China's plunge into capitalism was a "sensitive topic," but it tried to argue that it was a "fantasy" to believe that socialism could be built on a "backward level of productive forces."

Such efforts to convince veteran revolutionaries that Shenzhen was actually a hopeful development rather than a betrayal of the mother faith were not always persuasive. The best the paper could do was to urge these old-timers to remember that "a dozen years ago, Shenzhen was just a small worn-out town from which people fled across the border and sneaked into Hong Kong, whereas nowadays it has grown into a modern city that is treated with respect even by the people of Hong Kong." What is more, it boasted, "some of those who previously fled to Hong Kong have *even* returned to live and work here in peace and contentedness."

For Chinese who had been embarrassed by the hemorrhage of refugees risking their lives to escape to the British colony, this was, indeed, a gratifying change. But such pride did not answer the question of how good Marxists could support the dismantling of Mao's revolution, nor did it resolve ongoing tensions between reformers who wanted to see China's economy become marketized even more rapidly and hard-liners who believed that Deng's policy of "groping one's way across the river by feeling the stones" was a recipe for disaster. Instead of the forces of "national liberation" spreading out from China's rural hinterland and encircling the decadent cities of the capitalist world in what Mao's onetime heir-apparent Lin Biao had foreseen as a wave of international "people's wars," exactly the opposite was happening: The countryside was being engulfed by the urban capitalist world, and Mao's revolutionary base areas were being transformed into free-fire zones for entrepreneurs and tycoons. With official policy in such a state of irresolution, Deng now moved to end the ambiguity.

31

Deng Makes a Visit

In the middle of January 1992, Deng Xiaoping made his first public appearance in a year, popping up unexpectedly in Shenzhen. What made this trip so dramatic was not only that he chose an SEZ in which to resurface, but that at his age and frailty he now felt obligated to reemerge so publicly at all. For Chinese officials, his Shenzhen trip was a signal that a new power struggle was in process.

The object of Deng's *nanxun*, or southern sojourn, as the trip came to be known in Chinese shorthand, was Guangdong. Although it is not known who chose this name, it was both incongruous and fitting. Whenever the emperor traveled outside of the capital during ancient times, he was said to *xunxing*, or ''bring heavenly fortune'' to those local people along his route. Allowing his tour to be dubbed *nanxun* helped Deng to reinforce his image as an imperial and therefore unimpeachable ruler, which fit perfectly with his intention to send a series of bold new signals to the country. By choosing these economic hotspots as destinations, he was signaling reformers that he was once again ready to support a push toward further marketization of the economy. By his choice of rhetoric, he was signaling economic hardliners that he would not yield to their conservatism in economic matters, although he would continue to stand with them in ''exercising dictatorship'' over the Party's political enemies. And to the world, he was signaling that the boomtowns of the South China coast were henceforth to be taken as models for a new phase of high-speed, foreign-capital–driven development. Given the tenor of the times, Deng's appearance in the SEZs was comparable in shock value to the president of the United States showing up in Las Vegas to proclaim its glittering strip of hotels and gambling casinos the new American prototype of urban development.

For months prior to his departure from Beijing, Deng plotted strategy and made preparations. With Gorbachev's fall from power fresh in his mind and hard-liners led by Chen Yun threatening a new movement against "bourgeois liberalization" and marketization of the economy, Deng's intention was to launch a last blitz campaign in hopes of both erasing the stain left on his legacy by Tiananmen Square and saving the Party from the kind of ignominious defeat that fraternal parties had recently suffered in almost every other socialist country. Adding to Deng's sense of urgency was his awareness that at eighty-eight years old, he did not have much time left to restore his place in history. Moreover, with the Fourteenth Party Congress looming in the fall of 1993, he knew he had to make haste if he hoped to be successful in rallying his supporters to victory against hard-line resistance.

The outside world may still have viewed Deng as an all-powerful "paramount" leader, but he had been weakened by the rise of hard-liner influence after June 4 to the point that now when he needed to proselytize for his ideas on radical economic reform, he found himself shut out of the national media by the very men he had helped gain control of China's propaganda apparatus in 1989. As an alternative, he sought to rally support by holding a series of *shenghuohui,* or small gatherings of ranking Party leaders, to explain his plan privately and use his influence to personally convince them that having the Party embrace a new regimen of bold economic reform was the best hope for guaranteeing prosperity and stability.

"There is no other option open to us," he was reported to have warned at one Beijing meeting during the fall of 1991. "If the economy cannot be boosted, over the long run we will lose people's support at home and will be oppressed and bullied by other nations throughout the world. A continuation of such a situation will only lead to the collapse and disintegration of the Communist Party."

But while Deng wanted China to catch up with the West, he did not want to mimic it politically. The foreign models of development that he held up for emulation were not the industrialized Western democracies, but Asia's "Four Dragons." What made them such compelling models was not only their economic prosperity, but their success in maintaining stability. Deng's preferred model was Singapore, whose

Chinese patriarch Lee Kuan Yew tirelessly stressed social order over freedom of expression. "When you are hungry, when you lack basic services, then freedom, human rights, and democracy do not add up to much," said Lee.

"Singapore's social order is rather good," commented Deng dryly. "They exercise strict management. We should learn from their experience and even learn how to do a better job than they."

But even such conservative models of development failed to win Deng enough support in Beijing to launch his call for a new economic push through the media. And so, in mid-October 1991 a frustrated Deng left for Shanghai on a trip that was in many respects reminiscent of a trek Mao had made in the mid-sixties to launch the Cultural Revolution when he, too, had been forced to circumvent what he called the "impenetrable fortress" of the Party establishment in Beijing and take his case to Shanghai. Of course, while Mao intended to exhort Red Guards to "bombard the headquarters" of the Party and "make a tremendous proletarian uproar," Deng intended to goad Chinese to join him in a "second wave of reform" to transform China's economy. What was similar about the dilemma of both Mao and Deng was that each was forced by the exigencies of intra-Party politics to go around the existing leadership structure to mobilize "mass" constituencies in the provinces. The need for such stratagems was a reminder that even in totalitarian states, seemingly omnipotent leaders often find themselves constrained by cryptic systems of checks and balances that center not around institutions or laws, but around struggles between competing factions.

Deng chose Shanghai as a first stop because he viewed it as a key link in establishing more SEZ-like free-trade zones up and down the coast. It was also China's largest industrial city, and whereas Deng knew that Guangdong would be receptive to his new campaign, he was less certain about the rest of China. If Shanghai could be won over, he surmised, other parts of the country would certainly be more inclined to follow. To his relief, pragmatic Shanghai officials—who had been trying to develop their own "special area" in the Pudong section of the city as part of an effort to catch up with Guangdong's SEZs—were pleased when Deng arrived preaching that "everything should serve economic construction."

On January 17, 1992, Deng, accompanied by his son, daughter, and a coterie of advisors, left by train for Wuchang, where he stunned officials by criticizing Jiang Zemin and Li Peng for accomplishing so little over the preceding three years. Then on January 19 he rolled into Shenzhen, which he had last visited in 1984, and where he had left a stone inscription in his own calligraphy: "Shenzhen's Development and Experience Prove That Our Policy of Establishing Special Economic Zones Is Correct." Although not exactly in the tradition of inspired poetic inscriptions that Chinese of centuries past were fond of engraving into rocks at sites of great natural beauty, Deng's idea that China's SEZs were important catalysts of modernization had remained constant until 1992.

Despite his age, Deng spent the next three days in a whirlwind of meetings with local officials. He also posed for numerous "photo ops": against a background of loading cranes at the new Huanggang dock area; screening a documentary about Deng Yingchao, Zhou Enlai's widow, at the Xianke Laser Disc Company; standing in front of miniaturized versions of both the Tiananmen Gate and the Potala Palace at the Chinese Folk Culture Village; and touring the fifty-three-floor International Trade Building, which housed the nascent Shenzhen Securities Exchange. Deng had also arranged for Yang Shangkun, the former general who had helped him mastermind the 1989 military assault on Beijing, to make a special cameo appearance with him strolling through the Xianhu Botanical Garden. Because Yang was president and the most potent personification of China's military establishment as permanent vice-chairman of the Military Affairs Commission, his presence in Shenzhen created a perfect blend of images for Deng's new campaign.

"Without the achievements of reform and opening up to the outside world, we might not have been able to pass the test of the June 4 incident," Deng told local officials. "And if we had failed to pass the test, there would have been a chaotic situation that might have led to civil war, as was the case during the Cultural Revolution. The reason our country remained stable after the June 4 incident was that reform and opening up had already promoted economic development and improved the people's livelihood. Therefore both the army and the state government must continue to safeguard this line, this system, and these policies."

Deng emphatically reminded his hosts that the army and reform were integral mainstays of the Party's ability to remain in power. His prescription for avoiding what he called "the road to ruin" was a new "great leap forward" of reform that would hold up the SEZs and the Pearl River Delta as a model. "Reform and opening up require boldness and courageous experiments," he said. "They must not proceed like a woman with bound feet. . . . In this sense, making revolution means liberating the productive forces. . . . Areas that have developed first should bring along the less developed areas to achieve the final goal of common affluence.''

This was a far cry from Chairman Mao's notion of economically developing all sectors of society equally without allowing any region or any person to become wealthy ahead of any other. Ignoring all the egalitarian rhetoric that had been emphasized throughout the Party's long history, and dismissing the fundamental antagonism that the ideological hard-liners still presumed to exist between the bourgeoisie and the proletariat and between capitalism and socialism, Deng now reduced the definition of "revolutionary socialist struggle" to a single new materialist test: Did it produce more goods and services? However heretical these notions were, they were consistent with the pragmatism he had articulated as far back as 1978 after returning to power. "As long as we pay attention to economic efficiency, product quality, and foreign economic exchanges," he now reiterated, "we need not be worried about anything else."

Like an evangelical circuit preacher, Deng went from Shenzhen to Zhuhai sermonizing on the gospel of economic reform by calling on Chinese to erase old ideological distinctions between "socialist" and "capitalist" means of production. "A planned economy does not equal socialism, because planning exists in capitalism, and a market economy does not necessarily equal capitalism because the market exists in socialism," he asserted. "In order to make socialism superior to capitalism, we must boldly take heed of and absorb all accomplishments of every civilization achieved by the human race . . . [as well as] all advanced modes of operation and management techniques that have been developed by others, including those of the developed capitalist countries."

Before leaving Shenzhen for Zhuhai, Deng threw down an unmistakable challenge to Chen Yun and his hard-line allies. While China "must be on guard against rightism," he insisted that its "main task" was to "counter leftism," a code word for the various doctrines of the hard-liners. Claiming that certain "leftist things" were still very "deeply rooted" in China, Deng charged that "some theorists and politicians" have grown "accustomed to being able to level serious political charges against people in order to intimidate them." They had only been able to get away with such attacks, he said, because " 'leftism' does have a certain revolutionary color so that the more 'leftist' something appears, the more revolutionary it is considered to be." But, he concluded, leftism "has done terrible harm to our Party in the past."

Hard-liners were understandably offended by almost everything about Deng's *nanxun*. After all, Deng was implying that the dangers of Maoist "leftism" were far greater than those of capitalist "rightism." At the same time, his utterances gave reform-minded officials and entrepreneurs all across China canonic permission to experiment more aggressively than ever with the very capitalist-style ideas and market institutions that had hitherto been largely confined to SEZs.

Hard-liners struck back with the one defensive weapon still in their arsenal. For the moment they were able to mute the effect of his trip by refusing to give Deng any national media coverage. Even after papers in Hong Kong and around the world were running front-page stories about his *nanxun,* most ordinary Chinese did not even know that Deng was in Shenzhen, much less that he had launched a whole new era of reform.

32

Deng's Reformist Roots

Deng Xiaoping's unusual combination of reformism and conservatism have long had a way of confusing outsiders trying to make sense of him as China's leader. Indeed, in many ways Deng was an unlikely and contradictory figure for "strong man of China." "His mind is round and his actions square," Mao Zedong once said of him. After visiting his guerrilla base in the forties, American military observer Major Evans Carlson admitted being "astonished" at the knowledgeability of this "short, chunky, and physically tough man" whose mind was "as keen as mustard." Mao also described Deng as "a rare talent" who was like "a needle wrapped in cotton." Chen Boda, Mao's secretary, complained that because Deng always had "his own idea about everything," it was as difficult to sway him "as it was to reach heaven." Henry Kissinger reportedly dismissed Deng as a "nasty little man." Ordinary Chinese thought of Deng as *xiao pingzi*, or "the Little Bottle," a pun on his name alluding both to his ability to bob back up after purges and his four-foot-eleven-inch height.

As unassuming as he was short, Deng had none of the bravado and panache of Mao. Indeed, when he sat back in a large chair, his feet dangled almost comically off the floor. Seemingly unconcerned with image making, he chain-smoked Panda-brand cigarettes until his fingers were stained brown and was fond of expectorating in public, requiring that even at official meetings a spittoon always be close at hand. He was known for bursts of impatience and anger, but also for his straightforward and unpretentious manner. Unsentimental and humorless, he seemed to have few qualms of conscience, and little compunction to ingratiate himself with others through convivial chatter. When he spoke publicly, instead of using the jargon-ridden dogma of Party ideologues, he made terse homily-like utterances.

Deng was born Deng Xixian, meaning "Deng Who Aspires to Sagehood," in Paifang Village, Guang'an County, Sichuan Province, on August 22, 1904, to the first concubine of Deng Wenming, a well-to-do landowner. Although at the time the declining Qing Dynasty was being carved into spheres of influence by the Western powers and Japan, Deng himself appears to have grown up in a reassuringly stable home environment. As a teenager, however, he was sent to Chongqing to attend a preparatory course for a work-study program in France. "We felt that China was weak, and we wanted to make it strong," he later remembered. "We thought the way to do it was through modernization. So we went to the West to learn."

In 1920, at age sixteen, Deng left for Marseilles for what would be five rootless years involving a little study, occasional factory work (including a stint at the Paris Renault factory), and much political organizing among expatriate Chinese. Because of his reliability inscribing and mimeographing the Communist Youth League's overseas propaganda organ, *Red Light* (edited by Zhou Enlai), the young Deng soon won the sobriquet of "Doctor of Duplication."

By the time he left France for Moscow in 1926, Deng had become one of the most active members of the outlawed European Chinese Communist Party. He had also learned a smattering of French and acquired a love of croissants, a taste that evidently lingered, because during a 1974 stopover in Paris he ordered a large boxful to take back to Beijing. He had also gained a crucial awareness of how unavoidably important the West would be for China's future. Moreover, Deng's months in Moscow coincided with the end of Lenin's New Economic Policy (NEP), which called for decentralizing the economy by allowing *kulaks* (wealthy peasants) to engage in privatized agriculture and other kinds of small-scale private industry. It is not unlikely that his familiarity with the NEP helped lay the political framework for his own later reforms in China.

Deng returned home less than a year later, not long before Chiang Kai-shek turned savagely against the Chinese Communist Party and initiated the so-called "white terror." Along with other Shanghai-based Marxists like Zhou Enlai, Deng was forced both to go underground and to change his name to Xiaoping, meaning "Small Peace."

That same year he was appointed chief secretary of the Party Central Committee, a position that put him in constant danger of arrest. To make matters even more trying, a year later his new wife died in childbirth.

In hopes of fomenting uprisings that would help establish new "soviet bases" in cities away from the coast, the Party dispatched Deng to earthbound Guangxi Province. It was here in the southwest that he was initiated into the vicissitudes of guerrilla warfare. By 1930, the Seventh Army, in which he served as political commissar, had established a soviet around Bose that included twenty counties and more than a million people. But as he sought to expand the new soviet area and defeat followed on defeat, Deng mysteriously left his command and returned to Shanghai, raising questions of whether he had abandoned his troops in the field.

The early thirties were filled with many twists and turns as Deng and other revolutionaries struggled to come to grips with the growing rift between Mao's incipient peasant revolution and Moscow's Comintern, which despite the "white terror" ordered Chinese Communists to continue organizing urban workers. In 1933 after moving to Mao's rural-based Jiangxi Soviet, Deng was attacked by pro-Moscow elements in the Party, dismissed from office, forced to deliver a stinging self-criticism, briefly jailed, and then abandoned by his second wife. It was the first of what would be several bitter falls from official grace.

By the time the tattered remnants of Mao's forces ended their 6,000-mile Long March and straggled into Yan'an in 1935, Deng was exhausted and ill with typhoid. But as result of the ordeal, he had become a close confidant of Mao and formed a complex relationship that would both help and hurt him for the next four decades.

As war with Japan broke out, Deng was reassigned as the chief political commissar of the 129th Division commanded by another Sichuanese, the "one-eyed dragon," General Liu Bocheng, beginning a decade-and-a-half-long partnership that led to a string of important victories against Japanese forces. But at the same time that these years in the field steeled Deng in military strategy, they also gave him much valuable practical experience in governing. For Deng and Liu were responsible not only for military decisions, but for organizing the "government" that exercised de facto political control over large parts of North China. It was during these years that Deng acquired a practical sense of how abstract political policies affect ordinary peasants. What he saw caused him to launch a number of innovative programs, such as one to increase harvests by "rewarding the hardworking and punishing the lazy" with material incentives.

In 1943, Deng returned to Yan'an a military hero, and as a result of an increasingly close relationship with Mao was elevated to the Central Committee. He remarried, this time to Pu Zhoulin, the daughter of a wealthy Yunnanese. But with the outbreak of the Civil War in the mid-forties, Deng was soon back on the front with the "one-eyed dragon," this time fighting the Nationalists. By the fall of 1948, the 300,000 troops they commanded in Central China had defeated Chiang's forces in a series of battles known as the Huai-hai campaign, which ensured a Communist victory in the Civil War.

Following "liberation" in 1949, Liu and Deng were transferred to China's vast Southwest Military Administrative Region, which gave them command of their native Sichuan Province. Their orders were to defeat Nationalist remnants and establish a new Communist order, the heart of which was to be a land-reform program, which saw tens of thousands of "landlords" persecuted and killed and which gave Deng firsthand experience with one of the most tectonic and brutal aspects of Mao's revolution.

In 1952, at age forty-eight, Deng was summoned back to Beijing, where Mao conferred a host of prestigious new positions on him. For the next twelve years Deng had a hand in formulating most key Party decisions. Intoxicated with the idea of the new People's Republic and with his own new prominence and power, Deng enthusiastically threw himself into the task of carrying out Mao's "revolutionary line." The first major movement in which he participated was the collectivization of the very agricultural plots that he had helped liberate through land reform just a few years earlier. It was during these years that his third wife bore him a family of five children, over which Deng devotedly presided from a villa in Beijing's Zhongnanhai leadership compound.

At the Eighth Party Congress in September 1956, Deng's stature rose even higher when he was accorded a place on the six-man Standing Committee of the Politburo and was appointed general secretary of the Party. While he warned delegates that "serious consequences can follow from the deification of the individual"—he had just returned from Moscow where Khrushchev had launched his attack against Stalin's "cult of personality"—he nonetheless obediently praised Mao for all "our Party's victories." At the Congress, he also espoused a position that had the potential to put him at odds with his old comrade-in-arms. Since times have "drastically changed," Deng claimed, class struggle was no longer the main social contradiction.

It was also in 1957 that Mao called on the country's intelligentsia to let a "hundred flowers bloom and a hundred schools of thought contend" by freely offering criticisms of official policy. However, fearing that this eccentric call for "big democracy" would create a snowball effect and lead "rightist elements" espousing "bourgeois ideas" to challenging the Party's monopoly over thought, Deng resisted the Hundred Flowers Campaign. As far as he was concerned, when official policies needed rectification, they should be rectified from within the Party, not from without. Not surprisingly, when this interlude of "blooming and contending" turned into a torrent of attacks, Deng vigorously supported Mao's savage crackdown on the intelligentsia. Before the Antirightist Movement was over, almost 3 million intellectuals had been designated as "rightists" and some 500,000 of them had been shipped off to labor camps. So wedded had Deng been to this ruinous movement that even in 1980 when he finally acknowledged that it had been "broadened excessively," he still insisted that it was "necessary and correct."

Mao's next fevered move to push China into socialism was the Great Leap Forward. Rather than relying on the expertise of technocrats and intellectuals, whom he now viewed as ideologically suspect, in 1958, Mao turned to the revolutionary enthusiasm of "the masses" to communize agriculture. Controlling the Party Secretariat as he did, Deng found himself in a sensitive position between those who supported and those who opposed the magnificent madness of Mao's latest revolutionary scheme. By 1960, as the country fell into one of the worst famines in its history, Deng began to side with Premier Zhou Enlai and President Liu Shaoqi, who disapproved of much of what was happening. Although still artfully avoiding outright opposition to Mao, Deng seems to have been chastened by what he saw of the destructive power of an unrestrained leader acting out his spontaneous revolutionary whims on such a grand scale. Eschewing windy theoretical debates and ideological extremism, Deng now occupied himself with the pragmatic nuts-and-bolts work of trying to revitalize Party organization and revive the country's battered economy. "White cat, black cat, what does it matter as long as it catches mice?" was one homily for which Deng became well known during this period. He also began reintroducing private plots and free markets as a way to increase production of food. "In the past we have had too many political movements," he told the Communist Youth League in 1962. "When it comes to ways of optimizing the relations of production, I think we should take this attitude: Adopt whatever pattern will restore and develop agricultural output in each locality quickly and easily."

For the next four years Deng was able to navigate the treacherous political shoals of Party politics unscathed. But in 1966, as the Cultural Revolution began, Deng found himself in deep peril. The Cultural

Revolution was Mao's way of retaliating against those whom he suspected of maneuvering behind his back to control the organs of the Party and the state. It was also an expression of his belief that revolution must be "permanent" and constantly replenished through unending class struggle. As his tool, he used Red Guards, young students filled with Maoist ardor.

Ironically, it was Deng and Liu Shaoqi to whom Mao turned to launch his Cultural Revolution. But instead of initiating the kind of mass movement he envisioned, they sought to contain his call for class struggle within the preexisting political structure by sending Party-sponsored "work teams" into factories, schools, and universities to search for "revisionist tendencies." "If you don't make revolution," Mao ominously warned these foot-dragging officials, "the revolution will be directed against you." Although Mao had been Deng's main patron since the 1930s, he now turned on him, allowed him to be labeled China's "number-two capitalist roader" and accused of attempting to establish an "independent kingdom" within the Party. In October 1966 Deng was forced to make a humiliating self-criticism, repudiating his "bourgeois line," before the Central Committee.

"Now as I sit for the first time before the mirror and behold myself closely, a chill runs down my spine," he penitently said. "My real mistake is that I have not stood on the side of the masses and the revolutionary proletariat, and have pursued a line which is absolutely in opposition to the policies of Comrade Mao Zedong. . . . I can say with certainty that if from the start I had shown greater humility, had I listened to other people's opinions and asked for the Chairman's advice, I would have been able to correct my mistakes in time."

With a contrition at odds with his feisty independent nature, Deng continued, "My recent errors are by no means accidental or disconnected, they have their origin in a certain way of thinking and a certain style of work that has developed over a considerable period of time. . . . Ideologically, I must confess that not only have I not raised high the banner of Mao Zedong Thought, but I have not even lifted this banner up. . . . A prolonged neglect of Mao Zedong Thought in the past has now developed into a salient opposition to it."

Although in certain respects Deng's confession was probably a tactical ploy to propitiate the Red Guards, it was also a reminder of Mao's power to destroy opposition by making even the strongest of his colleagues submit meekly. If Deng's confession was not agony enough, the torment of being cast out of the leadership he had served for more than forty years most certainly was. And it was not long before physical abuse added injury to insult. In the summer of 1967, Red Guards stormed Zhongnanhai and held "struggle sessions" during which high leaders were taunted before huge crowds and then paraded through the streets in dunce caps. Unlike such unfortunates as President Liu Shao-qi, who was thrown into prison and left to die, Deng was only stripped of his official positions (save his Party membership), shipped off to Jiangxi Province, confined to an infantry school near Nanchang, and assigned to work at a tractor repair factory.

Why had Deng been given such special treatment? "Because Chairman Mao protected me," he later told Oriana Fallaci. Such protection was not, however, extended to his eldest son, Deng Pufang, a physics student at Beida, who was thrown from a fourth-floor window by Red Guards, paralyzed from the waist down, and then denied medical treatment.

Of all Deng's many experiences, his fall, exile, and separation from his children were the most traumatic. It left him more wary than ever of spontaneous political mass movements and convinced that, without stability, China was lost. "Historical experience has shown that no problem of mass ideological education has ever been solved by launching a mass movement instead of organizing exhaustive persuasion and calm discussion," he would later say.

Deng was not allowed to return to Beijing until 1973, when the unpredictable Mao finally responded to a series of personal pleas by Deng beseeching him for a chance to re-prove himself through "service to the Party and the people." With the ranks of the old leadership decimated and with Zhou Enlai ill from cancer, even Mao had grown concerned over the country's state of disarray, particularly over potential disaffection in the military, where Deng still retained great respect. As a result, he "rehabilitated" Deng and restored him to the position of vice-premier, the same position conferred on him when he first arrived in Beijing in 1952. Soon he was also appointed chief of staff and vice-chairman of the Military Affairs Commission.

In 1974 when Deng traveled to New York to address the Sixth Special Session of the U.N. General Assembly, it was the first time the outside world got a real look at him, and the first time since leaving Paris in 1926 that Deng caught a glimpse of the West. For him, the trip seemed to play an important role in highlighting China's backwardness. Convinced that without a change in direction China would never pull itself out of the state of chaos in which the Cultural Revolution had left it, Deng now turned his attention to elaborating the program of pragmatic economics that Zhou Enlai had sketched out in the early sixties.

It was not long, however, before Deng's emphasis on stability and production was once again antagonizing the increasingly addle-brained Great Helmsman. Warned by the radical "Gang of Four," led by Mao's own wife, Jiang Qing, that Deng was "China's Khrushchev" bent on trying to restore capitalism, Mao again "reversed the verdict" on Deng and let him be attacked, this time as the "king of counter-revolution." But, unlike in the Cultural Revolution when allies were not brave enough to stand by him, this time the commander of the Canton Military Region, Xu Shiyou, who had fought under Deng during the Sino-Japanese War, came to his rescue by flying him to safety in South China. "I have been deposed before," Deng reportedly said in defiance. "Do you think I am afraid of being deposed again?"

A month after Mao died on September 9, 1976, and shortly after former security chief Hua Guofeng was installed as president and Party chairman, the Gang of Four was arrested. From exile, Deng wrote the Central Committee. "I support with all my heart the decision of the Central Committee to appoint Comrade Hua Guofeng chairman," he proclaimed. "He is the most appropriate successor to Chairman Mao. This was a victory of the proletariat in the battle against the bourgeoisie. . . . Hurray for the victory!"

By the summer of 1977, Deng had been reappointed to all his former positions. His new rallying cries became "Seek Truth from Facts" and "Practice Is the Sole Criterion of Truth," down-to-earth slogans welcomed by most Chinese after all the ideologically inflated rhetoric of the Mao years.

Whereas formerly the Party had stressed "redness," Deng now called on it to stress "expertise." Saying that the influence of the Gang had created "an entire generation of mental cripples," he called on Chinese to "emancipate their minds" and to build a "modern socialist country" by the year 2000.

As Deng rapidly gained the upper hand over Hua—who continued to subscribe to the "whatever policy" ("Whatever Mao said should be defended, whatever Mao ordered should be carried out")—he began rehabilitating tens of thousands who, like himself, had been politically persecuted during the Cultural Revolution. Then at the historic Third Plenum of the Eleventh Central Committee in December 1978, he called for a radical two-pronged movement of reform: a major revamping of China's economic system and an "opening up to the outside world" so that Chinese "could compare the experience of other countries" and begin to formulate new "realistic plans" for the future. The Third Plenum launched China on one of the most dramatic courses of economic reform that the world has seen this century. Deng called it his "second revolution."

In January 1979, Deng's prestige rose even higher when he flew to Washington to normalize Sino-American relations. It was a visit that created a host of unlikely images: Deng hobnobbing at a cocktail party in the National Gallery with every American capitalist CEO who could wangle an invitation; Deng applauding John Denver and the Harlem Globetrotters at the Kennedy Center; and Deng in a ten-gallon hat circumambulating a Texas rodeo arena in a stagecoach. Deng's new reformism did not mean, however, that he intended to tear down the whole edifice of Maoist revolution. If the Party had made mistakes, it was best to forget them and move on. He was willing to assail such things as formalism and bureaucratism, but when students began putting up wall posters criticizing China's lack of freedom of expression at the end of 1978, Deng suffered them only so long as they served to help him against his own political opponents in the Party. When they ceased to serve this purpose, he unsentimentally turned on them, closed down Democracy Wall, and jailed those who had begun criticizing China's political system.

Although Deng did not rely on coercion as readily as Mao, he repeatedly showed his resolve to crush political opposition whenever he felt it necessary. In 1983 he joined hard-liners in a tough campaign against crime and "spiritual pollution" from the West, which included mass arrests, jailings, and executions. When student demonstrations swept across the country in 1986, he cracked down once again, proclaiming, "Firm measures must be taken against any student who creates trouble at Tiananmen Square. No concession should be made in this matter." His views on the democratization of China were unequivocal. "Democracy can develop only gradually, and we cannot copy Western systems. If we did, we would only make a mess out of everything."

While he had come to disagree with Mao on many issues, Deng was never willing to completely dethrone him. "We will not do to Chairman Mao what Khrushchev did to Stalin," he told Fallaci. Throughout the 1980s, Deng continued to insist that the Great Helmsman was 70 percent correct and only 30 percent in error. "Comrade Mao, like any other man, had his defects and made errors, but how can these errors in his illustrious life be put on a par with his immortal contributions to the people?" he asked.

Unlike Mao, who exaggerated political and personal differences, Deng was skilled at coalition and consensus building. China specialist

David Shambaugh has described his ability to manipulate factions through his extensive *guanxi wang* (network of personal relationships) as "not unlike a Mafia godfather ruling from behind the scenes." While Mao tended to revel in titles, Deng did not. In fact, he repeatedly refused to become the chairman of the Party, the premier of the State Council, or president. "The point was that formal political office would have limited his powers," observed political scientist Lucian Pye. "People were thus free to imagine him as being truly omnipotent, far more in command than if his powers were only those assigned to a particular position or job."

Part of Deng's strength derived from the fact that he rarely tormented himself over difficult decisions or allowed himself to be plagued afterward by qualms of conscience. Zhou Enlai was reported to have said that when making decisions, Deng's old mentor Liu Bocheng gave the appearance of "lifting something that is light as if it were heavy," while Deng always gave the appearance of "lifting something heavy as if it were light." Seemingly unaffected by ambiguity, Deng was ideally suited by temperament to be an autocrat. "The greatest advantage of the socialist system is that when the central leadership makes a decision, it is promptly implemented without interference from any other quarters. We don't have to go through a lot of repetitive discussion and consultation with one branch of government holding up another and decisions being made but not carried out," he candidly told Yugoslav Central Committee Presidium member Stefan Korosec in 1987.

While Deng could be opportunistic, he was also remarkably constant in his beliefs and predictable in his actions, especially when it came to his economic pragmatism and his conviction that, without stability, China would never succeed in saving itself. He debunked as "absurd" the Cultural Revolution slogan that it was "better to be poor under socialism and communism than rich under capitalism," saying that "poverty is not socialism." His self-confidence allowed him to take enormous gambles. First, he dissolved Mao's communes and leased the land back to private households, thereby transforming the face of agriculture. Then he began to reform industry by encouraging private business, upgrading antiquated management and technology techniques, implementing price reforms, and encouraging foreign investment and trade. It did not seem to matter to Deng that there was no clear plan for China's development. It was enough to try new things. "We have to be daring, or we will never be able to modernize," he told Alfonso Guerra González, the deputy prime minister of Spain, in 1987.

Sometimes Deng's economic boldness made it seem as if he understood people's urge to improve their own private lives far better than he understood the basic tenets of Marxism. Yet he eschewed any insinuation that he was making China capitalist. "I have explained time and time again that our modernization program is a socialist one," he insisted in 1986. "Our decision to apply the open-door policy and assimilate useful things from capitalist societies was made only to supplement the development of our socialist productive force."

Deng may have imagined that he could selectively pick "the best from the East and the West" and protect socialism with certain capitalist devices, but as his reform program proceeded, and as new and disruptive values such as individualism, freedom of expression, and democracy began filtering in and corroding China's once uniform socialist ethic, old revolutionaries became antagonized. Deng, however, remained unfazed. "There are those who say we should not open our windows, because open windows let in flies and other insects," he countered. "They want the windows to stay closed, so we will expire from a lack of air. But we say, 'Open the windows, breathe the fresh air, and at the same time fight the flies and insects.' "

Even after the 1989 debacle, Deng remained committed to his unique program of reform and openness to the outside world. And now in 1992, as he approached his ninth decade, he set out again to throw his weight behind one last effort to make these reforms irreversible.

33

Reform Returns

Not until February 20 when the maverick *Special Economic Zone News* succeeded in putting out a series entitled "East Wind Brings Spring All Around: An On-the-Spot Report on Deng Xiaoping in Shenzhen" did Deng get his first press coverage within China. But back in Beijing, where Chen Yun and other hard-liners who had been decrying Deng's showcase SEZs behind the scenes as "capitalist beachheads," the official press continued to refuse to give Deng's trip any coverage. "We should not turn the Propaganda Department into a production and construction propaganda team. The duty of the Propaganda Department is to publicize the theory and spirit of Marxism–Leninism–Mao Zedong Thought," said the director of the department, Wang Renzhi. At the same time an internally circulated *People's Daily* editorial proclaimed that what was needed was a "stimulant to wake people from their dreams in which Westerners are angels who rescue China."

In truth, Deng had been no more suited to a permanent coalition with such hard-liners than with Party liberals like Zhao Ziyang and Hu Yaobang. As ever, Deng belonged somewhere in between, where his command of the army and his ability to broker contending forces gave him independence and power. Now that Deng had again shifted his allegiances, China was once more thrown into a state of uncertain factional struggle.

It was not until after more than a month of jockeying within leadership circles that the stubborn *People's Daily,* which under the hard-line editorial direction of Gao Di since 1989 had been filled with diatribes against "bourgeois liberalization" and "peaceful evolution," was finally forced to relent on its total embargo. While it still failed to report on Deng's *nanxun* in detail, a series of editorials began to appear backing the gist of his new line. "Recent history shows that economically backward nations—especially those with long histories of feudalism—must correctly use capitalism rather than reject it out of hand," declared a February 24 commentary entitled "Be More Bold in Reform." "Only by critically absorbing those elements of Western culture that are useful to us rather than by disdaining them can we prosper and flourish."

In the meanwhile, Deng's supporters continued to maneuver behind the scenes and finally managed a clever end run around hard-liner–controlled media outlets by producing an edited compendium of the important points Deng had made while in Guangdong, and then distributing it to Party branches throughout the country via the Party's own internal information network. Presented in an almost chatty first-person style, Central Document No. 2 instantaneously galvanized national support for Deng's new campaign, especially among reformers and entrepreneurs who had been hopefully awaiting just such a policy change.

Signs that Deng was gaining the upper hand in his struggle were confirmed on March 10 when the Politburo met and issued a statement saying that "whether or not a move is considered 'capitalist' or 'socialist' will depend mainly on whether it will benefit the development of productive forces under socialism and will promote the people's standard of living." The *People's Daily* followed up with a headline proclaiming, "Firmly Grasp the Party's Basic Line and Do Not Waver for 100 Years! Seize the Opportunity to Speed Reforms and Opening Up to the Outside World in Order to Improve the Economy!" But it was not until March 31, after Deng managed to get a documentary film of his trip aired over CCTV, that the *People's Daily* printed a full account of his new pronunciamentos. By then the *fengpai* (wind faction)—so named because its members have a predictable tendency to blow expediently with any changing political breeze—had started clamoring to get on Deng's reform bandwagon. After a perfunctory reference to the perils of "bourgeois liberalization" during a speech on March 20 to the National People's Congress, even Li Peng declared that Chinese must "dare to innovate, and to take a bolder approach to reform and opening up." He made no reference, however, to Deng's urgent call to fight "leftism." That same month, Jiang Zemin, whom

Deng had reportedly criticized earlier for his "formalism," buckled and made a "self criticism" in which he admitted to having inadequately gauged the dangers of "leftism." And by May he was exhorting Party cadres to build a "brand-new social system" by "making use of all the productive forces and superior cultural fruits created by capitalist societies." As July arrived, reformist winds had reached such gale force that even Beijing Mayor Chen Xitong and Party chief Li Ximing, two of the Party's most hoary hard-liners, began trying to waft back into Deng's good graces. In one of the most dizzying displays of *fengpai* aerodynamics, Chen declared that "a mayor who does not make efforts to foster the market is not a qualified mayor."

Vice-Premier Tian Jiyun, a supporter of Deng's policies, injected one of the few notes of humor into this unctuous chorus of conversions. In a tongue-in-cheek April speech to senior cadres at the Central Party School, he facetiously proposed that if "leftists" didn't like the way Deng had made models out of the existing SEZs, maybe the Party should carve out another set of special zones in out-of-the-way places where hard-line policies could prevail and "no foreign investment will be allowed and all foreigners will be kept out." To make these inverted SEZs even purer, Tian suggested that they be run with "total state planning" and with all essentials rationed so that denizens would "have to queue up for food and other consumer products." Tian concluded by wondering out loud if outspoken hard-liners would be faithful enough to their creed of simplicity and sacrifice to give up their perks in the capital and move into these spartan preserves. His "modest proposal" was so well received by students that they began bootlegging videotapes of the speech and circulating them around Beijing as political opera buffa.

Mao had said that the Revolution had "two magic weapons": the organization of the Party, and its ideological propaganda. It now seemed as if both of these weapons were being beaten into plowshares to promote production rather than politics. As Deng told a Party work group that summer, "Development, and only development, is the sole irreversible central work from which we cannot deviate. Whoever does not understand this point, please stand aside."

Chastened by his close call with oblivion in Tiananmen Square, and by the failure of hard-liners to save the situation afterward with their retrenchment program, Deng seemed to have decided that the Party could survive only if the Draconian measures taken to maintain political stability could be complemented by greater prosperity. By turning Guangdong into a model and by giving ordinary people's dreams for a better standard of living new forms of expression, he hoped to head off the kinds of resentment that in the past had built into protest—even if, as some hard-liners feared, he was actually planting the seeds of the Party's ultimate destruction. While Deng had no desire to destroy the Party, he seemed to have realized that, with its reputation in tatters, the Party's only remaining path lay in its ability to deliver consumer goods. In Deng's eyes, the Party either had to lead the way to prosperity or be swept away by history.

In the short run Deng's new policies might delay that day, but in the long run the irreversible structural changes in the country's political economy that these policies caused also undermined the Party's ability to monopolize power. Entrepreneurs now had justification from on high to do almost anything to make money. "Whatever you want these days, you cite Deng Xiaoping," one official told Nicholas Kristof. "If you want to start a brothel, then you say, 'Well, Comrade Xiaoping says we should take bolder steps.' "

"Old Deng's prescription for reform is a little like *yingzhen zhike* (drinking poisonous wine to slake one's thirst)," a Chinese friend laughingly told me. Then she added, "But never mind. If he wants to kill socialism, it's fine by us!" But if socialism was fading, those who would rule in its name were far from allowing themselves to be completely vanquished. Moreover, hard-liners remained in waiting for the next interlude of "turmoil" so that they might once again reassert their leadership. In this sense, student protest served their purposes well. After all, it had been the eruption of demonstrations in 1986 and 1989 that had allowed hard-liners to form alliances of expedience with Deng, and regain power during the crisis of the moment. All they could do for now was once again to bide their time.

"China is moving toward a complete rejection of the basic theories of Marxism, Leninism, and Mao Zedong Thought," the Central Advisory Commission, the powerful but conservative council of elders led by Chen Yun, warned in a classified report that April. "Indiscriminate imitation" of foreign systems had resulted in "grave errors," it charged. To continue such wholesale borrowing, it warned, risked allowing the "entire national economy to race out of control and to cause social chaos." Since millions of workers and Party cadres in state enterprises stood to lose their "iron rice bowls" if Deng's reforms went forward, such dire warnings of chaos did not fall on deaf ears. Workers feared that unprofitable industries would soon start laying off employees who had neither the skills nor the experience to recycle themselves back into the privatized sector. True believers who had once taken pride in China's self-reliance were also offended by the way the country was now lapsing into what they considered a dangerous dependence on world markets. As the report warned, "Trade, exchanges, cooperation, and financial credits cannot be separated from actual political systems and the hegemonic world strategies of capitalist countries, because economics is the principal tool of hegemonistic nations in their foreign policies of coercion, subversion, peaceful evolution, and interference."

However, with Deng on the offensive and the media back under his control, by the summer of 1992 such cautionary voices were relegated to the status of background noise. Aware that the period of ascendancy for any political line was often very short, Deng pressed forward his reform agenda with a vigor that was surprising for someone of his age and fragility by boldly proclaiming that his new "basic line should be implemented for one hundred years without wavering." He understood that ordinary Chinese as well as hard-line leaders had been burned so often in the past when previous liberal lines had been reversed, they were now hesitant to jump too quickly in response to his new call. "Some comrades still have misgivings and get bogged down in the old 'surname question,'" explained a July article in the *Worker's Daily*. "When they approach anything, they first want to ask whether it's 'socialist' or 'capitalist,' whether it's 'red' or 'black' . . . [and they] think that they'd better be prudent when dealing with reform and economic construction, because they fear getting into trouble."

Intellectuals, in particular, were wary, not just because of past Party perfidy, but because nowhere in all of Deng's propaganda about economic reform were there references to the need for a commensurate restructuring of China's political system. During the mid-1980s many educated Chinese had come to view economic and political reforms as complementary parts of the same process. In 1986 even Deng himself had declared that "after reform of the economic system has advanced one step, we will feel the need to reform the political system." However, the two recent episodes of mass student demonstrations had changed his mind. Now he made it clear that any new reform efforts would be confined to the economic realm alone. He seemed to hope that he could sweep the country up in a new wave of economic progress that would make Chinese overlook politics. Nowhere was the success of his new policy more evident than in the way in which China's nascent stock markets began to grip the popular imagination.

34

The People Play
the Market

From out on the Huangpu River, the frieze of turn-of-the-century European-style buildings crowned with cupolas, turrets, clock towers, and domes that line the Shanghai Bund still radiates a glimmer of the power and elegance that were the city's hallmarks when it was the financial and cultural center of Asia during the early part of this century. From the Bund itself, however, the heavy toll that the intervening decades of neglect had taken on these once grand structures was by the beginning of the 1990s all too evident. Their battered entrances, desiccated wooden window frames, and patched roofs made them seem more like ruins than places of contemporary work and habitation.

For years the Pujiang Hotel, which lies just across the Garden Bridge from the Bund, was distinguished by its somber gray exterior and gloomy interior. During the twenties, when the hotel was known as the Astor House, it was one of the most luxurious in Asia. Managed by the Grands Hôtels des Wagons-Lits, it had 250 richly appointed rooms, a palm garden, liveried doormen, and some of the best French cuisine north of Saigon. When the PLA marched into Shanghai in 1949, the Astor House fell into decline, and its elegance was soon no more than an almost unimaginable memory.

It was not until Deng's open-door policy brought a new wave of Westerners to China in the 1980s that the hotel experienced a renaissance of sorts. This time, however, the guests did not arrive on P&O

liners accompanied by steamer trunks, but in third-class train coaches toting rucksacks and sleeping bags. For Western backpackers drawn to the Pujiang by its convenient location and dirt-cheap dormitory lodgings, the hotel was reborn as a hostel. As one guidebook warned, "the Pujiang is recommended only for travelers well prepared for 'roughing it.' "

On December 19, 1990, the Pujiang's faded fortunes took a turn for the better when a caravan of limousines arrived with a procession of luminaries. In the retinue were Zhu Rongji, Shanghai's mayor at the time (and later to become a vice-premier); Huang Ju, the vice-mayor (and later to become mayor); Liu Hongru, vice-minister of China's State Commission for Restructuring the Economy; Baroness Lydia Dunn, chairman of Hong Kong's Trade and Development Bureau; and an assortment of other invited foreign investment specialists. To enthusiastic applause, a brass plaque marking the hotel's rebirth as the home of the Shanghai Securities Exchange, China's first national computerized stock exchange, was unveiled.

During this milestone event, Mayor Zhu gave a speech in which he reminded the assembled guests that even after the political turmoil of 1989, China had refused to abandon its policy of modernizing and opening up to the outside world, and he promised that the city of Shanghai would continue to reform its financial institutions. Minutes later the opening gavel came down in a refurbished ballroom, and brokers wearing red waistcoats and sitting at computer-equipped desks arrayed around a new electronic "big board" imported from Taiwan began their first day of securities trading.

Long before December 19, word that Shanghai would open a new stock exchange had spread to other Chinese cities, where the news created no small amount of envy. Almost every other competing center of trade and commerce, it seemed, wanted an exchange of its own. In fact, on December 18, 1990—a day before the exchange in Shanghai officially opened—Shenzhen boldly decided to jump the gun. Without prior sanction from Beijing, officials unilaterally announced that they had converted the SEZ's existing over-the-counter market into an open exchange. Fearing that they might soon be challenged by other insurgent markets around the country, Beijing officials moved to control this unprecedented insurrection. But wanting also to avoid an open conflict, they decided to defuse the sensitive situation by granting permission to the SEZ to open an exchange in the spring if they would consent to postpone their official announcement for the moment. Shenzhen Securities Exchange authorities agreed to cover the brass plaque that had already been hung outside their offices with a piece of red cloth until after its formal opening, a concession that enabled Beijing leaders to maintain the appearance that they were still in control.

When the doors of the Shanghai exchange first swung open, only seven listings were available for trading, and most of them were unexciting fixed-interest bonds. At the close of 1991 the two "big boards" in Shanghai and Shenzhen were still offering only fifteen and seventeen listings, respectively. Given the government's discomfort with the idea of selling off its industrial infrastructure and the disorganization that reigned in China's incipient financial markets, only a few state-owned enterprises were allowed to list shares on the new exchanges. Most of the companies traded were collective enterprises, and regulators at the Bank of China limited the number of shares that these enterprises could sell to private investors, as distinguished from government entities, in order to maintain the appearance that state ownership still predominated in the People's Republic.

Nonetheless, by the end of 1991 the Shanghai market alone had already registered 100,000 individual investors—double the number of the previous year—and nobody had any idea how many more private punters had purchased shares in the numerous joint-stock companies that were not officially listed on the exchanges but were nonetheless seeking investors. The listings on the exchanges were actually only a tiny fraction of the thousands of Chinese enterprises throughout the country that were already marketing securities to their employees and to over-the-counter investors, and that were being traded outside of authorized channels. In fact, concern among reformers about this increasingly chaotic and unregulated market had been one of the main reasons for establishing the Shanghai and Shenzhen exchanges in the first place. But by linking the two exchanges electronically, the government hoped to lay the cornerstone of a disciplined national securities trading network. In the process, however, it was also making a highly symbolic admission—that the old system of state ownership, centralized planning, and government subsidies had failed.

By 1991 it was obvious to Deng that the economic-retrenchment program undertaken in 1989 to bring China's high inflation rate under control was dangerously depleting government coffers. Approximately 20 percent of the state's annual revenues were being used to prop up state-owned industries, two-thirds of which were unable to turn a profit and losing seven times more than a decade earlier. There were only four alternatives: Force these overstaffed, undercapitalized, and technologically backward state-owned industrial behemoths into bankruptcy, sell them outright to overseas investors, find foreign joint-venture partners for them, or let them finance themselves by becoming joint-stock companies. Needless to say, Marxist die-hards and "the proletariat" found the idea of forcing workers (30 million of whom were unnecessarily employed) out of their jobs by closing factories through bankruptcy procedures even more repugnant than saving them with capitalist-style stock markets.

Selling securities to generate capital was not entirely new in the People's Republic. China had been experimenting with such ideas since the mid-eighties when small, regional financial markets were first set up. By late 1986, China's new securities markets had even managed to capture the attention of the capitalist mother church. In November a pin-striped delegation from the New York Stock Exchange, headed by Chairman John J. Phelan, Jr., arrived in Beijing to spread big-board gospel to some three hundred enthusiastic Chinese acolytes gathered in the Great Hall of the People.

China's new securities markets gained additional legitimacy and momentum on October 1987, when the Thirteenth National Party Congress concluded that shareholding was a "legitimate form of property distribution in socialist enterprises." By March 1989 the government had gone so far as to establish a Stock Exchange Executive Council to study the question of solidifying the regulation and organization of China's future securities exchange system. Only a month after the council was formed, however, protesting students marched into Tiananmen Square.

The political crackdown and economic retrenchment that followed caused all plans to expand financial markets to be shelved, and it was not until the end of 1990 that they showed a flicker of new life. If the opening of the Shanghai Securities Exchange that December represented a small victory for financial reform, Deng's trip to Shenzhen in 1992 was a major triumph, for it was in Shenzhen that the idea of stock markets was brought back into the mainstream of public discourse. "Are such things as securities and stock markets good or bad?" Deng rhetorically asked a group of high-ranking Guangdong provincial officials accompanying him. "Is there a danger in adopting such things? Can they only exist under capitalism? Cannot they also be adapted to socialism?" For Marxists, these were questions of a very complex and delicate theoretical nature. But Deng had ready answers. He proclaimed that expanding organized financial markets was fine as long as they contributed to China's economic development.

As Deng regained control of the media that spring, the press bloomed with encomiums touting the curative powers of such markets. In March the *People's Daily* proclaimed that "active and prosperous financial markets will bring the country innumerable benefits" and called for "bold experiments and breakthroughs" so that "a joint-stock economy can serve our socialist construction."

For the sake of appearances, Party theoretical cosmeticians were called in to give this revisionism some semblance of congruity with Marxist canon. "A tangerine growing in southern Anhui is called a tangerine, but the same fruit is called an orange if it grows in northern Anhui," rationalized one commentary in the *New China Daily* during early May. "The same object may have different characteristics in different social environments. Securities and stocks are 'capitalist' in a capitalist society and are used by capitalists to exploit workers. But they can, however, be 'socialist' under a predominantly socialist environment."

As Deng's new political line was publicized, no one proved more enthusiastic than ordinary Chinese who, despite the small number of initial listings, queued up outside the new trading houses by the tens of thousands like teenage fans seeking tickets to a popular rock concert. Of course, relatively few had a very sophisticated understanding of how financial markets actually worked, much less an awareness of the downside risks involved in securities trading. Most simply reasoned that since Deng had anointed the exchanges with his blessing, stocks and bonds must be a sure thing—something like putting money in a savings account, except considerably more lucrative. And with one of the highest savings rates in the world, China was a dream come true for brokers and swindlers alike.

The country's savings rate had been running at over 30 percent, creating an enormous underutilized investment pool of some 1.3 trillion yuan ($260 billion) that had few places to go other than into low-yield bonds and savings accounts. For Chinese looking for new and lucrative investments, the Shenzhen and Shanghai exchanges seemed like a godsend, especially when demand for the limited number of securities caused the value of shares to skyrocket as soon as they were listed. Among the lucky investors who bought stock in the eleven companies originally listed on the Shanghai exchange during November 1991, most paid approximately 7,000 yuan ($1,400) for 2,000 shares. By August 1992, these same 2,000 shares were worth somewhere between 30,000 and 50,000 yuan ($7,000 to $10,000). With returns like these, it was hardly surprising that Chinese quickly became gripped by stock-market fever.

To accommodate the crowds flocking to trading counters, officials adopted a system of numbered tickets similar to those used at busy delicatessen counters in the United States. But rather than entitling an investor to actually buy securities, these so-called "share purchasing certificates''—each of which cost 30 yuan ($6)—merely allowed bearers to enter a lottery in which only those lucky enough to win were then entitled to register with a brokerage house to purchase a limited quantity of securities.

Eager investors were so determined not to be left out that many of them camped out overnight to get advantageous positions in line. Tens of thousands of Shanghainese queued up, bringing folding chairs, bedding, supplies of food and drink, fans, portable radios, umbrellas, and even children with them. Of course, it did not take long before speculators and *liumang* realized that there was as much money to be made in buying and selling lottery certificates on the black market as there was in stocks and bonds themselves. In Shenzhen, where a similar system had been introduced, fistfights broke out and two men were even murdered as gang members fought over positions in line, and on at least one occasion the PSB had to be called in to restore order. Certificates that originally cost 30 yuan ($6) sold on the black market for as much as 1,400 yuan ($275)—a premium of more than 4,000 percent. Of the lucky few who were able to get certificates, win the lottery, and then to reach a trading counter, many were disappointed to find that not only was the total number of shares they could buy limited, but they were unable to choose their own company.

In the middle of April 1992, a frisson went through the Shanghai market as a sudden downward correction created what one financial columnist (a new breed of journalist in China) characterized as a wave of "frenetic trading." For many Chinese who imagined that the market only went up, it was a rude awakening. The correction prompted Vice-Minister Zhu Rongji, who as mayor had presided over the opening ceremonies of the exchange, to worry that the "risk consciousness" of the stock-crazed public was still woefully underdeveloped.

"Of course, I'm concerned about the way the market is overheating," Gao Xiqing, the general counsel and executive director of the quasi-governmental Chinese Stock Exchange Executive Council told me shortly afterward. "It will take a few more market corrections and probably some bitter lessons before the mentality of people begins to change."

To help cushion the shock of such bitter lessons, the government took to printing warnings alongside stock quotations in Shenzhen papers: "The stock market involves risks." But by then a bull market had begun to move upward again and this vague admonition had no more effect than health warnings by the U.S. Surgeon General on packages of cigarettes. In fact, the craze to invest on the Shanghai exchange only gathered more momentum when that May officials removed the restrictions that had previously controlled the amount a share price could move up or down on any given day. On May 21 alone, the first day of trading under the liberalized rules, the market index soared to double the previous week's already record high. By then a weekly stock report had begun appearing in the English-language *China Daily,* and in market argot, columnist Wang Xiangwei declared that "the abolition of price controls on the Shanghai Stock Exchange last week flashed like a red flag to a ferocious bull, pushing prices to an historic record." One Chinese issue even reached a price-earnings ratio of 500 to 1—a spread which, according to one Chinese financial reporter, was worthy of a place in *The Guinness Book of World Records.* On Hong Kong's Hang Seng Index, ratios for most stocks remained at less than 20 to 1. In China the dramatic spread stemmed from one simple fact: Officially listed securities were in short supply while buyers were not.

Fearful that the market was out of control, authorities intervened in late May to reimpose trading limits. The combination of this news and rumors that the exchange was about to add thirty-four new share offerings sent the market into another tumble. By June 1 sell orders were pouring in so quickly that brokers were forced to open an annex in a city park. Before they had processed a small fraction of orders for those waiting, however, security police lost control of crowds shoving their way up to the trading counters and the annex had to be shut down. When panicky officials finally decided to scrap the new restrictions, the market regained some of its lost ground, but the frenzy hardly abated. Just a few days later, two people were killed and twenty others were injured when tens of thousands of crazed investors mobbed a Shanghai sports stadium where shares were being distributed.

The Shenzhen exchange was hardly more staid. In early June the index plunged when the government announced that it was going to look into allegations concerning illegal speculation by financial institutions involved in the securities trade. Things leveled off somewhat by July, but by then the weekly graphs charting the sharp ups and downs of the two new exchanges were as saw-toothed as a profile of the Himalayas. Even the People's Bank of China was warning that the "blind craze on stocks and bonds" might cause a collapse of the country's young securities market.

Contributing to the volatility of the situation was the absence of uniform accounting procedures, an overarching regulatory agency, or a business law to provide a juridical framework for enterprises planning to issue shares. Technically, it was the responsibility of the People's Bank of China to regulate the sale of securities, but the new market was growing so rapidly that it often seemed as if nobody was in control at all. Perhaps the most serious problem was that if the government could not limit the amount of funds raised outside the banking system, they could not regulate credit and control either economic growth or inflation.

By June 1992, more than 360,000 investors had purchased shares on the Shenzhen exchange, a number that was growing by approximately 20,000 every month. During the bullish first half of 1992, the total value of transactions made on the two exchanges was 5.2 billion yuan (nearly $1 billion) on a volume that was five times higher than the total for the entire preceding year. As the number of companies listed on the exchanges climbed from fifteen to thirty-two, more and more Chinese bought into the market.

Capital-hungry enterprise managers welcomed this investor interest and cheered government plans calling for more than half of all state-owned industries to be converted to a shareholding system within the next five years. For them, being able to issue shares and to raise unheard-of amounts of cash almost overnight seemed like divine providence. By the same token, many Chinese whose "work units" had previously forced them to buy bonds through payroll deductions in lieu of their full salaries during the post-1989 retrenchment, also underwent a sudden conversion with regard to their compulsory investments. In several well-publicized cases, like the Shanghai Special Steel Tubing Company, returns on these investments were suddenly looking spectacular. After the company was listed on the Shanghai Exchange on May 25, employees were stunned when the value of shares rose 471 percent during the day's trading, yielding an average windfall profit of some 20,000 yuan ($4,000) per worker. And then there was the Yuyuan Market Company, the only commercial firm listed on the Shanghai exchange. When its stock was first listed, it sold for only 100 yuan ($20). By the middle of March, it had shot up to 4,329 yuan ($865) a share. Such tales were the stuff from which fantastic dreams of wealth were made.

In July a *People's Daily* survey revealed that almost one-fifth of China's huge population now hankered to get into the market. Everything relating to stocks was suddenly in great demand. Tiny radios tuned in to special stock reports became the rage among information-starved investors. Radio stations and television channels rushed to include market reports in their daily broadcasts. A special twenty-four hour phone number was established in Shanghai to provide around-the-clock quotations, while several hotels in the vicinity of the Pujiang opened special "stock-exchange saloons" where market enthusiasts could meet to swap hot tips. Although the cover charge at such establishments was a hefty 30 yuan ($6), about a tenth of an average worker's monthly salary, the saloons were almost always filled to capacity. At times the clamor became so great that local residents complained; near one saloon someone was reported to have posted a sign: "We Wish That You Make Big Money, but Please Try and Be a Little Quiet and Not Disturb Us."

Trading houses soon began currying favor among the new set of high-rollers known as *dahu*, or "big players," by setting up special lounges where they could follow the market on computer screens and enjoying complimentary snacks and drinks while buying and selling. And as the stock craze gathered even more momentum, these privileged havens became both more numerous and lavish.

The Shanghai Saige International Trust and Investment Corporation is a trading house situated in a castle-shaped building that once belonged to the British army but which the Yan'an Middle School inherited after 1949. Desperate to find nongovernmental funds to support its educational activities, the school recently leased the building to Saige. When I visited its offices in March 1994, I found the old castle honeycombed with a whole array of private lounges ranging in size and extravagance depending on the financial ranking of the resident *dahu*. A 10 million yuan *dahu* got a private room with air-conditioning, a complete set of office furniture (including leatherette couches), several phones, dual computer terminals, and complimentary food and drink. The lounges shrunk progressively in grandiosity for investors with less robust accounts. *Dahu* who were unable to scrape up more than 300,000 yuan found themselves confined to a large common room with straightbacked chairs and shared computer terminals. And the hoi polloi were relegated to a large public trading area with an electronic quotation board and a counter downstairs that had direct access to the street and no chairs at all.

By early spring 1992, newspapers and magazines were filled with articles and columns giving advice on how to play the market. Getting a copy of the *Shanghai Securities Weekly*, a newsletter published by the exchange itself, usually involved standing in line even though its print run was up to 150,000 copies. In fact, any publication with the words "stocks" or "bonds" in its title tended to sell out almost before it hit the stands. One large bookstore was reported to have sold its complete stock of a thousand copies of the paperback *183 Tricks to Playing the Stock Market* in a matter of hours while the Xinhua bookstore in Beijing's busy Wangfujing shopping district could not keep copies of the *ABCs of Investing in Stocks* on its shelves. The Tianshan Film Studio was even inspired to make a movie, *Romance in the Stock Market*.

Private schools also sprang up to teach the mysteries of the stock market to potential investors. "I'm counting on this to make me rich," one unemployed youth told an NCNA reporter after registering at the Wanlong Securities Night School. The school was set up by Sun Puqin, an economics professor from Beijing's College of Finance and Economics, after one small newspaper ad brought him 120 eager students, each willing to pay 180 yuan ($33) to enroll in a three-month course. "In the past we didn't dare think about these things. But after what Deng Xiaoping said, we have greater faith," declared another of Sun's new students, a fifty-five-year-old pharmacist.

Professor Sun was not the only academic defector to the marketplace. A friend who had attended the Shanghai Finance University before becoming manager of Saige's new office told me that in a single month sixty-four professors had left his university to play the stock market. "Those that left were the best and the brightest," he added laconically.

The advent of computerized stock trading may have been a new beginning for many Chinese investors, but for others it was the end of the line. In early May a columnist for the *China Daily* only half-jokingly noted that "China's stock market won't truly be mature until a few people have jumped out of windows. You think I'm kidding? Just wait and see." The wait wasn't long. One week after the article appeared, Shanghai's *Liberation Daily* announced that a forty-one-year-old Shanghai man named Tang had hung himself in his home after losing $1,000 in the April market correction. It was the first reported stock-market–related suicide in China since 1949. (Alas, if Tang had been a little more patient, he would have more than recouped his losses during the bull market that began in mid-May.) Soon there were other casualties. In June a thirty-nine-year-old worker named Liu Xiaodong electrocuted himself after losing 4,000 yuan ($800) of borrowed money. When Lin Jianhua jumped to his death from a Hangzhou high-rise after losing 540,000 yuan ($62,000), his wife became part of the new "lawsuit fever" movement by suing a trading center for allowing her husband to abuse his margin privilege.

Officials in other cities watched Shanghai and Shenzhen ever more enviously. Even conservative Beijing showed an interest in getting in on the boom. By April, Chen Yuan, vice-governor of the People's Bank of China, announced that he favored opening an exchange in the capital, a particularly surprising turn of events given that his father, central planner Chen Yun, was the head of the hard-line Central Advisory Commission, which had consistently cast aspersions on Deng's reform policies.

Even though Beijing had not given local officials in Xiamen, Fujian Province, permission to establish an open market, on June 15, 1992, the Municipal Joint-Stock Experimental Unit Leadership Committee there authorized twenty-six companies to issue and sell stock publicly. By the end of the day some 400,000 share purchase certificates had been sold, and their black-market price had shot up from 5 to 110 yuan ($20) each.

That spring, in Hainan, a region known for acting first and seeking permission from the central government later, market boosters simply opened a securities exchange without bothering to notify Beijing, much less seek its approval. Less than a month after trading started, Vice-Premier Zhu Rongji had to fly to Hainan to close down the renegade exchange. "He swatted us like a fly," a Hainan official told Lincoln Kaye of the *Far Eastern Economic Review*. "He was worried that if we could launch a stock market on our own, soon they would be sprouting up all over the country." Nonetheless, Zhu's intervention did little to subdue the trading frenzy. Speculators simply set up a "gray bourse" and continued to sell securities through a decentralized system of independent brokerage houses.

"In the long run, I really don't think that the government will be able to control this thing," Gao Xiqing admitted to me. "The problem is that regional governments don't really listen to the central government. To get around their policies without approval, they simply interpret rules and regulations as they wish. If they want to allow local enterprises to sell stock, they just call it an internal offering to employees and then turn around and sell shares to the public on the sly."

In mid-June 1992, China's State Council and the Commission for Restructuring the Economy began issuing new administrative procedures for forming joint-stock companies and issuing, listing, and trading securities. "The urgent task now is to work on standardization, and to ensure that the experiment develops healthily so as to facilitate the exploration of a correct way to develop socialist shareholding enterprises and stock markets during the implementation of reform," wrote Liu Hongru, from the State Commission for Restructuring the Economy, in the *People's Daily*.

The governor of the People's Bank of China was ordered to oversee the new China Securities Supervisory Management Committee, which would review companies planning to issue shares and thereby ensure that markets operated according to the new regulations. The watchdog agency was also charged with controlling the rampant spread of unauthorized trading in the streets, sometimes in dance halls and restaurants, as well as the widespread speculation that was driving the markets to such dizzying heights. But the committee was too late with too little. Behind-the-scenes market manipulations by high government officials and the so-called *taizidang* (prince faction)—the sons and daughters of high-ranking Party officials who had already made millions in the international arms trade—were already widespread. With inside information they were able to make fortunes by buying early and then selling just after issues hit the market and prices soared under demand from small investors.

In late May 1992, China crossed another Rubicon when the country's first commodities exchange was opened in Shanghai to trade in contracts for nonferrous metals. Showing no signs of Maoist prudery, the banquet at the inaugural gala featured fifty seductively attired young female comrades brought in for the dancing pleasure of the Metals Exchange's male guests. "It's an historic event for China," Dale Lorenzen, a visiting first vice-chairman from the Chicago Board of Trade, was reported to have said, leaving it unclear whether he was referring to the presence of the young women or the futures exchange.

Speculators took quickly to this new investment medium, and within two months of its splashy opening, the daily volume of trade on the Metals Exchange reached over 150 million yuan ($30 million). Before the year was out, it had become the third-largest metals exchange in the world. (Only twelve months later China had spawned twenty commodities exchanges trading everything from oil and coal to timber and grain, making the establishment of full-fledged futures markets seem closer than ever.)

The eagerness with which Deng's allies responded to his call for these new financial institutions suggested a kind of extremism that, while different in emphasis from the past, was hardly new. It stemmed in part from the age-old tradition of obedience to a single ruler that the Communists inherited from China's imperial past. Another part of the phenomenon was rooted in the crisis of identity that has gripped China ever since the fall of the last dynasty in 1911—an event that left the Middle Kingdom vulnerable to manic shifts in political and economic ideology and periodic seizures of blind optimism followed by unalloyed pessimism. Economics happened to be the current focus of China's ongoing quest for salvation, but the quest for material wealth was being pursued with much the same ardor that had once been reserved for class struggle and mass political movements. As one local Shanghai broker wryly explained to the *New York Times*, "We're in a transition to capitalism, conducted under the leadership of the Communist Party."

Such statements must have made hard-liners see red. This time around, however, the reform faction took steps that would make it very difficult for anyone to reverse their latest innovations. After Deng's *nanxun,* select enterprises were granted approval to issue so-called B shares, a special series of securities designed specifically for sale to foreigners. With foreigners as investors it now became almost impossible for conservative Maoists to "reverse the verdict" on securities markets without seeming to attack the institutions of international finance.

When the Shenbao Industrial Corporation put $1.34 million worth of B shares on sale in mid-June, overseas investors inundated the Shenzhen branch of the Bank of China with some $112 million in subscription funds—more than eighty times the par value of the available securities. "Such a sensational subscription is rarely seen in any international stock market," said a dazed Liao Xiwen, general manager of the Stock Company of the Shenzhen Special Economic Zone, at a press conference. "It attests to the overseas investors' confidence not only in the Shenbao Industrial Corporation, but also in Shenzhen's stock market and the country's economic development."

Needless to say, Chinese enterprise managers were by this time transfixed by the idea of getting major infusions of hard currency simply by selling off a few thousand sheets of paper. Lincoln Kaye aptly described the situation as a "cargo cult mentality." "Most enterprise managers don't make any connection between selling stock and expanding the net worth of their business," a Shanghai think-tank director told me. "They see the issuance of stocks and bonds simply as a quick and easy way to get rich and to buy a new corporate car." The $67.5 million in proceeds the Shanghai Vacuum Electron Device Company had come by through a B share offering made Chairman Xue Wenhai begin fantasizing about constructing shopping centers in Beijing, factories in Mexico, hotels in Mauritius, and other assorted investments from Australia to the Virgin Islands.

With B shares being snapped up by foreign investors, in July, Zhou Zhishi, vice-president of the Shanghai branch of the People's Bank of China, left for Hong Kong to discuss publicly listing shares of Shanghai companies both on the colony's markets and in Australian and U.S. markets as well. Acknowledging that there was a vast difference between the accounting methods used by Chinese firms and generally accepted international practices, upon returning to China Zhou nonetheless expressed confidence that "some adaptation methods" would be worked out so Chinese markets could become more closely integrated with global financial institutions. No sooner had he spoken than a Chinese paint manufacturer made the Hong Kong grade, and shares tripled in value on the first day of trading. By mid-July foreign bankers had set aside some $2 billion for investment in the eighteen B shares listed, and the *Wall Street Journal* was reporting that some twenty different worldwide funds had already been established to focus exclusively on Chinese investment opportunities.

Another great leap forward occurred in October when a fully Chinese-owned company, Brilliance China Automotive Holdings—a manufacturer of minibuses that had been set up as a Bermuda holding company for tax and accounting reasons—passed muster and, with the First Boston Corporation serving as lead manager and Merrill Lynch and Salomon Brothers as secondary underwriters, became China's first listing on the New York Stock Exchange.

"As a whole, the situation is good and the development trend healthy," said Vice-Minister (and now head of China's Security Regulatory Commission) Liu Hongru. "However, some problems still remain." When I asked Gao Xiqing what kind of problems Vice-Minister Liu was referring to, he said, "Perhaps the biggest problem is that so many things are being done unilaterally and chaotically in these regional financial markets. If the cities continue to ignore the central government or if there is much more trouble with these new exchanges, it could be very bad not only for the stock-buying public, but for the country as a whole. And if hard-liners become tempted to try and regain their grip by closing the stock markets down, who knows where it will lead the reform movement?"

The securities and futures exchanges also accelerated the process of regionalization that had been dividing the country into economic satrapies beyond Beijing's control. This process raised questions that few people were eager to confront—at least not as long as so many of them were making so much money. What would the central government do if these regions began to translate their growing economic independence into political power, and what would happen if regional economic and political power ever merged with regional military commanders to form a network of opposition to Beijing? It was no accident that Deng was often forced to rotate, and sometimes purge, generals in each of the country's seven regional military commands to prevent them from becoming too politically or economically entrenched in any one area. With economics so dominating the agenda, it seemed very possible that, as Gao Xiqing had implied, the next major challenge to Beijing might revolve around questions of regional economic autonomy rather than issues of freedom, democracy, or human rights. Indeed, only a week after Gao's comments, a disturbance took place that made his warning seem prophetic.

On August 8, 1992, rioting erupted in the city of Shenzhen as thousands of people scrambled to buy certificates for an upcoming lottery that would allow winners to purchase shares in fourteen new companies listed on the Shenzhen exchange. Each of the 5 million lottery certificates cost 100 yuan ($20), with receipts purportedly going to municipal "welfare" programs. Only 10 percent of those applying, however, would win the right to purchase shares. Although the actual sale of certificates was not scheduled to begin until Sunday, on Friday, August 9 people started to line up at distribution centers, and by Saturday tens of thousands were queued up in the suffocating summer heat. Some were barefoot peasants from distant provinces, while others were workers from faraway cities bringing along the identity cards of friends and relatives back home so that they could buy extra certificates by proxy. There was such eagerness to play the lottery that people sold their places in line for as much as 2,000 yuan ($400), thereby creating pushing, jostling, and even gang fights.

When rumors began circulating that police had purloined a large portion of the coveted certificates and were making small fortunes selling them on the black market, on Sunday, a crowd waiting outside a local branch of the Bank of China became so rowdy that officials were forced to barricade entrances with filing cabinets to keep from being overrun. Ultimately police moved in using electric cattle prods, bamboo canes, and heavy leather belts to restore order. But there were still more than half a million people waiting in line when it was announced that all the 5 million lottery tickets had been "sold." Crowds turned angry, and one contingent marched on Shenzhen's municipal offices demanding to see Mayor Zheng Liangyu.

The next day, reports that two people had been killed in the rioting—an allegation that was promptly denied by the Chinese government and ultimately proved to be untrue—made angry mobs pour into the streets in an even more volatile mood. The fact that the official Chinese media refused to report on the event while Hong Kong television showed lurid footage of police beating those involved only incited crowds further.

Massing in front of the municipal offices, demonstrators smashed windows, overturned and burned vehicles, and waved placards and banners reading, "Fight for Justice!" and "Down with Corruption!" The scene was hauntingly reminiscent of the 1989 Tiananmen Square demonstrations. Although nervous police fired into the air, this time they relied mainly on high-pressure water hoses and tear gas to quell the disturbance. Nonetheless, more than a dozen people were injured before officials promised to distribute 5 million more application forms the next day. Deng, who had been among the hard-liners in 1989, now urged Shenzhen officials to keep their response well tempered. The last thing he wanted was for the Shenzhen protest to spin further out of control and possibly spark sympathetic demonstrations elsewhere, providing hard-liners with exactly the pretext they needed to condemn his reforms and initiate a crackdown.

"We won't deny that there are imperfections in the current sales method [of stock purchase certificates] since we are in fact very inexperienced," Mayor Zheng finally openly admitted on August 13 as he trooped off to Honghui Hospital with uncharacteristic contrition to visit those injured in the rioting. "We have made you go through all of this because we did not do well in our work. We are sorry for you, and express our apology."

Canton radio also seemed to bend over backward to be unprovocative. "The phenomenon of fraud did happen at some stations selling tickets," said an announcer during an August 22 broadcast. "Some Public Security cadres and policemen were not civilized enough in behavior while performing their duties. Yesterday afternoon the city paid great attention to the complaints of the masses, and organized a special force to conduct an investigation. Should fraud be verified, such cases will be dealt with resolutely."

The August riots were a vivid indicator of how economic reform could bring as much unrest as political reform. On his *nanxun* Deng had held up Shenzhen as a national model and promised that if the practice of opening financial markets "proves correct," it could be "spread across the board." He had also said that "if anything goes wrong," such markets could "either be corrected or closed." Then as a kind of afterthought he had added, "There is nothing to be feared. With such an attitude we will make no big mistakes."

Actually, there was much to be feared. The Shenzhen riots hinted at how ill equipped China was to deal with the consequences of the hyper pace of change that Deng had unleashed. To unknowing Chinese, the new stock markets may have at first appeared to be providential cash cows that could be milked endlessly by investors and enterprise managers alike. In fact, such markets were delicately balanced financial mechanisms capable of sending devastating shock waves through the Chinese economy when not managed properly. And it came as something of a surprise when shortly after the August riots both exchange indexes went into nosedives and even the seemingly indestructible B shares lost value. No one knew exactly what was causing this bear market, but as Ren Kan somewhat elegiacally wrote in his weekly market column in the *China Daily*, "Although it's still autumn, China's two securities markets are making investors feel winter's freezing cold." To those who were paying attention, it was a reminder that what goes up can also come down, and sometimes with sudden and disastrous consequences. It also showed what could happen when the central government lost control of important economic institutions.

35

Shanghai on Commercial Fire

My first acquaintance with Nanjing East Road, Shanghai's main shopping street, was one evening in early 1975 at the end of the Cultural Revolution, when I walked its length from People's Park to the Bund running along the Huangpu River. Gazing up at the ornate facades of the buildings that like the Astor House had been constructed during Shanghai's heyday in the twenties and thirties and had remained virtually unchanged since, I felt a little like an archaeologist stumbling on a lost city frozen in the past. Then the street's grand, European-style buildings had housed some of the most elegant department stores, hotels, restaurants, bakeries, photo studios, and haberdasheries in the Far East, and its sidewalks had been awash with stylishly dressed people from all over the world.

In 1975 the streets were filled with people in monochromatic Mao suits and the stores occupied by state-owned socialist enterprises. Although physically unaltered, the buildings were so run-down that their ambience had almost completely changed. Their once brightly decorated store windows had once been filled with fashions for ladies and gentlemen that made the street a nighttime spectacle. Now they displayed only grit-covered industrial products garnished with occasional banners proclaiming the latest five-year plan or posters featuring rosy-cheeked hammer- and sickle-wielding proletarians. Communist authorities had even stripped Nanjing East Road's stores of their old names. The famed Wing On Department Store had become the generic No. 10 Department Store, and the Sun Emporium the equally unevocative No. 1 Department Store. These gloomy retail outlets were presided over not by well-dressed shopgirls chosen for their smart looks, but by platoons of taciturn clerks with misshapen haircuts misanthropically slouching behind their counters and staring disinterestedly at customers not as clients to be served but as annoyances to be avoided.

Seven P.M. had become Shanghai's witching hour. All stores and restaurants slammed their doors shut regardless of whether or not customers were in the middle of a purchase or a meal. It was disconcerting to have the lights suddenly dimmed in the middle of dinner as surly waitresses began drumming their fingers on countertops and staring with barely disguised hostility toward still unfinished dishes on one's table. By nine o'clock the street was asleep with a completeness that made it hard to believe that Shanghai was an urban complex of over 12 million people that had once been the beating heart of Asia. What I still remember most vividly from that lonely stroll in 1975 was the shadowy stillness that made it seem unimaginable that the materialism of the pre-1949 era might ever be revived.

I returned frequently to Shanghai over the following years and watched it begin to evolve like one of those charts in biology texts that plot the stages of life up from the deep, starting with protoplasm, and moving on to cells, algae, marine life, and finally complex land-dwelling mammals. Whereas once the streets had been empty of commerce, private peddlers slowly began to reappear, followed by foreign joint venture stores, new hotels, and modern high-rise office towers. But it was not until Deng's *nanxun* that Shanghai's commercial evolution really began to accelerate. When I returned to take a stroll one Saturday evening during the spring of 1992, I found myself traversing a city that bore little relation to the one I had first known. Deng's trip had unleashed a madhouse of free-market economic activity. People spoke of *nanxun yihou*—"after Deng's trip south"—with the same historically definitive tone that they once used to refer to "after liberation" or "before the Cultural Revolution."

Shanghai's thoroughfares were now a nonstop hubbub of people, noise, food smells, music, and gaudy illumination. Craning out over the street was a canopy of blinking neon. Display windows were sporting mannequins draped in the latest fashions, favoring silk lingerie, body-hugging gowns, and shoulder-padded jackets for women, and brightly colored briefs, leather jackets, and stylish double-breasted suits for men. The facade of No. 1 Department Store was festooned with thousands of tiny lights arranged like theater curtains that looked as if some budding Chinese designer were trying to imitate Saks Fifth Avenue at Christmastime. Inside, the once sepulchral store was now suffused with bright light and music. During the first six months of 1992, sales at No. 1 climbed 30 percent over the same period the year before. The store was even planning to open several new branches with capital raised by listing shares on the Shanghai Securities Exchange. The sales staff, too, had also been miraculously transformed; gone were the lethargic comrades in dowdy Mao suits of yore, and in their stead was a staff of chicly attired and flawlessly made-up young women who now paradoxically carried out Mao's call to "serve the people" with far more vigor than had their ideologically correct precursors. The catalyst in this stunning alchemic change was a new system of incentives. Rather than working for straight wages, clerks now worked on a bonus system. The more they sold, the more they earned, and the more they, too, could purchase.

Like Canton, the city's skyline was almost unrecognizable. In addition to new tall buildings, rooftops sprouted huge neon signs bearing testimony to the commercial beachhead that Japanese companies like Toshiba, Panasonic, and Sharp had established on Chinese shores. The Shanghai No. 1 now boasted a tiara of advertisements touting Pond's facial cream and Vaseline Intensive Care skin lotion. Incongruously, these illuminated signboards competed with a long crimson banner hanging down the facade of No. 1 that proclaimed in bold white characters, "Struggle to Make Shanghai an Open-Style, Diverse, Highly Civilized, and Modernized Socialist City." That this hugely successful and profit-motivated enterprise still had a Party committee producing old-style propaganda was the perfect emblem for what was happening to the city. Like a teenager undergoing a hormone-induced spasm of runaway growth that mixes pubescent awkwardness with mature grace, Shanghai was still somewhere between its dour, socialist past and a brassy but still uncertain capitalist future. In this boiling cauldron of consumerism, such reminders of the past were increasingly difficult to find. But when one stumbled across throwbacks to the old regime, they highlighted all the more the city's transformation. After working through the crowds hovering around counters stacked with pop-music cassettes, karaoke videotapes, and books on cooking, travel, makeup, and fashion displayed on the ground floor of the Xinhua bookstore, I arrived upstairs. There were no throngs of shoppers here, only shelf upon shelf of dusty and faded volumes of Marx, Lenin, Engels, Stalin, and Mao still standing in undisturbed repose. Thumbing through these long-forgotten volumes was like pouring over relics from a Tang Dynasty tomb.

All along Nanjing East Road once money-losing state-owned enterprises were being reborn as for-profit businesses, many with the help of foreign joint-venture partners. Flush with overseas investment, they were emerging from socialist dormancy like so many brightly colored butterflies hatching from unprepossessing cocoons. Their once worn, creaking wooden floors had given way to smart checkerboard patterns of synthetic tile and masonry; their antiquated wooden display cases and cracked glass counters had been redone in gleaming chrome and stainless steel; dim single incandescent bulbs had been replaced with mercury vapor track lighting; and instead of the seedy back staircases that had once funneled glum masses from floor to floor in search of the barest necessities of life, some of these reincarnated palaces of consumption now even boasted escalators.

Even at night Nanjing East Road did not stop building. On new construction projects lit by the glare of enormous halogen lamps that suffused the smoggy air with ghostlike brightness, graveyard shifts worked on mazes of bamboo scaffolding, filling the dark with showers of sparks from arc welders and the machine-gun–like rat-tat-tat of rivet guns. Pile drivers pounded out insistent rhythms in syncopation with the beat of pop music being pumped into the street via outside speakers from nearby stores. High-decibel synthesizer versions of the "Moonlight" Sonata dueled with disco renditions of "Read the Works of Chairman Mao."

Whereas several years before, the idea of buying foreign name-brand goods had been no more than a fantasy for most ordinary Shanghainese, now such goods were all the rage. Television was ablaze with frenzied commercials for Tang breakfast drink, Nescafé instant coffee, Colgate toothpaste, Raid roach killer, Kodak film, Safeguard deodorant soap, Pledge furniture polish, and Head and Shoulders shampoo.

By 1992, the average annual income of a Shanghainese had risen to around 5,000 yuan ($1,000), more than three times the national average and roughly equivalent to what Hong Kong residents earned in 1973. With incomes rising and more discretionary funds in people's pockets, Nanjing East Road had become a grand procession of spending and consuming. Most upwardly mobile Chinese households had already acquired radio-cassette players, sewing machines, color televisions, refrigerators, and VCRs; the latest high-status consumer items were air-conditioners. At stores, floor models were piled up on top of each other like cordwood, each with little paper pennants tied to their grills fluttering like so many fishing lures in a rapid current as the machines pumped out their soothing coolness into the city's infamously muggy subtropical air. With Shanghai in the throes of a *kong-*

tiao re (air-conditioning fever), China had over two hundred factories producing more than 1 million units, a staggering 70 percent increase over 1991. In the four months prior to my arrival, Shanghai No. 1 alone sold some 6,000 units, a 117 percent increase over the same period the previous year. And sales would have been higher were it not for power shortages that plagued the city and prevented many eager consumers from getting their apartments rewired.

There was a time when socialist countries meant queues of shoppers waiting to buy scarce, poorly made goods. Now, however, Shanghai was facing too few people chasing too many goods, and the competition was forcing store managers to become innovative. Besides advertising and public relations—two trades that were booming—stores were turning to lotteries that entitled customers to enter drawings for "valuable prizes." A department store in Beijing made history by putting up three private cars and a minivan as a lottery jackpot. An electronics shop on Nanjing East Road tried to entice customers in off the sidewalk by positioning two pretty girls in its front window singing along with a karaoke video while their own images were projected onto a huge overhead TV screen. "A ramble down Nanjing Road puts strollers in a good mood," the *People's Daily* proclaimed enthusiastically. "The colorful neon lights match the new shining shopwindows, and the cheerful people in bars and inns have made the place a bustling nightless city again."

"People want to have some fun when they go shopping these days," said Xie Zhenhua, deputy general manager of Shanghai No. 1. "Price is not really important. They want style and they are willing to pay for it." Not surprisingly, by the end of the year, No. 1 had racked up a turnover of $237 million in sales.

Part of what made the street one of the most exciting places in China were all the smartly dressed young men and women enjoying the popular leisure-time activity of *guangjie* (strutting the sidewalks) in all their finery with shopping bags in hand, almost as their forebears had done sixty years before. Dolled up in the latest high heels, gold jewelry, studied coiffures, and flawless makeup jobs, young Shanghainese demoiselles were the rival of clotheshorses anywhere in the world. They sashayed arm-in-arm with young men sporting razor mustaches and wearing Ermenegildo Zegna and Giorgio Armani double-breasted suit jackets, expensive silk neckties, pleated slacks, two-tone saddle shoes, and gold Rolex watches. According to Wu Zhenglin, the general manager of the No. 1 Department Store, in the old days a garment was still considered new after three years of wear and serviceable for another six years or so after that. But now young people considered a piece of clothing old and out of style in a single year. For those who could not yet afford imports, Shanghai had also begun to manufacture its own knockoff versions of high-fashion garments, such as "Giorgio Giovanni" suits and lipstick and nail polish by "Bourjois," a trade name that seemed to be a mutant form of the most blasphemous, anti-Communist word of all—"bourgeois."

Already estimates put the number of Chinese *kuanye* (cash god) millionaires at 4 to 5 million. And then there were all the *geti hu* (private entrepreneurs) whose capitalist-style businesses formed the backbone of the burgeoning new middle class; the *dakuan* (big bucks) high rollers; the *dahu* (big players) from the stock market; and the *huanqiande* (money changers) in the streets. Each of Nanjing East Road's many money changers had a doorway or arcade entrance from which they worked their "territory." As soon as a foreigner appeared on their stretch of the street, they darted out from their hiding places like trout streaking out from under rocks to strike at floating insects. "Yooo lika sharnsha manee? OK!" one young man dressed in a white, Tom Wolfe–like suit hissed at me as I crossed Henan Road. Then doing an adept little two-step beside me as I edged back up onto the sidewalk, he repeated his proposition over again and again, sotto voce, like a mantra. Only seconds after Tom Wolfe broke off contact, another money changer—this one sporting a studied coiffure, a silk windbreaker, and a Marlboro clamped between his nicotine-stained teeth— materialized beside me. Like a pimp, he shadowed me the rest of the way down the block, making his whispered entreaties in the same fractured English. No sooner had he vanished than a third struck. All of these hustlers were part of a Mafia-like syndicate that was doing tens of millions of dollars in black-market currency exchanges. All that I could think was that if any of them had dared ply their trade in Shanghai's streets in 1975, they would have ended up in prison. But in the midst of this neon energy, prisons, especially the idea of political prisoners, seemed utterly remote.

Not everyone was sharing the wealth, however. There were beggars sitting along the sidewalks and sprawled out on the overhead pedestrian walkways spanning busy intersections, a reminder that even as some were becoming more prosperous, society as a whole was becoming increasingly delaminated and stratified. China was awash with a "floating population," mostly former peasants who had left the land when Deng broke up Mao's "people's communes" in the early 1980s and who had since drifted into areas like the Pearl River Delta and Shanghai in search of contract or piecework. While many had succeeded in finding better lives, others had fallen through the cracks, and with fewer and fewer socialist safety nets remaining, they often found nothing but destitution.

On many of Nanjing East Road's side streets, there were flotillas of small private stalls, often run by ex-prisoners or youths who had done time in reeducation-through-labor camps and could not get government jobs upon release. They sold everything from lingerie to shoes and hats to T-shirts, many emblazoned with English words and phrases. It was a hint of how drawn to things foreign—never mind if words were misspelled or meaningless—Chinese had become. "Compos," said one shirt, perhaps some sort of Dan Quayle–like exhortation to become an organic gardener. "Where We Are," another declared existentially. But perhaps the most enigmatic message was printed on a sweatshirt: "Nice Blrr."

No street market was complete without racks of glossy photo calendars featuring smiling Western movie stars, Caucasian musclemen, furry kittens, and, of course, busty, blond, bikini-clad women. In photo studios the vogue was for a different kind of Western affectation. Wedding portraits featuring smiling Chinese brides peeking out of white, Western-style tulle wedding gowns as if from giant bubble baths filled display windows. Grooms attired in formal wear stood at attention beside them with all the stiffness of the Japanese surrendering on the battleship *Missouri*. Virtually every photo shop had at least one of these nuptial costumes for rent—not for actual wedding ceremonies, but for the few minutes it took to snap an official studio portrait!

Now private Shanghai restaurants, where the decor of the day consisted of draping them with Christmas-tree lights and hanging them trattoria-style with bunches of plastic grapes, proliferated everywhere, and willingly remained open as long as there were people in the streets and money to be made. At one, where patrons could select their own live seafood from an aquarium, the line of waiting customers continued to spill out onto the sidewalk until well after ten o'clock. Another, advertising itself as "English Pub–Chinese Charm," was still full at midnight. And although the *spécialités de la maison* from Colonel Sanders's table were expensive by the standards of most Chinese, the red and white plastic cowling on the new Kentucky Fried Chicken outlet near People's Park was still glowing brightly late into the night. A little farther up the street, the towering Portman Shangri-La Hotel rose over the scene like the illuminated figurehead on the prow of an enormous ship. Through its magisterial brass front doors, one could gaze into its marbled lobby and past a grand chandelier to a sculpture of a huge gold nugget that looked as if it were part of the treasure in King Solomon's mines. With businessmen sitting around it in the lounge, sipping imported Perrier water while talking on cellular phones, this lobby seemed like the quintessential scene from new Shanghai.

By 1992, Shanghai had entered a consumer boom that some Chinese were starting to refer to as the "third wave." The "first wave" began in the late seventies when consumers emerging from the material desert of the Cultural Revolution snapped up electric sewing machines, tape cassette players, and black and white TVs. The "second wave" came in the mid-eighties as urban families made a run on color TVs, VCRs, refrigerators, and washing machines. The "third wave" began in the early nineties as air conditioners, telephones, and pianos became the latest status symbols. But even as Shanghai's incipient middle class was clamoring to get in on the "third wave," entrepreneurs were already trailblazing a "fourth wave" in which private cars, cellular phones, Italian suits, vacations abroad, and private homes were the yardsticks of having arrived.

The *shinei zhuangxiu re* (fever for interior decoration) was only one of many expressions of China's new infatuation with private rather than public pursuits. Just as Daoist hermits once escaped the secular state by retreating to isolated mountaintops, Chinese were now retiring into the insularity of their homes. They may not have been able to influence how their country was run, but for now, at least, they were permitted to upgrade their own living spaces without being labeled bourgeois renegades. To meet the demand, whole publications on home decor had begun to appear; designer furniture, kitchen cabinets, lighting fixtures, and drapery had become the rage. A 1992 survey of fifty households that appeared in one Shanghai magazine found that families spent an average of 3,400 yuan ($680) to decorate new apartments, a sum that surpassed most household incomes of only a few years before. What now was palpable in Shanghai among ordinary people was the feeling of relief that they could go about their private lives, even indulge themselves, without fear of being criticized or struggled against for being "too bourgeois."

However, having been deprived of any way to exercise their aesthetic appreciation for decades, Shanghai's sense of good taste was not at a high point. Overstuffed couches so strangely designed that they looked more like internal organs than pieces of furniture, faux Louis Quatorze–style dining-room sets, and crystal chandeliers with plastic dangles began incongruously appearing in people's homes. In the context of concrete floors and ceilings lit with fluorescent tube lights that had been de rigueur, such additions made interiors look as if they had been inspired by Diane Arbus rather than *House Beautiful*. Much of this craze for redecoration centered around bathrooms. Formerly, when government-issue apartments had had such conveniences at all, they usually consisted of dreary windowless concrete cells with Japanese-style squat toilets and no hot water. Now as whole bathroom speciality stores began opening, Shanghainese went on a buying spree for tile, hot water heaters, showers stalls, bath tubs, Western-style toilets, and even musical toilet-paper rollers.

After Deng's *nanxun,* consumer sales in Shanghai broke one record after another. During May 1992 alone retail sales climbed 4 percent over April, up almost 15 percent from the same month in 1991. One could not open a newspaper without being assaulted by dizzying arrays of impressive statistics. By 1993 the city boasted over two thousand projects, involving a foreign investment of more than $3.5 billion, almost seven times the amount invested in 1991. Gross industrial output was rising rapidly, too, from approximately $2.5 billion in 1989 to over $4 billion in 1992. Over 120 large multinational corporations, more than a third of which were American, had opened operations in Shanghai. The whole city was caught up in a cyclonic spiral of development. Even the Bund, Shanghai's celebrated waterfront, was undergoing a transformation. Zhongshan Road was being widened from six to ten lanes and a new pedestrian promenade was being constructed along the Huangpu River. But the most dynamic and rapidly changing part of the city by far was the area known as Pudong on the other side.

For years Pudong had remained undeveloped because the only way to reach it from downtown Shanghai was via boat. In 1990, Shanghai officials drew up plans to connect a 350-square-kilometer piece of land across the river to downtown Shanghai with a series of bridges, freeways, tunnels, and subways. With an investment of 50 billion yuan ($10 billion), the Shanghai government hoped to create a "special development zone" with an entirely new urban infrastructure. The Pudong Special Zone was Shanghai's attempt to catch up with the four SEZs and restore the city to its old position as commercial hub of China. When Deng visited Shanghai in 1991, he was reported to have told city officials that one of his "biggest mistakes" over the past decade was failing to include Shanghai as an SEZ. "Although Pudong was developed later than Shenzhen, it can start at a higher level," he then said. "I believe it can even surpass Shenzhen." Such encouragement from the country's paramount leader was music to the ears of city fathers, who took it as an invitation to speed up their already frenetic development plans to catch up with Guangdong, Fujian, and Hainan. In May 1992 gung-ho officials had won the same kinds of preferential policies enjoyed by the four SEZs, such as crucial permission for a tax exemption for foreign joint ventures and approval for a bonded zone through which duty-free materials could be imported. In the months following Deng's *nanxun,* boosters succeeded in getting some $900 million pledged for Pudong's new Jingqiao Export Processing Zone; $970 million for commercial buildings in the new Liujiazui Financial and Trade Zone; and $700 million for the Waigaoqiao Free Trade Zone. They were also successful in getting scores of substantial development projects underway, including such megaliths as a $2 billion commercial and residential complex funded by Thailand's Chia Tai investment group; a $100 million 1.3-million-square-foot shopping complex being built by none other than the Shanghai No. 1 Department Store in conjunction with Japan's Yaohan Group (which would be the largest one of its kind in Asia); a $100 million radio and television transmission tower ("Asia's tallest") being put up by Orient Broadcasting; and a new Shanghai Securities Exchange to replace the old Pujiang Hotel quarters (which by the end of 1993 boasted 2,500 seats scattered around the city in four different buildings, 500 Shanghai brokerage houses, and 5 million account holders). In 1990 Pudong posted a 6 billion yuan ($1.05 billion) GDP. By the end of 1993 the figure had more than doubled.

Shanghai was on commercial fire, and the influx of tourists and businessmen was soon stretching local facilities to the breaking point. In 1992 alone, Shanghai attracted as much foreign investment (approximately $3.3 billion) as it had throughout the entire 1980s, and in 1993 the figure was also destined to more than double again. To meet the rapidly expanding volume of shipping passing through the city, officials signed a $1.4 billion deal with Hong Kong taipan Li Kashing and the Hutchison Whampoa Company for a new container port.

Just as in Guangdong, this influx of foreign capital created a construction boom, drawing millions of migrant laborers from poorer parts of China to fill all the new jobs. Such a situation was a manufacturer's dream. As Peter Topp, supply manager for Shanghai Volkswagen, the city's largest joint venture, enthused to Patrick Tyler of the *New York Times,* "For all practical purposes the cost of labor in China is nothing." Having held off investing heavily in Shanghai because of the allure of the Pearl River Delta, many major overseas Chinese investors now started moving north. They came in such droves, in fact, that Shanghai Airlines set a record in May 1992 when almost 97 percent of its seats were occupied on its more than four hundred flights in and out of Hongqiao Airport. Officials at China Eastern Airlines reported that in June empty seats on its flights from Shanghai to Hong Kong and Japan had become so scarce that they had taken "emergency measures" to lay on larger aircraft. And passengers were not just foreigners. The Shanghai branch of the China Travel Service reported that wealthy locals applying to go on "shopping sprees" to Hong Kong had reached record numbers.

"Shanghainese have money," said Yang Honglin, manager of the service's Overseas Tour Department. "They want to spend it and see the outside world." With Hong Kong limiting the number of mainland Chinese it would admit, the travel service was impatiently awaiting the day when direct flights between Shanghai and Taiwan would make Taipei an alternative destination for wealthy Chinese shoppers. To handle the projected increase in air traffic, Shanghai officials drew up plans for a new airport in Pudong, the largest in Asia.

36

The Big Boom

Party leaders had planned to confine experiments with the market economy to the four SEZs established in 1980 and the fourteen other coastal cities including Shanghai that were ''opened'' in 1984. But Deng's *nanxun* signaled officials in every Chinese city that it was now permissible for them to join the scramble for foreign investment and development as well. The most popular strategy was to set up ''special development areas'' like the Pudong Special Zone to lure foreign investors with favored treatment. In 1991, China had only 117 of these urban zones, but by September 1992 the number had soared to 1,951, and these were only a fraction of a much larger proliferation of some 10,000 smaller development zones aimed at the domestic market that had sprung up in rural areas. Fierce competition among them prompted local officials to offer tax holidays, concessions on pollution controls, promises of inexpensive labor, guarantees of raw materials, and low-cost leaseholds in order to clinch key investment deals. ''Come to Our Zone and Enjoy More Benefits,'' trumpeted one typical headline in the blizzard of promotional literature that began appearing, this example distributed by the New Jinan High-Technology Industrial Development Zone in Shandong Province.

Since the 1950s, all land in China had belonged to the state and had been allocated rent-free to government enterprises, with no ownership allowed foreigners. Spurred on by Deng's reformist zeal, the Constitution was amended in 1988 to allow land-use rights to state-owned land to be bought and sold. By 1992 the State Land Administration (SLA) had further liberated the real estate market by adopting a nationwide policy designed to transform all land and buildings into income-producing assets through various leasing mechanisms, with value being determined by supply and demand. Local officials suddenly found themselves custodians of what one financial writer described as ''one of the country's most valuable and least recognized possessions.''

While the idea that land-use rights could be sold represented a monumental shift both in the theory and practice of landholding, it also opened vast opportunities for corruption and speculation. Perhaps the most common form was *chao di* (frying up real estate), where speculators bought and sold rights to land for profit again and again without ever putting it to productive use. With so much state property up for grabs and with local officials in charge of allocating leaseholds, possibilities for making private fortunes from the public trust increased exponentially. No piece of property was too sacred for profiteering. For instance, when officials in charge of the vast network of Xinhua bookstores began to realize that their stores occupied some of the most valuable commercial real estate in major cities, they not only started renting out space to book kings but even selling whole buildings. By 1993 all five bookstores in Lanzhou, the capital of Gansu Province, had been told to close their doors. In Zhengzhou, the capital of Henan Province, the main Xinhua store was closed to make way for a development project called the National Commercial and Trade City Center.

All over China state enterprises began to look at their holdings more in terms of the resale value rather than productive capacity. Many such properties were discounted by local officials to cronies in return for huge kickbacks and bribes. In one such case cited by the *China Business Times,* officials leased out a large parcel of land to a sweetheart development project for less than one U.S. cent per square meter for a period of seventy years! Other local officials raised large amounts of money from local banks by selling them land rights or using state land and buildings as collateral for loans. And since it was now politically correct to lease to joint ventures and foreigners, huge windfalls could be had if overseas investors were convinced to pay inflated prices in hard currency.

By the middle of 1992, surveys showed that government agencies were garnering some 50 billion yuan ($8.7 billion) a year through the lease of land rights, and that these revenues comprised upward of 80 percent of some local governments' annual incomes. Describing this change as a great "conceptual breakthrough," Zou Yuchuan, deputy director general of the SLA, predicted that soon there would be few "free users of land in China."

The rush of local governments to capitalize on their real estate holdings had its comic moments. In May 1992, for instance, the mayor of the port of Qingdao announced that the municipal government had decided to auction off the city's elegant old town hall, situated in a scenic part of town built when the city had been a German concession earlier in the century. Not surprisingly, the highest bidder was an international developer. In 1993, the Shanghai Religious Affairs Bureau rented out the Russian Orthodox mission church in the old French Concession to a stock brokerage house and a disco. Around the same time, local Jiangsu Province officials sold the land rights to the top of historic Lushan Mountain—a favorite retreat of both Chiang Kai-shek and Mao Zedong—to an investment group from Hong Kong. By 1994, Shanghai officials had also put up for commercial auction thirty-seven classical old buildings situated along the Bund, including the city's own headquarters in the Hong Kong Shanghai Bank building. Such commercial exploitation of government-owned shrines left one wondering whether the Forbidden City would not sprout a "For Sale" sign or whether Mao's mausoleum might not soon be auctioned off to a multinational entertainment conglomerate as an addition to some network of reptile gardens, Wild West ghost-town replicas, and amusement parks.

As more and more real estate was put on the block, a new kind of Chinese middleman appeared—realtors and real estate development companies. At the end of 1992 there were already estimated to be some 12,000 such companies, three times as many as the year before. Not since Mao's communization of agriculture in the 1950s and Deng's subsequent decollectivization in the early 1980s had Chinese society undergone such a profound change in patterns of property holding. But like so many anomalies triggered by Deng's *nanxun,* the new attitude toward land created a rip-off mentality that was increasingly difficult for Beijing to control. Still distrusting the durability of these new policies, many people grabbed every financial advantage from public property while they could, just in case the government again reversed its engines, as it had done so often in the past. Huge fortunes were made, but with so much power devolving into local hands, it sometimes looked as if China were being refeudalized. As regional autonomy increased, it became more and more difficult for the central government to rule effectively. As local government organs became more practiced at thumbing their noses at Beijing, even collecting federal taxes became a problem.

Another problem exacerbated by the real estate revolution centered around "housing reform," which aimed to relieve the government of costly upkeep for millions of state-owned urban housing units by converting them into what were effectively condominiums. While many nouveaux riches welcomed the chance to buy homes, those on small fixed incomes or pensions feared the consequences of these changes. Not only were they unable to buy their houses, but the reforms meant that their rents would be drastically raised.

One of the most incongruous features of Deng's new "planned commodity economy" was a revival of the notion of bankruptcy. As the private sector provided ever stiffer competition for the state sector, the percentage of the country's overall industrial output being generated by its state enterprises plummeted. Even though the state still employed nearly three-fourths of the urban labor force, bad management, Party interference, obsolete equipment, poor design, ballooning debt, and a listless workforce had by 1992 made the state's share of the nation's total industrial output fall below 50 percent for the first time in the history of the People's Republic. Since only 30 percent of these enterprises were profitable (another 40 percent operated at a net loss, and the remaining 30 percent barely broke even) this situation was not surprising. To keep the ailing state sector from collapsing entirely, the government was annually forced to expend tens of billions of dollars in subsidies—an amount that by the end of 1992 was variously estimated to constitute somewhere between 15 and 30 percent of all government revenue. State banks became giant cash registers dispensing "loans" not because it made economic sense to do so, but simply to "maintain social stability." Under the circumstances, it was understandable that economic-reform–minded officials might look upon bankruptcy as a welcome means of getting failing enterprises off the books, while hard-liners would look on it both as socialist apostasy and as a recipe for more political unrest.

In 1986 China had passed a "Trial Enterprise Bankruptcy Law" that allowed the "experimental" closing of some factories hemorrhaging red ink. Of course, dyed-in-the-wool Marxists recoiled in horror at the idea of the government throwing members of the proletariat out into the streets unemployed. Under hard-liner influence, officials backed away from using the new bankruptcy law after June 4. As economic reform gathered momentum after Deng's *nanxun* and as more state enterprises sank deeper into debt, however, cities from Canton to Shenyang once again began eyeing this uniquely capitalist way of solving their growing problem. As of August 1992 some sixty-six industrial enterprises, fifteen of which were state-owned, had been put out of their misery through bankruptcy. Although this was an infinitesimal percentage of the total number that needed to be restructured or closed, the fact that there had been any bankruptcies declared at all suggested how desperate the government was to find a way out of its impasse. It was an impasse which not even salvation by *gufenhua*—"stockification," or allowing companies to sell shares—could be expected to remedy.

Taken together, special development zones, privatized real estate, housing reform, and bankruptcy represented a major disjuncture with China's socialist revolution. After all, Marx and Engels had insisted that the theory of communism could "be summed up in a single phrase: abolition of private property." Adding to the inconsistency was the fact that the real estate being bought and sold with such abandon was property that had originally been righteously confiscated from private hands after 1949. The Chinese government, which had come to power by exterminating landlords, compradors, and capitalists and expropriating their property and businesses, was now being transformed back into the very image of everything it had once opposed.

Deng's *nanxun* had rammed Chinese society into reverse gear, stampeding the country into a form of unregulated capitalism that made the U.S. and Europe seem almost socialist by comparison. Instead of exhortations to struggle against "bourgeois liberalization" and "peaceful evolution," the official press was now filled with boosterish articles about economic development and "political stability." The *China Daily*, still the country's only English-language paper, now read more like a trade journal than a newspaper. Each week it produced a special trade supplement sponsored by a different city, province, or region, each featuring mug shots of beaming mayors and local honchos in Western suits and ties and photos of smoggy half-built industrial parks, highway overpasses, crowded docks, and clusters of showpiece high-rise office buildings and hotel complexes. Accompanying articles cited glowing economic statistics on local investment climates and extolled businessmen who had become self-made millionaires by trading in everything from AK-47 assault rifles and nerve gas to Santa Claus masks and Jockey shorts stuffed with herbal aphrodisiacs. The fields of advertising and public relations helped propel the boom like high-octane fuel. Not only did editors fudge the line between reportage and payola advertising, but journalists took bribes in return for product plugs. Even Party propaganda organs that once prided themselves on being unbesmirched by commercial taint now vied with each other to attract advertisers. In a first, Shanghai's *Liberation Daily* and the *Wenhui Daily,* both former mouthpieces of the radical Gang of Four, began auctioning off entire front pages to the highest commercial bidders for fees that sometimes topped $200,000. The returns were even higher on national television, where fifteen-second spots in prime time on CCTV cost $4,000 to $5,000, allowing the network to rake in an estimated $123 million annually. In quest of new horizons in outdoor advertising, *Changjiang Daily* even rented space on a cliff along the Yangtze River where it carved its name in the rock for all time. In a country whose media had had no commercials whatsoever only a few years earlier, by the end of 1992, there were suddenly upward of 17,000 advertising companies employing some 185,000 people. China's talent for political propaganda had, it seemed, simply been recycled into commercial PR.

Not to be left out of the boom, even the PLA and the PSB began setting up for-profit businesses that included enterprises to sell arms overseas, as well as thousands of other ventures ranging from livestock farms, shipping firms, and factories to luxury hotels, restaurants, dance halls, karoke bars, and even massage parlors and high-priced houses of prostitution. Some prisons even began charging fees for family visits, parole hearings, and reductions in sentences.

The Party now seemed willing to overlook any activity no matter how inconsistent with past Party dogma, as long as it was not overtly political. Every month brought new surprises. In late April 1992, Canton hosted the China Championship Gold Cup Race, the first horse race to be run in China since 1949, at its new suburban Huangcun Racetrack. "We are not organizing these races for the purposes of profit," insisted Huang Peizhen, an official with the Provincial Sports Commission, who emphasized that all proceeds would go to charity. The philanthropic urge did not, however, stop organizers from experimenting with a modified form of betting by making each 50 yuan ($9) entrance ticket eligible to win a 50,000 yuan ($9,000) prize, a ploy that persuaded many track enthusiasts to buy numerous tickets.

Not wanting to be outdone by their provincial confreres, the Canton municipal government put up 200 million yuan to open a track of its own at Tianho, and was soon holding races every Sunday. It featured unlimited betting on horses with such unlikely names as Ultimate Luxury and Freedom and Power, owned by institutions ranging from the Canton branch of the Bank of China to the Thousand Victories karaoke bar. Meanwhile, up in Beijing, an enterprising former peasant named Cheng Chunbo joined the racetrack sweepstakes with the Beijing Country Horse Racing Club, a complex complete with facilities for computerized betting, and promises of a clubhouse with an English bar, a French restaurant, a fitness center, a go-cart track, and an adjacent golf course.

When I visited the track one spring Sunday in 1994, I was stunned to find the parking lot out front filled with Mercedes, BMWs, Audis, and Lexuses, many with license plates from rural areas. Inside the clubhouse there were thousands of enthusiasts milling around and placing their bets at computerized betting windows while ear-splitting disco music reverberated over a tinny P.A. system. High above the track's capacious stands were floors of private rooms where, just as in Shanghai's trading houses, *dahu* could smoke, drink, eat, pore over the racing sheet, and urge horses such as Instant Wealth to victory as they galloped around the track below, which was incongruously bedecked with a banner proclaiming, "Resolutely Implement the Central Government's Order on Forbidding Gambling."

Horses, it turned out, were just the beginning of Chinese racing fantasies. In October 1992, the Malaysian firm Lamdeal Investment Ltd. signed a $100 million deal with the Zhuhai Longyi Industrial Corporation to open China's first Formula One grand-prix racecar track capable of seating 200,000 fans. That March, China took another step forward into the automotive future when it hosted its first Formula One auto rally, the China-Zhuhai Race Meet.

In 1978 there was not a single privately owned car in China. By 1993, however, the State Statistical Bureau reported that there were over 1 million, and the number was growing by 12 percent annually. The figure was more astonishing considering that the least expensive new car, the Charade, made in Tianjin with technology from Japan's Daihatsu, cost 110,000 yuan ($19,000), while a Santana made by Volkswagen's Shanghai joint-venture plant went for 190,000 yuan ($32,758).

Wealthy moguls who wanted something a little flashier in a domestic car got some curious news in March 1993 when the No. 1 Automobile Works of Changchun announced that it had been authorized to sell its Red Flag limousines, once reserved exclusively for officials above ministerial rank, to the masses. As leaders of the "dictatorship of the proletariat" had been seduced by Mercedes-Benzes and other imports, the fortunes of the Changchun plant had nosedived. With orders from the government reduced to a trickle, the plant stopped its assembly line entirely in 1980. It did not start up production again until 1992, when managers hoped that their homegrown product might find favor among entrepreneurs who, as one *China Daily* writer put it, wanted "instant and obvious social status."

The problem for the Changchun plant was that by then the Red Flag was a bit of a joke. Reviving these massively overweight and poorly designed socialist behemoths—they were almost twenty feet long, seven feet wide, propelled by huge, primitive straight-eight-cylinder gas-guzzling truck engines, and cornered with all the ease of super-tankers—was a little like cloning the woolly mammoth back to life. Red Flags had become the automotive equivalent of Lei Feng, and it was hard to imagine who but foreigners with a yen for high camp would shell out 410,000 yuan ($80,000) for one of these time-warped oddities.

Sure enough, when one of Mao's own Red Flag limos came on the block (at a Beijing antique auction!), it was bought for $170,000 by an American-Chinese woman decked out in gold high heels and a gold-lamé suit who signed the ownership papers with a gold pen. "I bought the car because it's beautiful just like me," she explained, leaving everyone to wonder what bourgeois indignity might next be visited on the relics of China's Communist escutcheon.

What the Chinese really wanted, however, were not Mao-mobiles, but sleek foreign-made luxury cars like the ones parked outside Cheng Chunbo's racetrack. In May 1993 a Beijing resident made history by coughing up $134,000 to become the first Chinese citizen to own a Ferrari. To mark the event, the car was shown off at the Temple of Heaven, where Italian fashion designers Gianfranco Ferre and Valentino had just recently held a rock music/fashion extravaganza. But nowhere was the mass fascination with opulence manifested more obviously than at the China International Exhibition Center, where that May the U.S. Fast Financial Corporation opened a show of fifty luxury European and American cars worth more than 6 million U.S. dollars. Tens of thousands of Beijingers flocked to view a thirty-seven-foot-long Cadillac stretch limo (with a built-in bar, TV, and Jacuzzi); a $500,000 Lamborghini; a $200,000 Ferrari; and an assortment of Rolls-Royces, Lincoln Continentals, and BMWs. Although none of the floor demos were for sale, nouveau riche "cash gods" aspiring to move into the upscale car market were helped by promoters to place orders directly with the foreign manufacturers. Few were surprised when by the end of the year Germany's BMW and Britain's Jaguar announced plans to open dealerships in Shanghai, Canton, and Beijing. "We see tremendous long-term potential for Jaguar in China," effused Nick Scheele, chief executive of the company. And to accommodate the proliferation of luxury automobiles, it wasn't long before Beijing had another first: the Dragon Emanation Automatic Car Wash.

Among the car wash's main customers were owners of South

Korean-made Hyundais, which were now being smuggled into North China by the thousands as commercial relations between Seoul and Beijing became increasingly robust.

With spiraling crime rates, an increasing number of wealthy entrepreneurs turned to bodyguards for protection. One of the most trendy fashion statements anyone could make was to hire a sexy young woman to play the role. The Wuhan College of Physical Education and the People's Liberation Army Physical Education College were only two of the many institutions that responded to new market demand for female protectors by opening special training facilities.

For those upwardly mobile young women interested in physical fitness, there were now places like Sophie Sun's Heavenly Bodies Aerobics Studio, where, clad in a brightly colored spandex leotard, Sophie barked out simultaneous translations to Jane Fonda workout tapes. Watching waistlines was particularly important to the growing class of *bangjia* (helper mate) mistresses whom wealthy entrepreneurs and businessmen from Taiwan and Hong Kong ensconced in expensive apartments. In a parody of the Party's penchant for characterizing political movements with sobriquets such as the Three Cleans or the Four Modernizations, wags soon proclaimed this fin-de-siècle period as the era of *yifu, yiqi, yibangjia,* or "one husband, one wife, and one helper mate," China's answer to "one man, one vote."

Another affectation that was becoming popular among China's new haute bourgeoisie was dogs, an unexpected occurrence since such animals had not only been viewed more as comestibles than as pets (southern Chinese are said to eat "anything with four legs except a table"), but had also long been banned in cities as unsanitary and decadent. Like almost everything else that was happening in China, the dog craze was driven by a combination of faddism and market forces. Like cellular telephones, expensive watches, remodelled bathrooms, satellite dishes, Italian suits, and private cars, house pets had become another hallmark of having arrived.

By 1994, the "Year of the Dog," there were reported to be half a million canines in Beijing alone. The estimated one hundred million dogs in the nation as a whole were believed to be consuming enough food to feed forty million people. This vast population of canines quickly created a whole support system of dog boutiques, dog hospitals, dog beauty parlors, dog TV programs, dog shows, and "dog brokers" to play matchmaker between man's best friend and future masters. Northwest Industrial University Press published *A Guide to Enjoying Purebred Dogs*, which featured fluffy little lapdogs with ribbons in their hair on the cover. Even mutts brought a good price, but imported purebreds, especially European breeds—doped up on vodka and pills and smuggled to Beijing from Moscow on the Trans-Siberian Railway by enterprising Russians—sold for as much as 100,000 to 150,000 yuan ($17,000 to $26,000). Such prices were so staggeringly high that ordinary Chinese complained that "dogs have become more precious than human beings." And canine *Kultur* was not limited to Beijing. While on a trip to Tibet in the fall of 1993, I was stunned to see svelte young women in stirruped stretch pants, tight sweaters, and full makeup strutting in the shadow of the Potala with leashed Lhasa apsos. By January 1994 the *People's Daily* was calling the dog craze "uncivilized and unhealthy," and demanding its end.

The embourgeoisement of urban society embraced everything from pawnshops and prostitute hotels to private hospitals and country clubs, and from beauty pageants and opium parlors to haute-couture boutiques and yacht clubs. As in love with statistics as ever, authorities continued to proudly compile figures, not, however, on the number of "people's communes" or "model workers," but on things such as private law firms (by 1993 there were estimated to be more than 4,000), golf courses (more than 30), futures exchanges (more than 40 officially registered and at least 30 more in the planning stages), and nonstate schools (more than 20,000, including 500 "private" institutions of higher education).

China's ideological about-face was all too evident in a photo essay that appeared in the *Beijing Review* on the first anniversary of Deng's *nanxun*. Glorifying what it called the "boom in consumer and capital goods markets," the spread included photos showing an enormous crowd of money-toting Chinese pushing and shoving its way toward a cashier's counter that was reminiscent of Henri Cartier-Bresson's famous shot of Chinese in Shanghai stampeding to exchange inflated paper money for gold back in 1948, only in this instance Chinese were trying to buy shares on Shanghai's new stock exchange; a pawnshop in Beijing with a client negotiating out front to hock his minivan for cash to open a karaoke bar; a bustling McDonald's hamburger restaurant; and a gleaming fleet of Cadillac limousines hired by the Tangshan Fuhao Mineral Water Company as part of a sales-promotion campaign.

Even gray culture was becoming so commercialized that it was questionable whether it still deserved to be called "underground." Cui Jian had become almost mainstream. He had had a baby with his American girlfriend and had settled down into the life of an established and prosperous rock superstar. By 1993 there were new pretenders to his throne as China's "rock king." One of them was the twenty-five-year-old singer Zhang Chu, who had pushed pop music forward another notch by combining the Mao craze with *zhongjinshu* (heavy metal) to create an album called *Red Rock 'n' Roll,* on which he updated such Party standards as "Socialism Is Good" and "Commune Members Are All Sunflowers" with a guitar track that did "Iron Maiden" proud and lyrics screamed out like a banshee. Whereas simple survival was once their goal, countercultural idols now looked to convert their art into wealth. Although it's unlikely that Party leaders had planned things this way, they had, in fact, managed to immobilize potential rebels and transform dissent into abstention with the lure of riches. Zhang Chu, who had himself made money doing TV commercials, caught the mood of the times when he remarked that if "Cui Jian is a high-class prostitute, we're mere street-corner whores."

China was now as drugged on business as it had once been on politics. Everyone wanted to get in on the action. The Plastic Surgery Research Center in Beijing even began doing sex change operations on foreigners. As one Chinese friend commented, "The last time I saw such extremism was during the Cultural Revolution, but then, of course, it was in the name of Maoism not economics."

On a trip to Shanghai during the spring of 1994, I was repeatedly stunned by the unlikely juxtapositions that this "socialism with Chinese characteristics," as Deng liked to refer to it, had created, especially in Shanghai nightlife. The PLA is joint-venture partner in J.J.'s, a massive smoke-filled cavern of a discotheque on Yan'an Road, where downstairs Chinese yuppies danced till dawn to ear-splitting music, while upstairs, on a shadowy balcony parked with couches, "bad elements" copulated to pulsing strobe lights. Also on Yan'an Road there was the Casablanca in the Rainbow Hotel, another PLA joint-venture enterprise where girls were available in private karaoke rooms. The Public Security Bureau was also in the swim of things with such places as the Shanghai Moon Club, a high-class brothel on Zhaojia-bang Road, and the Protect the Secret Club on Huashan Road, where admission was granted only to those who knew the secret password. Such places, ironically, were known as the safest nightspots in town, because nobody wants to mess with the PSB.

Not to be outdone by comrades in the military, the Shanghai Cultural Bureau had opened a bizarre nightspot called the Nights of Paris, located in the new Isetan shopping mall. Decorated with faux Greek statues and a set that seemed to depict a *bateau-mouche*, it featured a second-rate restaurant with a cabaret show boasting four young Ukranian women who did a dance of the seven veils and eight leggy Chinese models who, under the guise of holding a fashion show, stripped down to bikini-like contrivances and undulated around the stage to rock music.

When I asked one European cultural attaché how the frenzy for commercialism had impacted on serious culture, he bluntly retorted, "There is no serious culture here! Ninety-nine percent of so-called culture is leisure activities like discos and karaoke bars."

The ascendancy of commercial culture took a heavy, but from the Party's perspective not unwelcome, toll on the urban intellectual environment. With the exception of technical fields, academic study was coming to be considered a virtual dead end. In a 1993 survey of nine provinces and major cities, the *Beijing Youth News* reported that 40 percent of young contemporary Chinese did not own a single book. Since wealth was the new standard of success, it was not easy for a young person to rationalize struggling through school in order to become a teacher or a professor paid only $30 to $40 a month while others with far less education were making thousands, even millions, doing business. For anyone prizing the life of the mind or the fine arts, China in the early nineties was not an uplifting spectacle. With few people publishing, much less reading, the kind of poetry, politics, and literature that had aroused such excitement in the late eighties, most serious books were met with a yawn and tiny sales.

While the market had allowed for more freedom in people's everyday lives, it had also marginalized serious intellectuals and artists by making them increasingly irrelevant. As Er Dongqiang, a photographer who was trying to save the architecture of old Shanghai from the wrecking ball of developers, explained to me, "Yes, our standard of living is much higher now, but if someone like myself writes an article on a serious subject, no one will read it, much less buy it." Even the time-honored notion that men of learning ought to serve as the conscience of society was being eclipsed by the rush to commercialism. In Deng's new New China, it was "glorious" only to become wealthy, a change that left a huge tear in the country's value system.

China's obsession with production and consumption created a euphoria among foreign businessmen who, after Deng's *nanxun,* became possessed by what some investment analysts called "China fever." Every foreign company, it seemed, now wanted a grubstake in this erstwhile People's Republic. At last, China seemed on the verge of turning the nineteenth-century dream of hundreds of millions of new consumers into reality, and this created a near frenzy to get a foothold in the "China market." Battered by losses in the United States, in May 1992, General Motors began a $100 million joint venture with the Gold Cup Automotive Company in Manchuria and expected to produce some 30,000 trucks before the year's end. Struggling to find its balance after defense spending cutbacks in the United States, in June the Mc-

Donnell Douglas Corporation, which had already sold the Chinese about $3 billion worth of airplanes, announced a deal to supply more than $1 billion worth of new mid-range twin-engine jetliners to China. "The Chinese market for commercial aircraft over the next two decades is expected to be worth about $40 billion," enthused McDonnell's Washington manager Mark Schlansky.

That same month Motorola Inc. opened a $125 million semiconductor, pager, and cellular-phone factory in Tianjin. "We want to be ready here when this market takes off, and everything we see indicates that will come about," effused Richard W. Younts, a senior Motorola vice-president. He had every reason to be excited. Over the past year the Chinese market for pagers had quadrupled to 4 million. And after viewing China exclusively as a low-cost source from which to export its Robotech action figures, by 1993 even the Hong Kong–based Toy Corporation of America was considering a completely new strategy. With several hundred million Chinese kids beginning to act more like Western consumers, the company was targeting fourteen major cities in China not only as markets for action figures and spaceships, but as TV outlets for its toy-related video cartoons. "I am convinced that we are seing the building of an economic giant," said former secretary of state Lawrence Eagleburger, one of the many former U.S. officials who had *xiaxai*, or "jumped into the ocean of commerce," along with millions of their Chinese counterparts.

In its eagerness to win more new investors, the government began allowing failing enterprises to be *chushou* (sold off) to foreigners, which meant that outside investors could now own and control state businesses and factories. In June 1992, Hong Kong's Hongtex Development Company bought a controlling interest in Wuhan's foundering No. 2 Printing and Dyeing Works, making it the first foreign company to acquire a majority share in a state-owned Chinese enterprise since 1949. Then corporate raiders from China Strategic Investment Ltd., a Hong Kong venture-capital group run by overseas Chinese from Indonesia, marched into Fujian Province and spent $42 million to buy a 60 percent share in 41 of Quanzhou's 42 state enterprises. Pleased with their bargains, they advanced up the coast to Ningbo in Zhejiang Province, and then to Dalian in Manchuria, where they added another 152 shaky state-owned breweries, paper mills, shoe factories, and other industrial ventures to their growing empire. It was not long before this gospel of salvation by foreign buyout began to spread, creating a kind of fire-sale mentality among local governments eager not only to unload, but to cash in on, their failing state-owned enterprises. In the summer of 1993, the vice-governor of Hunan hurried to

Beijing to announce that his province was going to hold a kind of down-in-flames sale at which about 200 money-losing ventures would be auctioned off to the highest foreign bidder.

Foreign businessmen were dazzled by all the new possibilities. "There is a feeding frenzy here," said a friend working in Beijing. "Like the Chinese emigrants who went to California in the nineteenth century, foreign businessmen arrive here thinking the streets are paved with gold." And each new "deal" seemed more shocking than the last. Indeed, it was hard to know what to think when the Chinese government did something like signing a letter of intent with Las Vegas–based Tellus Industries to rent Wangfuzhou Island, an abandoned naval base fifty miles southwest of Macao, for seventy years at $4.6 million so that it could be developed with gambling casinos, yacht clubs, golf courses, and luxury hotels.

By the end of 1992, the Beijing government was able to dazzle Chinese and foreigners alike not with fireworks in Tiananmen Square, but with pyrotechnical displays of year-end economic stats. GNP had grown by almost 13 percent. The total number of newly signed foreign investment projects topped 40,000, an almost 100 percent increase over 1991 and more than the combined total of all such pledges since 1979. Industrial output increased by 19 percent. Foreign tourism was up to 37 million for 1992, with 8 million more visitors entering China than before the 1989 crackdown. Trade had risen $30 billion over 1991 to $165 billion, an increase of 22.1 percent.

If this burst of statistics was not impressive enough, the International Monetary Fund announced that after recomputing its rankings of the world's major economies, it discovered that China's national income of $1.7 trillion was third behind the United States and Japan in terms of actual purchasing power. Such figures led the British newsweekly the *Economist* to assert that, under Deng, China had enjoyed "the biggest improvements in human welfare anywhere at any time."

Despite the gloomy prognoses of almost every expert back in 1989, China had somehow managed to emerge economically stronger than ever from both the political calamity of June 4 and the economic slump that followed. In fact, in a way that almost no one had foreseen, the tragedy seemed to have proven a perverse blessing in disguise. By providing the government with an opportunity to implement an austere retrenchment program—something that ordinary Chinese would never have tolerated had they not been reeling from the massacre and paralyzed from protesting by martial law—the leadership had succeeded in bringing the country's badly overheated economy under control. Moreover, by jolting Deng and other Party leaders into a realization that nothing short of high-speed economic change would be enough to save their unilateral political rule, the tragedy had forced them to radical reformist action.

But by 1993 there was so much money being made that few had the time or inclination to reflect on 1989. As soon as one raised any question about politics—much less about dissent, dissidents in exile, or political prisoners—most Chinese businessmen immediately disconnected from the conversation. Not infrequently, they even condemned political dissidents as "troublemakers," as if it were they rather than the government who should be held accountable for what had happened. "Yes, people want to forget the past and politics and get on with their lives," one Chinese friend working for a foreign company in Beijing told me. "They only want to think about the here and now, hoping that after all these years of being deprived they can get something for themselves. And I say, 'Good for them!' Even if it's just fashion, food, and karaokes, the point is that at last they are thinking about themselves rather than the Party. In a curious way, this may be their first step forward to independence and individualism—a real break with the past."

Most foreign businessmen had also become ready supporters of the Party's status quo, vigorously lobbying Washington not to connect trade and China's MFN status to human rights conditions lest the Chinese leadership take umbrage and retaliate. (Sino-U.S. trade hit a record $40 billion in 1993, with China selling more than 30 percent of its total exports to America, creating a trade surplus with the U.S. of more than $22 billion, second only to that of Japan.)

For many the reservoir of political sentiment that had fueled the democracy movement appeared to have all but dried up. The Chinese and foreign businessmen who now overran the lobbies of five-star hotels and the corridors of high-rise office buildings seemed almost incredulous that anyone might still wish to dwell on the events of 1989. China seemed to have fallen under a different spell. Whereas once it had been Maoism and repression that had kept people from expressing dissenting views, now the Party had new and even more efficacious allies: capitalism and materialism.

Of course, if the economy were to take a turn for the worse, disaffection would probably reappear. But for now the order of the day was three-piece Western suits with ties and regimental briefcases rather than headbands and banners. Since the past could not be undone, and since the government that had perpetrated that past was not about to voluntarily step down, the only option was to forget. I don't know how many times during this period I heard Chinese cut off nascent political discussions with ''Let's not get into that! There's no point!'' By abandoning service to the people as the Party's official credo, and by sanctioning the creation of private wealth, Deng administered a powerful antidote to those Chinese who might otherwise have been inclined to confront the government as they had in Tiananmen Square. He also gave Chinese new hope, that after so many years of self-inflicted revolutionary turmoil, the country might now be edging toward greater prosperity and long-term stability, if not political openness.

37

Hints of Political Reform

Wh during the summer of 1992 word began circulating that Deng had been holding a new round of *shenghuohui* with key Party leaders and was calling for officials to take practical steps to help people "emancipate their minds," intellectuals who had felt short-changed by his agenda of economic liberalization allowed themselves to hope that reform might, at last, be on the verge of gaining a political dimension. "Regarding those intellectuals who are engaged in science, technology, and scientific and academic research, they should be allowed to have different value concepts, to believe in socialism and communism or not, and to express their own political and ideological tendencies," Deng was reported as saying. "As long as they do not go too far and violate the Constitution, intentionally challenge and jeopardize laws and decrees, or pursue antagonistic activities against the Party and the People's Government in an organized way, I suggest they be allowed to carry out a certain level of activity, such as debates, exploratory discussions, and exchanges with little or no administrative interference."

The government's attitude toward dissident students in exile also changed. With economic-development plans in high gear, China needed its trained professionals more than ever. Unfortunately, Party-sponsored repression had created a serious brain drain by making many of the more than 150,000 students who had gone abroad for study and work reluctant to return home. "We must rely on science, technology, and education," said Deng on his *nanxun*. "It is hoped that all people studying abroad will return to China. They can all come back no matter what political attitudes they held."

Deng's utterances launched a major government-sponsored public relations campaign to woo back as many hesitant students as possible. To reassure those abroad who still recalled Yuan Mu's characterization of the "contradiction" between the Party and protesters as "antagonistic," and who feared they might not be allowed to leave again if they returned to China, the government promised that citizens with valid passports would henceforth not be required to apply for exit visas in order to reexit the country. And as added bonus incentives for the brightest and best to return, those coming back "to serve the motherland" were not only permitted to bring in duty-free computers, printers, VCRs, and other electronic equipment, but to buy a car tax-free, no small consideration in a country where duties on private vehicles more than doubled their cost.

And there were other signs that seemed to suggest political relaxation. In July 1992, the relatively liberal Politburo Standing Committee member in charge of propaganda, Li Ruihuan, gave a speech that sounded more as if it had been delivered by a New Age California guru than by the propaganda boss of a Communist party. "The establishment of wholesome human relations is a basic requirement in the construction of a socialist ethic," gushed Li. "The cardinal principle for government lies in comforting the people, and the most important task in comforting people is to discern their hardships." Li then took a swipe at those who had fallen "under the influence of 'leftist' ideology" and used the pretext of class struggle to persecute people, thereby "seriously distorting human relations and causing unnecessary tension." That August, when the French paper *Le Figaro* interviewed Li, he became the first leader in some time to publicly link economic and political reform: "The two should go hand in hand, in order to improve and expand democracy, and give the masses greater freedom of speech, participation, and control." When the NCNA chimed in a few days later, it was even more emphatic. "The matter has become clear: The development and the reform of the economic system is strongly calling for a corresponding process of reform of the political system. If reform of the political system drags on for a long time, reform of the economic system will be subject to a bigger restraint."

That same month officials announced that, henceforth, authority to approve publication of several categories of materials—including ancient classics, photo calendars, and nude art!—would be transferred from the hard-line SGPPA to publishers themselves. The impetus behind this move grew more out of the government's urgent need to relieve itself of financial responsibility for debt-ridden state-run publishing houses by helping them find ways to become more profitable and self-sufficient (and better able to compete with the "second channel") than from any desire to promote freedom of expression. However, by allowing publishers to put out girlie calendars, seventeenth-century erotic novels, and books of nude Western art without restriction, officials were also allowing the marketplace to take another giant step into the heartland of state control over the printed word.

By the fall of 1992, other cultural fields also seemed to be undergoing a thaw. Theater, which had been even more moribund than publishing, began cautiously to respond to the warmer political breezes with a spate of new and yeasty productions. In September 1992 the Swiss playwright Friedrich Dürrenmatt's *Romulus the Great*, a tale loaded with allegorical significance about an imperial system on the brink of being overrun by barbarians, corruption, and madness during the waning days of the Roman Empire, opened in Beijing's Capital Theater. In October an even more unlikely production, Manuel Puig's *Kiss of the Spider Woman*, a story of homosexuality and imprisonment, was staged in Beijing. In film, too, there were signs of relaxation. The works of Zhang Yimou, whose movies *Red Sorghum*, *Judou*, and *Raise the Red Lantern* had been banned at home even as they won acclaim abroad, suddenly received official approval. However, when *Beijing Bastards* was released in 1993, it was promptly banned. But it was suggestive of the openness that culture now enjoyed that the film's director, Zhang Yuan, let it be known that his next projects would be even more provocative: a film chronicle of China's burgeoning gay scene and a documentary on "spiritual numbness."

The impression that the increasingly relaxed atmosphere being enjoyed in the economy might migrate into politics was reinforced when a series of high-visibility political prisoners were also released. By the end of 1993 the list included such well-known 1989 protest-movement activists as Bao Zunxin, a former researcher from the Institute of History at the Academy of Social Sciences and a member of Zhao Ziyang's brain trust sentenced to five years; Wang Dan, the Beijing University student leader who led the list of "most wanted" protesters and had been sentenced to four years; and Han Dongfang, leader of the Beijing Autonomous Workers' Federation, held for almost two years without trial. Several prominent members of an earlier generation of prodemocracy-movement activists were also released, including Wang Xizhe, Xu Wenli, and even Wei Jingsheng, who had all received long sentences for their participation in the Democracy Wall Movement. In early 1994 the government released Xiao Bin, who had been arrested for giving an interview to ABC-TV after the June 4 bloodshed and Wang Juntao, who had been given thirteen years as a "black hand" behind the movement.

At the same time, some of the country's best-known political dissidents were also permitted to go abroad. They included Han Dongfang; human rights activist Professor Guo Luoji, who had been suspended from his teaching duties at Nanjing University; editor and political philosopher Wang Ruoshui, who had been fired from the *People's Daily;* and essayist Wang Ruowang, who had been jailed in Shanghai for marching with students in 1989. Optimists tended to view these concessions as important symbolic steps which, when factored in with the growing freedom in the marketplace, were helping to lay the foundations for a society that would ultimately become both more prosperous and more open.

As the Fourteenth Party Congress approached in October 1992, the atmosphere in China was in certain ways reminiscent of the upswing in the last major cycle of liberalization that began around the time of the Thirteenth Party Congress in October 1987. Then, too, the Party leadership (under Zhao Ziyang) had encouraged a speedup in market reforms. However, Zhao had also made an explicit call for political liberalization, something that was distinctly missing when Jiang Zemin addressed the Fourteenth Party Congress. Instead, Jiang incanted Deng's name no less than thirteen times. Calling him "penetrating" and "brilliant," he declared that Deng had shown "tremendous political courage in opening up new paths in socialist construction" and "tremendous theoretical courage in opening up a new realm in Marxism." Jiang even grandiloquently proclaimed the new reforms "a revolution," thereby suggesting that Deng was on a par with Mao as an initiator of revolutionary change. "If we cling to outmoded ideas and remain content with the status quo, we shall accomplish nothing. Poverty is not socialism," said Jiang, paraphrasing Deng's Shenzhen homilies. "We must emancipate our minds . . . and not get bogged down in abstract debates over what is socialist and what is capitalist."

Then, in an effort to make Deng's economic line canon, his supporters rewrote the Party constitution to describe China as having become a "socialist market economy." To underscore how things had changed, the new constitution was altered to read, "the essential nature of socialism is to liberate and develop the productive forces." Nothing of substance was explicitly said, however, of the need for political liberation.

The congress had nonetheless been a masterpiece of behind-the-scenes manipulation that relied heavily on Deng's long-standing ability to build politically viable personal coalitions. Although there had not been a clean sweep of neo-Maoists, the period of ideological ascendancy they had enjoyed since 1989 had, for the moment, been ended. By the time the Congress closed, nearly half the members of the Central Committee had been replaced, including such archconservatives as former Secretariat member Deng Liqun. The reformist ex-mayor of Shanghai, Zhu Rongji, who had been dubbed "China's Gorbachev" and who had already been put in charge of the economy, was elevated to the new seven-member Standing Committee of the Politburo, half of whose members had been dismissed. Hard-liners Wang Renzhi, head of the Central Propaganda Department; Gao Di, editor of the *People's Daily;* He Dongchang, vice-minister in charge of the State Education Commission; and He Jingzhi, acting minister of culture, were all eased from office. Even the hard-line Central Advisory Commission presided over by Chen Yun had been dissolved.

That December the Politburo Standing Committee member in charge of security affairs, Qiao Shi, popped up at a rally commemorating the tenth anniversary of the Chinese Constitution and not only applauded the progress the country was making in differentiating Party and governmental functions, but urged that the "freedom and rights of Chinese citizens as stipulated in the Constitution be guaranteed." Qiao did not go so far as to mention Article 35, which guarantees "freedom of speech, of the press, assembly, association, procession, and demonstration," but after becoming chairman of the National People's Congress three months later, he did declare, "Without democracy and the rule of law, there can be no socialist modernization."

Foreigners living in China also began to notice the changing political climate when the Ministry of State Security and the Foreign Ministry took the unprecedented step of issuing an "internal" circular decreeing that security agents no longer needed to follow foreign reporters everywhere they went. This did not mean that gumshoeing and electronic surveillance would be completely suspended, but it did suggest a new sensitivity to the image of brute authoritarianism that China had been projecting abroad as a result of its often clumsy efforts to intimidate and control foreign journalists. Then in the fall of 1993 just before President and Party chief Jiang Zemin was scheduled to meet with President Bill Clinton in Seattle, Chinese Foreign Minister Qian Qichen announced that while he rejected the notion of "linking" human rights questions to trade, requests from the International Red Cross to visit Chinese political prisoners would receive "positive consideration."

While China was still far from a model of participatory democracy, in certain notable respects society had become more relaxed and open than at any time since "liberation" in 1949. A combination of freedom in the marketplace and response to foreign pressure made it possible for Chinese to buy what they wanted, enjoy private lives, speak more openly, and even to travel abroad more freely than ever before. At the end of 1993 the American ambassador to Beijing, Stapleton Roy, went so far as to say that "the last fifteen years are the best fifteen years in China's modern history" and that the last two years were "the best in terms of prosperity, individual choice, access to outside sources of information, freedom of movement within the country, and stable domestic conditions." The expansion of new fields of openness and the country's new prosperity did much to relieve the sense of despair that had characterized the post–June 4 period.

Whether such signs of relaxation were just so much cosmetic image polishing aimed at enhancing China's chances of assuring renewed MFN status and winning its bid for the 2000 summer Olympic Games or part of an ineluctable trend toward greater political liberalization was still not clear. But even the ambiguity came as a relief, and many Chinese allowed themselves to be soothed by a cautious optimism. Perhaps, they reasoned, if political confrontation with the government could be avoided while Deng's economic reforms took deeper root and the country gathered a new sense of dignity and self-confidence, aspects of a civil society, of which gray culture was a harbinger, might mature and slowly nudge the Party into accepting more openness and political pluralism. The hope of many of those who allowed themselves to be encouraged by such optimism was that since the Party was obviously not about to relinquish political control voluntarily, free markets provided the best available goad toward greater democracy. But few had forgotten that for Deng, development and political stability, not democracy, were the primary goals. He might allow a certain vague promise of political liberalization to be lofted about, but for him the ideal was still authoritarian politics combined with market economics. While there was no doubt by 1994 that life in Chinese society was in many ways becoming increasingly relaxed, there were few signs that the Party was any more prepared to tolerate real challenges to its political hegemony. Each time manifestations of even moderate political opposition arose, the Party moved to suppress then with a familiar thoroughness.

38

Shadows of the Past

W hat optimists tended to overlook was that in everything that happened in China there were such glaring contradictions that Mao Zedong, were he alive, would most certainly have viewed them as "antagonistic." Although the Fourteenth Party Congress in the fall of 1992 seemed to enshrine Deng's reforms as the "new line," Jiang Zemin's work report to delegates read more like a push-me–pull-you tugging in opposite directions than an integrated statement of policy. In effect, the Congress proclaimed that while it was time for a free exchange of goods and services, it was not yet time for a free exchange of ideas and political views. And lest any comrades jump to wrong conclusions and assume that economic license meant political license, the report was filled with warnings against "decadent capitalist and feudal ideologies," "peaceful evolution," and "factors that might lead to unrest and turmoil." China's economic revolution was "not intended to change the nature of our socialist system," Jiang reminded delegates. Nor was the Party about to soften its position on June 4. Instead of referring to the student demonstrations as "political turmoil," a term that had come into common parlance over the past few years, Jiang reverted to the harsher "counterrevolutionary rebellion" used during the crackdown.

In almost every sphere of official policy, there were conflicting scripts. Although Deng appeared to welcome the return of all students "no matter what political attitudes they held," there was one important caveat in the small print. "Those who joined organizations against the Chinese government and engaged in activities that were harmful to the state's security, honor, and interest are welcome to return home to work on condition that they withdraw from the organizations and no longer take part in any activities in violation of the Chinese Constitution or law or in opposition to the Chinese Government," said a State Council circular. All would be forgiven *if* returnees would just check their politics at the door.

Needless to say, some of those wishing to return home were unwilling to abandon their principles. When Gong Xiaoxia, a Harvard University graduate student, tried to return for summer vacation in 1992, he was denied entry. When Lü Jinghua, the BAWF activist who had been forced to leave her daughter behind when she fled after June 4, tried to return home the same year, she was denied entry at the Beijing airport and deported. And when Han Dongfang attempted to go back in August 1993, he was picked up by the PSB after crossing the border, beaten, and expelled to Hong Kong. Then his passport was canceled, leaving him essentially stateless. "Through the performance by this anti-China tool who betrays the nation, we can see the vicious intentions of the international hegemonists who hate China," raged the Beijing-controlled *Wen Wei Po* in Hong Kong. "He [Han] is entirely controlled by Western forces specifically to make chaos in China."

"My home is China," replied Han coolly. "It may take a hundred attempts to get into my country, but that is my intention."

As momentous as the economic changes were, China was still a one-party state. And as reform efforts in the past had repeatedly proven, it would be no easy task for a country as deeply rooted in the traditions of authoritarianism and Big Leader cultism as China to change politically, especially when the ruling leadership viewed such changes not just as a challenge to its power, but as an invitation to disorder. Deng was caught between the two conflicting sets of political purposes that Tiananmen Square symbolically represented: the tradition of broadly based liberal reforms first called for by the May Fourth generation, and the tradition of stubborn conservatism that since the failure of the Hundred Days Reform in 1898 had rejected almost all fundamental change. His solution was to adopt aspects of each side of this contradiction, and to goad one side of society into radical change while leaving the other frozen in place. In this sense he was much more in the tradition of those nineteenth-century reformers who had imagined that China could borrow technology and management techniques from abroad without affecting the existing society's culture and values, or political "essence." Now as then, such an effort depended on something of a split personality. For Deng, the contradiction manifested itself as an attempt to separate politics and economics in a way that led some observers to refer to his experiment as "laissez-faire Stalinism," "Confucian-Leninism," or "gulag capitalism." Such a bastardization might temporarily give the appearance of stability, but it was difficult to imagine how a system with such internal inconsistencies could long contain itself, especially when it was in such a dynamic state of unbalanced change.

In case anyone was inclined to forget the depths of Deng's aversion to political opposition, he dropped constant reminders. For instance, on April 27, 1992, even as he was stumping for accelerated economic reform, the *People's Daily* quoted him as saying that "liberalism and turmoil destroy stability" and that "as soon as elements of turmoil appear, we will not hesitate to use any means whatsoever to eliminate them as quickly as possible." One never had to dig too deeply beneath the surface of the economic boom and propaganda extolling the dawning of a new age of "opening up" to find the old, darker order of things. Even as calls to "emancipate thinking" were being trumpeted, those small but stubborn underground networks of dissidents that periodically managed to agitate for greater political pluralism continued to be arrested. The Liberal Democratic Party of China (LDP) was one such a group. It had been founded in 1981, managed to survive in various guises since, and had periodically issued communiqués to the foreign press in which it challenged the government. On March 18, 1992, just before the National People's Congress convened, the LDP issued a statement demanding that the government lift the press blackout on opposition political activity, cease persecuting those with dissenting political views, and release all political prisoners. In the view of LDP leaders it was futile to try to maintain "social stability" by "upholding dictatorship" because it was "unreasonable to pursue economic reform while enforcing totalitarian politics."

That May another group, known as the China Progressive Alliance, was reported by Asia Watch to have convened a secret congress in Beijing at which delegates called for vigorous political reform. Although the alliance eschewed what it called "large-scale social confrontations," it remained committed to an underground struggle in order to become "a democratic, strong, independent national organization" able to help "liberate the nation and the people" from having to live under "dictatorship, autocracy, corruption, and ossification."

In the context of the political silence that seemed to surround the economic boom, such rhetoric was jolting. Although it was impossible to know how widespread or firmly established these and other underground groups were, the fact that they existed at all was a reminder that not everyone in China had been silenced by the crackdown or bought off by the opportunity to become wealthy. And the way such groups continued to be relentlessly hunted down by the PSB signified the Party's ongoing concern. Leaders had not forgotten that it was from just such seemingly insignificant beginnings that the 1989 movement had sprung.

During the first few months of 1992 at least twenty intellectuals and workers who had participated in the 1989 protest movement were belatedly brought to trial. For instance, in February Zhai Weimin, a student at the Beijing Institute of Economics who was number six on the government's "most wanted" list and who had worked since with a clandestine organization known as the Democratic Front for the Salvation of China, was also given three and a half years for "counterrevolutionary propaganda and incitement."

In the middle of May 1992, the Beijing office of the *Washington Post* was unexpectedly raided and a young journalist Bai Weiji from the Overseas Edition of the *People's Daily* (whom Bureau Chief Lena Sun had known years earlier as a student at Beida) was arrested, charged with "leaking state secrets," and sentenced to ten years. Because this incident involved a large American daily, it made headlines around the world. But other incidents involving Chinese alone rarely attracted such attention, and thus the perception remained widespread that China was becoming a society of industrious merchants who cared little about anything but business.

That June, Liao Jia'an and Wang Shengli—two philosophy graduate students at People's University who had been publishing a student journal called *Everyone* that included articles on sensitive topics such as the massive Three Gorges Dam across the Yangtze River, foreign policy, and politics—were belatedly arrested by police for hanging protest banners out Beida dorm windows in May 1991 and for authoring handbills calling on students to wear black arm bands and white shirts as a memorial gesture on June 4. To assure that they would not organize commemorative events on June 4, 1992, several of Han Dongfang's BAWF colleagues, who had already spent time in prison, were again detained. And that July, Bao Tong, a senior official and aide to Zhao Ziyang was finally sentenced to seven years in prison for his role in the 1989 demonstrations.

During 1993, even as some long-imprisoned religious leaders were released, other Christian activists found themselves being harassed, detained, and imprisoned. And in the fall of 1993 two journalists, Xi

Yang, a reporter for Hong Kong's *Ming Pao*, and Gao Yu, the former deputy chief editor of *Economics Weekly*, who was about to leave for New York to attend Columbia University's Graduate School of Journalism, were accused of "stealing state secrets" and detained. Xi was later given a twelve-year sentence and Gao Yu was sentenced to eight years. At the same time NCNA editor Wu Shishen was sentenced to life in prison for leaking an advanced copy of Party Chief Jiang Zemin's Report to the Fourteenth Party Congress to the Hong Kong Press.

By the end of 1993, there was no sign of relaxation in government control over public expression and assembly. In November, eleven intellectuals in Beijing, Shanghai, and Wuhan who had circulated a "Peace Charter" (modeled on Czechoslovakia's Charter 77) calling for a dialogue on democratic political change were harassed by police, with three being arrested. These were just a few of the myriad Chinese who had stuck to their guns and were also harassed, detained, and sentenced in a strange counterpoint to the economic boom. Sometimes it seemed as if Chinese and foreigners alike had become so accustomed to such detentions and arrests that, far from being viewed as a particularly alarming state of affairs, they had come to be accepted as almost normal.

Nowhere in China was the ongoing political repression more severe than in Tibet, where followers of a highly nationalistic Tibetan independence movement continued to foment opposition to Chinese occupation and to be arrested in larger numbers. The profusion of privately run karaoke bars, clothing shops, video-game parlors, pool halls, and Chinese restaurants that proliferated as thousands of Hans flooded into Lhasa to make their fortunes was a deceptive veneer behind which deep anti-Chinese, pro–Dalai Lama sentiments continued to seethe. On May 24, 1993, one day after China celebrated the forty-second anniversary of the "peaceful liberation of Tibet" and shortly after several dissident Tibetans unsuccessfully sought to hand over information on political prisoners to a delegation of ambassadors visiting from the European Community, hundreds of Tibetan demonstrators took to the streets and battled with police. It was the worst public violence in Lhasa since martial law had been declared in 1989, just before the Tiananmen demonstrations erupted in Beijing. Among the more than 150 arrested was a Lhasa Travel Service employee named Gendun Rinchen who had served as a guide for such well-known foreigners as Harrison Ford, and whose arrest for "stealing state secrets," a crime punishable by death, generated a good deal of overseas publicity. Although Rinchen himself was ultimately released, Asia Watch reported that "the proportion of 'counter-revolutionaries' to common criminals in Tibetan jails today is almost twenty-one times higher than in China proper." When the U.S. State Department's annual human rights report on China came out in early 1994, it found that China's record "fell far short of internationally accepted norms as it continued to repress domestic critics and failed to control abuses by its own security forces." The Beijing government's fear that dissent or even pluralism would lead to instability was expressed by one of China's delegates to the U.N., Wang Guangya: "A tumultuous China would not only mean disaster to the Chinese people but would also have grave repercussions for Asia's stability, as well as for the whole world."

Such ongoing suppression of political dissent was only one of many dark shadows lurking behind the facade of Asia's newest economic miracle, and it caused a small group of Chinese, especially those intellectuals and professionals not engaged in business, to question whether economic growth alone would be enough to transform China into a society capable of peacefully mediating its own conflicts. Like Wei Jingsheng, who had been warned by the PSB not to meet with foreign journalists and forbidden by the PSB to publish anything after being released from prison, such intellectuals viewed democratization as an essential "fifth modernization" which, far from being a catalyst for disorder, would provide a safety valve for the inevitable buildup of new political pressures caused by the arbitrary exercise of state power.

"Now people look at the former USSR or Eastern Europe and they think that if democracy came to China it would mean that the country would split up," the well-known historian of science and translator of Albert Einstein Xu Liangying lamented to China specialist Allison Liu Jernow in 1993. "They prefer the Singapore model—economic success and stability, even if it comes at the price of democracy. But I despise Singapore! It has no freedom, no human rights. I don't want that for China! . . . The present compared to June 4 is worse in absolutely every way, except economically. Before we could air our views, now we are silent." Then seeming to relent a little, Xu added, "It's only natural that the growth of the middle class will be advantageous for democracy, but China also needs an 'Enlightenment.' " China may have been economically booming, but as Xu, in whose sitting room hang a poster of Einstein and his well-known quote "Great spirits have always encountered violent opposition from mediocre minds," pointed out, there were few reasons to be heartened by China's state of intellectual and cultural "enlightenment."

As Chen Kaige, the Chinese film director whose *Farewell My Concubine* won the 1993 Cannes Film Festival's Palme d'Or prize, succinctly put it, "Now there is economic reform going on in China with people having more chances to make money, [but] the point is: What kind of people are we going to be with a lot of money?"

When I raised the same question with writer and critic Wu Liang in Shanghai, he shook his head disparagingly and replied, "People are so excited and optimistic about the 'economic miracle,' but what I see is all business and no culture. The suffocation of culture is coming directly from blind worship of economic development. Here we have this huge city, but where are its great museums, concert halls, galleries, and bookstores? They are practically all gone."

With materialism the new standard of success, corruption–cum–self-aggrandizement running rampant, the old values of hard struggle and sacrifice sneered at and supplanted by unalloyed greed, state subsidies for everything from publishing houses to art troupes being slashed, and low-brow commercial pop culture rushing in to fill the vacuum, China did seem to be losing not only its intellectual, but also its spiritual soul. To resist what the NCNA unabashedly called a "cultural desert," some officials in Guangdong tried to impose a 3 percent vulgarity tax on bars, karaoke clubs, and dance halls in order to create a special fund to support "serious" art. But what the government really feared was not losing its culture or even its soul, but its political power. And while unsuppressed democratic opposition was an obvious danger, as the middle of the decade neared, Party leaders began looking with equal apprehension toward the social dislocation their own economic boom had begun to create.

While some Chinese were becoming astoundingly prosperous, others stuck on minuscule pensions and fixed incomes faced near dispossession. Where China was once a society that made social equality its raison d'être, it was now becoming highly stratified, and this social stratification was giving rise to a panoply of new and intractable problems. Millions of workers were still employed in unprofitable state enterprises. Since it was politically too dangerous to bankrupt them all, turn them into joint-stock companies, or sell them to foreigners, the government was still left with no choice but to begin reducing their bloated workforces.

Under the old system of centralized planning, once a worker was assigned a state job, he was guaranteed lifetime employment. But Deng's *nanxun* sent a signal that it was now permissible for managers to start firing excess or unproductive workers, who by some estimates comprised 30 percent of the total workforce. By mid-1992 the central government announced that over the next few years it intended to lay off a quarter of its 34 million employees. At year's end, the China National Coal Corporation, which had already laid off 100,000 of its

3 million workers, announced that in 1993 it would let another 100,000 go, and then continue the layoffs until one-sixth of its labor force was pared away.

While such layoffs—which government propagandists tried to prettify with the euphemism *youhua laodong zuhe* (optimizing the composition of the workforce)—made business sense, they enraged workers. The 1989 student rebellion had been disturbing enough to the Party, but the thought that the proletarian vanguard of the Revolution might rise up against the Party after being laid off was even more unsettling. It was in no small measure fear of worker unrest that finally caused the government to begin planning a new system of national social insurance designed to give dispossessed workers something to fall back on.

As layoffs and plant closures increased in 1992–93, and as money-losing enterprises halted wage hikes and bonuses, the country buzzed with stories about disgruntled workers retaliating against management and even sabotaging production lines. An employee who had been dismissed for incompetence by a reform-minded bank manager was reported to have firebombed his boss's house, severely wounding his wife and two children. A driver let go from a toothpaste factory that had adopted Western management techniques was reputed to have run over his boss and killed him. And a woman at a Tianjin watch factory was rumored to have immolated herself in protest when several thousand of her coworkers were laid off.

But the crisis was not just a matter of angry individuals taking matters into their own hands. Throughout 1992 and 1993, labor disputes led to thousands of work stoppages and wildcat strikes across the country. Disaffection even spread to some foreign-owned industries. By 1993 some dozen Korean- and Japanese-owned plants had been disrupted by wildcat strikes over poor work conditions. And what was even more threatening from the perspective of the government was that labor activists were again linking up in an organized fashion with intellectuals through such new de facto groups as the Association for the Protection of Labor Rights.

A sore spot for disgruntled workers was their inability to organize their own unions, the very kind of labor organizations for which Han Dongfang had been calling. Such reports made the Party nervous enough to issue a classified document ordering local senior officials to use force at the first signs of worker unrest. "Security work should be strengthened at factories, oil fields, mines, and other key state projects to prevent people with ulterior motives from stirring workers up to riot," it said. As China's chief of the General Staff, Chi Haotian, candidly told the NCNA, "The quicker the pace of reform, the greater the need for a safe and stable environment that is partly based on national defense.'' The lessons of Tiananmen Square had evidently been well learned.

Even for state workers not threatened with layoffs, the future did not appear rosy. Rising prices were drastically reducing the buying power of fixed incomes and it was impossible for money-losing enterprises to justify bonuses large enough to keep pace with inflation. According to official statistics, during the first half of l993, retail price inflation was up 20 percent in urban areas and up 16 percent nationwide, approaching the 1989 level of 25 percent. With a GNP growth rate of almost 13 percent—more than twice the original government forecast—the economy was dangerously overheated and threatening to spin out of control. As confidence in China's currency declined, some began engaging in panic buying. By July 1993, Chinese trying to hedge had driven gold sales up 27 percent over the previous year and millions were buying ''red slips,'' junk-bond–like issues in fly-by-night funds set up by individual companies promising interest rates as high as 40 percent annually as a way of beating the inflation. At the same time, Deng's supporters in Beijing knew that the political costs of tightening credit and cooling down economic growth—if, in fact, the central government still had enough control do so—might be even higher. Not only could such measures put millions out of work and frustrate the rapidly rising expectations of millions more who were eagerly anticipating entrance into China's new consumer class, but they might even derail the whole reform movement. For those who had forgotten how the last bout of high inflation ended, Chen Yun reminded them. ''The main cause of the 1989 political unrest was an overheated and derailed economy, which resulted in unbearable inflation,'' he said.

Whereas, before 1979, all Chinese had been rooted firmly either in rural People's Communes or in urban state-run enterprises by their household registrations, now the country was awash in a new underclass of some 100 million migrant workers and peasants known as the *liudong renkou* (floating population) who drifted around the country in search of pickup work. They occupied one of the bottom rungs of China's new socioeconomic ladder, the only class below them being destitute peasants in the poorest regions of the country and the growing numbers of beggars and homeless who had been chronicled by Jia Lusheng. It was a far cry from the idealized society that Mao's onetime successor, Liu Shaoqi, envisioned when he said in 1939, ''In such a world there will be no exploiters, oppressors, landlords, capitalists, imperialists, or fascists. There will be no oppressed and exploited people, no darkness, ignorance, or backwardness.''

By 1994, China was in rapid flux; even though it was far more prosperous, it was also far less stable than at any time during the previous four decades with the exception of the Cultural Revolution. Not only did the enormous number of contract and pieceworkers make society extremely vulnerable to even relatively small economic perturbations, but rates for serious crimes increased dramatically, up over 23% in 1993. Gangs and hoodlums operated with impunity. Thefts and robberies were increasingly common, often perpetrated by criminals bold enough to dress up in stolen police uniforms. (One official investigation conducted in Zhengzhou reported that of thirty-seven uniformed people surveyed, only seven turned out to actually be police!) Long-distance buses and trains were regularly held up by *chefei luba* (highwaymen) who could always count on a bountiful harvest because with bank checking accounts still uncommon, merchants had to travel with large amounts of cash. Theft and rape by bandits became so commonplace on the Trans-Siberian Railway that after a gang brandishing guns, knives, and axes took over a whole train in the spring of 1993 (even threatening to hack off the fingers of passengers who resisted surrendering rings) the PSB launched an extensive raid, arresting over seventy. Drug trafficking and use was so widespread that between 1991 and the middle of 1993 police claimed to have arrested 14,000 dealers and to have executed many of them. In May 1993, Central People's Radio was reporting that nearly a quarter million *yeji* (wild chickens) had been picked up during the previous year—a number they conservatively estimated to be only 20 to 30 percent of the total number of prostitutes in China. Pearl River Delta "barbershops" staffed with young girls for hire and hotels filled with cellular-phone–toting pimps servicing clients from Taiwan and Hong Kong who arrived on hydrofoils by the thousands in search of cheap, AIDS-free sex were ubiquitous. So lucrative was the Chinese flesh trade that even Russian women were stampeding to get in on it. Gambling at underground casinos led by crime syndicates and protected by government cadres on the take had become so commonplace that Shenzhen Police Chief Liang Dejun despairingly characterized it as an "issue of ultra-importance." And because the bribing of bureaucrats had become rife, such abuses went largely uncontrolled by the government. Ironically, it was easier to suppress political dissidents than dangerous criminals.

By the fall of 1993 unrest in the countryside also reached a danger point as cash-strapped local officials were unable to pay teachers and were forced to give farmers IOUs for grain they were obligated to sell at fixed prices to the state. In fact, the government was having such cash-flow problems—in 1993 China's budget deficit rose to $20.5 billion yuan ($2.4 billion), with a projected shortfall of 66.9 billion yuan ($8 billion) for 1994—that many rural post offices were also forced to issue IOUs to peasants receiving remittances in the form of postal money orders from relatives working in the more prosperous coastal areas. Needless to say, this de facto system of involuntary loans to the government did not go down well among the peasantry, whose standard of living was already substantially below that of city dwellers. By 1993 the average annual income of an urban resident was $365, while that of rural peasants was still only $140. And if this were not enough, scores of different taxes, corvées, tithes, and fees (including such levies as "movie-watching fees," "education taxes," "rodent extermination," "family planning," "toilet improvement fees," "land registry taxes," and "social stability tithes") were arbitrarily assessed by local officials on angry rural residents. It sometimes seemed as if the Communists were turning into carbon copies of their Nationalist precursors, who had themselves lost power by forfeiting the support of the peasantry. It was hardly surprising that in some localities a number of protorebellions soon sprung up. In June 1993 after a special road construction fee had been levied on peasants in Sichuan Province's Renshou County, thousands attacked government offices. That same month Deng was quoted as saying that "the peasants' burden has already passed the limits of their endurance." By summer even the *Beijing Review* was warning of the "alarming rate of deterioration in agricultural development."

Next to unemployment, inflation, and rural instability, perhaps the gravest social problem was official corruption. By 1994 it was almost impossible to do anything without using influence, presenting gifts, dispensing favors, or proffering bribes. With official position being regularly used as another means to riches, scandals—some of them grand in scale—erupted with increasing frequency. In June 1993, for example, it was revealed that corrupt officials from one branch of the Agricultural Bank of China had issued $10 billion worth of phony letters of credit. And Shen Taifu, the manager of the Great Wall Machinery and Electronics Scientific and Technological Industry Company, had made his contribution to "building socialism with Chinese characteristics" by duping some 100,000 investors into buying 1 billion yuan ($172 million) worth of high-yield bonds with an advertised annual interest rate of 24 percent. Instead of supporting research into new kinds of power generation as promised, however, the money was squandered on high living and luxurious offices. When this house of financial cards finally collapsed, more than a hundred other officials were detained and Shen was seized trying to flee China on a phony passport. "You can't get a Chinese person to do anything these days without providing a very major incentive," Baker & McKenzie law partner Eugene Theroux told the *National Journal.* "Corruption has reached very serious proportions in China. It's pervasive and demoralizing."

From a long-term perspective, the darkest side of this economic miracle was probably the exploitation of China's natural resources and the degradation of its environment. Traveling across the country in the seventies and early eighties, one often saw stacks belching clouds of bituminoid black smoke into the air and outfall pipes spilling untreated waste into waterways. Nonetheless, in most cities it was still possible to see the blue sky, and while rivers and harbors were far from pristine, the relatively undeveloped state of Chinese industry miligated against terminal pollution. China's proletarian politics and its Maoist vilification of material consumption turned out to have provided an inadvertent form of environmental protection. But now that everyone was answering Deng's call to "modernize," and going about it with the same unquestioning hell-bent energy with which they had once answered Mao's call to "make revolution," Mother Nature—which had not been particularly robust in China for millennia—was in serious peril. Leading the fall were the thousands of "township industries" whose proliferation was almost impossible for the central government to control.

As development surged, one saw signs of advanced environmental degradation almost anywhere one looked. In Guangdong, where only six of the province's twenty largest cities had any waste-water treatment facilities, inland waterways were foul with effluent; the Yangtze River, where the world's largest hydroelectric dam was planned, had become so industrially polluted that its rare fresh-water dolphin was almost extinct. In Manchuria and the foothills of the Himalayas where forests had been clear-cut of old growth, whole mountainsides had begun to wash away. Grasslands in Qinghai Province and Mongolia were so overgrazed and compacted by too many animals that they looked like putting greens. In suburban areas new factories and industrial-development zones not only gobbled up natural resources and polluted the surrounding air and water, but devoured large amounts of scarce arable land as well. By 1993 approximately 4 million acres of cropland had been consumed by such development, forcing some 16 million peasants out of agriculture. At the same time, the rapidly growing use of chemical fertilizers was further depleting already exhausted soils of tilth and helping reduce the country's annual grain harvest by approximately 3 billion kilograms.

But it was urban environments, each one marching down its own unique path to ecological ruin, that were most obviously being degraded. In the ancient city of Wuxi, the Grand Canal had become so befouled by chemicals that it looked more like an industrial-waste-treatment lagoon than a waterway; in Xining, state-owned stores were helping deplete stocks of rare wildlife by paying premium prices for such prize traditional medicaments as snow leopard bones, Tibetan brown bear paws, and blue bharal sheep horns; in Shanxi, cement plants emitted so much ash that workshop roofs appeared to be covered with gray snow; in Sichuan Province, tourists and loggers were threatening the habitat of China's last few pandas; in Beijing where skies were once renowned for their azure blueness, one could rarely see the sun through the pall of automotive smog from traffic jams of vehicles still operating on leaded fuel without any emission controls; in Liaoning, whole cities had become invisible from space satellites because of coal-burning factories; and in Dalian, the once pellucid green harbor had turned an inky blue-black from industrial waste.

By 1991, China was the world's largest user of coal, consuming over 1 billion tons a year and emitting over 16 million metric tons of ash (about 14 percent of the world's total) and over 15 million tons of sulphur dioxide (about 10 percent of the world's total), which caused acid rain as far away as Russia and Korea. Factories were annually discharging some 25 billion tons of untreated industrial waste, seriously polluting over 80 percent of the country's surface waters and 40 percent of urban drinking water.

Each year's environmental statistics were more disturbing than the last's. Although the central government had set up numerous bureaus and promulgated endless regulations—including a five-year plan to reduce pollution announced by the National Environmental Protection Agency in February 1994—the rapid slide toward ecological collapse continued because it was in so many people's short-term interest to allow it. Since the central government was so concerned with regaining popular approval by raising the level of material consumption, it was loath to impede the economic boom, much less to alienate increasingly powerful and boosterish regional governments—trying to win new industries for their regions—by enforcing environmental controls from above on local officials profiting from development. And the fact that living standards were rising made urban dwellers more indulgent about industrial pollution than they might otherwise have been. But even if a citizens' group had wanted to protest, government prohibitions against organized opposition made it virtually impossible to do so. When environmental hazards became so extreme as to directly menace life and property, ordinary people were left with no alternative but to take matters into their own hands, sometimes violently.

One such incident occurred in August 1993. After several months of official inaction against the Lanquan Chemical Factory's fouling of the waters of the Yellow River near Lanzhou, Gansu Province, with brightly colored, toxic acid wastes, workers from State Factory No. 471 (once a nuclear-materials plant) armed themselves with clubs, pitchforks, and spades and attacked the upstream plant in an effort to force it to halt production. Before the incident was over, two people were dead, scores wounded, and the provincial governor had been forced to resign. Such frustration with environmental decline was far from rare. A 1992 survey of the residents of Tianjin, which had itself created a highly successful new Economic Technological Development Area, found that 67.5 percent of respondents were "dissatisfied with China's current environmental situation."

By 1993 a handful of writers such as Dai Qing had begun to speak out, and several citizen environmental groups like the Beijing-based Friends of Nature were struggling to find a way to organize against abuses. But with so many constraints against a free press and the formation of nongovernmental organizations, these incipient groups made little headway. As Zhou Guangzhao, head of the Chinese Academy of Sciences, told Patrick Tyler in a classic bit of understatement, "China as a whole is weak in ecological stability, and society has not realized the seriousness of the problem." James Williams, a specialist in Chinese science and environmental studies at the University of California, Berkeley, put the matter more aptly. "The Chinese Government probably could not enforce environmental regulations even if it wanted to because they contradict short term economic growth interests, which, with 1989 still in their minds, remain a powerful motivation for leaders to ignore environmental problems," wrote Williams in an unpublished paper. And deprived of the kind of democratization that would allow a vox populi to ring the alarm and force the government to pay attention, it did not seem likely that environmental problems in China would soon receive the kind of attention desperately needed to mitigate their harmful effects.

As the country's economy continued its pell-mell pace into 1994, there was so much money being made that Chinese and foreign businessmen alike found it increasingly difficult to integrate environmental, cultural, political, and moral issues into the China equation. A few isolated voices within China joined dissidents in exile to urge the

United States to continue pressuring the Chinese government to halt political arrests and torture in prisons by retaining conditions on China's MFN status. "Without the annual review of most-favored-nation status, the Chinese government's behavior in the past four years would have been far worse," wrote Fang Lizhi from America, where he was now teaching physics at the University of Arizona.

39

Cycles of Weirdness

China's penchant for trying to reform a part of the existing system while clinging with stubborn conservatism to other parts echoed back to the waning years of the Qing Dynasty in the nineteenth century when reform-minded officials lobbied to adopt Western technology while maintaining the structural integrity and spirit of the old Confucian state. "Self-strengtheners," as they were known, advocated a policy of *zhongxue weiti, xixue weiyong* (use Chinese learning to support things pertaining to essence, and use Western learning to support things pertaining to function). It was as neatly divided a dichotomy as Deng's formula of borrowing capitalist techniques to reform the economy while maintaining China's Leninist system in matters of essential politics. The only problem with the equation, as Qing officials had discovered, was that reform had a way of refusing to be corralled within such a clearly defined perimeter. As China's whole *ancien régime* began crumbling, many early "self-strengtheners" ended up recoiling from their advocacy of reform to become deeply conservative. Although more determined than most of his precursors, Deng, too, waxed hot and cold on the scope of reform and the pace at which it should be pushed forward, and over time this ambivalence helped create a pattern of repetitive epicycles. The seventy-five-year-old exiled editor of the *New Observer,* Ge Yang, liked to recite a ditty spoofing these cycles. "Once things come alive, they fall into chaos.

Once they fall into chaos, the government tightens up. Once the government tightens up, everything dies. Once everything dies, the government loosens up again.''

What drove this unique dialectic in circles was not just the unresolved tension between reformers and hard-liners, but a deeper tension between the needs of the Leninist state and its dependence on expanding markets. While the hard-liners had been weakened as a bloc by Deng's manipulations at the Fourteenth Party Congress, they had not vanished any more than had China's age-old penchant for authoritarianism. After four decades of revolution, China still found itself relying on one larger-than-life leader rather than on a formal political system to mediate between warring political factions and contradictory interests. This particular Big Leader seemed convinced that economic development could somehow be quarantined from the country's existing political system. However, others felt that this presumption was problematic at best. For all their paranoia and myopia, this was one crucial cause-and-effect relationship that the hard-liners understood. After all, twice in recent memory economic reform and "opening up to the outside world" had, in fact, led to major political protest movements, and then crackdowns. By lurching from one extreme to another, then trying to settle somewhere in the middle, Deng may have imagined that in some novel way he was attaining the golden mean. But even as he was solving certain fundamental problems by economic growth, he was generating new and grave contradictions that would ultimately have to be resolved lest they lead China into yet another confrontation with itself that was even more disruptive than 1989.

"Cycles are not simply the product of Deng's reforms, but are the unavoidable consequence of the inner logic of the way things are set up in China's dictatorial political system," writer Wang Ruowang told me in 1992 after emerging from sixteen months of detention. "First the Party feels a need for opening up to invigorate the economy, then there is protest, then crackdown, then arrest and imprisonment, then a conservative interlude, and then, because the same need to invigorate the economy is recurrent, things start to open up again, and the process begins all over. We writers have started to call these patterns 'cycles of weirdness.' They may take two, three, or four years, but the cycle always reappears, and they will continue to reappear until the Party collapses.''

But there were some things that had undergone changes profound enough to influence this pattern of cycles. Having irrevocably joined the world market system, China was no longer an autarky and thus no longer able to isolate itself as before. For the first time since 1949, the outside world had economic, diplomatic, and strategic levers at its disposal to influence the course of its economic and political development. And while China had begun to generate real wealth which gave its burgeoning middle class more independence than ever, prosperity also gave it new reasons not to rock the boat, even to forget the May Fourth Movement's dreams of a more democratic society, which had found reexpression in Tiananmen Square in 1989. However, by trading the right to rule for the right to make money, this incipient middle class had struck a Faustian bargain with the Party. As long as the leadership was willing to modify its Stalinism and to maintain enough economic liberalization to allow people to go about their private lives, many Chinese seemed willing to forgo immediate confrontation over public politics. In fact, some who had been critical of the Party in 1989 now expressed real pride in their country's unanticipated economic accomplishments. Even many intellectuals who had once prided themselves on being "the conscience of society" were now willing to default and *xiahai*.

"I was very impressed by what I saw in Beijing this summer," a recent Ph.D. from MIT named Charles Zhang told me when I spoke with him in the fall of 1993 about his first trip home since 1986. "It made me proud to see what had happened. Yes, I was opposed to what the government did in 1989, but to keep this stability, maybe we have to put democracy on hold and wait while the economy develops." Even though he had received a degree in physics, Zhang was not planning to go into scientific research. What he had seen at home— where glistening skyscrapers were now rising in almost every big city, and where approximately three-quarters of all city residents owned color televisions and washing machines, and where a Chinese Academy of Social Science index system was listing twenty-four coastal cities as "well-off" seven years ahead of the previous target date of the year 2000 set by Deng in 1978—all made Zhang want to *xiahai*, and plunge into business in China himself along with everyone else.

Deng's new policies had, in essence, created two separate Chinas that now existed in parallel. On the one hand there was the new China of entrepreneurs with briefcases and businessmen with Italian suits; of neon night clubs and five-star hotels; and of Mercedes Benzes equipped with cellular phones. But just behind this impressive facade was the old China of failing state-owned factories filled with angry workers and belching pollution out over the landscape; of poor peasants in poverty-stricken rural areas dreaming of making it to the cities; of prisons where murderers and democracy activists were incarcerated together; of the Red Army whose loyalties were to feudal leaders not to elected officials; and of veteran revolutionaries weaned on Marxist-Leninist-Maoist doctrine who could conceive of no path to stability save political repression.

Nowhere was the dualism of Deng's policies rendered with greater metaphoric starkness than in his unique conception of the SEZs and his stratagem for the reversion of Hong Kong to China in 1997. In both cases, he proposed that even though China was a single country it should play host to two different political and economic systems. Missing from such a binary view was something that both Marx and Mao had keenly understood—the wholism of societies and the ultimate antagonism of opposites. As Marx had pointed out, economics has an ineluctable way of determining politics. If individual initiative was to be allowed in business, why not in politics? If SEZs could relate freely to the outside world, why not the rest of China? If Hong Kong could be allowed to remain politically autonomous, why not Tibet, or even Shanghai, for that matter? If merchants selling clothing and appliances were able to enjoy free markets, why not book kings and satellite-dish salesmen? And if artists and musicians were to be allowed a new quotient of independence and freedom, why not political activists advocating freedom of speech and workers organizing independent labor unions?

In March 1993 Deng's latest "heir apparent," Party General Secretary Jiang Zemin, was also appointed president. Whether Jiang would be able to preside over the contradiction of socialism coexisting with capitalism as well as Deng had was far from certain. It was difficult to see how he, Zhu Rongji, or Li Peng, whom the official press now tirelessly described as "the core leadership," would be able to continue Deng's balancing act, staying in power and keeping China from tilting irrevocably into the hands of either zealous reformers or conservative hard-liners. In trying to be both an economic reformer and a political Leninist, Deng sometimes seemed like a bigamist with two wives and two separate families whom he managed to placate only by dint of his uncanny skill at knowing when to switch attentions from one to the other. The real trick, of course, was to keep them apart, a very different enterprise from resolving the underlying contradictions that kept China revolving through one epicycle of *fang* (loosening up) and *shou* (tightening down) after another.

Hard-line economic planner Chen Yun used to describe China's economy-in-the-throes-of-reform as being like a capitalist bird growing within the confinement of a socialist cage. By 1994 this capitalist bird had grown so large that it had not only fractured its socialist cage, but was threatening to rupture the entire Leninist political structure as

well. No one, Deng included, seemed to know how it might be confined again, much less what this formerly caged bird might turn into as
it kept growing. But given China's history, it seemed more than likely
that it would only be a matter of time before a new crisis between this
rapidly mutating avian upstart and the old political structure erupted.
"Until the Chinese people have an opportunity to choose their own
leaders in free elections and stable democratic institutions start to be
constructed," predicted Zhang Weiguo, "China will remain vulnerable to the quixotic whims of Party ideologues and to cycles of spontaneous social unrest."

In fact, by the middle of 1994, there had begun to be new signs
of open political dissent. In early March, Wang Dan, who had continued to speak out, was temporarily detained. After the workers'
group the Association for the Protection of Labor Rights was announced, lawyer Yuan Hongbing, who had edited the *Tide of History*, and Zhou Guoqiang, who had helped Han Dongfang file a
lawsuit against the Chinese government, were arrested. A short while
later a group of seven Beijing intellectuals, including Xu Liangying,
publicly petitioned the National People's Congress to release all political prisoners. "We appeal to the authorities to bravely end our
country's history of punishing people for ideology, speech and writing, and release all those imprisoned because of the ideology and
free expression," proclaimed the petition. "Not everyone in China is
dead," Xu declared after releasing the petition, which represented
the first such public declaration made by well-known intellectuals
since 1989. One of the other signatories was Ding Zilin, a professor
of philosophy who had lost her seventeen-year-old son on June 4.
"We must come out and say something or they can continue to do
whatever they want," she said, explaining why she had risked signing the petition. Also in March two women were arrested while distributing leaflets in front of the Great Hall of the People while the
Congress was in session, and a group of fifty-four Shanghainese
signed another petition calling on the Congress to initiate constitutional amendments that would lead to a multiparty political system,
freedom of expression, and independent labor unions.

That same month, Wei Jingsheng, who had continued to ignore the
government's ban against consorting with foreigners, met with U.S.
Assistant Secretary of State for Human Rights John Shattuck. He had
also brazenly continued to speak out and write against the government.
In one article published in Hong Kong's *Eastern Express*, Wei declared that trying to plead with the Party by using "persuasion and
education" was tantamount to a lamb hoping to lie down safely with

a wolf. "It's not that the wolf doesn't understand reason," he wrote, "but rather that he isn't interested in discussing reason." On April 2, just before U.S. Secretary of State Warren Christopher arrived in Beijing, Wei was again detained. The next day, his Democracy Wall Movement colleague Xu Wenli was also picked up. And two days later, on April 5, a young man was arrested during the Qing Ming festival, when Chinese traditionally attend to the graves of their ancestors, while trying to lay a wreath in front of the Monument to the Martyrs of the People.

Despite this new wave of dissent, if and when another major upheaval came, it seemed just as likely that it would arise over economic as political questions. Worse, from the government's perspective, was that next time disenfranchised workers might unite with intellectuals to create exactly the kind of opposition coalition that Party leaders had so feared in 1989.

The Shenzhen stock market riots had, perhaps, been a hint of things to come. All that it would take to refocus attention on all the contradictions that had been arising was a downturn in the economic miracle. The CIA was warning that China's manic growth and inflation rate were "threatening to spiral out of control." By September 1993 even China's own economic czar, Vice-Premier Zhu Rongji, was using the words "relatively grim" to describe the situation in which his country's overheated economy found itself. "Inflationary pressure has gradually increased, the monetary system has been aggravated, regional disparities in economic growth have developed," he warned. "They demonstrate the real and present dangers of the macroeconomic imbalance that now exist." Despite a rigorous sixteen-point austerity program announced by Zhu that aimed to bring bank lending under control, curb corruption, rein in real estate speculation, and halt construction of luxury hotels, villas, resorts, apartments, and office buildings, by the beginning of 1994 the economy was still threatening to burn itself up with dangerous levels of unplanned growth. The State Statistical Bureau was reporting that during 1993 GNP had grown by 13 percent, gross industrial output by 21 percent with profits up 62 percent, and fixed asset investment by 46 percent. Foreign trade had risen 18.2 percent to $195.72 billion. This boom had been fueled by $27 billion in outside investments, making China the country attracting the largest sum of foreign capital in 1993, and it had spawned some 140,000 foreign-funded enterprises. Moreover, by 1994 tens of thousands of enterprises had adopted some sort of share-holding system; 123 issues were being traded on the Shanghai exchange and 96 on the Shenzhen exchange, turning twenty-five million Chinese into investors. Six Chinese stocks had gone public on Hong Kong's Hang Seng exchange and another four had been listed on the New York Stock Exchange. But at the same time that tremendous new wealth had been created for some, the cost of raw materials had soared, the inflation rate in many major cities had risen to around 25 percent, and for the first time in several years, China had a ballooning trade deficit, with exports up 8 percent and imports up 29 percent.

China, which had almost foundered on political divisions in Tiananmen Square, now seemed to be approaching a different kind of precipice, a crisis that was paradoxically the result of a surfeit rather than a lack of economic energy. Seeming to dismiss Zhu's efforts in the fall of 1993 Deng was reported as saying, "Slow development is not socialism." With this incantation from on high, efforts to modulate China's madcap growth came to a premature halt. In November the Central Committee had announced a new plan to raise state revenues through a revised tax structure (the central government had been receiving only 32 percent of tax revenues, because 90 percent of personal taxes and 50 percent of state enterprise taxes went unpaid); to reform the banking system (judged by Western standards, all thirteen state banks were considered insolvent); and to make the country's ailing state-owned enterprises (which by 1994 were running up almost $6 billion in annual deficits) responsible for their profits and losses by turning them into modern corporations controlled by outside investors and subject to the bankruptcy law. But with such restraints thrown off, a whole new wave of investment and development began to swell, and urban inflation continued to rise.

Because of his advanced age, Deng's supporters felt the need to establish something of a cult of personality around his rule in hopes of transforming his utterances into scripture sacred enough to endure as policies after his death. Official propaganda began referring to Deng as the "helmsman of the country," and, as if he were a commercial product being advertised on TV, his new revolutionary line started to be touted not only as "brilliant," but as "richer, clearer, more perfect, and systematic." Proclaiming the past fourteen years as the most stable and prosperous since the Opium War, an article in the *Beijing Review* declared that "Deng's theory" had "answered the fundamental question of how to build a modern socialist country in China . . . the problem to which Mao, the leading founder of the People's Republic, failed to find an answer."

Deng's hagiography continued apace with publication of the worshipful book *My Father, Deng Xiaoping*, by his daughter Deng Rong, and a third volume of his speeches and conversations with world leaders. Its selections merely highlighted Deng's conviction that only economic development could save China and that dissent was tantamount to turmoil. For instance, just before the spring demonstrations in 1989, he was quoted as telling President George Bush that China "must seize the opportunity to grow rapidly" even though such growth might sometimes be "chaotic and destabilizing." Just after June 4 he told Columbia University physics professor T. D. Lee, "If those people who caused the turmoil [in Tiananmen Square] had won, there would have been civil war . . . and who knows how many would have died."

The question that Deng's tenure as paramount leader raised was whether his strategy of so fearlessly liberating economics while so fearfully suppressing politics would help lead China into a new period of stability and prosperity that might ultimately elide into an era of greater openness and democracy, or whether it would end up creating uncontainable amounts of internal political pressure that would finally blow the country apart and plunge it back into one more cycle of chaos and repression. The answer would determine whether Deng went down in history as a savior whose astute understanding of China's uniqueness allowed him to ease his country into the modern world, or only a visionary manqué whose failure to understand the political dimensions of reform was his tragic flaw. It was a wager of enormous importance because as Singapore's former prime minister, Lee Kuan Yew, declared, "It's not possible to pretend that this [China] is just another big player. This is the biggest player in the history of man." Unlike Singapore's fellow "dragons," whose individual prosperity or poverty have had little individual consequence for Asia or the world as a whole, the fate of China, whatever it is destined to be, will have global significance.

It was possible that through his unique halfway reforms Deng had found the answer to his country's penchant for opening up only to become alarmed at the consequences and then to crack down again. Perhaps by drawing China so irrevocably into the global market, Deng had at last pulled his people free from their age-old tendency toward isolationism, had helped them forget the trauma of Tiananmen Square, and set them off on a new and unprecedented tangent that would break the old pattern of epicycles. That was the dream of many people, anyway. But it was important to temper any such optimism with an awareness of how deep the scars of 1989 were, how rooted most of China's backwardness still was, and how uncongenial both its traditional notions of politics and those set forth by Lenin and Mao were to democracy and the rule of law. By the middle of the nineties only one thing was clear: Because the present one-party system had no way to facilitate orderly succession and was increasingly unable to contain all the conflicts being generated by the powerful economic forces released by Deng's reforms, China needed a new and more institutionalized way to mediate its internal contradictions more urgently than ever.

40

Exile Dreams

To reach the Ranch House restaurant, one exits from the Bayshore Freeway just past San Francisco International Airport at the Redwood City Putnam Lexus dealership, turns left near the Chef Peking Chinese restaurant and the Miracle Auto Body Shop, and then stops in a parking lot where the sound of tractor trailers, trucks, and cars roaring down the freeway is as deafening as a jet plane taking off. As I walked past an outdoor illuminated sign proclaiming "We Welcome Large Party Functions," and stepped inside the Ranch House, Frankie B. and the Wolfman lit into Hank Williams's song "If You've Got the Money, Honey" from a small stage facing a bar overhung with Tiffany lamps. At the same time, a Muzak system in the dining room was blaring out a pop version of "Joy to the World."

Not long after the friend I had come to meet sat down with me for dinner, a booming voice broke through the dueling fields of music and, sounding like a cross between God speaking out of the whirlwind and a voice paging someone over a white courtesy airport telephone, said, "Will Kevin please come to the cash register. Kevin, please come to the cash register right away!" Kevin finished chewing a mouthful of prime rib, stood up, and in almost perfect English said, "If you will please excuse me for a moment."

As the night manager, Kevin was responsible for dealing with customer complaints, mediating disputes between employees, keeping track of receipts, and closing the place down at night—in short, for dealing with all the problems that arise at a large restaurant where the public comes to eat, dance, drink, and all too often drown its sorrows at the bar. In fact, at 2 A.M. the night before, just as he was about to lock the place up, Kevin had discovered a woman passed out in the ladies' room. Considering it part of his job, he revived her, phoned her home, and then waited until her angry husband finally arrived to retrieve her. Although each night brought new headaches, Kevin's authoritative manner and past experience dealing with crises and unruly crowds seemed to be standing him in good stead.

As I had passed the sign out front welcoming "Large Party Functions," it was hard not to smile at the thought of Kevin's new line of work. When I had first seen him, he was wearing a headband, had a bullhorn raised to his lips, and was standing in front of the Monument to the Martyrs of the People in Tiananmen Square blasting the Chinese Communist Party. "Kevin" was none other than student leader Wu'er Kaixi.

Watching him manage this American roadhouse, as revelers gorged themselves on enormous slabs of rare beef, drank mug after mug of beer, and honky-tonked until early morning, made the memory of Wu'er slouched in his pajamas in the Great Hall berating Li Peng seem almost chimerical. During those turbulent days, Wu'er's hair was longer and shaggier, his clothes were rumpled and often soiled, and fasting and sleepless nights had left him drawn and thin. Now he was resplendent in a pressed white shirt and tie, and a pair of stylish slacks, and his hair was neatly trimmed. Instead of the omnipresent bullhorn he had once carried as a badge of his authority, he now had a ring of keys that, among other things, opened the Ranch House's cash drawer. And replacing the gaunt, haggard look of yore, around his face and body there was now a suggestion of corpulence, which was perhaps not surprising given his stewardship over a chop house featuring prime ribs, steaks, and roast chickens garnished with baked potatoes slathered in butter and sour cream.

After several tumultuous years, Wu'er seemed to have settled down, but he had not completely changed. When I asked a provocative question, he still flashed the same naughty, boyish grin and gave the kinds of quick-witted answers for which he had become famous in the Square. At the same time, there was much less an air of braggadocio about him now. By day he was studying for his B.A. at Dominican College of San Rafael, a small Catholic liberal-arts school north of San Francisco. By night he rode herd on a new dominion of busboys, waitresses, fry cooks, cashiers, and bartenders. His no-nonsense mall-ner suggested that he had lost none of the confidence that had made him such an effective student organizer. But he now spoke more quietly and gave orders in a far less peremptory and theatrical manner. His attitude toward China had also undergone a metamorphosis. Whereas after escaping he had called Deng and his allies "bestial fascists," now Wu'er was able to acknowledge that in certain respects, at least, their reforms were a real step forward.

"It's quite amazing, but people in China can actually change their jobs now!" he said after returning to our table. "To be stuck with a lousy government-assigned job and not be able to do what we wanted used to be such a headache. So we exiles must admit that in certain ways the government is making progress. Sure, it is because of our pressure! And sure the level of freedom is still not yet up to our standards! But it is none the less doing many of the very things we demanded in the Square."

The Muzak system had just started murdering "O Little Town of Bethlehem" and the band had erupted into "Good Golly Miss Molly" when Wu'er was paged to the cash register again. When our waitress appeared in his absence with dessert, I could not resist querying her about "Kevin."

"Oh, Kevin's a real good guy," she replied with a uniquely Californian cheerfulness.

"Isn't it strange to find someone with a background like his at a place like this?" I asked.

"I'm not sure what you're talking about," she replied, suddenly eyeing me warily. "I mean, he's just Kevin." Then she tucked her order pad back in her apron pocket, turned and left with a briskness that suggested sudden wariness.

When Wu'er returned, I asked him what the other Ranch House employees thought of working with a person who had been so politically prominent. "Oh no! They don't know whom I am!" he said, laughing and waving the thought away. "The owner of this restaurant is a Chinese friend, and I promised that if he gave me this job I'd keep quiet and wouldn't create any bad publicity." Wu'er smiled beatifically.

When I asked him if he did not often find himself thinking back to Beijing, his friends there, and all that happened in 1989, for a moment he looked wistfully around the restaurant. By then the dining room was empty and only a few stalwarts were still slumped at the bar staring into their drinks. "Yeah," Wu'er finally said, exhaling a long sigh. "Each spring I still feel very depressed, and because I know they understand how I feel, I start calling friends who also escaped. When

June 4 rolls around, I can't help dreaming about Tiananmen Square and being back among my friends." He cradled his chin in his hands for a moment. "Once, I even dreamed that I had secretly returned to my old university in Beijing and started taking classes again. And, do you know what?" Wu'er's face lit up. "It took a whole month before officials discovered that I was there! When they realized it was me, they wanted to kick me out. But then, for some reason they relented and let me stay." He flashed one of his best bad-boy smiles. "And guess what? I started making trouble in Tiananmen Square all over again!"

As Wu'er spoke, my own memories of 1989 flooded back with such vividness that it was hard to believe that the events had happened almost four years before. At the time, the protest movement and the ensuing crackdown had loomed so monumentally large and felt so apocalyptic that it seemed unthinkable that their impact could fade or that China would ever be able to put those events behind it. But the Square had finally been "cleansed" of protesting students and returned to the Party, China had undergone an incredible period of development and change, and now here was Wu'er Kaixi, the *enfant terrible* of that historic movement, sitting before me in a California roadhouse eating prime rib. If nothing else, the scene was living proof that history always moves on, if in strange and unpredictable ways.

"Of course!" Wu'er exclaimed almost indignantly when I asked him if he still wanted to go home again. And what did he want to do? With the same cheeky candor that had made him such an appealing subject for foreign interviewers in the Square, he replied, "I want to go back and do one of two things. Either I want to do something that is really politically meaningful or,"—he grinned and hesitated for a moment—"or I want to become a billionaire!"

So, even here in California, Deng's strategy of rapid economic development had become a powerful antidote to opposition. But how long Chinese would accept having their politics subordinated to the dream of riches, or, at least, a better standard of living was the million-, even the billion-, dollar question.

As I said goodbye to Wu'er that night and walked back out to the roar of the parking lot, it did not seem unlikely that he would end up in business rather than politics. Given the way things were going in China, it was even imaginable that he might someday return home to open a string of prime-rib restaurants. After all, following his release from prison a short while later, fellow protest leader Wang Dan announced to the *Washington Post*'s Lena Sun that, in his view, "the pursuit of wealth is part of the impetus for democracy" because the "emphasis cannot always be on human rights." Then he added, "If I have a chance to go into business, I won't hesitate." To facilitate his entry into the world, and perhaps business, Wang had name cards made up with his electronic pager number at the bottom and, where such cards usually list one's occupation, he printed the words "Free Man." A few months later he was reported to have joined a consortium to buy land in Tianjin with money from overseas Chinese students.

As Wei Jingsheng observed upon emerging from almost fifteen years of solitary confinement, "People long for change, yet they despair of it, so they give up and go into business." For the moment, the Chinese were, indeed, throwing themselves into economics with a recklessness that made it seem as if 1989 had been all but forgotten. Of course, it hadn't been completely forgotten, nor would it ever be forgotten. People's University philosophy professor Ding Zilin, whose seventeen-year-old son, Jiang Jielian, was gunned down at Muxidi as troops closed in on the Square, still struggled against the anguish of her loss by collecting the names of as many of the dead as she could. "As a mother of a victim, there is no way for me to forget these boys and girls and men and women, including my own son, who died in pools of blood," she wrote in an open letter to the 1993 World Conference on Human Rights in Vienna. "I want the people of the world to know that they once lived in this world, that this world once belonged to them, and why and how they disappeared from it." Wu'er still dreamed of the Square and Wang still fasted each June 4 in memory of the dead, a ritual that he insisted he would observe the rest of his life. And yet, in the hurly-burly of new commercial activity that was once again uniting exiles with their homeland, for the moment few people seemed interested in pondering the question of how history would finally embrace the protest movement in which Wu'er, Wang, and Wei had figured so prominently and how it would ultimately influence the mandate of heaven. But if the history of Tiananmen Square taught any lessons at all, it was that China rarely overlooked such epic events for long, especially when they had taken place in this hallowed spot. China's next upheaval might be triggered by economics rather than politics, it might erupt in the provinces rather than Beijing, and it might be led by workers rather than students, but if the past was any guide, sooner or later the aftershocks would reverberate back into "the Square."

Notes on Sources

Newspapers and News Agencies

The *New York Times*, *Washington Post*, *Los Angeles Times*, *Wall Street Journal*, *San Francisco Chronicle*, and *San Francisco Examiner* in the United States; the *Independent*, *Observer*, *Times*, and *Financial Times* in Britain; the *South China Morning Post*, *Standard*, *Ming Pao*, and *Ta Kung Pao* in Hong Kong; and the *China Daily*, the *Shanghai Star*, *People's Daily*, *Guangming Daily*, *Wenhui Daily*, and *Liberation Daily* in China all provided valuable daily information. For English translations of Chinese press and radio broadcasts, I primarily used the U.S. Government's *Daily Report: China*, put out by the Foreign Broadcast Information Service, and the *Summary of World Broadcasts: The Far East—China*, published by the monitoring service of the BBC. I also drew heavily on articles published by Agence France-Press (France), Associated Press (U.S.), Kyodo News Agency (Japan), Reuters (Britain), and the New China News Agency (China).

Periodicals

Those periodicals and scholarly journals that I found invaluable included *Asia Pacific Issues* (U.S.), *Asia Week* (Hong Kong), *Asian Survey* (U.S.), *Australian Journal of Chinese Affairs* (Australia), *Beijing Review* (China), *Changing China* (U.S.), *China Exchange News* (U.S.), *China Focus* (U.S.), *China Forum* (U.S.), *China Information* (Holland), *Inside China Mainland* (Taiwan), *China News Analysis* (Hong Kong), *China Quarterly* (Britain), *China Rights Forum* (U.S.), *China Trade Report* (Hong Kong), *China Update* (U.S.), *Chingbao* (Hong Kong), *East Asian History* (Australia), *Far Eastern Economic Review* (Hong Kong), *Foreign Affairs* (U.S.), *Free China Review* (Taiwan), *Granta* (Britain), *Jiushi Niandai* (Hong Kong), *Minzhu Zhongguo* (U.S.), the *Nation* (U.S.), the *New York Review of Books* (U.S.), *Problems in Communism* (U.S.), *World Policy Journal* (U.S.), *World Politics* (U.S.), *Zhengming* (Hong Kong), and *Zhongguo Zhichun* (U.S.).

Books and Monographs in English

I owe a particularly heavy debt to those works indicated by an asterisk. Since they would not be of interest to nonscholars, I have not listed Chinese-language sources or specific articles from academic journals by title.

Amnesty International, *Political Imprisonment in the PRC* (1978) and *Preliminary Findings on Killings of Unarmed Civilians—Arbitrary Arrests and Summary Executions Since June 3, 1989* (1989)*

Asia Watch, *Repression in China Since June 4, 1989* (1990), *Anthems of Defeat* (1992), and *Detained in China and Tibet: A Directory of Political and Religious Prisoners* (1994)*

Barmé, Geremie, and John Minford, *Seeds of Fire: Chinese Voices of Conscience* (1989)* and Geremie Barmé and Linda Jaivin, *New Ghosts, Old Dreams: Chinese Rebel Voices* (1992)*

Beijing Publishing House, *The Truth About Beijing* (1990)

Black, George, and Robin Munro, *Black Hands of Beijing: Lives of Defiance in China's Democracy Movement* (1993)*

Brook, Timothy, *Quelling the People: The Military Suppression of the Beijing Democracy Movement* (1992)*

Byron, John, and Robert Pack, *The Claws of the Dragon: Kang Sheng—The Evil Genius Behind Mao—and His Legacy of Terror in People's China* (1992)

Che Muqi, *Beijing Turmoil: More Than Meets the Eye* (1992)

Cheng Chu-yuan, *Behind the Tiananmen Massacre: Social, Political, and Economic Ferment in China* (1990)

Ch'i Hsi-cheng, *Politics of Disillusionment: The Chinese Communist Party Under Deng Xiaoping, 1978–1989* (1991)

Chi Hsin, *Deng Xiaoping: A Political Biography* (1978)

Deng Xiaoping, *Selected Works of Deng Xiaoping* and *Fundamental Issues in Present-Day China* (1987)

Des Forges, Roger, et al., *China: The Crisis of 1989, Origins and Implications* (1990)*

Duke, Michael, *The Iron House: A Memoir of the Chinese Democracy Movement and the Tiananmen Massacre* (1990)

Evans, Richard, *Deng Xiaoping and the Making of Modern China* (1994)*

Fang Lizhi and James Williams, eds., *Bringing Down the Great Wall* (1990)

Fathers, Michael, and Andrew Higgins, *Tiananmen: The Rape of Peking* (1989)*

Feigon, Lee, *China Rising: The Meaning of Tiananmen* (1990)

Foreign Languages Press, *The Criminal Law and the Criminal Procedure Law of China* (1984)

Franz, Uli, *Deng Xiaoping* (1988)*

Gellat, Timothy, and the Lawyers Committee for Human Rights, *Criminal Justice with Chinese Characteristics* (1993)*

Goldman, Merle, *Sowing the Seeds of Democracy in China* (1994)*

Han Minzhu and Hua Sheng, eds., *Cries for Democracy: Writings and Speeches from the 1989 Chinese Democracy Movement* (1990)*

Han, Theodore, and John Li, *Tiananmen Square Spring 1989: A Chronology of the Chinese Democracy Movement* (1992)

Hicks, George, ed., *The Broken Mirror: China After Tiananmen* (1990)

Hodder, Rupert, *The Creation of Wealth in China* (1993)

Human Rights in China, *Children of the Dragon* (1990)*

Jakabson, Linda, *Lies in Ink, Truth in Blood* (1990)

Jane's Information Group, *Jane's Special Report: China in Crisis* (1989)

Jenner, W. J. F., *The Tyranny of History: The Roots of China's Crisis* (1992)*

Jernow, Allison Liu, and the Committee to Protect Journalists, *Don't Force Us to Lie: The Struggle of Chinese Journalists in the Reform Era* (1993)*

Jiang Zhifeng, *Countdown to Tiananmen* (1990)

Jones, Andrew, *Like a Knife: Ideology and Genre in Contemporary Chinese Popular Music* (1992)*

Lee, Ta-ling, and John F. Cooper, *Failure of Democracy Movement: Human Rights in the PRC 1988/89* and *Tiananmen Aftermath: Human Rights in the PRC, 1990* (1991)

Li Lu, *Moving the Mountain: My Life in China* (1990)

Link, Perry, *Evening Chats in Beijing* (1992)*

Liu Binyan, *China's Crisis, China's Hope: Essays from an Intellectual in Exile* (1990), *A Higher Kind of Loyalty* (1990), and, with Ruan Ming, *Tell the World: What Happened in China and Why* (1989)

MacFarquar, Roderick, *The Forbidden City* (1981)

Ming Bao, *June Four: A Chronicle of the Chinese Democratic Uprising* (1989)

Mok Chiu Yu and J. Frank Harrison, *Voice from Tiananmen Square* (1990)

Moran, Thomas, *Unofficial Histories: Chinese Reportage from the Era of Reform* (in manuscript form)

Nagel's Encyclopedia of China (1982)

Nathan, Andrew, *China's Crisis: Dilemmas of Reform and Prospects for Democracy* (1990), *Human Rights in China* (with R. Randle Edwards and Louis Henkin) (1986), and *Chinese Democracy* (1985)*

New Star Publishers, *Retrospective After the Storm* and *Rumors and the Truth* (1989)

Ogden, Suzanne, et al., eds., *China's Search for Democracy: The Student and Mass Movement of 1989* (1992)*

Oksenberg, Michel, et al., eds., *Beijing Spring, 1989: Confrontation and Conflict. The Basic Documents* (1990)*

Overholt, William, *The Rise of China* (1994)

Pang Pang, *The Death of Hu Yaobang* (1989)

Pasqualini, Jean, and Rudolph Chelminski, *Prisoner of Mao* (1973)

Saich, Tony, ed., *The Chinese People's Movement: Perspectives on Spring, 1989* (1990)*

Salisbury, Harrison, *Tiananmen Diary: Thirteen Days in June* (1989) and *The New Emperors: China in the Era of Mao and Deng* (1992)

Shen Tong, *Almost a Revolution* (1990)

Shirk, Susan L., *The Political Logic of Economic Reform in China* (1993)

Simmie, Scott, and Bob Nixon, *Tiananmen Square: An Eyewitness Account of the Chinese People's Passionate Quest for Democracy* (1989)*

Spence, Jonathan, *The Gate of Heavenly Peace* (1981), *The Search for Modern China* (1990), and *Chinese Roundabout* (1992)

Thurston, Anne F., *A Chinese Odyssey: The Life and Times of a Chinese Dissident* (1991)

Time magazine, ed., "Massacre in Beijing" (1989)

Turnley, David, and Peter Turnley, *Beijing Spring* (1990)

Unger, Jonathan, *The Pro-democracy Protests in China: Reports from the Provinces* (1991)

Wang Ruowang, *Hunger Trilogy* (1991)

Wasserstrom, Jeffrey, *Student Protests in Twentieth-Century China: The View from Shanghai* (1991)

Wasserstrom, Jeffrey, and Elizabeth Perry, eds., *Popular Protest and Political Culture in Modern China* (1992)*

Wu, Harry, *Laogai—The Chinese Gulag* (1992) and with Carolyn Wakeman, *Bitter Winds: A Memoir of My Years in China's Gulag* (1994)*

Yan Jiaqi, with a foreword by Andrew Nathan, *Toward a Democratic China: The Intellectual Biography of Yan Jiaqi* (1992)

Yi Mu and Mark Thompson, *Crisis at Tiananmen Square: Reform and Reality in Modern China* (1989)*

Special Note on Sources

I am especially indebted to the research of certain organizations and individuals. The staff of Human Rights in China Journal, which publishes the journal *Human Rights Forum,* provided me with much critical information about dissident activity within China as well as about issues related to freedom of expression in the post-1989 period. The archive of filmed interviews held by the Long Bow Group in Boston proved an invaluable source of material on the 1989 protest movement and its aftermath. The reports put out by Asia Watch were critical in keeping me informed about the activity of political dissidents after 1989. Robin Munro from the Asia Watch, Hong Kong office has been largely responsible for these well-researched, exhaustive, and informative reports on political prisoners and prison conditions. He has also written authoritatively about the events of June 1989 in Beijing. Timothy Brook's work on the army's role in the events surrounding June 4 was crucial to my understanding of what happened that night. To Timothy Gellat I owe a debt for his work on China's criminal justice system. Geremie Barmé's writing about the genesis of political dissidence in Mao's China and on journalist Dai Qing, his interest in the importance of popular culture, and his analyses of "gray" culture and the role it has played in contemporary Chinese society were all critical in shaping my own views on China's emerging underground. Harry Wu's research on the historical development of China's prison system was crucial in helping me understand how this shadowy but important institution works. Sophia Woodman and Allison Liu Jernow's examinations into the Chinese press, the Party's system of censorship, and the development of the "second-channel" played an important role in informing my own analysis of how publishing has been changing in China. And Andrew Jones's pathbreaking work on popular music gave me a key to understanding its significance in contemporary Chinese society. Four documentary collections—*Cries for Democracy; Beijing Spring, 1989; New Ghosts Old Dreams;* and *China's Search For Democracy*—proved particularly valuable sources. I wish also to thank Simon Leys, whose translation of the opening Lu Xun quote I have used.

Index

May Fourth Movement (1919), 22–
23, 27, 29–30, 36, 48, 63, 72,
102, 105, 106, 110, 132, 414,
430
May 16 Statement (1989), 110
May 17 Declaration (1989), 110
May Thirtieth Movement (1925), 23
Mayday, 89, 319
Metals Exchange, 374
migrant workers, 337, 389, 421
Military Affairs Commission, 134, 353
Military Museum (Beijing), 249–51
Mindszenty, Cardinal Joseph, 203
Ming Dynasty, 20
Mingbao, 302
Ministry of Justice, 224
Ministry of Public Security, 216, 226
Ministry of State Security, 411
mistresses, 399
Monument to the Martyrs of the Peo-
ple (Beijing), 25, 27, 234, 267,
433
  Hu Yaobang's death and, 45, 46
  military advance toward, 155, 157
  as site of hunger strike, 79, 81, 83,
  85, 88
  students' inscription on, 157–58
Moran, Thomas, 299
most-favored-nation (MFN) trade sta-
tus, 192, 205, 226, 405, 412,
427
Motorola Inc., 403
Munro, Robin, 124, 153, 154, 157,
172
Murdoch, Rupert, 307
Muxidi Bridge (Beijing), 140–41,
143, 252

Nanjing East Road (Shanghai), 380–
381, 383, 384, 385, 386
Nanjing University, 270–71
National Day (1989), 231–33
National Day (1991), 265–66
National People's Congress, 47, 173,
194, 219, 270–71, 411, 432
  Standing Committee of, 38, 95,
  129, 167–68
New China News Agency (NCNA),
76–77, 93, 173, 177, 218, 233,
248, 281–82, 283–84, 372, 408,
419, 420
New Economic Policy (NEP), 348
"New Long March of Rock and Roll,
The," 312

New May Fourth, 48, 66
New Observer, 53, 75, 93
New York Stock Exchange, 366, 376,
434
New York Times, 155, 166, 195, 226,
374, 389
Nie Rongzhen, 127
Nights of Paris (Shanghai), 401
1989 crackdown, 164–82, 220, 304
  arrests in, 168–73, 189–90, 211–12
  demonstrations restricted in, 194–95
  Deng's June 9 speech and, 167–68
  didactic films and publications in,
  177–78
  economic reforms and, 168, 331–
  332, 366, 404–5
  executions in, 171–72, 191
  Fang Lizhi's experiences in, 197–
  206
  forced labor in, 224, 225, 227
  foreign press corps' stories on, 253,
  264
  Han Dongfang's experiences in,
  188–96
  indoctrination and propaganda efforts in, 240–52
  June 5 proclamation and, 164–65
  June 6 press conference and,
  165–66
  official explanations and alibis in,
  178–82
  and official terminology for protest
  and bloodletting, 166–67
  within ranks of Party, 173
  rock music and, 317–18
  suppression of Chinese media in,
  175–77
  Wu'er Kaixi's experiences in,
  211–15
  see also Beijing massacre; People's
  Liberation Army
1989 I Love You, 317
Nineties, The, 239
Nixon, Bob, 138
"Nothing to My Name," 89, 313,
314, 317

open-door policy, 172, 286–87, 315,
334, 344, 357, 363
"Opportunists," 317

Paalvast, Heleen, 187–88
"peaceful evolution," 179, 180–82,
240, 247